NAGASAKI

ALSO BY M. G. SHEFTALL

Blossoms in the Wind

Hiroshima

NAGASAKI

THE LAST WITNESSES
Embers Volume II

M. G. SHEFTALL

DUTTON

An imprint of Penguin Random House LLC
1745 Broadway, New York, NY 10019
penguinrandomhouse.com

Copyright © 2025 by Mordecai G. Sheftall

Penguin Random House values and supports copyright. Copyright fuels creativity, encourages diverse voices, promotes free speech, and creates a vibrant culture. Thank you for buying an authorized edition of this book and for complying with copyright laws by not reproducing, scanning, or distributing any part of it in any form without permission. You are supporting writers and allowing Penguin Random House to continue to publish books for every reader. Please note that no part of this book may be used or reproduced in any manner for the purpose of training artificial intelligence technologies or systems.

DUTTON and the D colophon are registered trademarks of Penguin Random House LLC.

MAPS BY M. G. SHEFTALL
BOOK DESIGN BY ANGIE BOUTIN

Library of Congress Cataloging-in-Publication Data

Names: Sheftall, M. G. (Mordecai G.) author
Title: Nagasaki : the last witnesses / M.G. Sheftall.
Description: New York, NY : Dutton, 2025. | Series: Embers ; Volume II |
Includes bibliographical references and index.
Identifiers: LCCN 2025016069 | ISBN 9780593472286 hardcover |
ISBN 9780593472293 ebook
Subjects: LCSH: Atomic bomb victims—Japan—Nagasaki-shi |
World War, 1939–1945—Japan—Nagasaki-shi | Nagasaki-shi
(Japan)—History—Bombardment, 1945—Personal narratives
Classification: LCC D767.25.N3 S54 2025 |
DDC 940.54/2522440922—dc23/eng/20250407
LC record available at https://lccn.loc.gov/2025016069

Printed in the United States of America
1st Printing

The authorized representative in the EU for product safety and compliance is Penguin Random House Ireland, Morrison Chambers, 32 Nassau Street, Dublin D02 YH68, Ireland, https://eu-contact.penguin.ie.

To Kano Michiko, who taught me so much

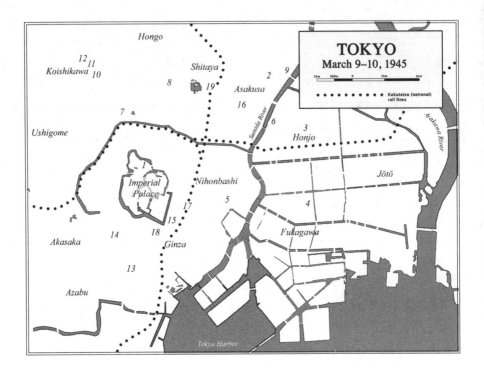

TOKYO MAP KEY

1. Eastern Military District Headquarters (Tokyo Air Defense HQ)
2. Aiming Point #1
3. Aiming Point #2
4. Aiming Point #3
5. Aiming Point #4
6. Lion Toothpaste Company
7. Kōrakuen Park
8. Tokyo Imperial University (Tōdai), Hongo Campus
9. Kototoi Bridge
10. Inoue Tetsujirō home, Kohinata, Koishikawa Ward
11. Atomi Girls' School
12. Tokyo Women's Teacher College
13. Radio Tokyo shortwave broadcasting facility
14. Prime Minister's Residence
15. Dai'Ichi Seimei Building (MacArthur's Occupation Era HQ)
16. Kiridōshi family home, Matsuba-chō
17. Tokyo Station
18. Ministry of Justice
19. Ueno Station

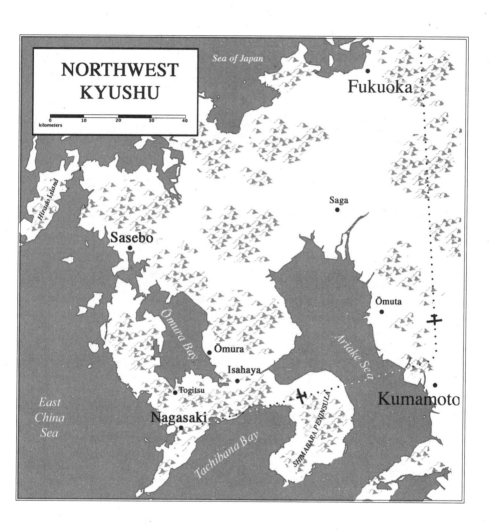

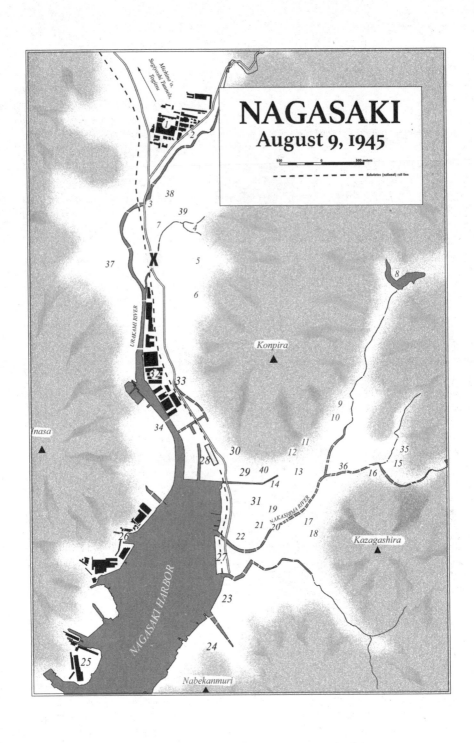

NAGASAKI MAP KEY

x. Ground Zero
1. Mitsubishi Ōhashi Plant
2. Junshin Girls' School
3. Ōhashi Bridge
4. Immaculate Conception (Urakami) Cathedral
5. Nagasaki Medical College
6. Nagasaki Medical College Hospital
7. Nagasaki Prison (modern-day Nagasaki Peace Park location)
8. Nishiyama Dam
9. Gunge brothers' boardinghouse
10. Nagasaki Prefectural Girls' School (Kenjo)
11. Suwa Shrine
12. Prefectural Civil Defense Bunker
13. Appellate Court Chief Judge residence (*kansha*), Katsuyama-machi
14. City Hall
15. Kiridōshi home, Nakagawa-machi
16. Keiho Girls' School (private)
17. Fukuro-machi bomb shelter dig site
18. Kōtaiji Temple
19. Tateno home, Fukuro-machi
20. Nigiwai Bridge (original designated Nagasaki Aiming Point)
21. Nagasaki Appellate Courthouse
22. Nagasaki Prefectural Office
23. "Consulate Row"
24. Ōura Cathedral
25. Mitsubishi Tategami Shipyard
26. Mitsubishi Akuno'ura Shipyard
27. Dejima (original location, connected by landfill since nineteenth century)

28. Nagasaki Station
29. Naka-machi Catholic Church
30. Nishizaka Slope
31. Shinkōzen Elementary School
32. Mitsubishi Mori-machi Plant
33. Mitsubishi Mori-machi main bomb shelter
34. Inasa Bridge
35. Nagasaki Middle School
36. Nagasaki Military Government Team (NMGT) HQ (postwar)
37. Shiroyama Elementary School
38. Yamazato Elementary School
39. Nagasaki School for the Blind and Deaf
40. Tateno post-evacuation home, Higashi'uwa-machi

Since Auschwitz we know what man is capable of.
And since Hiroshima we know what is at stake.

Viktor Frankl

No more forceful arguments for peace and for the international
machinery of peace than the sight of the devastation of Hiroshima
and Nagasaki have ever been devised.

United States Strategic Bombing Survey

The missions to Hiroshima and Nagasaki are nothing to be proud
of at all. But they are missions to be remembered. And never repeated.
Anywhere in the world. Ever again.

Abe Spitzer, 1946

NOTES ON NAMING CONVENTIONS, LANGUAGE USAGE, AND MEASUREMENTS

THIS BOOK FOLLOWS the Japanese convention for personal names—i.e., surname followed by given name(s)—unless the individual in question is already well known to readers by a Western name-order convention (e.g. Yoko Ono or Shohei Ohtani).

Female characters appear under their birth surnames unless they were already married at the time of their earliest appearance in the narrative timeline (or as otherwise noted).

For the transliteration of Japanese vocabulary items and proper nouns in the Roman alphabet, I have followed the Hepburn system that is standard in English-language Japanese studies, including the use of macrons for elongated vowels (e.g., ō, ū, etc.). Both macrons and *italic* font are used throughout the book for direct transliteration of Japanese speech, text, and vocabulary. Japanese terms (e.g. *hibakusha*) that are important in the context of the book but probably unfamiliar to most non-Japanese readers make their first appearance in *italic* font, then in regular typeface in subsequent appearances. For Japanese loan words like "kamikaze" or "kimono" and place-names such as Tokyo or Kyoto, with which readers are probably already familiar, regular typeface and English spelling is used throughout.

The insertion of an apostrophe in certain words or names (e.g., Kōno'ura, *tai'atari*, etc.) is used to indicate the glottal stop that can sometimes appear between vowels in spoken Japanese (similar to the pronunciation of "uh-oh" in English usage).

Metric system measurements are used in this book, with the exception of direct quotations from American material (in which case metric equivalents are added in parentheses).

NAGASAKI

PART ONE

INCENDIARY PRELUDE

"THERE ARE NO CIVILIANS IN JAPAN"

Tinian Island
0030 hours, August 8, 1945

THIRTY-THREE HOURS AFTER its roaring return to North Field, *Enola Gay* sat empty and crypt quiet on its macadam hardstand, the whirring movie cameras and cheering crowds of its August 6 mission-accomplished celebrations long since replaced by the ambient buzz of insects and the occasional passing sentry jeep.

Twenty-five hundred kilometers to the northwest, in the harbor city of Nagasaki, sixteen-year-old Gunge Norio was walking home after working a night shift at a Mitsubishi ordnance plant. Roughly two kilometers southeast of this factory, in Nagasaki's central business district, two of Norio's Mitsubishi coworkers, fifteen-year-old Kiridōshi Michiko and fourteen-year-old Ishida Masako, were catching their last few precious hours of sleep ahead of another day shift of thankless toil for Japan's rapidly collapsing war effort. So was thirteen-year-old Tateno Sueko, who, later that morning, would be helping to dig bomb shelters with other members of her neighborhood association.

In the northern Nagasaki suburb of Urakami, a twenty-one-year-old Catholic novice named Itonaga Yoshi would soon rouse in her convent room for Matins prayers with her fellow Sisters in the chapel of Junshin Girls' School.

Around and amongst these five adolescents, forty thousand men, women, and children were a few hours away from waking up to the last full day of their lives.

Across the Sea of Japan from Nagasaki, Kiridōshi Michiko's uncle, Tetsurō, was one of the million-odd soldiers defending the northwestern frontier of Japanese-occupied Manchuria. Along the border of this territory, the Red Army was using the cover of darkness to move more than five thousand tanks, twenty-six thousand artillery pieces, and 1.5 million men into final jumping-off points.[1] Thirty minutes later, these forces would spring into action, fulfilling Joseph Stalin's Yalta Conference promise to Franklin Roosevelt and Winston Churchill that the Soviet Union would officially join the war against Japan three months to the day after the capitulation of Nazi Germany.[2]

Four thousand kilometers southeast of Stalin's massing armor, and a few hundred meters from *Enola Gay*'s hardstand, scientists and engineers from the Manhattan Project's "Project Alberta" technical team were pulling an all-nighter in a purpose-built air-conditioned assembly shed.[3] Here, they were readying a second atomic bomb—a "Fat Man" (so called because of its rotund shape) plutonium device of the same type first ground-tested in the New Mexico desert barely three weeks previously. In a little more than twenty-four hours, this second Fat Man would be dropped from a B-29 on a Japanese city— either Nagasaki or the arsenal town of Kokura. While the "sure thing" and technologically much simpler one-off uranium device that had been dropped on Hiroshima had gone off, as expected, without a hitch, none of the Project Alberta team members were as confident about the odds of this far more complex and mechanically sensitive Fat Man device functioning as designed in the inherently chaotic conditions of a combat mission. Moreover, the probability of malfunction was further increased as the technicians were being forced to race against the clock; the second atomic strike was being timed to take advantage of the last remnants of a patch of favorable weather over the target area of western Japan.[4] After August 9, skies in this region were forecast to be socked in by clouds.[5]

In a strictly technical sense, the weather situation was not insurmountable for an all-weather bomber like the B-29. If necessary, the second mission strike force could drop its ordnance by radar, as per standard operating procedure for B-29s encountering inclement conditions during a conventional mission. But deployment of the atomic bombs came with a set of special rules: According to the field orders the 509th Composite Group had received from Twentieth Air Force, the atomic bomb was only to be dropped when its target could be clearly visibly identified,[6] and there were no mission parameters in the orders for radar-drop scenarios. If the August 9 window of good drop weather were missed, it would be nearly a week until the weather cleared enough for the 509th to get its next chance to drop a visually aimed second atomic bomb on Japan.

The Americans' meteorological urgency was a direct consequence of the strategic imperative to exploit the psychological shock value of Hiroshima. It was hoped that dropping a second bomb so soon after the first would lead the Japanese to believe that there were many more of these weapons in the American arsenal than there actually were, and that these would continue to be dropped on Japan until that country either surrendered or—as per Harry Truman's July 26 Potsdam Declaration threat (which the Japanese so far were refusing to acknowledge)—ceased to exist.[7] To ramp up the political and psychological pressure on Japan's national leadership, as well as its general populace, Twentieth Air Force B-29s—in between incendiary raids—had been dropping over Japanese cities in the wake of the Hiroshima bombing leaflets featuring a photo of Little Boy's mushroom cloud and bearing the following message translated into Japanese:

TO THE JAPANESE PEOPLE:

America asks that you take immediate heed of
what we say on this leaflet.

We are in possession of the most destructive explosive
ever devised by man. A single one of our newly developed

atomic bombs is actually the equivalent in explosive power to what 2,000 of our giant B-29's can carry on a single mission. This awful fact is one for you to ponder and we solemnly assure you it is grimly accurate.

We have just begun to use this weapon against your homeland. If you still have any doubt, make inquiry as to what happened to Hiroshima when just one atomic bomb fell on that city.

Before using this bomb to destroy every resource of the military by which they are prolonging this useless war, we ask that you now petition the Emperor to end the war. Our President has outlined for you the thirteen consequences of an honorable surrender: We urge that you accept these consequences and begin the work of building a new, better, and peace-loving Japan.

You should take steps now to cease military resistance. Otherwise, we shall resolutely employ this bomb and all our other superior weapons to promptly and forcefully end the war.

EVACUATE YOUR CITIES[8]

But even if the Americans' bombing schedule were met, and despite these air-dropped appeals to popular fear, there was still a possibility that the second bombing would prove as unconvincing to the Japanese leadership as the first apparently had been. In this case, the unlimited-bombs bluff would lose its teeth (assuming it had ever had any in the first place) long before a third bomb became available, which would be some time around August 19 to 21.[9] A lot could happen in ten to twelve days when an autocratic regime was facing an existential threat; exploiting this downtime, militarist hard-liners

"THERE ARE NO CIVILIANS IN JAPAN" 7

with access to the imperial throne might convince His Majesty that this new atomic wrinkle in the war situation—horrific as it was—was endurable in lieu of the unthinkable alternative of surrender, occupation, and the potential end of Japan's twenty-six-hundred-year-old imperial dynasty.[10]

As a matter of military prudence, the Americans could not dismiss out of hand official crowings that had featured center stage in Japanese propaganda content since the fall of Saipan a year earlier about possessing the ultimate strategic weapon of a populace that was prepared to die en masse in a final decisive battle—a so-called *hondo kessen*—to defend its homeland rather than dishonor it with surrender. Until the Americans began hitting the invasion beaches of Kyushu later that fall, they would not know if all of this Japanese talk about "a hundred million balls of fire" and flaming mass suicide was a sincere declaration of national resolve or mere propaganda bluster.

The Americans, then, were not the only players in this strategic standoff in which bluff and resolve were indistinguishable. The Japanese played their hand by raising in the American imagination the specter of a ground-combat and kamikaze-plane apocalypse that, if the Americans went ahead with their plans for a land invasion of the Home Islands, could have been akin in degree of ferocity to the bloodbath the Allies had just endured on Okinawa (where they had suffered some fifty thousand casualties and up to twice as many Japanese civilians might have perished), but potentially multiplied by orders of magnitude in terms of scale. The Japanese aim here was to get the Americans to blink first and cut a peace deal more generous than the unconditional surrender they had been demanding since the Casablanca Conference of January 1943.[11] In the early days of August 1945, Emperor Hirohito and his most trusted advisors—unaware not only of what was about to happen in Manchuria, but also of what the Soviet leader had promised in Yalta six months earlier—held out pipe-dream hopes that the still technically Japan-neutral Stalin might help to broker such a deal.[12]

In what can only be considered either a gross lapse of foresight or a fatal case of wishful thinking, no one at the highest levels of strategic decision-making in Tokyo seems to have advised the emperor—the only person in Japan capable of ordering an end to the war—of the possibility that a solemnly sworn threat of imminent Armageddon, rather than halting in its tracks the American juggernaut then headed for the Home Islands, might instead spur that enemy to deploy ever more effective means of indiscriminately slaughtering Japanese soldiers and civilians in their millions.

Although American field commanders at the in-theater operational level were contemplating using a third atomic bomb on Tokyo, higher-echelon decision-makers in Washington were coming around to the idea that there would be little strategic value in dropping another very expensive bomb just to rearrange the rubble in the imperial capital and kill another hundred thousand or more civilians, especially if the hearts of Japan's leaders were already inured to such sacrifice.[13] Instead, the third bomb and the rest of the next production run of plutonium Fat Man devices could be put to better use as tactical battlefield weapons for the upcoming invasion of Kyushu, prepping the landing sites and neutralizing Japanese command and logistic centers farther inland when the Allies began hitting the beaches there on November 1, by which time, General Leslie R. Groves assured Washington, the Manhattan Project organization would have ten or more such devices ready to go.[14]

In the meantime, the Allies would press on with their systematic dismantling of Japan's economy and infrastructure by conventional means and spare no collateral damage in the process. A passage from an official intelligence briefing for the Fifth Air Force succinctly encapsulated the operant mindset of this strategy:[15]

> [T]he entire population of Japan is a proper Military Target. . . . THERE ARE NO CIVILIANS IN JAPAN. We are making War and making it in the all-out fashion which saves American lives, shortens the agony which War is and seeks to bring about an enduring Peace. We intend to seek out and destroy the enemy wherever he or she is, in the greatest possible numbers, in the shortest possible time.[16]

"THERE ARE NO CIVILIANS IN JAPAN" 9

Toward this end, the country's sea-lanes, harbors, and inland waterways would continue to be blockaded and strangled by submarines, aerial mining ("Operation STARVATION"),[17] and air attack. The Far East Air Forces (FEAF) would hit tactical targets and immobilize the national railway network—an effort that would interdict enemy troop and supply movement as well as prevent the vitally important autumn rice harvest from reaching the main population centers on the Tokyo–Osaka urban corridor,[18] a development that would result in mass famine in the Home Islands by year's end.

Finally, Major General Curtis E. LeMay's XXI Bomber Command (XXI BC) would continue its incendiary campaign against urban areas and war industries, steadily increasing the size and frequency of its raids until there was nothing left to burn down. And if LeMay's B-29s left anything standing in the embers, the FEAF could swoop in afterward to bomb and strafe it.[19]

Outside of the barbed wire fencing of the 509th Composite Group's heavily guarded section of North Field, the 313th Bombardment Wing, XXI BC, was taking a prominent role in this agenda of destruction, busily preparing to help erase another line entry from the Twentieth Air Force's ever-dwindling target list of Japanese cities.[20] But unlike its secretive North Field neighbors, the 313th did not possess the ability to wipe out one of these targets in a blink with a single bomb. Instead, like the other four wings in LeMay's command, it waged its war by dropping thousands of tons of incendiaries and high explosives on Japanese urban and industrial concentrations every week or, in the case of maximum-effort outings like the great fire raids on Tokyo, sometimes even in a single night.[21]

Five months earlier, LeMay had begun this blitz by switching XXI BC's main tactic from daytime bombing of war plants to the incendiary-saturation "area" bombing of urban concentrations by night, as Britain's Royal Air Force had used to such great effect against Germany.[22] Since then, his B-29s had killed 300,000 civilians and "dehoused" some 30 percent of the Japanese population by either completely or partially burning down sixty-seven cities.[23]

Sustaining a campaign of such intensity and scale necessitated the creation of a dedicated global supply chain worthy of a giant multinational corporation. Sitting at the pinnacle of this organizational pyramid was management, housed in the Guam headquarters of XXI BC. Here, a small army of uniformed Ivy League MBAs (including a young statistician on loan from Harvard named Robert S. McNamara) used cutting-edge 1940s IT and scientific business theory to decide how much product would go out for each mission, when and where it would be delivered, and how much inventory had to be ordered from Stateside factories to sustain this incendiary momentum.[24]

Doing the heaviest logistical lifting for this enterprise, volume- and distance-wise, was an effectively proprietary merchant marine fleet that ferried product from manufacturers like Standard Oil of New Jersey and Permanente Metals across some ninety-five hundred kilometers of the Pacific Ocean to reach Guam and the other B-29 bases on the Mariana islands of Saipan and Tinian.[25]

Ensuring these bases operated smoothly was an in-theater maintenance and logistical apparatus of mind-boggling complexity.[26] This enterprise employed (and fed, housed, and clothed) thousands of engine mechanics, radar technicians, armorers, and other specialists who toiled around the clock in machine shops, warehouses, fuel tank farms, and bomb dumps.

Finally, there were the thousands of young men—typically eleven crewmen to each B-29—tasked with delivering product on time and on target. Operations at this end point typically incurred an overhead cost—due to some combination of enemy action, mechanical malfunction, and pilot error—of perhaps twenty planes a week during slow periods and more during maximum-effort phases.

From a certain perspective, the young aircrewmen who shouldered the ultimate burden of this operating cost were expendable cogs in a vast engine of indiscriminate industrialized destruction. Some of them might have even occasionally regarded and referred to themselves as such, either in private dark moments of the soul or in the time-honored military traditions of barracks kvetching and pre-mission gallows humor.[27] Nevertheless, cavalier nihilists or not, in their heart of hearts, they all wanted the same thing desired by the people they dropped fire on every night: to survive their current ordeal and return to their old lives as soon as possible. And the way the B-29 crews looked at it, the sooner they burned Japan to the ground, the sooner that would happen.[28]

Until that great dreamed-of day of deliverance, the aircrews of XXI BC had to live with the knowledge that each time they flew out to hit another target, they had a 1 to 2 percent chance of never coming back.[29] In the case of a more vigorously defended objective like a key military installation or an important war plant, those odds could worsen considerably, especially if the planes were flying by daylight to improve accuracy and bomb concentration. And although such loss rates were on the low side compared to the aerial slaughterhouse Eighth Air Force or RAF colleagues had endured for years in Europe, few of LeMay's aircrews flying multiple missions every week would have been comforted by such a comparison. Nor would they have found much solace in knowing that they had to beat these odds on thirty-five consecutive dice rolls to be able to catch a ride on "the magic carpet run" home to loved ones and safety.[30]

Anyone with a few missions under his belt was all too familiar with the fickle finger of combat fortune; all knew—or at least had heard chow line scuttlebutt about—rookie crews who had "bought it" on their first or second outings or homeward-bound veterans who had gone down on their thirty-fourth or thirty-fifth. There was no pattern or logic to any of it; while crew skill might have been a factor in avoiding midair collisions or laying defensive gun turret fire on incoming enemy fighters, it had absolutely no bearing on, or influence over, a mission hazard as randomly deadly as antiaircraft fire. A speeding piece of metal either missed a crew who lived to tell about it or it "had their number" and they went down to flaming death or to iffy survival chances in Japanese captivity. It was all dumb fate at its most brutal. There was nothing any of them could do anything about, and they knew it.

To keep their sanity in this daily environment, the crews learned to accept the fundamental condition of their own ultimate helplessness. Most were able to do this and get back into their planes for each new mission through some combination of soldierly swagger, peer pressure, horseplay, alcohol, prayer/superstition, and high adolescent testosterone.[31] Idealistic patriotism and dreams of medals and glory were for rookies—who would in any case be quickly weaned of such *Saturday Evening Post*-cover sentimentality the first time they saw a plane full of their buddies go down or caught the smell of burning people wafting up from a city they were helping to incinerate.

HIGH CITY, LOW CITY

Hamamatsu, Japan
February 2017

MY PHONE AT school rings. I barely make it through my standard Japanese *"Moshi-moshi, Shefutaru desu . . ."* telephone-answering protocol before the voice on the other end is swamping me with an interrogatory barrage of rapid-fire but age-slurred speech. After a few moments of audial confusion, I ascertain that the voice belongs to Seki (née Tominaga) Chieko, my primary *hibakusha* ("atomic bomb survivor") mentor.

"I want to introduce you to a friend of mine," Seki-san says. "She's a bit of a card, but I think the two of you will hit it off."

By the end of our brief but semantically dense exchange, I have received my marching orders: I am to be at the Odawara Shinkansen station at one p.m. the following Monday.

Bringing myself to the appointed place at the appointed hour, I wait for a few minutes outside of the Shinkansen gate. The westbound train from Tokyo arrives and passengers start coming down the stairs from the station platform. I spot Seki-san's small gray figure amidst the milling throng. Her face—which is large for her frame—is wearing its usual intense expression, determined in the set of the mouth but with some surprise/wonder in her perennially high-arched eyebrows.

Seki-san warms into the briefest of smiles at the moment our eyes meet. Then her game face returns and she is all business again. Adjusting course to make a beeline for me, she wields her cane with the vigorous, rhythmical swing of a Camino de Santiago hiker. Even though she is at least a head shorter than practically anyone else in the station over the age of ten, her bearing and very being exude such purpose and urgency that people practically jump out of the way at her approach. No one dares do otherwise.

I begin to go into my stock scripted, polite Japanese-greeting routine, but Seki-san waves this off with a *"Hai, hai"* while I am still in mid-bow. This is no time for formalities. There are places to go and people to meet.

"It's not too far from here, but it's still too far for me to walk," she announces, giving her cane a little wag for emphasis. "Let's take a taxi.

"Don't worry," she adds with a hint of harrumph. "It's on me."

At the taxi stand, I begin to raise my hand but Seki-san pushes in front of me and raises her cane. A car pulls up promptly. We get in, and Seki-san micromanages the driver from the back seat for the entirety of our brief journey into the steep hills pressing in close behind the station. After a couple of minutes, we arrive at a retirement facility in a leafy suburb surrounded by middle-class houses and mom-and-pop storefronts.

Off to the side of the entrance, an ancient man with a glassy thousand-yard stare is sitting on a little bench by an ashtray stand, blissfully puffing away on a cigarette. Wordless nods of recognition are exchanged.

"Every time I come here, that fellow is sitting there," Seki-san says with a note of noncommittal annoyance to no one in particular and not bothering to lower her voice.

A moment later a male caregiver in his early thirties shows up in the lobby to take us up to Kano (née Kiridōshi) Michiko-san's private room on the second floor. The young man is cordial and cheerful. On the way up, he peppers us with small-talk niceties that Seki-san hands off to me to field.

Kano-san—Michiko-san—greets us at the door. Even before she

speaks, I immediately pick up on an impish energy in her tiny eyes, and her small mouth has a slightly ironic twist to it, clearly primed to drop snark and mischief. She is somewhat bigger than I expected her to be—taller, more heavyset, and lighter-complexioned than the diminutive and ocher-skinned Seki-san. Her small-featured round white face is framed by a dark brown bob cut that makes the eighty-seven-year-old look closer to sixty-five. With the added accent of her cardigan and glasses, the overall effect is 1970s Catholic nun schoolteacher.

As I watch her brusque and familiar interaction with the male nurse, I see a facet of the *ojōsan* ("highborn young lady") trope that I have also noted in Seki-san. It is a manner of dealing with "the help" that is not intentionally condescending but more a sort of precocious imperiousness that kicks in on the part of the addresser when the addressee is deemed not to be a social equal, with the result that standard Japanese etiquette is removed from the conversational dynamic. Unlike the case where this attitude is assumed by a nouveau riche / arriviste matron, I do not get the sense in Michiko-san's and Seki-san's case that this attitude is calculated or even consciously assumed; old Japanese women of their dying breed grew up being doted upon by fawning family servants in a long-vanished Japan of more distinctly siloed sociocultural spaces, so this privileged way of dealing with others probably comes to them as instinctively and naturally as breathing. Unlike with Seki-san, however, it seems that Michiko-san does not take herself very seriously—the imperious shtick may all just be a bit of performance art, after all—but as with Seki-san, it is unlikely she could give a damn if anyone has a problem with that.

After the nurse puts out a tea set for us, Michiko-san dismisses him with a playful shoo-shoo wave and a parting quip that gets an indulgent laugh from its target.

Taking up a perch on the edge of her bed, Michiko-san shifts her attention to me, sizing me up with her little eyes behind her granny glasses and a slight smirk bending her tiny red lips.

Seki-san and I take chairs facing her, a little lower than eye level.

"They treat you pretty well in this place," Seki-san says.

"Yeah, they're all right, I guess," Michiko-san says with a bit of world-weariness. "We pay enough for it."

As we sip our tea, Seki-san mentions that I am working on a book about Hiroshima and Nagasaki, then segues into a long rundown of my research and linguistic bona fides for the benefit of our host, who punctuates the monologue with the occasional *"Ah so desu ka,"* as nonchalant about the exchange as if entertaining American visitors in her room is a daily occurrence.

Sensing that our hostess might be getting bored—and wanting to move things along—I intercede during a lull in the conversation to steer the discussion toward Michiko-san. As tactfully as possible, I begin probing into the circumstances of her residence in an assisted-living facility. As I have assumed that there is backstory involving bereavement and loneliness, I am a bit taken aback when Michiko-san informs me that her husband and son are alive and well and living in the family homestead in Suginami, Tokyo. Her smirk widens as she lobs this over the conversational net and waits for me to return the serve. I play along as the straight man to her comic by asking the prompted question.

"Why live here, then?" I say.

"I prefer living alone," she says. "I always have."

"Don't you miss your family?"

"Now and then I do, and I go back to Tokyo. But when I get tired of them again, I come back here."

This punch line gets a big laugh from Seki-san, who flashes me a quick *I TOLD you she was a card* glance. She has heard all of this before—and may, in fact, have just helped Michiko-san set me up for it—but apparently she still finds it hilarious.

Michiko-san notes my theatrically exaggerated surprise reaction and gives a low, slow devil-may-care chuckle, satisfied that the gag has landed as intended.

The back-and-forth continues for a few more rounds, with Seki-san bringing her veteran-interviewer chops into play here, adroitly emceeing the conversation so my host and I can continue sizing each other up.

It turns out that Michiko-san and I have a lot in common. Like me, she is a lifelong cutup and enfant terrible, but also, paradoxically, a to-the-bone introvert. As a child, she loved reading but hated formal classroom learning, so naturally she ended up working in education. She also shares with me a fascination with Spain that flowered, in both our cases, in our early fifties. We exchange some stories about visits to Guernica and the Basque Country before we start talking about her privileged prewar-Tokyo childhood.

The densest area of Tokyo's hectic urban concentration is centered around the abruptly and extravagantly spacious, moated grounds of the Imperial Palace. And it has always been so. Tokyo has followed this general pattern of development since the city was still known as Edo and this Palace compound—in its former incarnation as the castle home of the Shoguns—was the actual and not merely symbolic and spiritual locus of Japanese political authority. And as in days of samurai yore, one rule of thumb for gauging the importance and prestige of any given institution, home, or other space in the city is to measure its proximity to this geographic and symbolic focal point.

In addition to the yardstick of Palace proximity, there is a second important demarcation of the capital's sociocultural space—topographically delineated, in this case—that can be visualized by imagining the Palace occupying the center of a circle superimposed on a map of Central Tokyo that is divided into northern, southern, western, and eastern quadrants.[1] The terrain in the first three of these quadrants is characterized by ridges and gentle hills radiating up and away from the low-lying Palace. After some kilometers of slow but steady climb, these elevations eventually flatten out to merge into the great plateau of the largest expanse of level land on the main Japanese island of Honshu: the roughly Connecticut-sized Kantō Plain, which is home to most Tokyoites (and about a third of the nation's population) today. The fourth quadrant extends eastward a few short kilometers from the Palace to reach the shores of Tokyo Bay and the alluvial plain of the Sumida River. This area is pool-table flat and barely a couple of meters above sea level at its highest points.

When the old city began to cluster around Edo Castle from the early seventeenth century on, the Shoguns' retainers and their respective samurai retinues set up homes and clan-branch compounds in the easily defended hilly areas of the northern, southern, and western quadrants around Edo Castle. In time, these districts came to be referred to collectively as the "Yamanote," or "High City"; in the twenty-first century, they form an area that boasts the city's priciest residential real estate.

The flat lands to the east, however, were settled by the artisans, merchants, and assorted castle town camp followers who gravitated to the Shoguns' capital to attend to the needs—and exploit the opportunities—of this new center of power and economic activity. In time, this part of Tokyo came to be known as the "Shitamachi," or "Low City"—a naming that was a reflection not only of its terrain vis-à-vis the Yamanote but also of its residents' relative status in the Shogunate Era caste system pecking order.

In the late Meiji Era—as Japan's latecomer industrial revolution kicked into high gear and dynamited the old caste system with mass literacy, nationalism, money, and technology—the capital's exploding population spilled willy-nilly out into suburbs along new commuter rail lines, with the most important of these stretching far out into the Kantō Plain. In short order, Tokyo transitioned from a city of samurai bureaucrats, teahouse girls, merchants, and artisans into a booming metropolis of salarymen, café waitresses, and semiskilled factory workers. Yet throughout the course of this geographical (and socioeconomic) evolution, the Palace remained, and continues to be, the placid eye at the center of the frenetic urban storm that is Tokyo, just as the Yamanote-Shitamachi divide has remained the most significant demarcation in the city in terms of how the residents of Central Tokyo regard the world and their place in it.

Until well into the Meiji Era, the Shitamachi was the heart of the energetic and vital bourgeois culture of Old Edo that gave birth to many of the art forms—e.g., Kabuki theater and wood-block prints—that modern-day Japanese revere as central elements in their country's pantheon of venerated "ancient" cultural traditions. In its Edo and Meiji Era heyday, the district's plucky denizens had a reputation for working hard and playing harder—hustling by day in their cramped wooden storefronts and workshops and partying by night in red-lantern-lit teahouses while staid samurai counterparts (and, later, their imperial bureaucratic descendants) stoically scowled through hours of administrative drudgery and stilted ceremony in the leafy precincts of Yamanote. But this began to change with the mechanization and acceleration of the city's transportation network, which essentially rendered moot the topographical tyranny of the Yamanote. Once this happened, the retail, commercial, and entertainment activity that had traditionally been the purview of the Shitamachi began shifting steadily westward and upward into the increasingly energized and dynamic financial and political power mecca of the High City, and there it would stay.

But the Shitamachi was not necessarily forlorn and forgotten—merely repurposed. Decades of Meiji and Taishō Era waterfront development stretched the Shitamachi far out into Tokyo Bay and shored up the Sumida's alluvial plain with landfill (much of it incorporating old garbage dumps), creating new space for warehouses and factories and for the homes of the hundreds of thousands of people who would toil in them. By the turn of the century, the Shitamachi had become one of the most important manufacturing centers in Japan and one of the most densely populated spots on the planet—no mean feat considering that practically none of its jam-packed houses or factories rose higher than two stories and that it was constructed almost entirely of wood.[2]

The conspicuous susceptibility of Japanese urban concentrations to destruction by fire was the subject of worldwide news coverage when the Great Kantō Earthquake wrecked and burned down most of Tokyo and neighboring Yokohama in September 1923, with the capital's most horrendous conflagrations and a sizable portion of the disaster's 100,000 casualties occurring in the Shitamachi.[3] Among the global audience for this catastrophe, Japan's hypothetical future enemies were taking careful notes; likely inspired by Kantō earthquake news stories, military aviation visionary Brigadier General William "Billy" Mitchell was one of the first Americans to latch onto the idea of someday firebombing Japanese cities, calling them "the greatest aerial targets the world has ever seen."[4]

A year after the Tokyo calamity, Mitchell was warning colleagues as well as the general public that rising Japanese military capabilities posed the clearest and most present danger to Western hegemony in the world order. As he saw it, America's only sane course was to fully prepare for an inevitable transpacific clash between "the white and yellow races . . . to determine which shall prevail." In such a contest, he proclaimed, mastery of the air (as well as submarine warfare, he noted) would be essential to victory.[5]

Predicting several years later that the opening move in the coming great transpacific race war would be a massive Japanese air strike against Pearl Harbor, Mitchell mentally war-gamed a scenario in which Alaska-based bomber formations conducted incendiary raids on Japan's "congested . . . and easily located" population centers, whose "structure . . . of paper and wood or other inflammable substances . . . ma[de] their country especially vulnerable to aircraft attack."[6] In 1934, amidst a contemporary news backdrop of Japan's ongoing domestic political plunge into ultranationalist militarism and its increasingly ambitious and aggressive imperialist adventurism on the Asian continent, Mitchell made another prediction: this time in the form of a boast to a *New York Times* reporter that it would take no more than three modern military aircraft to "demoralize and destroy Japan."[7]

Seven years after Mitchell's interview in the *Times*—and a mere three weeks before the Japanese fulfilled his 1928 prophecy by bombing Pearl Harbor—the rhetoric was unmistakably incendiary when Army chief of staff General George C. Marshall told a gathering of influential journalists that in the increasingly likely event of war with Japan, America would "fight mercilessly" and that B-17 bombers based in the Philippines would be "dispatched immediately to set the paper cities of Japan on fire. There won't be any hesitation about bombing civilians," the general promised. "It will be all out."[8]

But it would be a long wait before Marshall's vision could be put into action. Dramatic gains by the Japanese military during the Sino-Japanese War and in the opening rounds of the war that followed the Pearl Harbor raid—including devastating preemptive strikes against the same Philippine B-17 bases name-dropped in General Marshall's threat—seized every bit of East Asian and Western Pacific real estate from which American bombers might have been able to hit the Japanese Home Islands. Moreover, the Soviet-Japanese Neutrality Pact secured by Foreign Minister Matsuoka Yōsuke eight months before Pearl Harbor denied what would have been ideal locations in the Russian Far East for carrying the air war to Japan; the neutrality stipulations of the treaty were, in fact, followed so strictly by the Soviets that, until the very last days of the war, they did not even share Northeast Asian and Northwest Pacific meteorological data with their ostensible American "allies." As a result of these military and diplomatic masterstrokes, Japan's cities were given nearly three years of breathing room from a full measure of American wrath from the air.

The sole exception to this respite was an audacious one-off attack on Tokyo and other Honshu targets on April 18, 1942, by sixteen carrier-launched B-25 bombers, led by Lieutenant Colonel James Doolittle. Although Doolittle's mission was tactically insignificant in terms of measurable damage of Japanese war-making potential, it was played up as a triumphant feat of martial derring-do by the American press. As intended, the news electrified an American public still thirsty for Pearl Harbor revenge and heretofore frustrated by five months of relentlessly unsatisfying news from the Pacific. News that some of the Doolittle Raiders had been captured by the Japanese and subjected to "severe punishment," however, was withheld from the American public until October of that year.[9] And another six months would pass before the news that three of the Raiders had been subsequently executed by their Japanese captors[10] was announced in an official White House statement.[11]

A similar temporary blackout was imposed on news of the

successful escape of ten American and two Filipino prisoners from a Japanese POW camp on the Philippine island of Mindanao in April 1943.[12] The prisoners concerned had endured over a year in captivity following the fall of Bataan and Corregidor in the spring of 1942, during which time they witnessed and experienced what *The New York Times* would later term a "calculated Japanese campaign of brutality" against American and Filipino prisoners. In their post-rescue debriefings, the prisoners described a litany of atrocities exacted upon their fellow prisoners by their Japanese captors, including beheadings, live burials, forced labor resulting in death from exhaustion, regular beatings, and denials of food and water for extended periods.[13] When the story was finally released to the American public in January 1944, coverage introduced a new catchphrase that would become a mantra for focusing and fleshing out visceral desires for retribution against the Japanese—against their military and government, against their country, and, most ominously, against their people and race.[14] That phrase was "Bataan Death March."

As historian Michael Sherry has pointed out, there were two primary reasons behind the American authorities' news blackout regarding the Japanese military's atrocities against Allied POWs. Most immediately, there were concerns at the top levels of leadership that any big media campaign devoted to exploiting such stories for propaganda value might cause the Japanese to lose face, thereby exacerbating their ill-treatment of their captives.[15] A second reason was a matter of timing. As one of Marshall's staff members put it, such reports should be held back until they could be used to "steel public opinion to the damage which . . . we are about to inflict upon the Japanese homeland."[16] Americans, after all, were supposed to be the "good guys" in the current conflict, and "good guys" were not supposed to be raining fire down on women and children—even "enemy" women and children. The American government and media establishment had railed against such acts after Guernica, during the Spanish Civil War, and when the Japanese began indiscriminate bombing of Chinese cities after 1937, and during the Nazi Blitz against London in 1940. Criticism had been considerably more muted when the British—via RAF Bomber Command—began returning the favor against German cities in 1942, but the tacit understanding still stood among the American public that their fighting men were better sports than to engage in such behavior. However, the time would come when that same government and media establishment would be asking the American public to sanction their own young men committing just such acts and at far greater scale. Accomplishing this acceptance, it was believed, would require popular sentiment to be stoked to what Marshall termed a "storm of bitterness" and wrathful rage. The Japanese POW atrocity stories would have great utility toward this end.

By late 1943, after a virtually uninterrupted string of American land, sea, and air victories, Pentagon strategists were at last approaching the point where undertaking actionable mass-scale retribution against the Japanese homeland was becoming militarily feasible. In this vein, they began to entertain at length and in increasingly specific detail their incendiary visions for Japan's wooden cities.

Some of these concrete preparations were underway at Dugway Proving Ground in the Utah desert, where painstakingly detailed movie-set-like re-creations of Japanese urban spaces were firebombed with different types of incendiary devices to measure optimal burn rates and napalm-splash-dispersal patterns before being rebuilt and bombed again.[17] Eventually, a napalm bomblet designated the M69 was determined to be the American weapon of choice against wooden Japanese housing. Concurrently, at closely guarded Stateside Army Air Forces bases, after carefully selected long-range Army bomber aircrews traded in their B-17s and B-24s to begin transitioning to the new wonder weapon Boeing B-29 Superfortresses, they underwent special intensive training to fly these massive, gleaming airplanes over vast expanses of featureless ocean to hit far-off targets.[18]

At the Pentagon, a study group—the Committee of Operations Analysts (COA)—began planning in earnest for the razing of what they deemed to be Japan's six most important cities in terms of war matériel production: Tokyo, Kawasaki, Yokohama, Nagoya, Kobe, and

Osaka. Initial targeting lists and tactical maps for these Japanese cities were drawn up, printed,[19] and distributed to need-to-know personnel. Each of these maps featured an outlined and shaded area marked "Incendiary Zone #1," showing the district of the city determined to be most vulnerable to firebombing. On the COA's maps of Tokyo, Incendiary Zone #1 was the Shitamachi.

SHITAMACHI GIRL

KANO MICHIKO WAS born Kirodōshi Michiko in 1929 in Asakusa, a Tokyo commercial and entertainment quarter located in the northwest corner of the Shitamachi. At the time, its real estate was some of the most densely populated in the world.[1] Similar in both atmosphere and economic function to Times Square in New York or Piccadilly in London, Asakusa was a lively (if somewhat sketchy), nonstop money machine through which coursed rivers of cash borne in the purses and pockets of the tourists and other visitors who thronged there in search of thrills and love. Accordingly, over its long history, the district's denizens had devised innumerable ingenious, enticing, and usually legal ways to disencumber these visitors of as much of that cash as possible. This hungry energy kept the district's narrow wooden warrens ringing with the calls of merchants and pushcart hawkers by daylight and blinking and clattering with neon-glowing amusement arcades, red-light alleyways, beer halls, and taxi dance joints after dark.

Michiko's grandfather, a physician, was the progenitor of the Tokyo branch of a proud old samurai family from Fukuoka Prefecture. After medical school, he set up a successful practice in Matsuba-chō, Asakusa, in the district's late-Meiji heyday, and there have been Kiridōshis in the capital ever since.

While Dr. Kiridōshi tended to Matsuba-chō's medical needs, his wife ran his household with full control of its purse strings, as was customary for well-to-do families of the era. After the doctor's demise in the 1920s, his widow invested a sizable chunk of the family fortune in Asakusa real estate, eventually putting up on their holdings some thirty-five rental properties complete with a proprietary maintenance staff. This investment continued to provide a healthy income stream for the family long after the late doctor's medical clinic was shuttered.

In addition to exercising her business acumen, Mrs. Kiridōshi lived up to her traditionally prescribed dowager role in an upper-middle-class household by carrying out a long-term campaign with the aim of furthering her grandaughters' marriage prospects. One ongoing effort in this vein—requiring daily vigilance—was to keep Michiko and her sisters culturally quarantined from Shitamachi ways and prevent them from inadvertently picking up the district's distinctive dialect and streetwise swagger from classmates, neighbors, and household help.

When twelve-year-old Michiko graduated from Matsuba Elementary School in March 1942, the adults in the family decided that it was time for her to get out of the Shitamachi—at least for eight hours a day. Toward this end, she sat for the entrance exam to Atomi Jogakkō—a private girls' school atop Tomisaka Slope in the upscale Yamanote ward of Koishikawa that had been established in 1875[2] by its namesake founder, Atomi Kakei, a Meiji Era pioneer in women's education.

In the 1940s, Atomi remained faithful to its founder's vision of providing its female charges with a Japanese-themed liberal arts curriculum emphasizing subjects like poetry, painting, and the tea ceremony, all underpinned with a firm basis in home economics, gender-appropriate samurai ethos and morality, and Shinto-heavy patriotic indoctrination. Although the school produced some rare convention-bucking graduates who later went on to accomplished professional careers in overwhelmingly male-dominated prewar Japan, Atomi was still in essence what it had always been: a finishing school for upper-middle- and upper-class girls being groomed to become dutiful housewives and self-sacrificing mothers in upper-middle- and upper-class households. Although the Atomi campus was only a half hour from Asakusa by streetcar, it might as well have been on the far side of the moon in terms of sociocultural distance.

Accordingly, it must have seemed an answer to the Kiridōshi family's prayers when Michiko passed her entrance exam. Now she would at last be able to associate with other girls of good family, safe from the pernicious influences of the dodgy Shitamachi. A few weeks after Michiko's triumph, however, her father, Kunitake—a bank executive—was transferred to a branch office back in the Kiridōshis' ancestral hometown of Ōmuta, Fukuoka Prefecture. For Michiko to accompany her father on his transfer would have entailed an utterly unconscionable cultural banishment to the Kyushu boondocks for her—a fate worse than death for any self-respecting Tokyo *ojōsan*—and understandably, she balked. Grandmother Kiridōshi must have agreed, because a panicked scramble ensued to find alternate living arrangements in the capital for her eldest granddaughter. The temporary crisis was resolved when a spot was secured for Michiko at the last minute in the Atomi dormitory—accommodations that were normally reserved for girls from distant prefectures. In due course, the rest of the family—with Grandmother Kiridōshi in tow—left Tokyo for Fukuoka. The home in Asakusa was sold to a local trucking company owner's family—the Kurofuchis—and the nearby rental properties were left in the care of a business agent.

Atomi's dormitory was a two-story wooden structure across the main Tomisaka Slope thoroughfare from the school's campus. Headmistress Inoue-sensei and dorm mother / maid / cook "Sumiko-san" lived in private rooms on the first floor of the dormitory, which was also the location of the boarders' dining room, Sumiko's kitchen, a communal bath, Inoue-sensei's office, and a large recreation room with a piano and a radio. The students—who ranged in age from twelve to seventeen—boarded on the second floor, eight per room. Each of these tatami-matted rooms was overseen by a senior-year student resident assistant whom the other residents of the room customarily and affectionately referred to as *Kā-chan* ("Mom").

Michiko adapted to her new circumstances with her usual aplomb, immediately resuming her normal modus operandi of doing whatever she wanted to do whenever she wanted to do it. Although she had friends, she also had personal boundaries that she expected to be respected. She spent most of her time alone in the school library, where she would pore over racy novels by Tanizaki Jun'ichirō instead of studying.

Michiko was in the library when sirens began sounding across the city one April afternoon in 1942. Though she was vaguely aware of some commotion going on outside, this did not raise her concern. It was a Saturday—perhaps the local ward was holding another scheduled air raid drill she had not heard about.[3] If so, it would certainly not be the first time she had missed the memo for such an event. She paid no more mind to the matter and went back to her book.

The next morning, the dormitory was abuzz with the news of the previous day's events: Some American planes had shown up out of nowhere and dropped bombs on the city. Although damage was not extensive, an Atomi girl—the star of the school volleyball team—was among the raid's victims, killed with her mother while the two were out shopping in the fashionable Ginza retail district.[4] For Michiko, the incident marked the first instance of losing a personal acquaintance to the war. It also got her to thinking that Tokyo was perhaps not as safe as she had assumed and that she might have been better off joining the rest of her family in the sticks of Kyushu.

In terms of tactical impact, the Doolittle Raid on Tokyo of April 18, 1942, was little more than a shin kick to the Japanese war effort, and at least for the next twenty-six months, it would be a one-off event for the Home Islands.[5] From strategic and psychological standpoints, however, the raid was a slap in the face—a rude awakening that rattled Japanese complacency about the oft-touted invulnerability of their homeland to enemy attack. As the grievously humiliated Japanese military blundered into fatefully ill-advised retaliation in force against the American-held Central Pacific island of Midway, it blustered to deflect attention from—and shift blame for—its dropping the ball on the home front, calling for greater vigilance and fighting spirit on the part of the populace, as if lack of the same had somehow contributed to the debacle of American bombs violating the sacred precincts of the emperor's capital. In the post-raid, media-driven national mood swing that followed, constant air defense awareness and strictly enforced nightly blackout regulations became watch-words, particularly so for the residents of Tokyo and the other big Pacific coastal cities in Honshu.

In the same breath, the populace was reminded to keep calm and carry on, reassured that the military had everything under control again. When some of Colonel Doolittle's men were captured in China, there was breathless reportage claiming that several American bombers had shot up a schoolyard during the raid, and reassuring coverage was given to the speedy courts-martial and subsequent executions of the purported offenders.[6] In the narrative pushed by the Dōmei News Agency–led mass media, justice had been served, nothing like the raid would be allowed to happen again, and all was right again with the empire.[7] But these and other official reassurances aside, the incremental encroachment of privations and restrictions on movement, activity, and personal time over ensuing months made it increasingly difficult for Michiko and her schoolmates to ignore the reality that the war was edging closer to the once inviolate sanctuary of their own backyards.

In October 1943, as the war steadily drained the nation's supply of prime working-age men, the Japanese government canceled classroom instruction for all formerly draft-deferrable male college students enrolled in "nonessential" humanities majors to free them up for immediate military service. In April 1944, the classroom cancellations were extended to every child in the country fifteen years or older in order to mobilize this demographic for war labor. Three months after this edict—immediately after the deeply shocking news of the fall of Saipan—the war-labor-mobilization age was dropped again to twelve.

In accordance with government directives, regular classroom instruction at Atomi was duly suspended, and students were divided by year into eight-girl labor squads christened with patriotically themed names. (Michiko's labor squad was the "Akebono Squad.")[8] On campus and under direct teacher supervision, the youngest students—the twelve- to thirteen-year-old first-graders—did unpaid "volunteer" war work, tending vegetable patches on the school grounds or assembling cartridge magazines for machine guns in the school workshop. The higher-grade girls were farmed out as *dō'in gakuto* ("mobilized student") laborers, receiving modest salaries as essentially full-time employees of private enterprises involved in war production.[9] Atomi's sixteen- and seventeen-year-old fifth-graders, for example, had several work squads assigned to the vast (and by late wartime otherwise long-dormant) Takarazuka Revue Theater, which had been converted into a plant for the manufacture of giant *Fu-Gō* paper balloon bombs. These had been designed to be fitted with an incendiary payload and gassed up with hydrogen before being lofted into the stratosphere. Once there, the global jet stream was supposed to carry them across the Pacific to start fires in the great forests of the American Northwest. Although these late-war vengeance weapons never accomplished anything in the way of measurable combat results, their mere existence—and newspaper photos of happy, determined-looking girl workers building them—made for great propaganda copy, and they gave student laborers like the Atomi fifth-graders a tangible sense of helping to strike a blow against the loathed enemy now preparing to set fire to their homes.

For Michiko and her Akebono Squad workmates, however, their contributions to the war effort were not so romantic and exciting. Since the spring of 1944, they had been commuting every day to work at the main factory of Lion Toothpaste Company. This facility was about twenty minutes away by streetcar, deep in the heart of the Shitamachi and almost precisely at the geographic center of Tokyo Incendiary Zone #1. Although no Pentagon planner would have regarded bombing a toothpaste plant to be a high-priority strategic objective, Lion's Honjō factory was nevertheless designated "Target 184" in the U.S. Army Air Forces' Tokyo Target Folder.[10]

On Lion's factory floor, the Akebono girls' daily drudgery involved using wooden paddles to thwack tubes of toothpaste—actually tooth *powder*—into packing crates earmarked for military destinations. At the end of each workday, the girls would ride the streetcar back to Atomi dusted white with the stuff from head to toe. But despite the boring slog of their work and the steadily worsening privations of their daily lives in general, their morale was usually good. And Kiridōshi Michiko could always be counted on to keep the laughs coming with her narrow-eyed, poker-faced snark through thick and thin, even by the lean season of early 1945, when the food began to run out in earnest and the air raids on Tokyo became more frequent and severe. The Japanese, after all—as their leaders and mass communications media never tired of reminding them—were a race of natural-born warriors, samurai who faced adversity and hardship not only bravely but enthusiastically.

A YOUNG MAN OF PROMISE

BY THE MID-NINETEENTH CENTURY, Japan had passed two and a half centuries in jealously guarded isolation from the outside world. But this leisurely and politically stable cultural and technological slumber would come to an end with the dawn of the Age of Imperialism; Great Britain and other Western powers were beginning to exploit the sclerotic decline of East Asia's traditional Chinese hegemony to make significant military, economic, and eventually colonial inroads into the region. With Chinese power in free fall after its First Opium War (1839–1842) humiliation at British hands, it was only a matter of time, it was feared, before the Western barbarians came pounding at Japan's gate.

That time arrived on July 8, 1853, when a flotilla of U.S. Navy ships steamed into Edo (now Tokyo) Bay and their commander, Commodore Matthew C. Perry, demanded parley with local leaders. After several days of discussion, the Americans vowed to return the following year with treaty documentation, informing their stunned, affronted, and unwilling hosts that they expected all preparations to have been readied by that time for a hospitable welcome for a resident American consul.[1]

Assessing the advanced military technology of these uninvited visitors in the wake of this diplomatic bombshell, the samurai leaders of the Shogunate were forced to realize that they were not going to be able to run these foreign interlopers out at the tip of a katana sword, as their ancestors had done in the early seventeenth century when they had rousted a thriving community of Portuguese Jesuit missionaries and their merchantmen hangers-on from their Nagasaki enclave and sent them skedaddling back to Manila and Macao on their barques and carracks.[2]

Faced with the present strategic dilemma, a bolder, more forward-thinking Shogunate might have committed to a mad national mobilization dash over the next twelve months so they would be in a position to tell the Americans where to stick their demands the next time they steamed into Edo Bay with their smoke-belching ships, oversized bodies, and matching attitudes. But bold new ideas had never been in the nature of this political beast, and conservative counsel ended up winning the day. A rapid modernization effort, after all, might have delegitimized the Shoguns' power base and plunged the country once again into open conflict between rival samurai fiefdoms—a scenario that would leave the archipelago wide open to divide-and-conquer exploitation by Western intruders, as in the bad old days of the sixteenth century. With what was happening in the rest of Asia at the time, these were valid concerns, and the possibility of impending colonization by one or more of the Western powers could not have been dismissed out of hand.

Bereft of better options, the hidebound and politically hamstrung Shogunate's least bad response was a feeble delaying strategy of humiliating piecemeal appeasements through the Ansei Five-Power Treaties (the so-called Unequal Treaties) it signed first with America, then with the Netherlands, Russia, Britain, and France in 1858.[3] Ceding ever more port access and trading concessions with each treaty it signed, the Shogunate sought to buy time for an eventual soft-landing modernization on its own terms, thereby preserving its domestic political power.

But there were increasing numbers of samurai who could see the writing on the geostrategic wall, and they were quickly losing patience with the ruling regime's go-to diplomatic tactic of passive-aggressive foot-dragging vis-à-vis the impertinent Western interlopers. Taking pains to avoid the Shoguns' ubiquitous secret police and nationwide snitch network, scattered discontents gradually found and created clandestine alliances with like-minded confederates. A coalition of disaffected samurai from the western Japanese domains of Satsuma and Chōshū rose to prominence in the anti-regime movement and decided to take action. Raising the rallying cry of "Revere the Emperor, Expel the Barbarians," they lined up powerful allies behind their cause and eventually secured the blessing of Emperor Kōmei (1831–1867). Arming themselves with advanced Western weaponry (primarily imported through British middlemen in Nagasaki), they overthrew the Shogunate and set up a new national state in the name of Kōmei's successor, the teenage Emperor Meiji (1852–1912).[4]

Learning their statecraft on the fly in their new capital of Tokyo, the successful coup plotters embarked on the kind of bold policy the Shogunate had been too timid and conservative to take: a crash program of modernization that upended centuries of political, social, and cultural practice. One of the most significant of the resulting reforms was the abolition of Japan's hereditary four-siloed samurai-peasant-craftsman-merchant social caste system. But this was not a policy taken out of some enlightened desire to elevate the lot of the common man; rather, its aim was to centralize authority in, and better unify society behind, the figure of the newly "restored" emperor.[5] Once this was accomplished, the new nation would steadily build up and increasingly and aggressively assert its economic and military strength, the humiliating Ansei Treaties could be renegotiated—if not abrogated entirely—and Japan would assume its rightful place among the other imperialist powers then busily engaged in the process of rapidly carving up the rest of the world amongst themselves.

In a modernizing, social-engineering sense, samurai culture had not been "abolished" so much as it had been simplified for popular consumption and expanded to include all of the emperor's subjects, regardless of station of birth. In return, these newly ennobled subjects were expected to prove themselves worthy of this honor and privilege by following to the letter every line and stage direction contained in the newly formulated life scripts the regime handed down to them.

The basic stage directions for these scripts were simple enough for any functionally illiterate peasant or child to grasp: The emperor expected that every man, woman, and child in the New Japan would perform their duty with unquestioning loyalty and stoic endurance of any hardship and self-sacrifice—up to and including one's life or the lives of loved ones—for the greater good and glory of sovereign and country. In their fulfillment of these strictly gender-specific roles and obligations, men would dedicate their lives to the emperor state as soldiers, either literally or figuratively, and it was women's sacred role to support this male duty and give birth to the next generation of imperial warriors. Personal activities and aspirations falling outside these parameters were tolerated only upon the strict understanding that such pursuits were contingent upon the generous indulgence of the emperor qua state and that they were subject to sudden suspension or termination whenever the prerogatives of duty demanded as much.

As the common foot soldiers of the Sino-Japanese and subsequent Russo-Japanese Wars soon went on to prove, the populace responded to their initially involuntary samuraization with sincere enthusiasm.[6] This revolutionary formulation of mass national consciousness would make possible the mobilization of the entire population toward the regime goals of modernization, overseas imperial expansion, and, eventually, the retooling of society from top to bottom toward the pursuit of modern, industrialized total warfare.

In the span of less than two generations, Japan's (ex-)samurai "founding fathers" succeeded in transforming the country from a provisionally cooperative feudal network of self-interested agrarian fiefdoms into a centrally governed, world-class military power fueled by a burgeoning export economy. Much of the nuts-and-bolts spadework for this transformation was the handiwork of great mercantile houses like Mitsubishi, Mitsui, Sumitomo, and Yasuda. Accordingly, the entrepreneurs and financiers leading these firms—mostly members of the former (and socially lower) Shogunate Era merchant caste—went on to amass great fortunes and political influence.

Despite their wealth and contributions, however, Japan's new captains of industry and finance did not occupy pride of place in the nation they had contributed so much to build. Neither did the members of the reconfigured aristocracy orbiting the throne—a mixed bag of extended imperial family relatives, old Kyoto retainers, and newly ennobled former samurai fiefdom chiefs. Instead, the summit of power, prestige, and cultural influence in New Japan was steadily ceded, over the first few decades of the Meiji Era, to the military and bureaucratic elite of the new imperial state's executive branch.[7]

The members of this elite—the direct institutional successors of the original Meiji Restoration coup plotters—considered themselves the flame keepers of the old hereditary samurai ethos they revered as Japan's spiritual backbone. As such, from the late nineteenth century on, one of the most important tasks of this cohort was to oversee the regime's aforementioned samuraization project for the general populace through military conscription, public ceremony / pageantry (the main function of the new religion of State Shintō), media overwatch, and, perhaps most important of all, centrally controlled compulsory education.[8]

The new imperial state was tooled for totalitarianism by a theocratic ideological foundation based on worship of the emperor as a living deity. The implementation of this ideology and the machinery of state it legitimized were overseen by a core cadre of national leaders who in their heart of hearts mistrusted the principle of democracy, who tolerated no genuine political opposition (which could have been interpreted as apostasy when it was at the convenience of the theologically legitimated state to do so), and who sought to guide/police every aspect of the individual and collective lives of the emperor's subjects.

Nevertheless, this totalitarianism was generally perceived as paternalistic and benign by the populace on its receiving end, and in its way, this system of social governance was as egalitarian and progressive as those of any of Japan's ostensibly democratic Western rivals—perhaps even more so, considering the state's dedicated efforts to banish class prejudice from the national psyche (albeit for pragmatic strategic purposes). If fundamentally unassailable political authority was the state's stick, the promise of meritocratic social mobility for all Japanese—within carefully prescribed boundaries—was its carrot.

Under the new meritocratic Japanese social system, each one of the emperor's subjects—to borrow a Napoleonic metaphor—carried a marshal's baton in their haversack; the regime was on a constant lookout for new talent to cultivate and then elevate into its managerial ranks. Toward this end, the state provided two "royal roads" (ōdō) by which any young Japanese man of ability and ambition might rise to membership in the ranks of the national executive elite. For those who would serve their emperor in uniform, one of these roads led through the imperial service academies—either Etajima in Hiroshima for the Navy or Ichigaya in Tokyo for the Army. For those who preferred to serve the emperor from the safety of a bureaucratic desk, the second road—leading to the highest ranks of the civil service elite—began with admission to the University of Tokyo (Tōdai).

Access to either road started from early adolescence with a grueling regimen of rote memorization and intensive cram studying for entrance exams—provided, of course, a boy's family situation afforded the time and a modicum of household resources to be devoted to this pursuit. Naturally, there were certain cases—as in any meritocracy—where an individual's circumstances of birth might have conferred a certain edge in this competition.

Ishida Hisashi (1895–1962) was one such individual. As the son of a district court judge and the descendant of a long line of Okayama samurai scholars, young Ishida started out with a strong and steady wind at his back to propel him toward a stellar academic future.[9] After graduation from Shūyūkan Junior High in Fukuoka, he was accepted into Daigō Kōtō Gakkō (National High School Number Five) in Kumamoto.[10] This was one of the eight so-called Number Schools located around the country; directly administered by the Ministry of Education, and serving as regional feeder schools for the nation's elite imperial universities.[11] With Hisashi's place on the institutional escalator to highflier status thus secured, it was almost a matter of course when, three years later, he won the grand prize of Japanese academic meritocracy: admission to Tōdai's Faculty of Law.

Hisashi had a charismatic and garrulous personality that set him apart from the sort of colorless grind typical of so many of his Tōdai classmates. The combination of this temperament with a broad range of cultural interests, including literature and the theater, soon saw him develop into a big man not only on but also off campus, where he rubbed shoulders with literati in the capital's salons of cultural influence and with kingmakers in its corridors of institutional power.

After his graduation from Tōdai, Hisashi was hired into an elite executive track at Mitsubishi. But this career path lost its luster for him after only two years. Eschewing the lure of the corporate ladder, he followed his father into a career with the Ministry of Justice, where he reached jurisprudent rank while still in his late twenties.[12] By the 1930s, his name was appearing regularly in the national daily newspapers in coverage of numerous famous courtroom trials.

One critical personal contact Hisashi had made during his time at Tōdai could have served as a poster boy for the Imperial Japanese meritocracy: Hirota Kōki was the son of a stonemason who, at the turn of the century, had battled his way up and out of the Fukuoka working class and into Tōdai through sheer talent, chutzpah, and force of will. By the time he took Hisashi under his wing, he was an up-and-coming bureaucrat in the prestigious Foreign Ministry.

A second key contact Hisashi made during his days of high-flying Tōdai hobnobbing was Inoue Tetsujirō (1855–1944)—yet another Fukuokan academic prodigy who, in the previous century, had also made his way to the capital via Tōdai. He had gone on to become an accomplished literary figure while still in his twenties and, in 1882, was hired as the first native Japanese instructor of philosophy at his alma mater.[13] Once securely ensconced in his ivory tower after a six-year-long study sabbatical in Europe—during which he developed a deep suspicion of, and psychologically near-crippling inferiority complex toward, the West and Westerners—Inoue quickly threw in with other conservative public intellectuals working to sort out what they saw as the spiritual and ideological confusion that had been created by Japan's headlong importation of Western ways during its breakneck modernization.[14]

Inoue made a name for himself in this regard in the 1890s when he penned an official commentary on the recently issued Imperial Rescript on Education, which codified in absolutist moral and religious terms the regime's expectation that its subjects should prioritize their obligations to the emperor in all aspects of their lives.[15] He also contributed to the critical Establishment goal of checking the challenge to regime loyalty then posed by a renascent Japanese Christianity, which had begun to flourish again—after two hundred fifty years of brutal Shogunate suppression—under the freedom of religion ostensibly granted to imperial subjects as a modernizing social reform, but more accurately regarded as something the Meiji Regime had promulgated under the Western gaze (while holding its collective nose) as cultural window dressing toward eventual renegotiation of the despised and humiliating Unequal Treaties.[16] From mid-career, Inoue also played a Rudyard Kipling–esque role in support of Japan's ideological mobilization goals, using prolific publication and frequent appearances on lecture circuits to promote for popular consumption an aggressively nationalistic new ethos—heavy on geopolitical social Darwinism and samurai-esque values like self-sacrifice and thrift—that was a perfect fit for the spirit of spartan mystical militarism then beginning to build up ideological steam in the country in the wake of the Russo-Japanese War.[17]

In 1924, Inoue married his daughter Takako[18] off to the young Fukuokan up-and-comer in the capital named Ishida Hisashi. After tying the knot, the young couple moved into a rental house near the Inoue family compound in Koishikawa Ward. Grandchildren for the renowned professor soon arrived, beginning with the Ishidas' son, Jō'ichi, followed by three daughters: Masako, Yasuyo, and Shizuko.[19]

YAMANOTE GIRL

FOR A BRIEF time during the postwar Allied occupation of Japan, Judge Ishida's eldest daughter, Masako, was one of the most famous hibakusha in the country. She was never comfortable in this role, however, having never sought it in the first place, and when the shelves of Japan's bookstores began to fill with other hibakusha testimonies from the 1950s on, a much-relieved Masako stepped out of the limelight and slipped into comfortable anonymity as an ordinary mid-twentieth-century homemaker.

Despite her hasty exit from the public stage, the few short years she had spent upon it as a living symbol of her country's phoenixlike rise from the ashes of defeat have ensured her a place in the history of early-postwar Japan. This is the context in which I first came across her name not long after beginning my research on hibakusha. One spring day in 2019, I decided to find her.

Japanese-language Google searches of both "Ishida Masako" and "Yanagawa Masako" turn up dozens of hits—mostly academic papers, library holdings, and the like for the former name and journalistic profile pieces for the latter. However, I cannot find any immediately actionable contact information; Japanese telephone search sites give me numbers for numerous individuals named "Ishida Masako" and

"Yanagawa Masako," but none are written with the exact kanji ideograms ("elegant" and "child") used in the historical figure's first name. Thumbing through a book about her, I come across mention of her brother, Jō'ichi, whose name employs the rather unusual ideograms "bumper crop" and "one." When I do another Japanese white pages search, this name gives me two hits: one in Tokyo and another in Okinawa. Steeling myself to be on my best polite Japanese linguistic behavior, I pick up the phone, dial the Tokyo number first, and get a recorded "This line is no longer in service" message. I try the Okinawa number, and an elderly woman answers. I go through my Shizuoka University credential self-intro spiel and then ask if I have reached the home of Ishida Jō'ichi. I have, and in a minute, I am talking to the master of the house.

The voice on the other end of the line is that of an individual of advanced senescence, but it is garrulous and bright, and its speaker is unmistakably cognitively sharp—something of a chip off the old block apparently. We enjoy a quick and entertaining conversation about what has brought Ishida-san to Okinawa. It turns out, he spent his professional career following in his father's illustrious footsteps at the Ministry of Justice. After retirement in the 1990s, he moved to Okinawa in search of a more hospitable climate and laid-back environment to focus his remaining years on poetry and writing about his lifelong passion of train watching.

In the midst of our conversation, I realize that Ishida-san thinks I have called to interview him. As tactfully as possible, I inform him that I am, in fact, looking for his sister Masako. We share a little nervous laughter, as my intent is clarified, before he graciously offers to contact his sister and see if she is willing to talk to me. I leave my phone number with him before we end the conversation with mutual courteousness—me encouraging him to continue his research and writing in good health and him wishing me *ganbatte kudasai* ("the best of luck and tireless efforts") with my own.

Scant minutes later, my office phone rings. I answer it and an elegant elderly female voice says, *"Hajimemashite, Yanagawa desu"* ("Nice to meet you. This is Yanagawa."). I experience an electrifying jolt of excitement, and after several long and stammering seconds to recover my composure, I finally manage to explain who I am and what I am trying to do.

"I've heard about what you are doing from other Tokyo hibakusha," she says. This gives me a little rush of accomplishment, but I am floored by what she says next.

"I've been waiting for you to contact me."

Bunkyō Ward, Tokyo

May 2019

The following Saturday, I am interviewing Ishida Masako in her apartment, which is less than two kilometers from where she was born in the Manchurian Incident year of 1931. During our talk, Ishida-san—Masako-san—reveals that in her youth she was the spitting image of her mother. If this is true, Inoue Takako must have been quite stunning, because Masako-san is one of the most beautiful elderly women I have ever met, with long, expressive eyes set above prominent cheekbones and a sharp, exquisitely sculpted jawline that belies its owner's eighty-eight years. In her speech and mannerisms, she is the very embodiment of an elegant Japanese *ojōsan*. If I have been able to identify her as such this quickly, I imagine that after no more than a minute or two of interaction, any Japanese interlocutor—even without knowing any of Masako-san's biographical details and perhaps even without an exchange of words—would immediately recognize her as an individual of privileged and cultured background.

We begin talking about her oldest memories.

In March 1936, her father's old Tōdai benefactor Hirota Kōki had just finished a stint as foreign minister and was about to succeed to the post of prime minister.[1] To help him navigate the byzantine complexities of his new job, he was in need of capable and trustworthy staff. This second qualification was perhaps especially important, given the extremely unstable nature of Japanese politics at the time. To wit, a bloody coup attempt by radical right-wing Army officers in late February 1936 had just brought about the downfall of his predecessor's Cabinet. Now, in setting up his own, Hirota needed a personal secretary whom he would literally be able to trust with his own life. Remembering his old Tōdai protégé, Hirota called in some favors to borrow Judge Ishida Hisashi from the Ministry of Justice.[2]

Masako-san's earliest memories date from around the time her family moved into the prime minister's official residence compound in Nagata-chō, the walls of which were still pockmarked with fresh bullet holes from the recent military insurrection.[3] It was a heady period of high living for the Ishidas, but it would also prove short-lived: during his time in office, Hirota had earned the ire of an Imperial Japanese Army (IJA) establishment impatient with what it regarded as his lack of enthusiasm about its ongoing and ever more audacious adventurism in China. This friction—echoed and egged on by the Army's ultranationalist allies in politics and business circles—led to Hirota's Cabinet being dissolved after less than a year and to Hirota himself being relegated to his former post as foreign minister.

In the wake of his benefactor's demotion, Judge Ishida had no choice but to return to his post at Tokyo District Court and move his family back to their old place in Koishikawa.[4] Before he could settle back into his jurisprudent duties, however, Hirota had one more job for his protégé: to undertake a nearly yearlong fact-finding mission in America and Europe; Japan, with Nazi Germany and Fascist Italy, had recently signed the Anti-Comintern Pact—the diplomatic precursor to the fateful Tripartite/Axis alliance of 1940. Nevertheless, in light of the war in which Japan was already up to its neck in China, it seems safe to assume that Hirota was anxious to avoid further military entanglements, thus not unreasonable to speculate that in tasking Judge Ishida with hand-delivering personal notes to Benito Mussolini and Adolf Hitler, he did so in hopes of getting these fascist leaders to understand the delicacy of Japan's present circumstances. With his English and German skills, legal knowledge, and engaging personality, Judge Ishida was a natural for the mission, which by his own account at least was a resounding success. Upon his return to Tokyo, he celebrated his behind-the-scenes diplomatic triumph with armfuls of souvenirs for his children and autographed photos from his private audiences with *Il Duce* and *der Führer*.[5]

Once the household settled into a more familiar domestic routine, the judge's son Jō'ichi—a budding scholar and writer, taking after his father and both grandfathers in that respect—boned up on his studies to embark on his own institutional march to Tōdai and beyond. Meanwhile, Masako and her younger sisters, Yasuyo and Shizuko, stayed closer to home, attending elementary school a short walk away at Tokyo Women's Teachers College.[6]

The four Ishida children were comfortably shielded from the vagaries of the outside world both by the socioeconomic bubble of their family's privilege and by their father's fierce overprotectiveness. And as they had never known a Japan that was not in constant preparation for engagement in total war, nothing would have seemed particularly out of the ordinary to them about the streets always being filled with Rising Sun flags, patriotic slogan banners, and parades, or for the radio airwaves to be dominated by strident announcements of military triumphs and an incessant playlist of martial music.[7]

The outbreak of war with the West in December 1941 did not have much direct impact on the Ishidas, even when, half a year after Pearl Harbor, some American planes dropped a few bombs on the Shitamachi commercial district and waterfront area in the eastern part of the city. Things began to change from mid-1943, however, as Japan's steady loss of naval supremacy across its empire saw the supply of food and general consumer goods in the capital begin to plummet precipitously. But so far, that was about the extent of tangible wartime hardship for the household.

Later that year, however, the family's fortunes took a dark turn when Masako's mother developed a nagging cough that she could not seem to shake. Doctors eventually gave her the dreaded diagnosis of tuberculosis—a perennially common Japanese ailment of the era,[8] particularly in the country's hopelessly overcrowded cities.

In peacetime Tokyo, the procurement of antibiotics to arrest or even reverse the progress of the illness would not have been an issue for the wife of an important Ministry of Justice official. But by this point in the war, medical supplies—like every other conceivable resource—were earmarked and prioritized for the military.[9] Mrs. Ishida's doctors did what they could with what they had, but their patient's condition steadily worsened through the autumn, no doubt exacerbated by the chronic malnourishment that was the lot of most mid- and late-war Japanese civilians. In November 1943, Ishida Takako died at the age of thirty-seven.[10] Her esteemed father, Inoue Tetsujirō, would follow her in death a year later.

Around this time, the Ministry of Justice informed Judge Ishida that he was being considered for promotion to the post of chief judge of the Hiroshima District Court the following spring.[11] But these plans ended up being deferred in light of the Ishida family's recent loss and the domestic upheaval it had precipitated in a household with four young school-aged children now headed by a widowed father. For the time being, Judge Ishida would remain at Tokyo District Court while Jō'ichi proceeded apace on his path to Tōdai at the elite private Seikei High School and Masako continued her studies as a first-year student at the *jogakkō* (girls' school)[12] attached to Tokyo Women's Teachers College. Yasuyo and Shizuko were evacuated out of the city with their elementary school classmates half a year later, in the summer of 1944, after the American capture of the Mariana Islands put Japan within American bomber range.[13] Yet despite their private tribulations and family tragedy, the war, for the Ishidas, was still something happening far away.

Since the Tokyo metropolitan government began conducting air raid drills in the early 1930s, the moans and bleats of civil defense sirens had become a familiar feature of the city's soundscape. But when they began wailing on the beautifully sunny afternoon of November 1, 1944, they announced the arrival of the war at the city's doorstep. On that day, the ironically christened *Tokyo Rose*—a special F-13 photoreconnaissance B-29 flying out of one of the new American bomber bases in the Marianas—leisurely circuited high over the city for several hours, taking thousands of high-definition photographs of the landscape and infrastructure below,[14] its altitude rendering it impervious to flak or the fighters that scrambled to intercept it. Upon *Tokyo*

Rose's return to its Guam home base, this film was processed and used by the operations staff at the headquarters of General Haywood S. Hansell's XXI BC to identify priority industrial targets for the daylight-precision-bombing campaign that was about to commence against the capital.

Regular air raids on Tokyo began on November 24 and would not let up for the next nine months.[15] In the first phase of their campaign, the Americans expended particular fury (and many thousands of tons of inaccurately dropped high explosives) against the Nakajima Aircraft Engine Factory—a massive industrial complex near Jō'ichi's high school in the northern suburb of Musashino. While Jō'ichi regularly returned from school with stories about hunkering down in shelters with his classmates as American bombs exploded nearby, Judge Ishida and Masako—and their Koishikawa home—were for the most part out of immediate danger, and the most stressful consequence of the raids for the family's quality of life was sleep deprivation. Although bombs usually fell on the city in the daytime, the existence of American bomber bases in the Marianas meant that B-29s might appear over or near Greater Tokyo at any time, day or night.[16] And whenever this happened, regardless of the hour or the strength of the American formation, sirens and emergency radio broadcasts would compel the residents of the city to head for air shelters.

NORTH FIELD, GUAM

ON THE UNSEASONABLY warm morning of March 9, 1945, Kiridōshi Michiko and the other Akebono Squad girls were getting ready to descend into the Shitamachi once again for another eight-hour shift at Lion Toothpaste. After a typical late-war breakfast of barley rice gruel and whatever scraps of vegetables Sumiko-san had managed to scrounge up for her undernourished charges, the girls boarded an eastbound No. 17 streetcar. As the conveyance negotiated a long, curving descent down Tomisaka Slope, it unknowingly crossed into what the American enemies called Incendiary Zone #1 a few blocks past Kōrakuen Park.[1] After traveling east another four kilometers—with a good stretch of the trip passing through areas of Kanda and Shitaya, wards that had been destroyed by an earlier raid—the girls got off the streetcar in Asakusa before crossing the Umaya Bridge on foot to reach the Lion Toothpaste plant on the far bank of the Sumida.[2]

A few hundred meters to the north of Atomi Jogakkō, Ishida Masako also got ready for another day of war labor—in her case, soldering circuit boards and polishing metal avionics parts in lieu of classwork. Tying on a white cotton Rising Sun *hachimaki* headband, she said goodbye to her father and Jō'ichi and set out for her streetcar commute to the Anritsu Electrical Company factory in Minami-Azabu, a Yamanote neighborhood in Minato Ward nearly six kilometers away to the south.[3]

By late afternoon, the balmy sunshine Greater Tokyo had enjoyed during the morning was replaced by weather conditions more seasonally appropriate for the capital in early March. Now there was a dry, bitingly cold wind blowing in hard from the northwest—exactly the conditions XXI BC meteorologists had been hoping for this evening.[4]

Twenty-five hundred kilometers from Lion Toothpaste and not far from the HQ compound where the XXI BC weathermen toiled over their maps and charts, hundreds of revving Wright Duplex-Cyclone engines were heat-shimmering the tropical air over the macadam and crushed coral of Guam's North Field, their lower notes reverberating with an earthshaking rumble. As this sound rose a step in pitch and chest-rattling power, gleaming aluminum B-29s of the 314th Bombardment Wing began to roll off of their hardstands and merge into long lines to taxi toward takeoff position at the southwest end of the field's parallel twin runways.[5]

Two kilometers to the northeast, at the opposite end of the runways, Major General Curtis LeMay stood next to his jeep in the slowly fading light, silently chomping one of the unlit cigars he was rarely seen in public without.[6]

Although LeMay was still only thirty-eight, he could have easily passed for a man in his mid-fifties. Stockily built and dour-faced, he cut a decidedly uninspiring, even frumpy figure, and a tendency toward corpulence caused his khaki uniform to cling to his heavy frame for a sweaty-schlub effect—a cross between Louisiana sheriff and Maytag repairman. With the exceptions of his lushly profuse pompadour, which he wore for the entirety of his adult life parted and pomaded in 1930s-matinee-idol fashion, and the omnipresent cigar, which helped to hide the Bell's palsy that partially paralyzed the right side of his face,[7] no other aspects of the general's wardrobe or physique betrayed any evidence of any concern on his part about his physical appearance.

But LeMay's looks belied the fact that at the time he was the youngest major general in any branch of the U.S. Army. He had commanded a wing of B-17s in the Eighth Air Force with distinction, flying missions out of Great Britain against Germany and Nazi-occupied France and helping to perfect the combat box formation for defensive aerial gunnery that went on to become a standard tactic in American bomber operations.[8] In Pentagon circles he was regarded as America's best frontline bomber man—a driven, iron-willed, motivated, and motivating leader credited with helping turn the tide of the air war in Europe. Along the way, he had acquired a reputation as a seat-of-the-pants miracle worker—a sort of one-man managerial fire brigade who specialized in swooping in to take over underperforming units and whip them into fighting shape in short order.[9]

It was this specific set of skills that put him on the radar of Pentagon decision-makers and eventually resulted in his being sent to take over XX Bomber Command in China and India in August 1944. This transfer was followed by another just a few months later, when he was transferred to the Mariana Archipelago for his current assignment heading up XXI BC, which at the moment was arguably second in terms of influence, impact, and importance in the overall context of the American air war only to General Henry "Hap" Arnold's post as commanding general of the Army Air Forces.

Another secret to LeMay's success was undoubtedly his nearly superhuman ability to work through extreme levels of stress while revealing to others as little of his internal dialogue as possible. As a habit, LeMay preferred receiving information to giving it, offering very little in the way of communication with others that was not directly relevant to some pressing matter immediately at hand and then only in utterances he delivered primarily in monosyllables. As his onetime staff officer and later secretary of defense Robert McNamara recalled, LeMay's working vocabulary seemed to consist primarily of three words: "Yes," "No," and "Yep."[10]

In rare moments he might have let his guard down to engage in brief "Where are you from, son?"-type exchanges with some random enlisted man, or to respond to someone else's witticism with the quick, single-beat snort that was the closest he could manage to a sincere laugh, but on the whole, prevailing opinion seems to have it that he was generally not a very pleasant person to be around.[11] St. Clair McKelway—another member of XXI BC headquarters staff and a *New Yorker* magazine columnist in civilian life—recalled of his former commanding officer that "he ... was what, by civilian standards, would be called rude to many people," and that when he did speak, it was "through teeth that had obviously been pried open only with effort, an effort with which the speaker had no real sympathy."[12]

On this balmy, tropical late afternoon of March 9, 1945, LeMay was even more taciturn than usual. Although he had his chief of staff and an entourage of staffers and journalists in tow—as major generals usually did when a history-making event was afoot—LeMay did not attempt to engage any of them in conversation, and his silence was reciprocated.[13] In the tense quiet of the moment, the rapt attention of all present was focused on the opposite end of North Field, where long lines of B-29s stuffed to groaning with napalm clusters were converging on the far ends of the runways.

In just a few more minutes, those planes—joined by an additional 271 B-29s flying out of nearby Saipan and Tinian—would begin taking to the skies to carry out "Operation MEETINGHOUSE."[14]

During the previous four months of operations against the Japanese Home Islands, XXI BC had adhered to an institutional and regularly publicly self-trumpeted moral commitment to avoiding the deliberate targeting of civilians, concentrating instead on the daytime precision bombing of war production facilities. But that policy—which had not brought about any appreciable results against Japan—would officially end tonight.

LeMay had once remarked that in order to win a war, "you've got to kill people, and when you've killed enough they stop fighting."[15] With MEETINGHOUSE, he was going to put that principle into practice. Toward that end, he was committing the bulk of his B-29s and some three thousand aircrewmen to an unprecedented nighttime, low-altitude, mass incendiary raid against the most flammable city in the world.

Ultimate responsibility for the success or failure of this venture rested with LeMay alone, and this was certainly weighing on his mind as he waited for the 314th BW to begin taking off from North Field. Any number of undesirable developments over the course of the mission could result in catastrophe: His overloaded B-29s might crash on takeoff; the antiaircraft fire over Tokyo could be much heavier and more accurate than LeMay's intelligence people had predicted; enemy fighters might make an appearance in unexpected force; some unforeseen sudden front of perilous weather—always a possibility in this part of the world—might materialize out of nowhere to assail the assault force at some point during its fourteen hours in the air to and from the target area, causing planes to collide in the murky darkness or crews to lose their way, run out of fuel, and end up ditching in the Pacific at night with meager hope of rescue.[16] A thousand different things could go wrong, the contemplation of any one of which was enough to put sweat on the brow of even the toughest, most emotionally withdrawn commander.

If it had been up to him, LeMay would have been at the controls of the lead plane tonight, as he used to do on big raids in Europe and as he had done on several occasions flying out of Chengdu with XX BC.[17] But there would be no more of that kind of derring-do for him; as part of his briefing before taking over command of XXI BC from General Hansell, he had been told about the ongoing development of some kind of top secret superbomb that would in all likelihood be staged from one of his Mariana bases when it was finally ready for deployment—by current estimates, sometime in the summer of 1945. LeMay had been briefed to a level of need-to-know detail—a broad-stroke sketch of scale, timetable, and delivery method and no more. But that was still enough to permanently ground him from any further participation in combat missions over enemy territory.

With no more planning and preparations to attend to, his role for the rest of the night of March 9 to 10 would be limited to sitting around headquarters, waiting for the first aircrews to break radio silence over the target and then, seven or so hours after that, when he would be back out here by the runway again, waiting for the planes and their crews to come back. It was going to be a long fourteen hours.

For the rank and file of the XXI BC, March 9 had already been a long day before a single B-29 was wheels up. While Ishida Masako and Kiridōshi Michiko and tens of thousands of other student workers were toiling away on cold Tokyo factory floors, tens of thousands of LeMay's ground support personnel and aircrew members sweated under a tropical sun, getting more than three hundred B-29s ready for the night's mission. This activity was centered on the hundreds of baseball-infield-sized, asphalt-paved circular hardstands—one per bomber—that carpeted the airfields on Guam, Tinian, and Saipan. At and around each hardstand, pilots, copilots, and navigators went over flight plans, maps, target assignments, timetables, and preflight checklists. Flight engineers checked and rechecked circuits and fuel mixture settings, mentally juggling data from dozens of dials and switches on their telephone-operator-switchboard–like cockpit consoles. Radio operators made sure that their gear was in working order and that their frequencies and codebooks were up-to-date. Mechanics clambered over and under gleaming silver aluminum wings and nacelles, making last-minute adjustments to engines that would have to power the giant planes that carried the eleven-man crews all the way to Tokyo and, they hoped, back.[18] To keep those engines running for the fourteen hours from takeoff to landing, ground crews on the three bases would pump enough aviation fuel into the B-29s of the XXI BC that afternoon to fill four Olympic-sized swimming pools.[19]

Doing XXI BC's heaviest lifting on this day were the weaponeers, who were responsible for loading bombs onto the planes. They hauled and broke open mountains of shipping crates to unload nearly two thousand tons of incendiaries and hoist them up and into the bomb bays—roughly seven tons per plane.[20]

The day's preparations for the armorers—who maintained and loaded the planes' defensive armament of .50-caliber machine guns— involved something new and, at least to the crewmen who would be flying into combat, bordering on heretical madness.[21] Although the B-29s were already capable of carrying the largest bombloads in the

American arsenal, LeMay wanted his bombers to carry even more ordnance for the upcoming mission. Accordingly, he ordered his armorers to remove the defensive machine-gun armament from the planes so they could be loaded with an extra dozen clusters of M69 bomblets.[22]

When the no-guns directive was first announced at crew briefings the day before—practically in the same breath as the equally disquieting information that the upcoming operation was going to be a low-altitude night raid against the enemy's capital—the news had resulted in gasps of disbelief and despair.[23] The assembled aircrews, most of whom were already veterans of numerous daytime combat missions against Tokyo, had an obvious personal interest in having fully functioning defensive armament when flying over this typically fiercely protected target. But the word had come down from the very top, and it was final: The B-29s would be going in without their guns.[24]

Two kilometers from where LeMay was watching his assembling bombers, the boss of the 314th BW and overall commander of tonight's mission—the wired, wiry, and Hollywood-handsome Brigadier General Thomas Power—sat in the copilot's seat of lead plane *Snatch Blatch* waiting for the takeoff signal.[25] Lined up behind *Snatch Blatch* was the rest of 43rd Squadron, which would fly tonight's mission as Pathfinders for the 314th BW. This role—and that of the Pathfinder squadrons in the 73rd and 313th BWs now preparing to take off from the other Mariana bases—would be essential to the execution of MEETINGHOUSE.

The Pathfinders' job tonight would be to mark four aiming points in Tokyo's Incendiary Zone #1 with high-visibility M47A2 napalm bombs.[26] These coordinates had been carefully selected with the objective of igniting "appliance fires"—blazes requiring the attention of professional first responders with specialized firefighting equipment like hose and ladder trucks. If all went according to plan and the weather cooperated, the fires started around the aiming points would quickly overwhelm attempts on the ground to get them under control. While Tokyo's front line of firefighters[27] was preoccupied by the appliance fires, the long streams of B-29s following on behind the

Pathfinders would use these marking fires as homing beacons. Once over the target area, their bombardiers would not even have to use the precision features of their Norden bombsights—they'd just have to ballpark-aim their bombloads at any dark spots remaining in the sea of fire below that weren't rivers, canals, or Tokyo Bay.[28]

On a map, the aiming points occupied the corners of an oblong quadrilateral encompassing the most densely built-up (and thus optimally flammable) districts of the Shitamachi incendiary zone. The northernmost of these—Aiming Point #1—was in the heart of the congested, old-city wooden maze that was Asakusa. Two-thirds of the squadrons put up by the 73rd BW tonight would drop their ordnance on and around this spot after its marking by their Pathfinders.

A third each of the 73rd and 313th BWs was assigned to Aiming Point #2, which was in Honjō Ward on the east bank of the Sumida (and not far from Lion Toothpaste). This was a newer part of the city—like Fukagawa Ward to its immediate south, the result of rapid Meiji Period urban and industrial development. Unlike the organically evolved and chaotically convoluted Edo Period buildup that had grown over centuries on the west bank of the Sumida, the East Shitamachi was laid out on a grid pattern. But not all of the grid-forming lines here were roadways; nearly as many were canals originally dug to irrigate the rice paddies that had once covered this part of Old Edo before being widened, deepened, and straightened to service cargo barges for the factories and warehouses the sprouted up here during Japan's late nineteenth- and early twentieth-century industrial revolution. The "squares" of Honjō and Fukagawa dry ground so demarcated were connected with narrow bridges and packed tight with wooden structures almost right up to the edges of these waterways. A few long firebreaks had been cleared through the East Shitamachi since the summer of 1944, but the IJA engineers who had originally mapped and cleared them had not done so envisaging conflagrations springing up simultaneously across the entire area.[29]

Aiming Point #3 was in the harbor district of Fukagawa Ward, directly south of Honjō Ward, and it was assigned to the remainder of the 313th BW.

The final aiming point—#4—was located back on the west bank of the Sumida, in Nihonbashi, at the southwest corner of Incendiary Zone #1. Similar to Asakusa, Nihonbashi was another Times Square–like Shitamachi pleasure-and-retail district, though more upscale due to its history as the former economic and cultural heart of Old Edo and, more recently, on account of its high-rent proximity to Tokyo Station and the Imperial Palace. *Snatch Blatch* and the other Pathfinders of the 43rd Squadron would mark this aiming point for the rest of the 314th BW.[30]

As the bombardiers were briefed, each plane in the main (i.e., non-Pathfinder) force would carry forty E-28 or E-46 cluster canisters, each of which contained thirty-eight M69 bomblets. The intervalometers ("time × speed = distance"–calculating devices) in the planes' bomb salvo systems would be set to fifty feet, causing them to electrically release their entire payloads of clusters one at a time in just over six seconds (a rate of fire approximating that of a .50-caliber machine gun).

The cluster canisters were fused to pop open and release their incendiary cargo at preset altitudes of between six hundred and seven hundred fifty meters in order to provide an optimal saturation density of bomblets over the target. With cooperative weather (dry and windy) and sufficiently dense urban buildup below, one B-29 could set fire to an area the size of twelve laterally stacked American football fields.[31] At Shitamachi population densities, this would mean a single aircraft could kill or, at a minimum, dehouse some twenty-five hundred people on the ground.[32]

Tonight, LeMay would be sending more than three hundred of these aircraft against Tokyo.

MEETINGHOUSE

AT 1736 HOURS Mariana Time (1636 Japan Time), the North Field control tower cleared *Snatch Blatch* for takeoff.[1] Acknowledging the signal, General Power and aircraft commander Captain George Simeral stomped hard on their respective brake pedals while Simeral pushed the engines to full throttle. When the takeoff officer standing on the tarmac next to the plane dropped his flag, pilot and copilot released the brakes and the B-29 jumped off into its takeoff run. The last human faces *Snatch Blatch*'s crew and their VIP copilot would see on solid ground for the next fourteen hours were North Field's Protestant and Catholic chaplains standing together by the takeoff start line and blessing each plane before it roared off into the late-afternoon sky.[2]

Out at the opposite, Pati Point end of the field, LeMay stood in silence for nearly half an hour watching the 314th BW take off from its parallel runways, two bombers at a time, each sending up clouds of coral dust that barely settled before the next two planes in line began their runs. When the general set off back to his headquarters at Tumon Bay to begin his long night of listening and waiting by the radio, planes of the 73rd and 313th BWs were beginning to take off from nearby Saipan and Tinian, which were several hundred kilometers closer to the target.

By the time the last planes were aloft, the strike force was a pair of airborne aluminum daggers, each hundreds of kilometers long and speeding at low altitude over the Pacific, pointed straight at the heart of the Japanese Home Islands.[3]

The air defense of Greater Tokyo was coordinated at Eastern Military District Headquarters, a purpose-built bunker near the northern tip of the Imperial Palace grounds.[4]

The bunker's nerve center was its belowground and bombproof operations room, which was laid out like the tiered surgical gallery of a medical college.[5] Down on the floor, plotters worked a large map table with croupiers' rakes and contact information cards. Encircling this area, mobilized schoolgirls manned phone desks, standing by to receive field reports and send out alert calls as needed.

Taking up one wall of the room was a giant electrically operated information board featuring a map of the Kantō region and the main sea-lane approaches to the area. Whenever any observer post, radar installation, or offshore picketboat picked up an enemy contact headed toward Honshu, the estimated size, bearing, and altitude of the contact would be marked on the plotting table, and the information board would illuminate its position with red lights so that its progress could be ascertained at a glance from the shift commander's desk on the highest tier of the room. If this high-ranking officer determined that the contact posed a legitimate air raid threat, the phone operators would notify airfields and flak emplacements to go on alert, local municipal authorities throughout their region would sound sirens in their respective jurisdictions, and the civilian NHK radio announcer on duty in the operations room would cut into Radio Tokyo's main AM broadcasting signal from his special microphone desk to read reports and updates[6] written by his military minders.

On this evening, there was some concern about recent rumors that the Americans were planning something big to disrupt the capital's celebrations for Army Day, a national holiday observed every year on March 10—the anniversary of the decisive Battle of Mukden in the Russo-Japanese War.[7] But even if these rumors were true, March 10 was tomorrow, and everyone in the operations room—if not everyone in Tokyo by this point in the war—knew the Americans appeared over the capital in force only by daylight, when they would usually go after the aircraft plants they had been obsessively targeting since the previous November. When they did fly over at night, it was only singly or in small formations, carrying out their usual sleep-interrupting nocturnal harassment raids, which the Americans referred to euphemistically as "weather missions." Once Eastern Military District learned not to get too concerned about the weather missions, these might be cause for *keikai keihō* ("warning alert") sirens, but not for subjecting the entirety of Greater Tokyo to a full-on *kūshū keihō* ("air raid alert"), which would entail, at a stroke, the loss of literally millions of man-hours' worth of labor for the region's hard-pressed war industries while night shift workers were either huddled up in bomb shelters or in transit to or from the same.

As the operations room wall clock ticked toward 1800 hours, the soldiers and schoolgirls on duty at Eastern Military District Headquarters settled into the rhythm of what most probably expected would be another uneventful four-to-midnight watch.

—————

Three kilometers south of Tokyo's air defense HQ bunker, at NHK's overseas broadcast facility near Shiba Park, microphone switches were flipped on at precisely 1800 hours and Radio Tokyo's shortwave signal began bouncing the opening bars of the circus-brassy romp of Arthur Fiedler and the Boston Pops' rendition of "Strike Up the Band" off the ionosphere.[8] Across the far reaches of the Pacific—in the Marianas and the Philippines, from the Aleutian Islands to New Guinea, on land, at sea, and in the air—hundreds of thousands of Allied servicemen within earshot of shortwave sets listened in, as they did every night at this time, to catch their favorite Japanese propaganda radio program, *Zero Hour.*

Zero Hour had been a runaway hit with its specifically targeted GI audience since going on the air in late 1943, not only because of its playlist of big band numbers and torch songs, but more than anything else for its English-speaking female disc jockeys, who filled the airtime between songs with wryly twisted propaganda and flirty, innuendo-laden banter. The girl who worked the microphone most nights delivered her lines with an unmistakably sunny (and genuine) Southern Californian accent,[9] which she played up to exaggerated juvenile effect, especially when she was openly mocking her captor employers with an over-the-top pidgin routine that kept her GI audience in stitches but to which the NHK censors apparently never caught on.[10] On-air, the girl referred to herself as "Orphan Annie" (often adding "your favorite playmate, the little sunbeam whose throat you'd like to cut"). But in the American imagination, she would forever be known as "Tokyo Rose."

As Orphan Annie's sassy chatter reverberated through the ether on the evening of March 9, 1945, three-hundred-odd B-29s were flying low and fast in the exact opposite direction of the Radio Tokyo signal carrying her voice.

Although these bombers were part of the largest formation of aircraft yet seen in this theater of the war, this notion would have felt like little more than intellectual abstraction to the men on board the planes, each one of which was for all intents and purposes flying alone in the dark. In this particular formation, each B-29 was surrounded by twelve kilometers of (the aircrewmen hoped) empty space, with the next plane up the bomber stream six kilometers ahead and essentially invisible under blacked-out combat conditions, as the planes were flying toward enemy airspace without their usual nighttime navigation safety lights. As a precaution, every member of each crew not directly engaged with actually flying the airplanes would spend most of the fourteen-hour mission on anti-midair-collision watch, staring out at the gloom through Perspex windows at their respective workstations.[11] Outside of rare occasions when a sudden and rapidly developing situation would involve a screamed lookout warning over the intercom and corresponding violent evasive maneuvers, this was monotonous duty. Eyelids could get heavy, and minds could wander. To help pass the time and keep everyone on their toes, the radio operators on some of the planes tuned their shortwave gear to Radio Tokyo when *Zero Hour* came over the airwaves, patching the signal through their planes' intercom so their crewmates could listen in. According to at least one former XXI BC crewman's account, Orphan Annie's playlist for March 9, 1945, was a darkly and, presumably, unintentionally prophetic one that included such numbers as "Smoke Gets in Your Eyes," "His Favorite Flame," and "I Don't Want to Set the World on Fire."[12]

Two thousand kilometers to the north, most of the residents of the Japanese capital were also within earshot of radios, which in their case were uniformly tuned to Radio Tokyo playing its typical AM band fare of military marches, fake war news, and, when necessary, air raid information.

In Koishikawa, the radio in the Atomi rec room had been left on every night since the first B-29 raids on the city the previous November, and the dorm's residents had long since learned to sleep with one ear open, listening for the announcer to interrupt regular broadcasting to deliver air raid bulletins. But like most people living under American bombs in Tokyo and other cities in Japan, the Atomi girls primarily relied on neighborhood sirens to warn them of air raid danger. When the sirens sounded any kind of alert—whether of the *kūshū keihō* or the less urgent *keikai keihō* variety—dorm protocol required the girls to open all of the windows, regardless of the weather, before taking refuge in the bomb shelter downstairs. The window policy was supposed to minimize damage from near-miss explosions, both in terms of avoiding flying glass and by letting blast wind simply blow straight through the building, in one side and out the other, instead of having the structure take the full brunt of the shock—at least in theory. Nobody knew if this measure would actually work, but Inoue-sensei and Sumiko-san—who had probably read about it in an air defense article in some women's magazine—insisted that it had to be done, so it was.

There was, however, one resident of the dorm who never took the sirens seriously. Whenever they sounded at night (for the usual weather mission / harassment raid), the other girls dutifully performed their window-opening routine before heading to the shelter, but Kiridōshi Michiko would inevitably complain about the cold and wave off entreaties to participate in the evacuation before rolling over on her futon and pulling her blanket over her head. For some reason, this insubordination was never reported to nor punished by Inoue-sensei. And in any case, Michiko was always confident that no bombs were ever going to fall on staid, leafy old Koishikawa.

A few hundred meters northwest of the Atomi dorm, Judge Ishida had also worked out a protocol routine for emergency nighttime evacuation for himself and the two adolescent children still living under his roof. His daughter Masako had long since taken to sleeping in her work clothes with a steel Army helmet next to her pillow. That way, when the sirens sounded or the radio announced approaching enemy aircraft, she could roll off of her futon and jump into her *geta* sandals and then into the family's backyard foxhole with her father and brother within seconds. If the all clear signal sounded before too long, she might be able to get back to sleep. But she was not always so lucky.

At 2230, sirens throughout the Greater Kantō region began sounding the intermittent bleats of a warning alert. This put the populace on notice to be ready to take shelter if or when the more urgent (and, as per the National Air Defense Law of 1941, legally binding) air raid alert sounded. The warning alert signal also meant that strict light discipline regulations automatically went into effect; Tokyo went dark in an instant as metropolitan authorities threw a switch to turn off the city's streetlights. In homes and any places of business that were still open at this hour, citizens had already, per regulations, drawn heavy blackout curtains across the windows thirty minutes earlier, at the prescribed nightly hour of 2200.

Against this background wailing of sirens, radio sets within range of Radio Tokyo's AM signal simultaneously crackled with the repeated phrase the NHK announcer always used when interrupting the broadcast for air raid information: "This is a bulletin from the Eastern Military District.... This is a bulletin from the Eastern Military District...."

In his next breath, the announcer informed his audience that American bombers had been detected approaching from the south and were believed to be headed toward the Bōsō Peninsula—the landmass forming the eastern shore of Tokyo Bay.[13] Several updates later, however, he reported that the aircraft appeared to be turning away. Eastern Military District issued an all clear, the sirens went silent, and nocturnal life in Greater Tokyo returned to wartime normalcy.

The American bombers *were* turning away in a literal sense, but only temporarily; because the success of the mission would depend on the main incendiary force being able to see the aiming points marked by the Pathfinders, LeMay's tactical planners had determined that from the visual angle of the bombers' altitude relative to their targets, attacking from downwind would be optimal in terms of avoiding the otherwise obfuscating effects of smoke from previously ignited fires. For tonight, LeMay's meteorologists had predicted that typically seasonal westerly winds would be blowing across the target area—a forecast that had been confirmed by a weather plane flying over Tokyo earlier in the day.[14] Accordingly, around 2230 hours, Japan Time, and about ninety minutes out from their target, the XXI BC's twin bomber streams executed a big wheeling right turn away from the Kantō region and back out over the Pacific[15] to set themselves up for a downwind run on Tokyo. On board the planes, the pilot / aircraft commanders at this point would have ordered their crews to don battle gear—steel helmets and flak jackets—as a final preparation for entering hostile airspace.[16]

After a second wheeling turn—hard port/left/west in this case—the B-29s, still spaced one minute apart, commenced individual bomb runs that would take them west across Chiba Prefecture and Tokyo Bay at staggered altitudes and headings to avoid midair collisions and to confuse enemy fighters and antiaircraft defenses.[17]

Lulled into a false sense of security by the all clear announcement, no one on the ground in Incendiary Zone #1 had any clue that anything

MEETINGHOUSE 63

was wrong until they heard the chest-rattling drone of low-flying B-29s approaching from the east a few minutes after midnight.[18] When the first bombs of the raid fell on Aiming Point #3 in Fukagawa Ward at 0008 hours, some Shitamachi residents were already running around in the streets, trying to figure out what was going on.[19] Four minutes later, Aiming Point #2 was hit. This was followed in quick succession by Aiming Point #1 and Aiming Point #4.

On the ground, the first sirens had only begun to sound at 0015, nearly ten minutes after the narrow streets of the Shitamachi began echoing with the sound of approaching B-29s, and seven minutes after the first of those streets began to go up in flames steadily fanned by the night's strong prevailing winds.

While the 43rd Squadron Pathfinders finished marking Nihonbashi, *Snatch Blatch*—which carried extra fuel tonight in lieu of a bombload—took up a circuiting orbit at high altitude over the city. From this airborne eagle's aerie, Brigadier General Power began sketching the progress of the mission on a sheaf of crude mimeographed maps of Incendiary Zone #1.[20] Every ten minutes over the next three hours, he would record the conflagration pattern he observed below on a new map, coloring burning areas in red pencil. He would go through several pencils before the night was through.[21]

At lower altitudes, the sight of the Shitamachi succumbing to flame was viscerally impressive. To an intelligence observer aboard one B-29, the landscape he saw two thousand meters below his Perspex window "looked like all the open hearths in Pittsburgh."[22] And every minute, two or three new bombers would fly in from the southeast to drop their rapid-popping daisy chains of napalm clusters, feeding more six-hundred-meter-long shovelfuls of white-hot coals into this blast furnace.[23]

Released from their clusters, the M69s—1,520 of the 2.7-kilogram bomblets in each planeload—built up enough velocity to easily punch through the tile or pressed asbestos roofs of the wooden homes and factories below. According to an eyewitness on the ground, M69-perforated structures were ablaze "[w]ithin minutes"—just as the Dugway Proving Ground technicians had predicted eighteen months before—"lighted from the inside like paper lanterns."[24] Repeated many thousands of times across the target area, each one of these single-structure blazes—whipped up by the constant strong wind from the northwest—quickly joined up with neighboring fires to form great advancing palisades of flame consuming everything in their paths, burning hot enough to melt glass and even concrete.[25]

Within half an hour after the first bombs landed on Fukagawa, the entire Shitamachi was ablaze end to end,[26] and Tokyo's already beleaguered professional firefighters were now powerless to stop the destruction.[27] The incalculable thermal energy generated by the conflagration grew and evolved like a developing hurricane system, eventually forming a kilometers-wide dome of red- and orange-glowing smoke and superheated air over the target. Sucking in all of the oxygen it could grab from the surrounding atmosphere, this man-made microclimate of flame generated winds that screamed through the narrow wooden alleys of the Shitamachi at up to a hundred fifty kilometers per hour.[28] This blast of inrushing superheated air blew burning structures to splinters and knocked fleeing people off their feet, sucking one and all into the flames. The conflagration generated such intense air turbulence that XXI BC pilots were hard-pressed to keep control of their planes as they flew over it.[29] Crews reported their planes being impacted by pieces of burning houses—doorframes, corrugated metal sheets, tatami matting, and the like—rocketing up to formation altitude on rising thermals.

Among the night's gallery of visceral and incalculable horrors, many crews reported that in addition to their cabin air filling with smoke from a million wooden houses burning below, it also carried the unforgettable and utterly stomach-churning smell of burning people.[30] As he circuited Tokyo, even the normally empathy-challenged Brigadier General Power appeared to struggle to emotionally process what his planes were doing to the human beings on the ground; one *Snatch Blatch* crewman later attested that at one point he saw the young general gaze down at the inferno below and mutter, "Poor bastards."

LeMay and his planners had gotten their firestorm.

Throughout Incendiary Zone #1, untold thousands were trapped in homes or blocked alleyways to be incinerated in place while the Shitamachi's able-bodied adults—compelled by the Air Defense Law of 1941 to assist in local firefighting—were running about outside in the blizzard of sparks and flame, trying to organize bucket brigades or attempting to put out the fires with tatami mats and handheld bamboo-tube squirt guns.[31] Almost no one who stood their ground like this would survive the night.

Those who were lucky enough to escape their burning neighborhoods to make it to the nearest firebreak thoroughfare were given an at least temporary lease on life in terms of evacuation options. Many who managed to do so attempted to make it to their designated neighborhood evacuation points—usually local elementary schools whose steel-reinforced concrete external construction and relatively spacious schoolyards offered some faint hope of sanctuary.

In Honjō Ward, many made their way to Futaba Elementary School—some seven hundred fifty meters west of Aiming Point #2. A three-story steel-reinforced concrete structure, it was one of the most modern elementary school campuses in the Shitamachi and the only one in the district with its own swimming pool.

One Honjō resident who sought refuge at Futaba was a thirty-year-old restaurant worker named Akabane Kazuo. After being awakened by the sound of B-29 engines just after midnight, he hurriedly roused his mother and three sisters, urging them to go on ahead of him to take shelter at the school while he made last-minute preparations to close up their house. When Akabane showed up at the school, however, his mother and sisters were nowhere to be found. As he searched for them one classroom at a time, he stopped to look out of an upper-story window; Honjō Ward had been transformed into a sea of fire that stretched as far as he could see.

Before long, Akabane's horrified window-side reverie was interrupted by the increasingly urgent exigencies of his own survival; making his way back down to the first floor, he ran outside and jumped into the school's swimming pool—which was already packed tight with other people, bobbing up to their necks in the water, gasping in the superheated and increasingly oxygen-starved air. A moment after he hit the water, the wooden interior of the school seemed to spontaneously combust, the building's windows exploding outward to disgorge what Akabane later described as "waterfalls of fire" that poured directly into the swimming pool.[32]

The next morning, Akabane found the body of his sixteen-year-old sister, Tokiko, in the now corpse-clogged Futaba pool. She had apparently been within arm's reach of him the whole time he had been in the water. For the rest of his life, Akabane would be tortured by the possibility that he had kept his head above water during the raid by standing on his sister's submerged body.[33] None of his other family members survived the night.

Elsewhere in the Shitamachi, people instinctively headed for the Sumida River, either to jump into its near-freezing water or with the intent of crossing it, in the not-unreasonable but fatally mistaken assumption that only their side of the river was on fire and that the opposite shore therefore offered sanctuary from the flames. Many people in neighborhoods along both banks of the Sumida seemed to have come up with the same idea simultaneously.

In Asakusa, on the west bank of the river, people fled east toward the five bridges that connected their neighborhood with Honjō Ward. Simultaneously, thousands of people attempting to evacuate from the equally furiously burning Honjō made their way to the same crossings, heading west. When the two tidal waves of panicking people (many with pushcarts piled high with household possessions) met at mid-span on the narrow bridges, traffic became hopelessly jammed. Baggage, vehicles, and people began to catch fire as M69s landed in their midst and the surrounding air itself reached organic-matter-combustion temperatures. Anyone who did not make it over the railings and into the water to drown or die of hypothermia ended up as the lumps of charcoal and scorched grease puddles first responders found on the bridges' roadways the next morning.[34]

MEETINGHOUSE

Looking at the numbers, MEETINGHOUSE was a resounding success for XXI BC. Forty-one square kilometers of Tokyo had been wiped off the map. Nearly 82 percent of Incendiary Zone #1 had been transformed into a vast field of ashes, heat-twisted steel, and carbonized corpses. Somewhere on the order of 100,000 Tokyoites had perished, succumbing in the fires, suffocating from smoke and lack of oxygen in the ensuing firestorm, or drowning or dying of exposure after seeking refuge from the fires in the freezing waters of the Sumida or the East Shitamachi's grid of barge canals. More than one million survivors were rendered homeless by the raid, which lasted two hours and fifty-three minutes and dropped some 327,000 M47 and M69 incendiaries on the emperor's capital.[35]

Not one of LeMay's bombers had been lost to enemy fighters, and only two had fallen to the moderately heavy but ultimately ineffective flak the capital's defenders had thrown up into the gloom against his low-flying, zigzagging force.[36] Of more long-term and momentous import, the radical change of Twentieth Air Force tactics from daytime precision bombing to RAF-style indiscriminate firebombing that LeMay and Brigadier General Lauris Norstad had been brainstorming for at least half a year now had just been spectacularly validated.[37] With the proof in this incendiary pudding now plain for all in the Pentagon to see, a Pandora's box was opened, shifting the entire moral tone of the war; civilian populations in Japan's cities were now fair game, and if their leaders continued to refuse to come to their senses and sue for peace, then LeMay was going to burn down the whole damned country.

PART TWO

THE ROAD TO NAGASAKI

TRAVEL ORDERS

Koishikawa Ward, Tokyo
March 10, 1945

ONCE THEY REALIZED that the Americans' fury was focused elsewhere, many Yamanote residents emerged from their shelters to watch the raid while it was still in progress. Like spectators at a fireworks display, some even oohed and aahed in wonder as each B-29 entered the target area to drop its stick of napalm cluster bombs.[1] After falling far behind and below the plane, these canisters would crack open a few seconds later with a rapid popping sound like ripping canvas, each producing a shimmering firefly curtain of streamered M69s fluttering to earth.

In Koishikawa, Ishida Masako opted not to participate in any rubbernecking at the Shitamachi's agony. Instead, she stayed hunkered down on her haunches in her family's backyard bomb shelter for the duration of the raid. Occasionally, she would gaze straight up at the sky overhead, which the inferno to the east had transformed into a red-and-orange aurora borealis that dusted her neighborhood with small embers and a steady snowfall of light gray ash. She did not stand back up from her crouch until the all clear signal finally sounded across Greater Tokyo a little before 0300.

Later that morning, with a smoke-pallid sun rising over the city, Masako watched from the front gate of her family's house as an endless, silent parade of scorched Shitamachi survivors slowly wended their way through Koishikawa, heading west. Many trundled wheelbarrows carrying possessions—or infirm family members—they had managed to save from the flames the night before. Most escaped with only the clothes on their backs. The scene caused Masako to experience a very Japanese sense of shame at her own unblemished survival and self-conscious embarrassment over her family's conspicuously intact house.

But the previous night had not been entirely consequence-free for the Ishida family. Some of the raid's incendiary tentacles had reached out of the Shitamachi and found their way into the bureaucratic precinct of Kasumigaseki, in the far southeastern corner of the Yamanote. There, less than a kilometer from where Emperor Hirohito was sheltering in a bunker with his family and staff, the Ministry of Justice compound and Judge Ishida's workplace at Tokyo District Court[2] had burned to the ground.

In the wake of the raid, personnel administrators at the ministry (or what was left of it) expedited the judge's reassignment to a new posting. Effective April 1, 1945, Ishida Hisashi would become chief judge of the Nagasaki Appellate Court. It was a prestigious posting—unmistakable recognition of highflier status for a magistrate who was just a few years past fifty. But from the perspective of an ambitious man who had just spent the past thirty years making a name for himself in the imperial capital center of the Japanese universe, it could also have been interpreted as a consignment to the boondocks, for Nagasaki was about as geographically far as it was possible to get from Tokyo without leaving the Japanese Home Islands proper.

The judge would be allowed to bring his family members along to his new posting, where they and any servants in their employ would be housed at public expense in a manner befitting an imperial servant of such lofty rank. However, it was decided that Jō'ichi would stay behind to hold down the fort in Tokyo so he could keep up with his Tōdai entrance exam preparation. He would board with maternal relatives at the old Inoue Tetsujirō compound in Koishikawa, checking in from time to time on the nearby Ishida home, which the judge was lending to the Ministry of Justice to use as a temporary dormitory for some of its incendiary-displaced personnel.[3]

In late March, rail passage was secured for the judge; his three daughters; their twentysomething personal tutor, Hayashi Akiko; and Hayashi's mother.[4] The household members spent their last night in the capital at Jō'ichi's new lodgings, taking the occasion to express their gratitude and farewells to the Inoue family.

After an arduous and continuously delayed rail journey, the traveling party—including Hayashi-sensei and her mother—moved en masse into the *kansha* ("official residence") of the Nagasaki Appellate Court chief judge. The *kansha* was an ornate Meiji Era mansion that—appropriate to its age and the cultural atmospherics of its location—was a hybrid of Japanese and European styles. Located in the downtown neighborhood of Katsuyama-machi, it was within an easy twenty-minute walk of the judge's courthouse in Banzai-machi. This, in turn, was less than two hundred meters from the Nigiwai streetcar bridge—the main artery of the theater and high-end-retail district at the geographical and cultural heart of the city. It was also USAAF cartographers' designated aiming point for Nagasaki Incendiary Zone #1.

When the air-raid-alert sirens had first sounded across Tokyo at a quarter past midnight on March 10, Kiridōshi Michiko, as usual, had waved off her roommates' pleas to evacuate with them to the Atomi Jogakkō dormitory bomb shelter. Instead, she chose to stay in her now-empty eight-bed room, watching the sky over the Shitamachi from her wide-open second-story window. As the city's sirens continued to wail, searchlight beams and arcs of tracer bullets from antiaircraft guns made furtive stabs at the low-flying intruders, whose silvery skins gleamed against the rust-colored sky with all of the reds and oranges of the burning city below.

After a while, Michiko tired of the spectacle, rolled over on her futon, and went back to sleep. When she woke up, the Shitamachi half of Tokyo was gone.

In due course, Michiko's adult minders in the Atomi Jogakkō dormitory came to the conclusion that it was only a matter of time before the Americans would return to burn down the Yamanote half of Tokyo as well. Given the high likelihood of such a development in the near future, Inoue-sensei determined that she could no longer guarantee the safety of the student boarders on campus. Accordingly, Atomi made the painful but necessary decision to shut down the dormitory.

Tokyo girls whose family homes were within commuting distance—or who could find alternative lodgings—could stay on at Atomi, working at their mobilized labor sites (assuming these had survived the firestorm of March 10) and occasionally assembling for classroom instruction on campus. Anyone else who could not make such arrangements would have no choice but to leave school for the duration. Families of the latter category of students were contacted and instructed to get their daughters home by whatever means they could manage. The fortunate were able to secure train tickets for their children. Everyone else's children either had to embark on cross-country forced marches or wait in place until Inoue-sensei could figure out what to do with them. Michiko fell into the latter category of marooned Atomi boarders.

A tenant in the Kiridōshis' rental properties in Asakusa could perhaps have been paid or otherwise persuaded to let Michiko board with them, but these houses had all gone up in flames with the rest of the Shitamachi on March 10.

The Kurofuchis, the family living in the old Kiridōshi homestead in Matsuba-chō since 1942, might have been approached for help had they not also perished in the raid along with their home and most of the neighborhood.[5]

Alternatively, Michiko might have boarded with a maternal aunt who had lived in Honjō Ward, near the main Tōdai campus, located just about midpoint between Atomi and the no-longer-extant Lion Toothpaste. But this aunt had been incommunicado since her house was lost to a smaller daytime raid on February 25—a Tokyo incendiary test run for more ambitious American arson soon to come.

TRAVEL ORDERS

Theoretically, it might have been possible to lodge with a commuting Tokyoite schoolmate, perhaps paying for room and board, but what with the increasingly dire living conditions in the now half-incinerated and half-deserted capital, food was quickly becoming something that not even money could always secure. Under these circumstances, it would have been too much of an imposition to ask someone else's family to take on another mouth to feed.

With the mass evacuations of the city after the raid, there were no other relatives or close family friends left anywhere else in Greater Tokyo who could take Michiko in. There was no other choice: Michiko could not stay in the capital. But "home" was now in Nagasaki, where Mr. Kiridōshi had taken up a new posting as bank branch manager the previous year, and getting there from Tokyo—a trip of some nine hundred kilometers—would not have been a simple matter of going to the Kokutetsu (National Railways) office and buying a ticket. While a bigwig like Judge Ishida might have been able to secure rail passage to the western Kyushu harbor city with relative ease, it would have been a different matter altogether, by this point in the war, for a "regular" civilian like Michiko to even contemplate, let alone acquire a ticket for, a train journey of such ambitious distance.

As her dormitory steadily emptied of other residents, Michiko whiled away her involuntarily indolent hours waiting for a resolution to her situation. She read mostly—in the library by day and behind blackout curtains in her now tomb-silent bedroom at night. By late March, only she and two other girls—daughters of families stranded in overseas Japanese colonies—were left in the Atomi dormitory.[6]

Deliverance finally arrived for Michiko when Inoue-sensei, through some miraculous combination of finagling and luck, managed to secure for her an unreserved-seating ticket to Nagasaki. The train would leave on March 23.[7]

Michiko made her final preparations for the trip before sunup on the morning of her departure. Her most significant challenge in this respect was posed by new official travel regulations: In view of the severe overcrowding conditions prevailing on the trains as civilians streamed out of Tokyo, rail passengers were now being restricted to a single item of handheld luggage per person.[8] This posed a serious problem for Michiko, as she possessed far more clothes than she could possibly fit in the cloth shoulder bag that was her sole piece of travel kit; neither she nor her family had foreseen the need for her to ever have to move the entirety of her possessions in one go all by herself. Moreover, due to the worsening war situation, having her belongings commercially shipped to Nagasaki was completely out of the question.

Initially resigned to abandoning the lion's share of her wardrobe in Tokyo, Michiko finally hit upon a brilliant solution to her conundrum: She would simply layer her clothing, one outfit atop the previous one, and salvage her best pair of leather shoes by wearing them on the trip. By the time she finished with donning her last layer of clothing (Kiridōshi-san claims there were twenty-four in all), she was barely able to move her limbs.

At the dormitory gate, Inoue-sensei's sister, Sueko, pressed a small cloth-wrapped package of steamed bread into Michiko's hands. It represented all of the food on hand in the dorm kitchen that morning, but at least according to the plan, this was supposed to be sufficient to hold the young traveler over—with frugal pacing—during what was scheduled to be a thirty-hour rail trip to Nagasaki. Upon thanking Sueko and saying her final goodbyes, Michiko—who must have looked like a miniature Michelin Man in her dense, bulky layers of clothing— waddled off into the predawn gloom to begin her journey.

When she arrived at Tokyo Station, she waded into a chaotic mob scene of dehoused air raid survivors desperate to get out of the city, ostensibly to seek refuge with relatives in the provinces.[9] The fortunate had the official police paperwork they needed to buy rail tickets. The unfortunate, who were in the majority, rolled out blankets or tatami matting to await the slow gears of bureaucratic salvation in the unheated passageways of the station or on the sidewalks outside.

With her own precious ticket clutched tightly in hand, Michiko navigated the crowds to make her way to the platform of the westbound Tōkaidō Line, which would get her as far as Kobe for the first leg of her trip. She arrived on the platform early, beating the long line of fellow passengers that soon formed behind her. This meant she was able to grab her desired seat—a spot on the left side of the train she wanted so she could enjoy views of the Pacific Ocean during her journey to points west.[10]

Before she set out on the trip, Michiko had assumed that she would be able to buy food along the way, as she had always been able to do during rail travel in happier times. She had not given it a second thought, then, when she hungrily gobbled down the last of Sueko's steamed bread mere hours into her journey. But the severity of this oversight soon became evident; while stops and long layovers at various stations on the way to Kobe allowed Michiko to replenish her water supply and use toilet facilities, there was no food to be had anywhere—not a grain of rice nor a crumb of bread.

Adding to her travails, there were innumerable and seemingly interminable delays, many of these between stations. Several of these occurred when Michiko's train was strafed by American carrier planes. Similar attacks on trains or rail facilities farther down the line—plus sundry other manifestations of general fog-of-war chaos—added delays on top of delays. As a result, the rail trip to Nagasaki ended up taking three and a half days, the last three of which Michiko had to endure with nothing but a stale canteen's worth of water sloshing around in her otherwise empty stomach. By the time she reached her family's new "home," in the semi-suburban east Nagasaki neighborhood of Nakagawa-machi, she was dead on her feet.

GEOGRAPHICAL DESTINY

AS KIRIDŌSHI MICHIKO, the Ishida family, and centuries of other travelers before and since have learned firsthand, Nagasaki is exceedingly difficult to approach by land—so much so that one may be forgiven for wondering why anyone ever thought to build a city there in the first place. But when the remote spot was still known as Tamano'ura, and it was a pirate cove for corsairs preying on Chinese merchantmen, its isolation and inconvenience were not bugs—they were features.

Nagasaki lies tucked into the corner pocket of a peninsula on Kyushu's craggy East China Sea coastline. This peninsula, in turn, is attached to a larger, oddly shaped blob of land that dangles from northwest Kyushu's chin like a laterally distended turkey wattle.

To its south, Nagasaki can be approached only by sea. On its other three sides, it is shrouded by deep belts of mountain ranges. North of these semi-encircling highlands lies Ōmura Bay, which puts yet more craggy coastline at Nagasaki's back and adds a massive thirty-five-kilometer-wide water obstacle to the city's line of natural defenses.

Pinched between Ōmura Bay to the west, the Amakusa Sea to the south, and Tachibana Bay to the east is a narrow, mountain-choked isthmus that is the city's sole natural overland connection to the rest of Kyushu. This terrain feature in particular—and the region's harsh topography in general—has rendered the Nagasaki region a nightmare for generations of Japanese railway engineers,[1] with subsequent consequences for the city's modern urban evolution and history.

Nagasaki itself is mercilessly vertical, dominated by a trio of three-hundred-meter-plus peaks. Each of these mountains is surrounded by a mazelike network of foothills, ridges, and canyons that severely limit how the city's land can be used; collectively, they put a low cap on the size of the population (some 400,000 today; about 250,000 in pre-high-rise-apartment-building 1945) the locale can sustain without serious overcrowding. In their geological absence—and even taking into account the spot's geographical isolation from the rest of Japan—Nagasaki would likely have eventually evolved into a million-plus-population metropolis. But these mountainous hills—or hill-ish mountains—are where they are, and as a result, Nagasaki ended up a middling-sized regional city, at least in terms of population, and was so even in its economic heyday nearly a century and a half ago.

To the east of Nagasaki's fjord-like harbor, two of these landscape-dominating peaks—Mount Konpira and Mount Hōka—squeeze the Central Business District (CBD) from the north and east, respectively, while a smaller but still substantial (hundred-fifty-meter) hill, Kazagashira, presses in from the south. The third three-hundred-meter peak, Mount Inasa, forms a giant sunset-spoiling (but also typhoon-blocking) wall on the harbor's opposite, western shore.

Of the three, Mount Konpira is urban Nagasaki's topographical centerpiece. Wending their way around its base are the city's two main rivers: the Urakami, passing the mountain on the west; and the Nakashima, flowing past the mountain's southern foot. These rivers, by way of their respective valleys, provide the city with most of its industrially and commercially viable (i.e., topographically level) real estate, outside of the thin belt of wharfs, quays, and landfill ringing the upper reaches of the harbor.

The Urakami is the more substantial of the two rivers in terms of flow volume. Even so, it is barely a hundred meters across at its widest stretches, near its mouth at the head of the harbor. Only the estuarial, southernmost third of the river's nine-kilometer-long course is navigable, and there only by small craft and flatboats. Upstream from Mount Konpira's foothills, the river quickly narrows into little more than a concrete-lined creek before vanishing into its headwaters deep in the densely wooded mountains northeast of the city.

Despite the Urakami's meager flow volume, its floodplain averages about 1.5 kilometers in width. The sides of this belt of level land are lined, like bleachers at a racetrack, by Mount Konpira and its foothills to the east, and by Mount Inasa and more hills and ridges to the west.

In previous eras, the Urakami Valley was dominated by agricultural activity, and settlement centered on several farming villages. It was also home to the largest and oldest continuous native Catholic community in Japan—a story with origins in the peculiar circumstances of Nagasaki's European Age of Exploration provenance.

However, after the valley's 1920 incorporation into Nagasaki proper—coincident with the Mitsubishi Corporation's transformation of the city from a maritime- to a manufacturing-based economy—it became dominated by industrial plants.[2] Its population density also rose dramatically.[3] Today, the valley floor is blanketed by factories, warehouses, and supply yards. These are interspersed with schools and housing that extend far up into the surrounding high ground. With the exception of the occasional modern-day high-rise apartment block or hospital complex added to the mix, the overall feel of this landscape—in terms of the general pattern of habitation and population density—has changed little since 1945.

Due to its flat terrain, the Urakami Valley has always served as a major conduit for the overland movement of goods and people. In 1945, before automobiles dominated and when trains were still the most important mode of ground transportation in Japan, the city's sole rail link to Mainland Kyushu—the Nagasaki Line of the Kokutetsu—ran along the floor of the valley. Just past the suburb of Michino'o, some 7.5 kilometers north of the CBD, the tracks turned abruptly to the east to traverse a narrow land bridge of mountain passes, tunnels, and zigzagging stretches of the jagged southern shoreline of Ōmura Bay to reach Isahaya, Ōmura City, and other points north-northeast.[4]

Along its southernmost five kilometers, the Nagasaki Line was paralleled by a busy branch of the city's Nagaden streetcar system that connected the CBD with the Urakami suburbs. The northern terminus of this line was Ōhashi Station, located near a massive (and eponymous) Mitsubishi shipyards expansion facility (today, the main campus of Nagasaki University).[5]

Finally, an important vehicular and pedestrian traffic thoroughfare—the old Togitsu Road—straddled this streetcar line before running the remainder of the full length of the valley, connecting the CBD in the south with the small Ōmura Bay fishing harbor of Togitsu some nine kilometers to the north.[6] Today, this stretch of roadway—still straddling the tracks of Nagaden's No. 1, 2, and 3 lines—is part of National Highway 206, which connects Nagasaki with Sasebo, a Newport News–like traditional naval harbor some fifty kilometers (as the crow flies) to the north-northwest.[7]

Aside from this industrial and transportation infrastructure, there are two other Urakami district landmarks that deserve mention here because of their significance in the events of August 1945. The first of these is Immaculate Conception Cathedral, aka Urakami Cathedral, a handsome, twin-bell-towered redbrick edifice built atop one of the northeast foothills of Mount Konpira. The cathedral's first incarnation was funded by local parishioners' donations and built largely with their volunteer labor between 1895 and 1925. From the time of its completion until 1945, it was the largest Christian ecclesiastical structure in East Asia.

Between 1958 and 1959, the cathedral's second incarnation was erected on this same site. Urakami's by then mostly destitute Catholic community—reduced to less than half of its 1945 population—pitched in once again to build the second cathedral. But this time, primary funding for construction came not through local parishioners, but rather through an international charity drive spearheaded by American Catholic organizations. As with its architecturally nearly identical first incarnation, the 1959 cathedral, which still commands a sweeping view of the valley, was one of the region's most visually conspicuous landmarks until Urakami's sky was shrunk by late twentieth-century gentrification.

A second important Urakami landmark is the nearby Nagasaki University School of Medicine (known until 1949 as Nagasaki Medical College). Founded in 1858 by Dutch physicians specially chartered by the Shogunate, the school is one of the oldest and most prestigious institutions of modern (i.e., Western) medical education in Japan. Originally located closer to the CBD, it moved to its present site on the western slope of Mount Konpira in the 1890s.

In 1945, Nagasaki Medical College and its attached hospital complex enjoyed an even more spectacular view of the surrounding area than Urakami Cathedral. These impressive facilities were visible from either end of the Urakami Valley and virtually everywhere in between. This was particularly true of the towering twin smokestacks—then the tallest man-made structures in the valley—of the hospital's waste incinerators. Fatefully, these smokestacks—painted in bright white and red bands as an aviation safety measure—were also conspicuously visible from the air.

Nagasaki's other main river, the Nakashima, has been dammed in the eastern suburb of Hongōchi since 1891 to create a drinking-water reservoir for the city.[8] In 1904, a second dam in the Nakashima's catchment was built in Nishiyama, at the eastern foot of Mount Konpira.[9] Since then, the dam-strangled Nakashima has been barely a Los Angeles River–esque trickle by the time it wends through the heart of the CBD to empty into the east side of the harbor. Today, the water level of the Nakashima in this part of town is often low enough for tourists to clamber down the river's stone-walled embankments to frolic and pose for selfies on its concrete-paved streambed. Belying this meager flow volume, but necessitated by its redundant high stone embankments, the Nakashima is spanned in the CBD by numerous bridges. One of these—the Nigiwai streetcar bridge in the heart of the city—is particularly readily identifiable from the air.

The overall feel of the CBD can be likened to that of San Francisco—another famously vertical harbor town. In terms of its topography and land use, however, it may be more useful to think of central Nagasaki as a cross between the canyon-gouged Hollywood Hills and the cheek-by-jowl, steeply stacked residential density of Hong Kong's Kowloon District.

In the CBD, almost all of the city's office space, department store retail, and socioeconomically elite private housing (e.g., Judge Ishida's official residence in Katsuyama-chō) are crammed onto the floor of the extensively landfill-augmented Nakashima Valley. Some of this urban buildup spills over onto the floors of the various canyons formed on the periphery of the valley by the southern foothills of Mount Konpira, the western foothills of Mount Hōka (e.g., the Kiridōshis' neighborhood of Nakagawa-machi), and the northern slopes of the smaller Kazagashira and Nabekanmuri Hills.

The steep sides of all of these canyons, slopes, and hills are terraced with narrow, twisting roads that would have barely accommodated two farmer's wheelbarrows abreast in times past, let alone passing automobiles or delivery trucks today. Here, middle- and working-class residences are perched with such gravity-defying audacity that some of them can seem suspended in midair. Dotting these precariously perched and difficult-to-access residences are Buddhist temples and cemeteries, a smattering of slowly and gracefully dying Christian churches, and numerous school and small private college campuses (often Protestant or Catholic affiliated).

Charming as such sites are—and offering, as most do, spectacular harbor views—this centuries-old pattern of Nagasaki habitation entails certain drawbacks. One of these is its susceptibility to landslides—a danger that is exacerbated by the heavy rainfall that is a perennial hallmark of the region's humid climate. Another drawback is less immediately life-threatening and more literally pedestrian: the physical challenges this terrain poses for those members of Nagasaki's rapidly aging (and shrinking) population who have to navigate this vertically oriented and distinctly car-unfriendly part of the city on foot or bicycle.

My favorite vantage point for taking in the grand convoluted physical tapestry of Nagasaki—and contemplating the history that created it—

has always been atop 170-meter-high Nabekanmuri Hill, which dominates the lower-harbor-waterfront district of Ōura-machi, site of Japan's oldest (1865) Catholic cathedral.[10]

Although Nabekanmuri is barely half their height, the hill offers the sightseer certain advantages over Mount Konpira and the city's two other landscape-dominating peaks. One of these is its nearly equidistant proximity to the harbor to the west and to the CBD to the north. Another is that it is (relatively) easily ascended these days, thanks to a municipally operated funicular car system—the Glover Sky Road, named after famed nineteenth-century British merchant Thomas Blake Glover—that goes halfway to the hill's summit. Although this apparatus was ostensibly built to promote foot traffic to the Glover Garden tourist attraction on the harbor side of the hill, it seems likely that it also exists for the benefit of local residents, who now no longer have to endure the sweaty slog of the old stairway system up from the CBD street level to reach homes perched high on Nabekanmuri. In the half dozen or so times I have availed myself of this conveyance, I have seen far more fellow passengers carrying grocery bags and staring at their phones than toting cameras and glancing around at the scenery.

From the topside terminus of the Glover Sky Road, the remaining half of the ascent to Nabekanmuri's observation deck must be climbed on foot, up concrete staircases and winding, sharply sloped alleyways— barely wide enough to accommodate motor scooters—that wend their way through the neighborhood's tightly clustered housing. But upon reaching the summit, intrepid hikers are rewarded with a magnificent panorama of the harbor and the CBD. To the north, the CBD sprawls along the floor of the Nakashima Valley, dwarfed by the giant Mount Konpira at its back and dead-ended to the east by the equally massive Mount Hōka. On the harbor side, the CBD ends abruptly in wharfs and quays on the waterfront.

To the west, Nagasaki's famed deepwater harbor spreads out like a finely rippled glass tabletop, backdropped by the majestic dark green mass of Mount Inasa. By day, the water's surface is herringboned by the crisscrossing wakes of Japan Coast Guard cutters, deep-sea fishing trawlers, and high-speed ferries to outlying islands—an effect that is particularly beautiful under low, late-afternoon sunlight. After dark, the man-made lights and colors of the cityscape below are heart-achingly romantic, and the soothing thrumming of ships' engines and the plaintive bleats of their steam whistles waft up on the night air to reach Nabekanmuri's summit with poignant clarity.

On the near shore of the harbor, and seemingly almost straight down from Nabekanmuri's summit, lies the four-hundred-meter-long, ruler-straight wharf of the Matsugae International Terminal. A century and a half ago, this strip of waterfront was the center of for-eign institutional activity in Nagasaki—the location of the British consulate, various mercantile banks, and the offices of the Great Northern Telegraph Company, a Danish firm that opened the first submarine communication cables here between Japan and the Asian mainland, and thence to Europe, in 1871.[11] Today, it is the mooring spot for enormous cruise ships—giant gaudy amusement parks on top of floating, ten-story hotels—that disgorge hundreds of thousands of Chinese tourists upon the city every year.[12]

The opposite shore of the harbor is dominated by factories and the famed Mitsubishi shipyards of Akuno'ura and Tategami, site of the building of the *Musashi*, one of the two white elephant *Yamato*-class su-per battleships the Imperial Japanese Navy squandered nearly 4 percent of Japan's gross domestic product constructing in the early stages of World War Two.[13] Today, the giant dry dock facilities where the *Musashi* and two IJN aircraft carriers were built still exist but are now mostly used for the construction and refitting of big freighters and oil tankers.

Finally, to the south, the elegant support towers and suspended roadway of the Megami Bridge span a narrows in the lower harbor, marking the gateway to Nagasaki's original raison d'être: the East China Sea.

———

The geographical destiny of Nagasaki's proximity to the Asian main-land has afforded the city a rich blend of trans-global cultural influ-ences over its roughly five centuries of existence.

The first heyday of Nagasaki's intercourse with Western cultures occurred from roughly 1550 to 1650, during the so-called *Nanban bōeki* ("southern barbarian trade") era of contact between Portugal and feudal Japan.[14] In this context, the Japanese pirate cove and loose conglomeration of fishing villages that would eventually become Nagasaki were developed from 1571 by Portuguese Jesuits and traders chartered under official *Padroado* sponsorship of the Kingdom of Portugal and the Vatican. The Jesuits had been a presence in western Kyushu for some ten years by this point, with their initial base of operations in the region in the small Shimabara Bay fishing port of Kuchinotsu, some fifty kilometers to the east. But the Nagasaki site presented the Portuguese with an opportunity to establish a settlement on a grander, more lucrative scale—and with an unprecedented degree of both politically and geographically protected autonomy so they could conduct their business at a safe remove from meddling by the powers that be in Mainland Japan. And for a while, the Portuguese got exactly what they wanted.[15] The final piece for the project fell into place with the visionary imprimatur of—and a generous land grant from—the Nagasaki region's samurai *daimyō* lord, Ōmura Sumitada.[16]

The occasional bloody clash with their samurai hosts aside, the Portuguese settlement in Nagasaki thrived over the next half century. And while this span might have been brief, set against nearly two thousand years of recorded Japanese history, the legacy of this contact has been broad and enduring. Among the many material cultural and technological artifacts the Portuguese introduced to their counterparts are bread, cake, and other sugar-based confectionaries; deep-frying (which the Japanese perfected with tempura); trousers, jackets, and brimmed hats; velvet fabric and other textiles; globes, maps, and compasses; clocks; grape wine; tobacco; and Western-firearm technology.[17]

The cultural DNA of the Nagasaki settlement also lives on in the genome of the modern Japanese language in the form of a rich lexicon of Portuguese loanwords. These items include words for "glass" (*bīdoro*), "velvet" (*birōdo*), "balcony" (*beranda*), "flask" (*furasuko*), "soap" (*shabon*), "pumpkin" (*kabocha*), "playing cards" (*karuta*), "bread" (*pan*),

"Catholic mass" (*misa*), "Christian" (*Kirishitan*), and the names for England / the United Kingdom and the Netherlands (*Igirisu* and *Oranda*, respectively).

Paradoxically, but certainly not coincidentally, Nagasaki's *Pax Portuguesa* overlapped the final half century of Japan's Warring States period—the hundred-fifty-year-long struggle between rival samurai warlord armies vying for control of the Japanese archipelago.[18] Riding the tiger of this fluid political environment, the Portuguese in Nagasaki managed to keep their heads above water—and, with notable gruesome exceptions, their necks attached to their shoulders—by maintaining a steady enough stream of goods and revenue coming into the port to satisfy all interested parties.

As a charter condition of their *Padroado* patronage, Nagasaki's Jesuits were tasked with winning local converts to the Catholic faith as part of their order's global Counter-Reformation founding mission to stem the spread of Protestantism beyond Europe. Eventually, and coincident with the pursuit of this mission, the Nagasaki Jesuits acquired so much financial and political influence—particularly after converting Ōmura Sumitada and his family to Catholicism—that commerce through the port began to take a back seat to ever more ambitious and aggressive proselytization. In this effort, the Jesuits were even more successful at soul saving than they were at business; it is believed that, at one point, they and their compatriots in other Jesuit missions in Kyushu and Honshu might have converted as many as 300,000 Japanese to Catholicism.[19] But the very success of these proselytization efforts ended up sowing the seeds of Portuguese Nagasaki's eventual doom.

The writing was on the wall by the first decade of the seventeenth century, when the Shogunate was consolidating its rule over the Japanese archipelago after emerging victorious at the end of the Warring States period. Initially, the new regime had been open to allowing the Nagasaki settlement to continue flourishing and bringing in foreign goods and gold; the Christian proselytization, however, stuck in its craw. Increasingly, the steady growth of Japanese Christianity that accompanied this trade and foreign cultural intercourse began to be perceived in Edo as a Trojan horse for eventual colonization[20] of Japan itself.

This suspicion eventually led the Shogunate to issue the infamous *kinkyōrei* (1612, expanded in 1614) ordering the banishment of Christianity and the expulsion of all Westerners from the country.[21] When these proclamations were not obeyed with sufficient alacrity, a spasm of official violence followed, resulting in the deaths of possibly as many as forty thousand *Kirishitan*—the vast majority of whom were recent Japanese converts.[22]

In a spiteful symbolic mockery of the now forbidden religion, victims of the Shogunate's anti-*Kirishitan* pogrom were sometimes literally crucified, their bodies left to rot in place in public spaces as a warning to the living.[23] Suspected *Kirishitan* who wanted to avoid such a fate were forced to participate in annual *efumi* ("picture-trampling") apostasy rituals—before a captive audience of peers and a specially dispatched Shogunate inquisitor—involving the trampling of stone or bronze tablets depicting either a crucified Christ or the Virgin Mary (typically cradling an infant Jesus in her arms).[24]

In Nagasaki—Ground Zero of what the Shogunate perceived as the Christian menace—the apostasy rituals were held once a year for the next 240 years on the very spot now occupied by Urakami Cathedral. These were particularly showy and notorious productions, known far enough afield of Japan's borders by the early eighteenth century to merit satirical mention in Jonathan Swift's *Gulliver's Travels*.[25]

Despite its firm ban on Christianity and contact with the West, the Shogunate nevertheless allowed a trickle of bureaucratically micromanaged and jealously surveilled foreign trade to continue in Nagasaki, limited exclusively to Chinese and Dutch merchants. As Swift acidly suggests in *Gulliver's Travels*, the Dutch were perhaps tolerated by the Japanese authorities because they appeared to harbor far more zeal for lucre than they did commitment to Christianity, with the English satirist hinting that they even participated in *efumi* rituals to stay in the good graces of their Shogunate hosts.[26] Be that as it may have been, the Shogunate's official tolerance of these Westerners had its limits: While the culturally familiar and Christianity-averse Chi-

GEOGRAPHICAL DESTINY

nese were allowed to live and trade freely ashore, the Dutch were restricted to "Dejima," a small man-made island near the mouth of the Nakashima River. This fan-shaped spit of land, connected to shore by a narrow, closely guarded wooden footbridge, was purpose-built to keep Dutch crewmen and business agents in quarantine whenever one of their merchant ships made port of call.[27] Here the Dutch seafarers would remain, essentially under lock and key and round-the-clock surveillance, until their ship weighed anchor to take them away whence they came (usually Batavia in the Dutch East Indies / present-day Indonesia).

Belying all of this hypervigilance by local authorities, the actual amount of Dutch commerce that moved through Dejima was rarely more than a trickle. (There were some years when not a single Dutch ship laid anchor in the harbor.) The Shogunate perhaps maintained whatever little contact it did with the Westerners there more to keep open a source of information about developments in the outside world than to conduct any trade of actual economic significance. Whatever the Shogunate's ultimate motive for building Dejima might have been, its consequence was clear: Nagasaki's role as an international commerce hub and window on the West would remain moribund for the next two centuries of the Shogunate's isolationist policy.

Nagasaki's second and more significant period of international commerce, in terms of creating the city as it exists today, began on July 1, 1859.[28] On this date, the harbor was officially reopened as a stipulation of the Ansei (Unequal) Treaties signed with the Western powers in the dying days of the Shogunate. This event saw Nagasaki transformed in short order into an important maritime commerce hub and coaling station for transpacific shipping.[29] Within five years of its opening to foreign trade, the city's population surpassed seventy thousand residents, most earning livelihoods either directly or indirectly connected to the burgeoning economic activity generated by the harbor.[30]

This was the golden era of the culturally eclectic Nagasaki that fired romantically inclined (and often erotically charged) Western imaginations in the late nineteenth and early twentieth centuries, and was perhaps most famous, in this context, as the setting of Giacomo Puccini's beloved opera *Madama Butterfly*. During this period, large-scale foreign-investment capital saw European and American businessmen build sumptuous homes (some of which, like the mansion preserved in the aforementioned Glover Garden, survive to this day) in the city's designated Foreign Settlement District, which extended inland from Ōura-machi to climb high up the slopes of Nabekanmuri and Kazagashira.

The blue-eyed mandarins who made their homes in the Foreign Settlement were protected by extraterritoriality clauses for Westerners stipulated in the Ansei Treaties, meaning that they essentially operated as they pleased, completely immune to Japanese legal prosecution. Any transgressions for which they were responsible were answerable only to the local consulate of the offenders' country of origin.[31]

The only exception to this was traffic in opium. The Shogunate had seen the chaos and misery wrought upon Chinese society by this British-pushed dope and was adamant, during the Ansei Treaty negotiations, in seeing agreements put in place that banned any trade in the substance on Japanese soil. Still, there were plenty of other ways for the otherwise immunity-protected Westerners in Nagasaki to get rich, and not all of these were strictly legal. The more upstanding among these pioneers (or Shogunate-decline-exploiting carpetbaggers, if one prefers) took advantage of their unbridled privilege and freedom to amass fortunes importing Western industrial machinery and exporting Japanese tea and silk. The less reputable reaped ill-gotten gains running guns and other non-opiate contraband. Some, like Thomas Glover, dabbled in all of the above.

Concurrent with—and largely as a result of—the activities of these freewheeling foreign captains of commerce, Nagasaki was a busy international port of call. American and British whalers, as well as warships of every major world naval power, regularly laid anchor in the harbor to reprovision and send their crews ashore for a little well-earned rest and relaxation. Prowling the narrow alleyways of the city's notorious red-light district of Maruyama, sailors from these ships rubbed elbows with an international potpourri of local natives and fellow Westerners—a Kiplingesque rogues' gallery of swaggering fortune hunters and fellow sea dogs, alcoholic journalists and starving writers, eccentric Orientalists and disowned ne'er-do-wells, and sundry other *gaijin* scalawags of widely varying talent and character. Depending on the season, the city could be host to as many as seven thousand Westerners at a time, both resident and visiting, drunk or sober, keeping the local magistrates and foreign consulates busy maintaining the peace, but also keeping Nagasaki's tax coffers—and its pleasure quarters—flush with foreign coin.[32]

The most outrageous excesses of Nagasaki's period of Wild West free-for-all wound down abruptly with the end of extraterritoriality— a result of renegotiation of the Ansei Treaties—at the end of the nineteenth century. But maritime commerce in the harbor enjoyed several more decades in the economic sun before eventually falling victim to the vagaries of international trade and technological evolution.

A particularly bruising body blow landed in the first decades of the twentieth century when oceangoing merchant shipping plying the Pacific and Japan-to-continental-Asia routes began transitioning from coal- to oil-fueled engines—a need Nagasaki did not possess the infrastructure to service.[33]

Accelerating Nagasaki's decline was its slow strangulation at the hands of Fukuoka, a rival regional city some hundred kilometers (as the crow flies) up the western Kyushu coast whose political influence and economic fortunes were on the rise in the opening decades of the twentieth century (as seen in the contemporary personal career trajectories of Hirota Kōki, Inoue Testujirō, and Ishida Hisashi). From the 1930s, Fukuoka's swelling (and oil-refueling-capable) Hakata port facilities began poaching ever larger shares of international freight traffic to western Japan that had once been the near-exclusive purview of Nagasaki.

Nagasaki's economic coup de grâce was delivered by steadily improved rail infrastructure linking Fukuoka, its now world-class

Hakata harbor, and the nearby Yahata Steel Works with Honshu's Tokyo–Osaka industrial and population megalopolis. In terms of its own meager potential as a major ship-to-rail connection point player, Nagasaki was doomed by the topographical destiny of its notoriously mountainous inland terrain, convoluted waterways, and wildly irregular coastline.[34] For nearly a century, the city would have to make do with its single rail connection with the outside world.[35]

As Fukuoka took away more and more of its maritime raison d'être, Nagasaki entered a slow decline into a sort of East Asian Valparaiso—a decaying elegant relic of bygone days. Meanwhile, the city held on to whatever was left of its economic relevance through tourism and, far more important, by revamping itself into a Mitsubishi factory town for naval munitions production, electrical machinery manufacture, and shipbuilding,[36] with most of the new infrastructure for this activity concentrated on the western shore of the harbor and along the floor of the Urakami Valley. By the outbreak of the Pacific War, some 80 to 90 percent of Nagasaki's labor force was either directly or, via subsidiaries, indirectly employed by Mitsubishi.[37] Still, for what had once been one of the most important ports in East Asia, Nagasaki was, by 1945, only a shell of its former self and of only modest significance in the overall picture of Japan's war effort, accounting for some 10 percent of IJN shipbuilding/outfitting and 7 percent of munitions production.[38]

This was more than enough, however, to put Nagasaki on the radar of Pentagon air war planners.

ACCULTURATION

Nagasaki
Spring 1945

EVER SINCE HER father's first posting to Ōmuta three years earlier, Michiko had dreaded ending up in the *inaka* ("the sticks") of Kyushu. Once there, though, she found that it was not quite as bad as she had feared, but the cosmopolitan Tokyo girl's sudden immersion into this provincial environment still involved a degree of culture shock.

One manifestation of this was linguistic. The idiosyncrasies of the local *Nagasaki-ben* dialect were alien and disagreeable to her ears, and as a result, she never really managed to become conversant in it. Instead, Michiko stubbornly (and perhaps a bit snobbishly) hung on to the speech mannerisms of her Tokyo upbringing. Nevertheless, the resulting "language gap" vis-à-vis age peers and neighbors did not faze her in the least. Because she was inveterately and preternaturally immune to the pressures of social convention that straitjacketed the lives of most of her contemporary compatriots, conformity for its own sake had never been a personal priority for her in Tokyo, nor was it one in her current venue. And, after all, she was not planning on sticking around Nagasaki for very long, anyway.

Another cultural adjustment annoyance for her was having to get used to wearing *geta* everywhere in her daily comings and goings, like nearly everyone else in Nagasaki seemed to do. After a pampered

Tokyo childhood shod in good-quality leather (including her entire Atomi career and the ten months she had worked at Lion Toothpaste), Michiko regarded as hopelessly hayseed the wearing of the clunky wooden sandals for any outing involving more than a quick clippity-clopping saunter down to the corner mailbox and back. She eventually accepted the unavoidability of the footwear transition, but this was less a matter of following local custom (and the uniform policies of her new school) than it was a pragmatic concern; the only pair of decent leather shoes she had managed to salvage from her Tokyo wardrobe had been on her own two feet, and with the war situation being what it was, she did not know when or if she would see another pair.

Such minor issues aside, Nagasaki nevertheless had its amenities. The Kiridōshis' home in Nakagawa-machi—rented from a Mitsubishi shipyards executive—was one of them. It was a large, well-built two-story dwelling in the southwestern foothills of Mount Hōka. Redolent of sophisticated taste and money, the house featured a lavishly roomy staircase—a heretofore unknown luxury for someone who had known only the submarine-ladder stairways of Tokyo dwellings. There was even a maid's bedroom, although this was redundant in 1945 Japan; the nation's domestic servants had long since been hauled away to work in war plants, giving upper-class Japanese women like Michiko's mother dishpan hands for the first time in history.[1]

Just as Michiko's parents had promised in their letters from home, Nagasaki itself was peaceful, its quaint temples and churches picturesque and its famous harbor postcard pretty. In dramatic contrast to the city Michiko had just escaped, there were no vast brown fields of burned ruins stretching to the horizon. The air did not reek of corpses. There were no endless lines of homeless refugees filing out of their destroyed city to points unknown, pulling the entirety of their worldly possessions in rickety wheelbarrows. If one could ignore the sprawling, gantry-tangled Mitsubishi shipyards and machine factories dominating the western shore of the harbor, the massive Mitsubishi munitions plants smudging the northern approaches to the city along the floor of the Urakami River valley, and the omnipresent propaganda posters and banners ("Until Final Victory, Go Without," etc.) lining otherwise quiescent, narrow wooden downtown streets, it was hard to believe there was a war going on.[2]

This was not to say, however, that Nagasaki did not have its share of wartime inconveniences and concerns, the most immediately dire of which was food. This was true even for a financially well-off family like the Kiridōshis, whose daily existence was now spent hovering at or just above the lowest level of Maslow's pyramid, their lives increasingly focused on desperate efforts to find food and a dwindling ability to enjoy what was found when these efforts succeeded.[3]

Geographically remote Nagasaki had always been heavily dependent on the shipborne delivery of foodstuffs and other supplies, but American submarines were now regularly sending Japanese merchant shipping to the bottom of the East China Sea.[4] Moreover, since March 1945, in pursuance of the Twentieth Air Force's grimly and aptly named Operation STARVATION, B-29s had been lacing the shipping-lane approaches to the city (and the rest of the coastline of Kyushu and Honshu) with a mixture of magnetically, acoustically, and pressure-triggered mines.[5] The sum consequence of this effective blockade of Nagasaki was that, outside of provisions brought in on small fishing boats—whose wooden hulls, put-put engines, and light displacement rendered these vessels essentially immune to the mine hazard—precious little food was making it into the harbor anymore, and malnutrition was quickly becoming a major public health problem in the city.[6]

As Michiko already knew firsthand from her time at Atomi, being able to acquire food on a regular basis in Japan had long since ceased to be a simple matter of having the cash to buy it—even if one were willing to resort to the black market. One had to know people—good local-grapevine-information sources for where and when something was going to be available. Food was running out everywhere, and under the circumstances, people would take whatever they could get from their local rationing cooperative or from some farmer relative or from a blanket rolled out in some dark alley—and they would consider themselves lucky to have anything at all, regardless of what it tasted like.

At home, Michiko's mother did what she could with the meager measures of dried sardines, cucumbers, and *katakuriko* potato starch[7] that made it down through the rationing cooperative system to reach Nakagawa-machi families via their neighborhood association. Occasionally, there would be welcome variation in the usual grim menu when Mrs. Kiridōshi or one of her daughters came home from shopping in the CBD with a watery, flavorless pumpkin or a skinny sweet potato.

Plain white rice, that normally indispensable traditional staple of their diet, was but a fond memory for the Kiridōshis—as it was for most any Japanese not in military uniform—by the lean summer of 1945. In an attempt to compensate for this keenly felt absence, Mrs. Kiridōshi was forced to get creative with *katakuriko*.[8] She would often mix the starch powder into a dough and knead some ground-up dried sardines into it to make dumplings. Serving options were limited to boiling or open-grill roasting; deep-frying—which might have coaxed a bit more umami flavoring out of the dumplings—was out because cooking oil was no longer available. Neither were spices—even something as ordinary and normally taken for granted as black pepper. Meat was yet another fading taste memory for the Japanese palate by 1945. Michiko never once saw any—not even a bit of pork or chicken— during the entire span of the war.[9] Everyone knew that whatever little meat there was in the country had been earmarked for the military, whose soldiers' protein needs clearly got priority over everyone else's. Yet few civilians complained about this, at least not in public. People had been known to be hauled into the back rooms of police stations and smacked around for lesser displays of defeatism and lack of fighting spirit.

As for enemy air attacks on the city, so far there had been only one raid of any consequence; this had occurred in August 1944, when twenty-four B-29s flying out of China had dropped some high explosives and incendiaries around the waterfront area, killing fifteen people and setting a few fires at the eastern foot of Mount Inasa, behind the Mitsubishi shipyards and electrical machine factory.[10]

Then, for the next eight months, there was nothing.

The city's run of luck ended one month after Michiko's arrival. On April 26, at around 1100, a single B-29 slipped unnoticed through the region's air defense grid and dropped its bombload on the Nagasaki Station / Ōhato Wharf area, killing some 129 passengers on a large ferry that had just pulled in to dock.[11]

After that, air raids on the city proper dropped off to zero again. Large B-29 formations still frequently passed over on their way to hit the IJN air station at Ōmura, some twenty kilometers (as the crow flies) to the northeast, or the major IJN base at Sasebo. But these planes never dropped so much as an empty beer bottle on Nagasaki, and the city's residents, on the whole, learned to ignore these flyovers, as well as the cacophony of air raid sirens that would sound—on orders of Western Army HQ air defense command in Fukuoka— whenever American aircraft were detected flying anywhere in the vicinity of Kyushu.[12]

Michiko was pleasantly surprised at how lax most people in Nagasaki seemed to be about blackout protocol, evacuation to bomb shelters, and other civil defense regulations—that is, when these were followed at all.[13] Perhaps, she thought, the city would not be such a bad place to lie low until she and the rest of her family could reestablish their lives back in Tokyo. Barring slow starvation and/or a big B-29 incendiary raid, it seemed the Kiridōshis were all going to be able to see out the rest of the war in relative safety.

Within days of her arrival in Nagasaki at the end of March, Kiridōshi Michiko had matriculated at "Kenjo," the prefectural girls' school.[14] Under normal circumstances, admission to the elite five-year program was awarded only to candidates who passed a battery of rigorous entrance exams. But the times being what they were, Michiko's status as the daughter of an important man was sufficient, in a pinch, to get her shoehorned into Kenjo on the merit of an ad hoc admissions interview alone to begin as a new fourth-year student on April 1, 1945.[15] After some desultory registration formalities, Michiko was informed that, from April 2, she would be dispatched as a mobilized student laborer to the Mitsubishi Steel and Arms Works (USAAF Target 546) in Mori-machi, three streetcar stops north of Nagasaki Station (USAAF Target 1842).[16] She would barely see the inside of a Kenjo classroom again for the rest of the war.

For her first day on the job, Michiko donned the prescribed Kenjo mobilized labor outfit—typical of the era—of patriotic-slogan-emblazoned *hachimaki* headband, school uniform blouse, school-name-emblazoned armband, baggy homemade cotton *monpe* work trousers, and the inevitable *geta*.[17] She also carried a khaki canvas shoulder bag. This was supposed to contain only a padded cotton *bōsaizukin* protective hood, a roll or two of cotton gauze bandage, and perhaps a small bottle of disinfectant tincture, but for most girls, the bag also doubled as a purse, lunch box, and canteen holder.

In keeping with official ordinances for civilian clothing, Mrs. Kiridōshi had sewn civil defense personal identification patches—a cloth equivalent of GI dog tags—onto the left breast of her daughter's blouse, one leg of her *monpe*, her *bōsaizukin* hood, and her shoulder bag. This was done so Michiko's body could be identified in the event of an air raid or some calamitous mass mortality workplace accident like a factory fire or explosion.

While some other Nagasaki schools—for example, the Catholic Junshin Girls' School in Urakami—had their students march to their mobilized labor sites every morning en masse and in cadenced military fashion, Kenjo girls from second year and up were left to their own devices to get to their war plant jobs every day on time. In Michiko's case, her daily morning commute was a breeze—taking barely twenty minutes from her living room to her worktable in Mori-machi. Hotarujaya, the eastern terminus of the Nagaden streetcar system, was a mere minute's walk from her house. After she had gotten a few rides under her belt, Michiko learned that if she made it to Hotarujaya early enough, she was almost guaranteed a seat for her morning commute. This was critically important, because by the time the streetcar reached Shindaiku-machi or Suwa Shrine, only a few stops farther into the CBD, it would be filled to standing room only. Once it reached the city hall stop, passengers would be practically hanging from the windows.

Michiko would get off the jam-packed car at Zenza-machi, three stops past Nagasaki Station, cross the busy Togitsu Road to the factory gate, salute the uniformed Mitsubishi man who was always on guard there, then proceed to her assigned workstation.

The Mori-machi works was built in the final year of World War One to produce torpedoes for the IJN, which was then a combatant on the side of the Western Allies.[18] The facility remained in operation postwar, albeit at a reduced peacetime capacity. However, fueled by IJN production contracts—a consequence of Japan's rapid military buildup from the 1930s on—the Mori-machi complex grew by leaps and bounds. Soon, operations expanded to include a steel-rolling mill supplying armor plating for IJN warships under construction or dry-docked for refitting in the harbor's busy Mitsubishi shipyards.[19] And to keep up with skyrocketing demand for torpedoes[20] at the outbreak of the Pacific War, the management of Mitsubishi Shipyards was compelled to construct an annex plant (USAAF Target 2022) at Ōhashi in Ieno-machi, a Urakami Valley suburb some six kilometers (and six streetcar stops) to the north.

Flush with naval cash and ever-burgeoning production orders, the Mori-machi operation and its various subsidiary facilities eventually occupied an industrial park that straddled the lowermost kilometer and a half of the Urakami River.[21] On an average late-war day shift, some twelve hundred fifty workers toiled at the complex.[22] The overwhelming majority of this workforce consisted of mobilized war labor—adults dragooned into munitions plant service from homemaking or non–war-essential industries; Korean migrants; and junior high / girls' school students aged fourteen to eighteen.

During the first year or so of the conflict, IJN submarines, destroyers, and cruisers were using Nagasaki-produced torpedoes to consign American, British, and Dutch sailors to watery graves with gruesome regularity. But once those heady days were gone, Mitsubishi's production priorities were compelled to evolve in step with the shifting fortunes of Japan's war. From June 1944 on, with the Allies' steady decimation of the IJN in full swing, Mitsubishi's shipyards switched over from warship construction and refitting to the production of suicide weapons. These included *Marure* (IJA) and *Shin'yō* (IJN) special-attack motorboats, *Kaiten* manned torpedoes, and *Kōryū* two-man midget submarines.[23]

Concurrent with this shift, the Mori-machi works and the huge Ōhashi expansion plant prioritized operations to supplying the Akuno'ura and Tategami shipyards with parts and finished assembly sections for these specialized weapons. The conventional-torpedo production lines at these plants required little in the way of retooling for this task, and their machinery could be operated with minimal on-the-job training for Mitsubishi's primary labor force of mobilized amateurs.

FACTORY GIRL

Mori-machi, Nagasaki
1.9 kilometers northwest of Nigiwai Bridge

BY THE SUMMER of 1945, Michiko had been working in the torpedo finishing section (*shi'age kōjō*) building at Mori-machi for some three months. There, she toiled along with fourth-year Kenjo classmates, several hundred *dō'in gakuto* students from other schools, and about an equal number of *jokō* (adult *teishintai* women) who lived in nearby company-run dormitories. Overseeing this semiskilled labor force was an outnumbered and overworked skeleton crew of professional Mitsubishi craftsmen.

Occupying the lowest rung of the Mori-machi labor ladder was a small army of male Korean workers who, when not on the factory floor, boarded in Korean-managed shanty dormitories known as *hanba* (literally, "meal place").[1] These workers, who were ostensibly imperial subjects on paper but very much colonial subjects in practice and treatment, were living and working in Nagasaki in 1945 as a consequence of Japanese policy put in place some six years earlier, when the ongoing conflict in China was rapidly escalating into an industrialized total-war effort.[2]

In 1939, the Japanese government—eager to free up military-aged Japanese men for Imperial Army and Navy service—approved a labor-mobilization plan that would bring Koreans to Japan to work in coal mining, munitions factories, shipbuilding, and other essential war industries.[3] Recruitment was based on a mobilization system under which Japanese war production firms would make formal requisition requests for Korean labor to the Ministry of Health and Welfare. After a request received official approval, the Japanese governor-general of Korea would handle the matter locally—for example, determining from which provinces and counties the requisitioned workers were to be recruited and mobilized.[4] Once in-country, these workers would become the responsibility of their employers, and a local network of *hanba* and Korean drinking places and the like would be in place to see to their needs off duty. As a final layer of accountability to the arrangement, these Korean worker communities would be closely surveilled by local police authorities (and their neighborhood snitches, including *hanba* management) on the lookout for criminal moonlighting and the possible presence of Communist agitators, potential labor organizers, and other troublemakers. Punishment was harsh for those Koreans who forgot their place and stepped out of line.

When the recruiting process was still largely voluntary, prospective workers were sometimes lured with the promise of on-the-job training through which they could acquire Japanese technical qualifications that would move them toward more lucrative careers upon their eventual return to Korea. In other cases, the simple prospect of better pay than what the workers could earn in their impoverished farming hamlets or fishing villages—or even just the promise of three square meals a day and a *hanba* flop—might have been sufficient to get them to sign on the dotted line on the labor agents' paperwork and cross the Sea of Japan to begin new lives.

From September 1944, however, as Japan's war fortunes worsened, the recruiting system assumed a more openly coercive character.[5] In either case, be it voluntary or forced, the recruitment program saw the Korean population in Nagasaki Prefecture soar from 8,852 in 1938 to 61,773 by August 1945, with almost the entirety of the newcomers engaged at war production facilities like the Gunkanjima coal mines and Mitsubishi enterprises such as the Akuno'ura and Tategami ship-

FACTORY GIRL

yards, the Steel and Arms Works plants in Mori-machi, and the torpedo-production expansion facility at Ōhashi.

On the job, Michiko never had any contact with the Koreans, as none of them worked on the Finishing Section floor. Instead, they tended to be assigned menial, dirty, and dangerous tasks at Mori-machi such as carting away waste, digging air raid shelters and underground storage spaces, and toiling away in the fiery bowels of the steel rolling mill and the plant's various casting shops, raking away smelter slag without the benefit of protective gear.[6]

The Koreans were assisted in their "grunt" work by Dutch, Australian, and British internees from Fukuoka POW Camp No. 14.[7] This facility—which was named after the IJA Western Army HQ that oversaw it and other Kyushu POW camps—had been built in September 1944 near the southern limit of the Mori-machi works. Most of its prisoners had been in Japanese captivity for years by this point, since the IJA's early war triumphs in the Dutch East Indies, Burma, and Thailand.[8] The Westerners—who actually received tiny daily stipends from Mitsubishi to buy cigarettes, tea leaves, and the like—mostly worked in Mori-machi's casting shops, where some performed semi-skilled labor tasks such as drilling holes in steel plates.[9] But none were employed in the torpedo finishing section, where security-sensitive work was underway, so Michiko never had any contact with them on the job either, though she occasionally caught a glimpse of them through briefly opened doors or lined up in formation behind the fences around their compound when her streetcar was pulling into the Zenza-machi stop.

Michiko's Finishing Section workstation was located in a huge airplane-hangar-like building where lathes, drill presses, and various other workstations covered floor space about the size of an American football field.[10] While the original World War One–era Mori-machi facilities had been of brick construction, the Finishing Section was a steel-frame structure clad in sheet metal walls and roofing of corrugated asbestos—common building materials in the rudimentary style of construction typically seen in hastily erected mid-war Japanese industrial plants.[11] In terms of function, the building was in essence not much more than a giant raincoat to protect the machinery within from the elements, as well as a cloaking shroud to keep prying eyes outside of the plant from seeing what was going on inside.

Being freezing cold in winter and sauna-like in summer, the building offered little in the way of creature comforts for the workers who toiled under its cavernous roofs. During the region's interminable and suffocatingly steamy summers, the security measure of keeping the doors and frosted safety glass windows shut at all times added to the misery of Nagasaki's sweltering climate by preventing any potentially cooling breezes from entering the space. This same practice trapped inside the building air that permanently reeked of burned steel from all of the welding and grinding going on at the various workstations; the ventilation system was never quite up to the job of flushing the air out.

Seventy-two years later, Kiridōshi-san still remembers with displeasure the smell of that air and its scorched metallic taste.

From the building's high ceiling hung countless pulley chains, high-voltage power cords, and an extensive tracked system of wheeled gantry cranes, the latter of which frequently derailed, showering the workers below with sparks. These cranes were used for transporting torpedo or minisub sections from one workstation to the next, thence to the loading dock for flatboat transport to the Mitsubishi shipyards in Akuno'ura and Tategami for final assembly into finished weapons. From there, these would be transported by ship to the Sasebo Naval Anchorage, where they would be fitted with their massive explosive warheads by IJN ordnance specialists.

Against the northern wall of the building, near the Togitsu Road entrance, was an interior loft that offered its occupants a commanding view of plant operations. Here, the Finishing Section manager worked at a comfortably safe remove from the spark showers, toppling torpedo sections, flying metal shards, and the general cacophony of the factory floor below. Also safe and comfortable in the manager's loft was the plant's administrative staff, which included a mobilized student worker named Honda Sawa.

FACTORY GIRL

Sawa-san, as she was known to Michiko, had been chosen for her cushy job instead of the sweaty, dangerous work on the factory floor because of her demure demeanor and her acuity with numbers and paperwork.[12] She was also one of the few friends that Michiko had managed to make so far among her Kenjo classmates, and the two introverted girls used to enjoy spending their lunch breaks together outdoors, away from the peer group social politics of their respective work teams.

Michiko, for whom arithmetic and penmanship—let alone social diplomacy—had never been personal strong points, worked on the factory floor with a team of five or six other Kenjo girls, ten *jokō* from the eastern Nagasaki Prefecture town of Obama, and a single *kumichō* ("section boss") who was a career Mitsubishi craftsman.[13] This team was mainly tasked with using hand files and electric sanders to deburr bolt holes and finish the rough edges of steel minisub and *Kaiten* bulkheads from the plant's casting shops. Job performance was assessed at the end of every shift by tallying how many bolt holes each worker had managed to file, poke, and grind smooth. The work was done without the benefit of eye or ear protection or even gloves, and it was rote, monotonous, and repetitive-strain-injury-inducing for the protein-deprived girls and women who had to perform it.

Despite their chronic malnutrition, the physically arduous aspects of their work, the ugly gray environment of the plant, and the morbid nature of what they were helping to build, the girls in the bolt-hole-deburring section maintained a relatively high level of morale. Listening to motivational speeches, participating in orchestrated group slogan chanting, and singing at *chōrei* morning formations helped in this respect, as did their knowledge that they were doing their bit for their country in its time of need. Ordinary workaday comradeship played a part as well: The mobilized fourth-year Kenjo students at Mori-machi—inclusive of Sawa-san—had been employed full-time at the plant since May 1944.[14] And in the case of Michiko's work team, the Kenjo girls had formed tight bonds with one another during their time together on the factory floor, where, to help pass their hours of manual drudgery, they kept up a continuous stream of

Nagasaki-ben banter—which if not encouraged, was at least tolerated by the Mitsubishi cadre.

Michiko did not usually join in her classmates' running conversations. Instead, at least while on the company clock, she kept her nose to the grindstone—literally, in her case—regularly outstripping her chatty classmates and the *jokō* in the job performance metric of turning out well-polished, inspection-passing bolt holes. One day, at the end of the shift, the bolt-hole-deburring-section *kumichō* called his work team together and singled out Michiko for praise, holding her up as an example for the other girls to follow. This might not have helped Michiko much from the standpoint of fitting in with her Kenjo peers, but she found it thrilling nonetheless, as she was pretty sure it was the first time in her life that anyone had ever praised her for displaying self-discipline and perseverance in any kind of work or other task-performance situation.[15]

Regardless of the presence of diligent workers like Kiridōshi Michiko on the factory floor, the Mori-machi works could not keep churning out *Kaiten* torpedo and minisub and suicide motorboat parts without steel for its crucibles and casting shops. By July 1945, freight tonnage reaching Nagasaki by rail had dropped to barely 4 percent of mid-war levels.[16] This was not a local issue of the direct targeting of Nagasaki or Kyushu rail lines but rather was primarily a national supply chain problem—a result of the Allied naval blockade and sea mining of the Home Islands. With ships no longer able to make it across the Sea of Japan with Manchurian and Korean iron ore and coal, output was strangled at steel mills like Yahata, Nagasaki's primary source of the metal.[17] As a result, work at Mori-machi and Mitsubishi's other Nagasaki facilities slowed to a crawl by late summer.[18]

This did not, however, mean that Michiko and her Kenjo classmates would be released from their labor commitment to return to their classrooms and studies. On days when there were no actual bolt holes to be deburred—days that increased with frequency as July wound down—the girls were instead given make-work tasks such as redundantly polishing already finished metal components or endlessly sweeping and re-sweeping the factory floor.

The obvious big-picture implications of this change in their working conditions, and in the overall moribund mood shift at the plant in general, were not lost on the girls, who occasionally shared amongst themselves—and always out of earshot of their adult male colleagues—whispered conjecture that none of what they were seeing every day bode well for the fading chances of Japanese victory. For her part, Michiko was particularly chilled when a new catchphrase—*ichi'oku gyokusai* ("the glorious immolation of the hundred million" [i.e., the entirety of the Japanese race])—joined the canon of the other stock propaganda phrases that Japan's mass media had employed to sustain the morale of the populace through the four years of its war against the West. Nevertheless, Michiko had no intention of being immolated, whether for emperor and homeland, for the Mitsubishi Corporation, or for anyone else.

ŌHASHI

Nagasaki harbor
0803 hours, July 29, 1945

NAGASAKI WAS ECHOING with civil defense sirens for the fifth time in seven hours.[1] The longest stretch free of sleep-ruining sirens during this interval had been between a 0149 warning alert and a release from same at 0505.[2] Going by the letter of civil defense guidelines, a warning alert was technically a mandatory take-shelter evacuation directive only for the very young and/or infirm and their caregivers, so most adults in the city had probably only rolled over on their futons and grumbled a bit when these particular sirens blared.

The 0803 siren, however, was of the more urgent air-raid-alert variety, indicating compulsory evacuation to the nearest shelter for all but military personnel and first responders. Therefore, anyone in Nagasaki who was following this directive faithfully had been squatting in some hillside or backyard bomb shelter for nearly four hours when, eleven minutes before noon,[3] thirty-two A-26 attack planes of the Seventh Air Force swooped into the city's airspace at high speed and low altitude to strafe and bomb the harbor and the CBD. The raid, a quick hit-and-run affair that lasted only some twenty minutes, was the first on the city in more than three months.

It was also never supposed to have happened.

Eleven weeks earlier, at the May 10 and 11 meeting of the joint civilian-military Target Committee held in Los Alamos (with J. Robert Oppenheimer in attendance), a list of four candidate cities to be attacked with the first combat-deployed atomic bombs had been finalized to include Kyoto, Hiroshima, Yokohama, and Kokura Arsenal.[4] After some Pentagon tweaking, in-theater USAAF commands received a directive from Washington that three cities—Kyoto, Hiroshima, and the Sea of Japan port of Niigata—were now "Reserved Areas" and thus not to be subjected to conventional strategic attacks.[5] Somewhere in the mix, it seems to have been determined that Yokohama was already slated for a major XXI BC operation, so it was removed from Reserved Area designation. The decision was emphatically finalized when the city was devastated by a mass incendiary raid two weeks later, on the night of May 28 to 29, three days after another XXI BC attack had burned down the Yamanote half of nearby Tokyo.[6]

When Secretary of War Henry L. Stimson was informed of the Target Committee's "final" recommendations, he expressed his opposition to Kyoto's inclusion on the target list. By way of argument, he offered several political, cultural, and diplomatic justifications for his stance. These were all connected in some way with Kyoto's historical background as the pre-Meiji capital of Japan, during which time it had been a locus not only of political power but also of the Buddhist religion and traditional Japanese arts. With the ultimate outcome of the war already a given, Stimson held that the atomic destruction of the uniquely beautiful and culturally irreplaceable city would, in addition to killing a sizable portion of Kyoto's one million overwhelmingly civilian residents, also result in horrendous optics for America, which would shortly be faced with administering the military occupation of eighty million Japanese people. In a bigger, longer-range picture, it would also be a bad look for a country that was poised to become the standard-bearer of Western civilization in what was shaping up to be a long-game ideological competition with Communism for the hearts and minds of the postwar world.[7]

Equally adamant that Kyoto should not only stay on the target list but do so as its top-priority line item was Manhattan Project chief General Leslie Groves (technically, Stimson's subordinate), whose opinion was both informed and backed by the unanimous consensus of the Target Committee's members. In support of his case, Groves offered that the city was the last major Japanese war production center that was still relatively intact by this point in the conflict. Moreover, he had also been advised by the Los Alamos members of the Target Committee that Kyoto's topographical characteristics—a wide, flat area of dense, wooden, urban buildup surrounded on all sides by steep mountains—would make the city an ideal target for demonstrating the power of the new weapon. One of the quirkier justifications offered up by the Target Committee for atom-bombing Kyoto was based on the belief that the city was an "intellectual center" whose residents would be "more apt to appreciate the significance of such a weapon . . . ," so, assuming any "intellectual" witnesses survived the event, their testimony could ostensibly be used in the aftermath to convince Japanese policymakers that continued resistance was futile in the face of such technology.[8]

Debate over the matter went back and forth for more than two months until President Truman, then attending the Potsdam Conference, finally came down on Stimson's side. Kyoto was officially removed from the atomic-target list while retaining its Reserved Area status protecting it from any XXI BC incendiary or other air attack.[9] When the list was finalized on July 25, Kokura was restored to atom-bombable status and a fourth location—the western Kyushu harbor city of Nagasaki, which had formerly been considered too militarily insignificant to merit a $2 billion atomic bomb—was added to replace Kyoto, perhaps as a face-saving sop for Groves.[10]

Likely due to an omission in Washington's communications to Pacific Theater air commander General Carl Spaatz regarding the updated target list, several in-theater chains of command—including that of Seventh Air Force—seem to have missed the memo on Nagasaki's updated no-touch status.[11] As a result, in addition to the above-mentioned July 29 strike, the city's CBD and harbor area were hit by two more tactical strikes by Seventh Air Force elements on July 31 and August 1. But the communications snafu was cleared up in time to prevent any further damage to the city after this, and even with a few of its waterfront neighborhoods badly shot up and the Mitsubishi shipyards and Mori-machi works bomb damaged, Nagasaki still presented a near-pristine (albeit relatively small and topographically unfavorable) target on which to observe the effects of an atomic weapon on a densely populated urban area.[12]

Stimson's intervention to spare Kyoto was only the second in a series of bitter ironies that would go on to seal Nagasaki's fate in August 1945. The first of these had actually come nearly a year earlier, in October 1944. At the time, then XX BC commander Curtis LeMay and his immediate Twentieth Air Force liaison, Brigadier General Lauris Norstad, were finalizing preparations for a major incendiary raid the following month against Nagasaki, which, along with the larger but much less densely populated Fukuoka, was the only major Japanese urban concentration XX BC bombers could reach from their forward Operation MATTERHORN bases in Chengdu, China.

Nagasaki, it was hoped, would provide a spectacularly flammable stage for demonstrating the full capabilities and return-on-investment value of the jaw-droppingly expensive B-29 program (the Twentieth Air Force's raison d'être), which had so far been something of a disappointment. Moreover, showing what a large incendiary raid could do to a densely populated wooden Japanese city would strengthen the argument—then championed by Norstad and LeMay (and opposed by "Bomber Mafia" acolytes of the Norden bombsight)—for a switch in American tactical policy from the theretofore canonical daylight precision bombing of military and industrial targets to RAF-style indiscriminate area-bombing incendiary attacks against urban concentrations.[13] If the raid had gone through as originally planned, it is unlikely that Nagasaki would have been deemed worthy of consideration when the Target Committee in Washington was finalizing its list of pristine candidate cities for atomic destruction.

However, in late 1944, Washington decided to pull the plug on the ineffective, costly, and increasingly IJA-ground-campaign-threatened Operation MATTERHORN. As a result, the Nagasaki mass fire raid was scratched, and the incendiaries that had been stockpiled for it at forward Chinese bases were instead dropped on the important IJA logistical center of Hankow, China[14]—the destruction of which was a parting American gift to Chiang Kai-shek, slowing down for a spell the IJA Operation *Ichi-gō* campaign then threatening the region, thereby giving the Americans time to carry out a relatively orderly evacuation of their forward bases. The XX BC's lone operational wing, the 58th, was soon merged into the new XXI BC then being set up in the Marianas.[15]

Mitsubishi Shipyards Ōhashi plant

Ieno-machi, Urakami Valley

4.5 kilometers north of Nigiwai Bridge

August 2, 1945

Even with the recent steel-drought strangulation of weapons production, the Mitsubishi Shipyards Ōhashi plant in the northern Urakami Valley neighborhood of Ieno-machi still employed some seventy-five hundred workers on a typical day shift. While this was more than four times the size of the labor force at Mori-machi,[16] both plants had a proportionally similar breakdown in worker category. Full-time Mitsubishi professionals constituted perhaps only 10 percent or so of this force, while the remainder consisted of *jokō* and both male and female *dō'in gakuto* student laborers and *chōyōkō* adult laborers.[17] That last group had been conscripted from non-war-essential occupations (e.g., service and hospitality industry workers, maids, gardeners, and other domestic positions, etc.) under the National Service Draft Ordinance (*Kokumin Chōyō Rei*) of 1939 and loaned, as such, to Mitsubishi for the duration.[18]

Ishida Masako worked at the center of activity at the plant, the Main Torpedo Assembly Shop. There, her section was tasked with waterproofing *Kaiten*, minisub, and conventional torpedo tail sections by flattening rivets with hammer blows. It was a noisy, arduous job—performed, again, without any protective gear—and it left the girls and women in the team with chronically sore muscles and low-grade tinnitus.

The assembly shop itself was a sprawling operation, occupying a cluster of conjoined hangar-like structures. Together, the rectangular complex these formed covered a total floor space roughly equivalent to six American football fields.[19] As with Kiridōshi Michiko's Morimachi building, this Ōhashi structure was also a rushed wartime affair—basically a gargantuan tent of sheet metal roofed with corrugated, semitranslucent asbestos that allowed dingy gray natural light to filter down to the factory floor on sunny days. This "tent," in turn, was suspended on a skeletal framework of steel girders and lattices that doubled in function to support the system of overhead gantry cranes that did the heavy lifting at and between the factory floor's various workstations.

When Ōhashi's lathes, drill presses, and hammers fell silent that summer, the focus of activity at the plant was shifted from weapons production to safeguarding vital machine tools and other supplies in line with government orders—standing since the previous autumn—for munitions producers to disperse their means of production at a remove from their main factory facilities. The purpose of this dispersal was to mitigate the effectiveness of Allied daylight precision bombing of industrial targets.[20] Some of Ōhashi's operations had already been moved to the nearby campuses of Shiroyama and Yamazato elementary schools and the Nagasaki School for the Blind and Deaf (*Nagasaki Mō'A Gakkō*) to comply with this policy.[21]

A more ambitious dispersal measure had been undertaken from September 1944 when excavation began for underground factory facilities in Sumiyoshi, some 1.2 kilometers northwest of the main plant. The new complex consisted of six parallel tunnels, each approximately three hundred meters long and 4.5 meters wide. Each tunnel was spaced about ten meters from the next, and all were perpendicularly interconnected by communications passages at the hundred- and two-hundred-meter marks of their lengths.[22] By April, most of the heavy lifting on the project had been completed, with only finishing touches to attend to—including ongoing work to outfit the complex with rails for hand-pulled mine carts to be used in lieu of the electrically powered overhead gantry crane systems employed at the main Ōhashi plant.[23] By August, the mine cart rail system was finished and some metal-part machining jobs had been transferred to the tunnels.[24]

Remarkably, no heavy tunneling equipment had been involved in this massive excavation. It had all been hand-dug over a period of eight months with picks and shovels by a work crew of some one thousand Koreans who were put up nearby in hastily purpose-built *hanba* clusters.[25]

For anyone at the plant with even a shred of situational awareness, the implications of Ōhashi being moved into dank tunnels had to have been experienced, at least on some level of consciousness, with a heavy undertone of cognitive dissonance: A nation in control of its own airspace—a nation winning its war—did not have to hide its factories underground. Such considerations lent the ostensibly urgent bustle of all of this dispersal activity a rearranging-deck-chairs-on-the-*Titanic* aspect that even student workers had enough strategic savvy to grasp, though the constant patriotic-song recitations and slogan chanting helped somewhat to keep such thoughts away—or at least left publicly unvoiced.

Every morning at *chōrei* assembly, when the official Ōhashi anthem was chanted, it was difficult not to feel a little surge of pride at the verse about the aerial torpedoes deployed in the Pearl Harbor attack having been built at the plant. And while there was pride, there was still hope; for purehearted, patriotic girls like Ishida Masako, a scenario in which Japan could actually lose its "holy war" (*seisen*) was utterly inconceivable despite the undeniable reality of American planes now flying overhead day and night, seemingly at will and unmolested by Japanese defenders. Surely the responsible adults—the *erai hito*—in Masako's world knew what they were doing. And if they were not expressing doubts about the war, then children like her had no business harboring them. Rather, their job was to wake up every morning, tie on their headbands, show up for work, and toil tirelessly and uncomplainingly until final victory was at hand.

But the flurry of raids on Nagasaki between July 29 and August 1 was different. This time, instead of just flying over as they usually did, the Americans had swooped in low—almost angrily—to shoot up and bomb the city. For Masako, the attacks heralded an intimation that the war might be entering a dangerous new phase, and she felt this most keenly on the day after the August 1 raid. As she walked past the Mori-machi works during her morning commute, the sight of some bomb-collapsed walls and smoky rubble piles at the plant raised the possibility in her mind that the next raid might hit Ōhashi.[26] Nagasaki, she realized, was not quite the sanctuary she had come to believe it was since escaping with her family from fire-destroyed Tokyo.

Not all of the Ishida family had made the move to Nagasaki; Masako's brother, Jō'ichi, had stayed behind in Tokyo, boarding with relatives at the old Inoue Tetsujirō mansion so he could continue with his preparations for the Tōdai entrance exam. At least, that was the original plan; but the Tokyo incendiary raid of May 25–26 had destroyed much of the Yamanote half of the city and, with it, both the Ishida and Inoue homesteads.[27] In early June, Jō'ichi endured an arduous rail journey, punctuated by multiple train strafings, to Nagasaki to report this bad news to the family in person. He also had to report that, given these developments, his Tōdai entrance exam preparations were now on hold, as he no longer had a place to stay in the capital. His journey from Tokyo, then, had also been made because of the contingency that this temporary evacuation to Nagasaki might become permanent.

Judge Ishida, however, was having none of it. He was going to ensure that his son followed in his footsteps—using the springboard of Tōdai to bound up to the highest elite circles of the imperial bureaucracy—and he was prepared to use every bit of personal and professional influence he had to make that happen. The judge, aware of the terrible shape Tokyo was now in, particularly in terms of food supplies, decided that it would be untoward to impose his son on the household of any of his many personal friends and associates in the capital. Instead, he managed to get Jō'ichi into a private dormitory— in the so far relatively un-bomb-scathed Suginami Ward—for the exclusive use of Tōdai students hailing from Fukuoka.[28] Once these arrangements had been secured (notwithstanding the fact that Jō'ichi was not yet a Tōdai student), the judge sent his son back to the capital to continue his studies; the nearly daily air raids there would just have to be endured.[29]

Judge Ishida was somewhat more circumspect, however, when it came to Masako's younger sisters, Yasuyo and Shizuko. Out of concern for their safety in the Ishidas' densely populated and almost entirely wooden Nagasaki CBD neighborhood, he had sent the girls off in July to stay with Ishida relatives in rural Fukuoka. This move rendered the position of the girls' live-in tutor, Hayashi-sensei, unnecessary for a second time—the first time being when Yasuyo and Shizuko had been evacuated from Tokyo with their elementary school classmates in mid-1944. Regardless of the now nonexistent nature of her tutoring work (Masako had no studies to speak of, being essentially a full-time munitions worker at Ōhashi), Hayashi-sensei was kept on (along with her mother) as a sort of governess and household manager and to provide well-educated-female companionship for Masako.

In the meantime, Masako's Nagasaki routine continued. Each morning, she would get up at 0500 and be out of the house by 0600—an early-rising schedule that was necessitated by the circumstances of her five-kilometer commute to Ōhashi. Unlike the case of Kiridōshi Michiko, whose home location near Hotarujaya Station allowed her the luxury of a streetcar seat every morning, Masako was effectively precluded from such transportation arrangements. The location of her own home in Katsuyama-machi, deep in Nagasaki's CBD, meant that westbound streetcars were hopelessly overcrowded by the time they rolled through her neighborhood. For a while, she attempted to ride them anyway, but she eventually gave up and began doing her commute on foot. Having to do this shod in *geta* was arduous—she faced the same initial Tokyo *ojōsan* footwear challenges as Kiridōshi Michiko had in this respect—but the ninety-minute hike between Katsuyama-machi and Ōhashi became a little easier to bear once she made friends with other Kenjo girls living in the CBD who could serve as traveling companions. During these hours of daily *geta* marching, conversation was generally light and cheerful, usually dominated by fond reminiscences about the types of food they missed from the prewar era—mostly sweets of some kind—and vocalized fantasies about how they were going to be able to enjoy all of those delicacies once again after the media-promised "divine wind" blew and the war ended in inevitable Japanese victory.

<hr>

Many Nagasaki-area secondary and/or vocational schools[30] were sending their students to work as de facto full-time employees at Ōhashi. Kenjo, for example, had committed its entire third-grade class—Masako and perhaps two hundred or so of her classmates—to serve as *dō'in gakuto* workers there.[31] Keiho Prefectural Junior High School, which was actually much closer to Mori-machi, was represented by some three hundred fifty of its male students.[32] Keiho Girls' School—a private institution in the CBD unrelated to its public male namesake—also had students at the plant, including some in Masako's waterproofing section.[33] But by far the largest institutional contributor of *dō'in gakuto* muscle to Ōhashi operations was Nagasaki Junshin Kōtō Jogakkō, a Catholic girls' school that every day sent some five hundred second- to fifth-graders to the plant's Main Torpedo Assembly Shop.[34]

While their work might have been tedious, the Junshin girls were at least fortunate in having a very short commute. Their school was located directly opposite Ōhashi's main gate, occupying a long strip of land sandwiched between the Nagayo Road[35] and the Urakami River (which was closer to a creek by this point in its course). Even by suburban Nagasaki standards, the campus was luxuriously space endowed; inclusive of its athletic fields, it covered almost as much ground as Ōhashi's torpedo assembly works.

The centerpiece of the campus was Junshin's hundred-meter-long, two-story main classroom and administrative building: a handsome white-stuccoed, Art Deco–inflected Gothic structure that directly fronted on the Nagayo Road. It was one of the most architecturally modern school facilities in Nagasaki, and its steel-reinforced concrete construction would have made it ideal as a Mitsubishi dispersal facility had its extreme proximity to Ōhashi not rendered such a function redundant.

Fundraising efforts for the Ieno-machi campus' 1937 construction—and the real estate it occupied—had been organized by the Nagasaki Sisters of the Sacred Heart of Mary (aka Junshin Sisters), the women's religious order that administered the school and filled most of its faculty roster.[36] The bulk of contributions for the school's construction came from the families of students, many of whom belonged to the local working-class Catholic community that had just toiled and scraped and tithed over the previous five decades to build the recently completed Immaculate Conception (Urakami) Cathedral.[37]

In peacetime, the campus—along with the cathedral—had been the pride of the neighborhood. But as with most everything else in the city—and in the country as a whole—a distinct patina of late-war shabbiness had long since descended upon Junshin's formerly grand and expansive grounds. What had once been airy open spaces between the school buildings, the student dormitory, and the Junshin Sisters' quarters were now striated with slit trench bomb shelters. The athletic fields were vegetable farms tended by the nuns and students between Ōhashi shifts toward some measure of food self-sufficiency. But as the school's principal often reminded her charges during *chōrei* morning assemblies, even Catholic schoolgirls had to make sacrifices for the nation in this time of war. Rest could come after victory.

HIDDEN CHRISTIANS

FROM A LONG-VIEW perspective, the Catholic community in Urakami Valley owed its continuous, centuries-long existence to a uniquely unlikely series of historical factors. The first of these was the Portuguese penetration of this part of Kyushu in the late sixteenth century.

A second factor was a matter of incompetent governance on the part of the Edo Period Shogunate. Had its nearly two-hundred-fifty-year-long anti-Christian pogrom been pursued with efficiency proportionate to its passion and fury, Urakami's Catholic community would have been wiped out centuries ago, and Junshin Girls' School and Immaculate Conception (Urakami) Cathedral would never have existed.

The most recent factor—eighty-five years before a Junshin girl had ever swung a hammer in a munitions plant or thumbed a rosary praying for kamikaze pilots to sink American aircraft carriers—was the Shogunate's signing of the Western-gunboat-backed Ansei Treaties in the twilight of the Edo Period.

As a stipulation of these treaties, the port cities of Hakodate, Yokohama, and Nagasaki were reopened to foreign trade and residence.[1] Among the various concerns of Japan's rulers regarding these externally coerced accommodations, one of the more worrisome was that subjecting these cities to a locust plague of carpetbagging Westerners would entail exposing Japanese cultural space once again to the potentially destabilizing influence of openly practiced Christianity. To shield the local populace from any anticipated pernicious effects of this exposure, Shogunate treaty negotiators had secured a prohibition against any Christian proselytization activity targeting the native population and a guarantee that any Christian activity on Japanese soil would stay within the boundaries of the officially designated Foreign Settlement Districts in each of these "open" port cities,[2] with participation in the same restricted to the residents therein.

Treaty-limited and geographically quarantined though it might have been, the foreigners' religious activity was nevertheless kept under close surveillance by the Shogunate. Despite the official abolition of mandatory public *efumi* apostasy rituals—a cosmetic policy adjustment begrudgingly enacted to gloss the optics of the port openings—the official edict against native Japanese practice of Christianity still stood.[3] While violators were no longer being crucified, they were still subject to arrest and harsh punishment,[4] including interrogation under torture to betray compatriots; imprisonment; forfeiture of property; and even mass banishment under the Shogunate's *goningumi seido* ("five-household system") legal policy of collective criminal responsibility—a sort of Edo Period RICO statute that could be applied to entire villages or neighborhoods suspected of hosting or even merely tolerating clandestine practice of what the Japanese state was still officially referring to as a *jakyō*, or "demonic religion."[5]

As there were, for obvious reasons, no Japanese clergy members qualified to administer to the liturgical needs of the Foreign Settlements, the Shogunate was compelled to allow foreign Christian clerics into the country to perform this function. In the case of Nagasaki, the city's first openly administered Catholic parish in more than two hundred years was established in the Foreign Settlement in 1863 by Father Louis-Theodore Furet, a priest from the Société des Missions Étrangères de Paris (MEP)—the missionary order specifically tasked by the Vatican with reviving the Catholic community in the recently "reopened" Japan.[6]

The Vatican was at this point still concentrating its Japanese foothold efforts in Yokohama, as near as it was allowed to get to the Edo power center of the Shoguns' capital. In the grand scheme of the Church's strategy for eventual open proselytization in the country, Nagasaki—its peerless deepwater harbor aside—was a demographically insignificant provincial burg in comparison with Edo, Osaka, Kyoto, and the other great population centers of Honshu. Nevertheless, given the fabled Jesuit roots of its history, the city had long held a special symbolic significance for modern Catholicism, with accounts of the tribulations, humiliations, and martyrdom endured by the clerics of the Portuguese settlement and their Japanese converts long the stuff of legend—as reverential as it was dark—in Catholic lore.[7] And of particular sentimental interest and iconic status in this mythical canon was the story of the Twenty-Six Martyrs of Nishizaka, an incident that occurred during a brief but bloody earlier, pre-Shogunate anti-Christian pogrom carried out by late Warring States–period warlord Toyotomi Hideyoshi.

In 1597, on Hideyoshi's orders, a mixed group of Western clerics and Japanese Christians were arrested in the Kyoto-Osaka region and ordered to renounce their faith. When they refused, they were publicly mutilated and then force-marched over a six-hundred-fifty-kilometer-long *via dolorosa* from Kyoto that went across the western half of Honshu and northern Kyushu. Eventually wending their way down the Togitsu Road to Nishizaka—a rocky bluff at the head of Na-gasaki harbor,[8] the symbolic ground zero of Japanese Christianity at the time—the unrepentant Christians were crucified and administered coups de grâce by lance, Golgotha-style.[9]

Underscoring renewed ecclesiastical interest in the story co-incident with the reopening of Japan, Pope Pius IX carried out a canonization of the Twenty-Six Martyrs that made world news in 1862[10] and gave Catholicism its first Japanese saints. Additionally, the Vatican was intrigued by rumors of an underground community of "hidden" native Catholics (*kakure Kirishitan*) in the Nagasaki region who were said to have survived the long centuries of Japan's isolation and the Shogunate's mercilessly pursued campaign of extermination against their faith.[11]

The secular governments of the Western powers might have assured the Japanese authorities that they would keep Christianity restricted to the Foreign Settlements, but the Catholic Church itself—whose transnational nature the Shogunate never seemed to grasp—had never made any such promises. In 1863,[12] a second MEP priest—Father Bernard Petitjean—was posted to the city, ostensibly to help Father Furet administer the new Nagasaki parish. But Petitjean's marching orders also included a second mission not included in his official portfolio: to assist his colleague in confirming the existence of the *kakure Kirishitan* community and, once this had been done, to establish contact with the same.

As the first step in this diplomatically sensitive (and legally perilous) mission, the French priests decided to send up the nineteenth-century ecclesiastical equivalent of a Bat Signal. With the enthusiastic help of Léon Dury—the French consul of Nagasaki and a devout Catholic—Furet and Petitjean (soon joined by a third MEP priest, Father Joseph Laucaigne) set out to build the first Catholic church in the city in more than two hundred years.[13] Following Shogunate guidelines, they would build the church safely within the confines of the Foreign Settlement. The site chosen for the new church was in the waterfront district of Ōura, about one-third of the way up the northwest slope of Nabekanmuri. The spot offered a commanding view of the surrounding landscape, but more important, it was conspicuous; this vantage point would render the crucifix-topped church a veritable beacon of Catholicism that would be visible from anywhere in the harbor and from most of the downtown districts. To drive home the operant symbolism of this in-your-face high visibility, Father Furet's architectural plans had the foundation of the church oriented so that its front entrance would point directly at Nishizaka[14]—a none-too-subtle "We have returned, at long last and as promised, and we are open for business again" message whose meaning would be immediately clear to an audience—including, he hoped, *kakure Kirishitan*—privy to the pertinent historical provenance of that rocky outcropping.

Work on the project proceeded slowly at first, hampered primarily by a lack of qualified native carpenters willing to help build what was coming to be known in the city as the *Furansudera* ("French temple"). But after Father Petitjean agreed to help the local Shogunate authorities set up a French-language training facility in the city, a flood of highly skilled Japanese carpenters appeared at the Ōura construction site[15] within days, ready and eager for work.

The completion of Ōura *Tenshudō* (literally, "pavilion of the Lord of Heaven," i.e., "church") was commemorated with a dedication ceremony on February 19, 1865. This event was attended by everybody who was anybody in the Foreign Settlement, by the captains and crews of several European warships that happened to be making ports of call in Nagasaki harbor at the time, and by very few Japanese.[16]

The new church began holding masses for the local faithful forthwith. Although these were attended only by Catholic residents of the Foreign Settlement, they were nevertheless kept under close watch by Shogunate authorities and neighborhood snitches to ensure that no Japanese participated, as well as to see that the front entrance of the church was kept shut and locked when services were not underway.[17] But it was to prove impossible to keep secret for long the goings-on at the exotic "French temple" rising high over the southern reaches of the city. And this was just as Father Furet had intended.

On March 17, 1865, Father Petitjean looked out of his rectory window to see a group of "12 to 15 [Japanese] . . . men, women, and children" standing motionless in front of the church,[18] assuming a seemingly anticipatory, reverent posture in the direction of the entrance. Petitjean, disregarding the official injunction against allowing Japanese onto church premises, unlocked the gate and bade the party enter. Leaving their *geta* at the entrance, the visitors padded barefoot up into the apse of the *Furansudera*, gazing about in awe and wonder.

Although Petitjean, like his clerical colleagues, had a working familiarity with spoken Japanese from earlier postings in the Ryukyu Islands and Yokohama, the challenges posed by the visitors' rustic dialect were daunting. Although the conversation that ensued pushed and occasionally exceeded the limits of his linguistic skills, he was eventually able to ascertain that his visitors were peasants from the village of Urakami who, after hearing rumors that there was a statue of what they called "Santa Maria" at the *Furansudera*, had walked all the way to Ōura to see her.

Petitjean assured the visitors that there was indeed such a statue in the church, and when he led them to it, one of the middle-aged women in the party astonished him by asking whether he and his people, like the villagers of Urakami, also celebrated the birthday of the Lord of Heaven's son on the twenty-fifth day of December.[19] Petitjean knew in that moment that his visitors were not merely curious local sightseers—he was face-to-face with *kakure Kirishitan*, descendants of the first Japanese converted by Saint Francis Xavier's Jesuits nearly three centuries earlier.

Deepening his rapport with the Urakami Catholics in ensuing months, Petitjean was able to piece together the theretofore unwritten history of their remarkable community. Enduring long centuries of official persecution and the annual humiliation of *efumi* apostasy rituals, these simple, stalwart peasants had still somehow managed to maintain their Christian faith, secretly observing Catholic holy days and holding mass in the shadows with a phonetically memorized pidgin-Latin liturgy and Portuguese clerical terminology (e.g., "Santa Maria") passed down generation to generation through jealously guarded oral tradition. Given the staggering improbability of this saga, the *kakure Kirishitan* community's survival was nothing short of miraculous. It is said that when news of Petitjean's discovery reached the Vatican, Pius IX wept.[20]

Unfortunately, news of the miracle at Ōura also reached the ears of the Shogunate, despite Petitjean's having taken pains to prevent this. In the wake of the disclosure, Japanese authorities commenced a dragnet for *kakure Kirishitan* in Urakami, Hirado, the Gotō Islands, and other suspected Christian enclaves in the Nagasaki region in a wave of persecution that persisted even after the regime change of the Meiji Restoration.[21] Eventually, in an official act that resulted in a storm of international protest, 3,290 Urakami Christians were forced from their homes and exiled, piecemeal, to far-flung provinces around the Japanese archipelago in January 1870.[22]

Four years earlier, thirty-seven-year-old Father Petitjean had been consecrated to the rank of bishop—a rare honor for a cleric of his relative youth and one no doubt bestowed in recognition of his important work in Nagasaki. Concurrently, he was also appointed to the post of vicar apostolic of Japan.[23] After assuming this office, Petitjean exercised his authority as the senior in-country Catholic clergyman to move the seat of the vicar apostolic from Osaka to Nagasaki, where he would be better positioned to help the embattled Catholic community there, with the most urgent task being to put pressure on the Japanese state to repatriate the exiled Christians to Urakami. With Petitjean serving as the Church's boots-on-the-ground point man for a yearslong campaign of intense diplomatic and international media pressure, the new Meiji government was eventually compelled, in 1873, not only to restore the Urakami Catholics to their home village but also to repeal the nationwide ban on the practice of Christianity by Imperial Japanese subjects.[24]

Riding the wave of these triumphs, Petitjean continued his tireless work in Nagasaki for the remainder of his years, establishing facilities for the training of native novitiates and cementing the region's status as the center of Japanese Catholicism.[25] In 1878, he also oversaw the reconstruction of Ōura Church (later Cathedral) into an ecclesiastical edifice befitting its official status as a bishop's seat. He was buried there in 1884.

Nearly half a century later, in 1927, the long reach of Petitjean's efforts to cultivate domestic clerical talent achieved their greatest triumph to date when Father Januarius Hayasaka Kyūnosuke became the first Japanese to be elevated to bishop rank in the history of the Catholic Church.[26] The year before donning his scarlet prelate's robes, Hayasaka had been chosen as one of the participants in the Religious Legislation Investigation Commission, an advisory body formed by the Ministry of Education to find common ground—and clarify mutual interests—between the Japanese state and the nation's most influential religious groups.[27] Establishing his seat as the new head of the

Diocese of Nagasaki at a time when the country was taking the first steps of its hard-right lurch into ultranationalism and militarism, Hayasaka might have been tapped for his bishopric because of his demonstrated ability to walk the increasingly precarious tightrope between the canonical and apostolic demands of his office on one hand and the rapidly developing political and ideological situation in Tokyo on the other.

Once ensconced in Nagasaki, Hayasaka continued in the Ōura parish tradition of grooming Japanese Catholic leadership talent. In 1929, he reached out with a proposal to Ezumi Yasu, a Kyoto schoolteacher and novice of the School Sisters of Notre Dame: He wanted to establish the first native Japanese women's religious order, and he thought Ezumi had the right stuff to lead it. To seal the deal, he sponsored the novice to complete her novitiate at the elite Convent of the Sacred Heart in Marmoutier, France.[28] After four years there, she took her final vows to become Sister Mary Maddalena Ezumi Yasu, then set off back to Japan to assume her lifework.[29] On the way, she made a stop in Rome for a private audience with Pius XI to pass on greetings from the bishop of Nagasaki and receive the coveted imprimatur of a papal blessing for what would become Ezumi's new Sacred Heart–affiliated all-Japanese-religious-order project.

With encouragement from Hayasaka, Ezumi resolved that the new order should be based in Nagasaki, the site of the martyrdom of the Twenty-Six and the most hallowed Catholic ground in Japan. On June 9, 1934, Ezumi was sworn in by Bishop Hayasaka as the founding Mother Superior of the Nagasaki Junshin Seibokai ("Nagasaki Sisters of the Sacred Heart") in an investiture ceremony held at Ōura Cathedral.

THE NOVICE

Junshin Girls' School / Junshin Sisters' residence
Ieno-machi, Nagasaki
4.4 kilometers north of Nigiwai Bridge
Summer 1945

WHEN MOTHER EZUMI took the helm of the Junshin Sisters order,[1] Christianity was hitting the roughest patch of Japanese road it had seen in generations. Putting wind at the back of this latest wave of Christophobia was the ultranationalist "Imperial Way" (*Kōdō*) political philosophy then gaining traction around the country. A self-reverential fascistic mélange of emperor worship, collective narcissism, and long-simmering populist hostility vis-à-vis Western-tainted, capital-*M* "Modernity," the movement was originally championed by a motley ideological crew of militarists, mystics, nativists, and other far-right mountebanks. Initially dismissed as such by the Tokyo power elite, the movement ceased being a punch line in the early 1930s, simultaneously shocking and thrilling the country with a series of close-run coup attempts and spectacular assassinations in the capital.[2] By the time Mother Ezumi was organizing her new order, the *Kōdō* movement was enjoying substantial and growing support not only in the Tokyo halls of power but also—fanned by a sympathetic and sensationalist mass media—among the populace in general.[3]

This xenophobic wave in national sentiment directly and negatively impacted the Junshin Sisters because, in the *Kōdō* worldview, Christianity was an "un-Japanese" (*hikokumin teki*) threat to the State Shintō

civic religion on which the sacred national polity (*Kokutai*) was based[4]—
an insidious spiritual Trojan horse of suspect foreign provenance. By
the mid-1930s, *Kōdō* thinking was beginning to take hold even in traditionally multicultural Nagasaki, where Christianity had until recently
been tolerated and even celebrated (at least as an exotic tourist draw),
but where its followers were now dogged with harassment and innu-
endo painting them as potential spies and fifth columnists.

Steering the Junshin Sisters through these treacherous shoals,
Mother Ezumi was savvy enough to grasp that a favorable public image was going to be crucial for her fledgling order's survival. And as a
first step toward securing this positive PR, the young Mother Superior
would have to decide what kind of order the Junshin Sisters were going to be.

In the Catholic tradition, there are two categories of female religious orders that, in terms of form and function, correlate roughly to
the respective roles and missions of monks and ordained priests. The
members of what are known as "contemplative" orders are technically
classified as "nuns." Like monks, they live in literally cloistered environments maintained to protect them from the distractions (and
temptations) of the outside world. Aside from work chores necessary
for the physical upkeep and operation of their respective convents or
abbeys, their daily activities are inwardly focused on prayer, meditation, study of the scriptures, and contemplation/adoration of the Holy
Spirit. To give a somewhat trite encapsulation, nuns regard their
activity—particularly their daily hours of silent prayer—as manning
the phone banks, so to speak, of humanity's Hotline to Heaven. One
drawback to such an orientation in a predominately non-Christian
and traditionally hardworking culture such as Japan's is that, from the
critical perspective of nonbelievers, its practitioners can come off as
out-of-touch duty shirkers. In the historical context of a Japan gearing
up for military mayhem in East Asia and expecting all of the emper-
or's good subjects to kick in and help on the home front, this would
obviously not have been a good look for the Junshin order.

Members of the second, "apostolic" category of female religious
orders are referred to in Church terminology as "Sisters."[5] In contrast

THE NOVICE

with nuns, Sisters are more actively engaged "down in the trenches," promoting God's work out and about in the secular world, much like parish priests. These deeds are typically performed in the fields of education, charity work for the poor, nursing, and—where allowed by local political climate—social justice.[6]

As an intensely spiritual and intellectual person, Mother Ezumi admired the contemplatives' commitment, as brides of Christ, to passing consecrated lives in prayer, meditation, and contemplation[7] of the glory of the Holy Spirit. Had the Junshin Sisters been formed in postwar Japan, it is quite possible she might have opted for more focus on this orientation for the order. But Mother Ezumi did not enjoy that historical luxury.

That said, neither was her hand entirely forced in the matter; she had come up in the apostolic tradition with the School Sisters of Notre Dame. Moreover, as a Japanese of her generation, she did not need to be convinced of the spiritual value of good, honest work. Just as important, from a pragmatic PR standpoint, hard work and community service—out there for all to see—would be a good look for the Sisters in a cultural milieu where the hoary folk maxim of *ichinichi fusaku fushoku* ("Those who do not work do not deserve to eat") was still a bedrock ethos for most Japanese.

In the end, Ezumi would follow both her heart and her head, cherry-picking the best from both orientations. Her Sisters would spend normal "business hours" engaged in community outreach as schoolteachers—a pedagogical focus for the order that was natural, given Ezumi's qualified professional background in high school education. But "off duty," the Sisters would lead the consecrated and rule-bound lives of contemplatives. Accentuating this duality at the core of the Junshin identity, Ezumi chose *Sapientia et Servitium* ("Wisdom and Service") as the new order's religious motto.[8]

In 1935, Ezumi successfully petitioned the Nagasaki prefectural government to charter the Junshin Sisters as an officially approved educational enterprise. With this credential, she was able to establish Junshin Girls' School, which would serve as a venue for the Sisters' apostolic work in the Nagasaki community.

The school was small and woefully underfunded at first, dependent for its classroom space on the generosity of Naka-machi Church, a parish in a well-heeled residential district in the CBD. Despite these financial and physical challenges, it quickly garnered a reputation for academic and moral education excellence in the Nagasaki region, not only among Catholics but also among nonbelievers (whose money was as good as anyone else's and whose daughters were thus free to apply for admission upon passing a competitive entrance exam). Only two years after the school's founding, it acquired the means and bureaucratic influence to move the campus (inclusive of the Junshin Sisters' dormitory) into more impressive facilities in the Urakami Valley neighborhood of Ieno-machi.

One advantage of the original Naka-machi operation was something Mother Ezumi and the other Sisters would not miss until it was lost: In its original location and configuration, Junshin had been shielded from the unwanted attention of patriotic cranks and xenophobes by its very physical inconspicuousness. In this regard it was also protected by the sociocultural buffer zone of the upper middle class and comparatively cosmopolitan Naka-machi neighborhood surrounding it.

However, this anonymity was lost with the April 1937 opening of the Ieno-machi campus—which entailed the misfortune of overlapping with the onset of all-out war with China in July of that year. Moreover, its new surroundings, although located in Urakami, were not exclusively or even overwhelmingly Catholic in terms of demographic composition. Illustrative of the challenges posed by this environment, an early source of friction vis-à-vis Junshin's new neighbors was the sound of praying and hymn singing leaking out through the open windows of the school chapel. These windows were the regular targets of shouted taunts and insults from Nagayo Road pedestrians (Junshin's rear flank was safe—protected by the natural barrier of the Urakami River), with an occasional rock thrown for added emphasis.[9]

As the rapidly intensifying China war (and frantic media coverage of the same) ramped up local xenophobic sentiment, the Junshin Sisters' clerical uniforms of gray work habits and veils (black for full-fledged members and white for novitiates) made the Sisters frequent targets of harassment when they were out and about off campus. Eventually, things got so bad that Mother Ezumi had to ban the wearing of the habits and veils in public; whenever venturing into hostile "pagan" territory outside of school/convent grounds, the Sisters would instead don the dowdy mufti of work blouse and baggy cotton *monpe* trousers that was quickly becoming standard for adult women in a Japan gearing up for total war.[10]

Increasingly, Junshin students—readily identified by their uniforms—were also harangued in public by superpatriots and other self-appointed defenders of *Kokutai* purity. This was particularly the case for girls who used the streetcar for their commutes.[11] Still, Mother Ezumi never considered doing away with school uniforms as a way of evading the simmering low-grade persecution; the situation would be endured by her girls for an additional seven years, resolved only when the mass student labor mobilizations put the Junshin student body into factory work outfits full-time from mid-1944 on.

The heating up of the China war also brought unwelcome attention from the authorities. Particularly irksome were agents of the Special Higher Police (*tokkō keisatsu*), the Home Ministry's law enforcement branch tasked with the monitoring, exposure, and punishment of political "thought crime" (*shisōhan*).[12] Soon after the school's opening, Special Higher Police agents began regularly coming around to Junshin to grill Mother Ezumi about the provenance and loyalties of the institution. Openly dubious about the ability of the fledgling religious order to finance such a grand new campus, they were particularly interested in exposing what they suspected were foreign sources of the school's funding.[13] Despite Mother Ezumi's protestations that these sources were exclusively Japanese, the Special Higher Police harassment along these lines continued for months.

While this was still underway, Mother Ezumi's Home Ministry tormentors were joined by officers from the Nagasaki IJA garrison Kempeitai detachment, whose official inquisition was of a more blatantly ideological nature. During the Kempeitai's first intrusion on the Junshin campus, Mother Ezumi was cornered in her little office and asked whether she thought Christ, in some framework of grand universal hierarchy, was superior to the emperor. Mother Ezumi deftly parried away this obvious loyalty/"Japaneseness" probe by responding that the question was meaningless, from both political and theological standpoints.[14] At this rebuff, the temporarily tongue-tied head Kempeitai officer—no doubt incensed at having just been bettered by a *jakyō*-believing woman—abruptly rose to leave. With the best parting-shot retort he could come up with in the time he took to walk to the office door, the fuming Kempeitai man wheeled around and barked, "So if you Sisters are really Japanese, why don't you behave like it and worship Japanese [i.e., Shintō] gods? Put a *kamidana* [Shintō altar] in your faculty room and pray facing Ise Shrine . . . Every morning . . . You people pray to Christ every morning, right? Well, when you do that, pray to Ise Shrine, too."[15]

Mother Ezumi's immediate reaction to this demand was to reject it as a preposterous—not to mention blasphemous—intrusion on the freedom of religion ostensibly guaranteed all imperial subjects by the Meiji Constitution of 1889. But she was also a practical and pragmatic leader who had a school and a religious order to protect; if both were to survive the current straits in which Christian institutions like hers now found themselves, it would be in Junshin's interest not to buck state policy on a political matter. Accepting that compromise was the better part of valor in this situation, the Sisters put a *kamidana* up in the faculty room, as ordered, and from thereon out would bow to it with hands together in a praying pose every morning before beginning the day's work.[16] This ethos of dual theological loyalty—precariously balanced between allegiance to Catholic canon on one hand and to State Shintō on the other—would soon filter down into the student body as a whole, eventually becoming a central pillar of Junshin's wartime identity.

Once Mother Ezumi had gotten her school up and running, any girl who wanted to win a spot as a full-fledged Junshin Sister had to bal-

THE NOVICE

ance heavy teaching loads against long hours of devotional contemplative duties and arduous daily maintenance chores for the order (which included agricultural toil). In addition to fostering spiritual discipline, this grueling lifestyle was a harsh but effective way to separate the order's wheat from its chaff, talent-wise, ensuring that only the strongest in body and spirit among the Junshin Sisters' perennially sleep-deprived and physically challenged trainees survived the postulant and novitiate phases of their candidacy to take their final vows and join the order as lifelong members.

In the late summer of 1945, the most promising novice in the Junshin Sisters community was twenty-two-year-old Sister Itonaga Yoshi.[17] Many of the other girls on the rolls of the Junshin novitiate at the time were first-generation Christians, having converted to the faith as secondary-school or college students; some, like Mother Ezumi herself, might have done so after encountering a charismatic clerical mentor who steered them toward a life of the cloth. But Sister Yoshi stood out from the others as a pure Nagasaki Catholic thoroughbred.

According to Itonaga family lore, Sister Yoshi's ancestors had escaped the cauldron of anti-Christian persecution and surveillance that was Edo Period Nagasaki and fled some seventy kilometers to Hirado, a near-shore island on the northwestern periphery of present-day Nagasaki Prefecture. Factoring in its geographic isolation and economic and political insignificance, Hirado was well suited for *kakure Kirishitan* looking to go to ground after the *kinkyōrei* ban on their religion. Its eponymous harbor was the site of an early Jesuit foothold in the late sixteenth century and a failed English East India Company trading post in the early seventeenth.[18] Although these foreign settlements had eventually come to naught, the Christian seeds they sowed during their Hirado sojourn went on to sink deep roots in the local culture. Enjoying the relative safety of this sanctuary over the next two and a half centuries, Sister Yoshi's forebears eked an existence out of Hirado's rocky soil by day while practicing their faith with a cautiously clandestine community of fellow believers by night.

When Yoshi was born in the Hirado farming and fishing village of

Himosashi in 1923, the local Catholic community had been legally and openly practicing its faith for exactly half a century. Belying their influence in this community, the Itonagas were far from financially well-off. The family's financial situation compelled them to follow a frugal lifestyle, not only because of the considerable burden of having so many mouths to feed and bodies to clothe, but also because Yoshi's parents—like the extended Itonaga clan on Hirado as a whole—were dedicated to investing in solid Catholic educations for their children and paying parochial school tuition to do so. To make ends meet, Yoshi, her parents, and her ten siblings toiled in a relative's stone quarry during agricultural offseasons.

Like her siblings, Yoshi received her legally compulsory six-year primary education at the Catholic parochial Himosashi Elementary School. When, at age twelve, she declared to her parish priest her intent to enter a religious order, the Sisters of a local convent subjected her to a battery of oral examinations to determine the sincerity of her aspirations and her suitability for a life of the cloth. When her candidacy was approved, the convent sponsored her for an additional two years (seventh and eighth grades) of attendance at Himosashi's higher-education course before she transferred, as a third-year boarder, to the then new Junshin Girls' School in Ieno-machi, Nagasaki.

Upon graduation from Junshin two years later, Yoshi joined the Junshin Sisters community, with Mother Ezumi's blessing, at the entry-level rank of postulant. After proving her mettle in two more years of postulant grunt work, Yoshi stood for and passed the entrance examination for the School of Education at the elite Nihon Joshi Daigaku (Japan Women's University) in Tokyo in the spring of 1941.

While most of the Sisters on the faculty at Junshin Girls' School had only junior-college-level academic credentials and were thus qualified to teach only such subjects as preschool education, sewing, or home economics, Ezumi had bigger plans for her protégée; Yoshi would board at a Tokyo-area convent and the Junshin Sisters would bankroll the entirety of her university tuition so that upon her return to Ieno-machi she could join the Junshin faculty with a full-fledged Ministry of Education–approved high school teaching license. Her

THE NOVICE

homecoming would also mark the official beginning of her novitiate—the last stage of training (and screening) before taking final vows to become a lifetime member of the Junshin order.

Graduating in September 1944, a semester early due to a war-accelerated university schedule, the newly minted novice returned to a Junshin community and culture much changed in her absence. Despite her hard-earned bachelor of arts degree and education qualifications, she would not be standing at the head of a classroom anytime soon. The entirety of the student body—with the exception of the first-year girls—was now mobilized as war labor, and Sister Yoshi and her Junshin colleagues were obligated to perform chaperone duties for them.

Every day at 0430, the entire Junshin student body would assemble on the school grounds and recite the same prayer, ostensibly sotto voce enough to avoid waking and spooking the rest of the neighborhood with the *jakyō* incantations of a thousand schoolgirls:

Holy Mother Mary,
Please deliver unto Japan victory in this war.
Mary, Mother of God,
Have mercy on us sinners,
Now and forever.[19]

After their victory prayer, the students would march in formation a kilometer and a half south to Urakami Cathedral, where mass would be celebrated and more victory prayers incanted. Returning to Junshin, the girls would eat breakfast, then line up in formation for their *chōrei* morning assembly in front of the school gate. There, Mother Ezumi would deliver her daily send-off lecture, usually working some Christian learning point into war-effort motivational messages, ever hyperconscious of the need for everyone in the Junshin community—from herself down to her youngest charges—to constantly prove their unimpeachable and enthusiastic Japanese spirit and cultural loyalty at all times when within sight and earshot of their non-Christian countrymen.[20]

At the conclusion of the *chōrei*, the students would form up into their assigned labor mobilization units (with the Ōhashi detachment vastly outnumbering all others) and march off to their workplaces, chanting slogans and singing patriotic songs. Mother Ezumi's favorite was the stirring "Ballad of the Mobilized Students," the opening verse of which proudly proclaimed:

Budding cherry blossoms are we,
And small though we may be,
We are martyrs for our country's great cause,
That is the duty of all students,
Ah, our young blood burns with ardor.[21]

As each girl reached the gate, she would pause briefly to deliver two bows before falling back in formation and step with her classmates. The first would always be given to the school's *hōanden*—a sort of outdoor concrete *kamidana* where a photograph of the imperial couple was safeguarded for daily veneration.[22] The second bow would be to Mother Ezumi, who reciprocated with a slightly shallower-angled version of her own to each rank of girls, always wearing her trademark beatific smile as she sent her young charges off for another day of making suicide weapons for the *Kokutai*.[23]

By August 1945, Sister Yoshi was halfway through her novitiate. In another year, she would stand before an altar, at Immaculate Conception or Ōura, to take her final vows and graduate from her white novitiate's veil to don the black veil of full-lifetime Junshin Sisterhood. But she would not have much need for either type of veil as long as the war continued. Since returning to Nagasaki eleven months earlier, she had been wearing female factory worker's duds as a faculty chaperone for mobilized Junshin girls. For the first nine months of this assignment, she had supervised third-graders at Ōhashi—fairly light duty involving practically no commuting distance and requiring

THE NOVICE

her to do not much more than sit in the plant manager's office reading when she was not making the rounds on the factory floor to check on her students. From June, however, a new requisition request for war labor had gone through Nagasaki Military District from two small metalworking shops—one in Michino'o and the other in Togitsu. Junshin was tapped to provide the required work teams.

Sister Yoshi and another novice, Sister Uchino Chito, alternated days escorting these work groups;[24] when one was with the students, the other would stay behind at Ieno-machi, doing administrative work at the nearly empty school or tending the athletic ground truck patches for the order's meager vegetable supply with the first-graders. The new chaperone posting involved long walking commutes—a three-kilometer hike to Michino'o, with another three tacked on to get to Togitsu—but that was really its only drawback, and the physical environment at the shops was far less noisy and hectic than that of the sprawling factory floors at Ōhashi.

Since the midsummer production slowdown, there had been hardly any work going on at all at any of the Junshin labor sites, including Ōhashi. At the Michino'o and Togitsu metal shops, Sister Yoshi and her colleague had to get creative in coming up with ways to keep their girls busy; recently, they had had them digging slit trench shelters on the grounds of their workplaces. While this had originally been time-filling make-work, the start of American attacks on Nagasaki proper now meant that they might prove to be of practical use after all. The enemy planes had yet to venture as far north up the Urakami Valley as Michino'o or Togitsu, but that might change any day. And if it did, the metal shops would make tempting targets for low-flying strafers, as their small smokestacks probably rendered them identifiable from the air as industrial plants.

On the morning of August 6, 1945, the metal shop teams were walking north on the Togitsu Road, about to reach their first stop at Michino'o, when, some three hundred fifty kilometers to the northeast, a formation of three high-flying American B-29s entered Honshu airspace and wheeled west to assume a straight-line course for Hiroshima.

PART THREE

THE BOMBS OF AUGUST

FIRST BRIEFING

509th Composite Group compound
North Field, Tinian
1600 hours, August 8, 1945

IN THE 509TH Composite Group's briefing hut, a group of need-to-know pilots, bombardiers, and navigators stood around a large map table, waiting for the start of a meeting called by their commander, Colonel Paul Tibbets. As they waited, each man was handed a mimeographed copy of field orders for "Special Mission #16"[1] which had been issued by LeMay's Guam HQ the previous day.

At the appointed hour for the briefing, Tibbets—never really at ease in public-speaking situations—made no opening remarks beyond a quick command to get his crewmen's attention. Once this was accomplished, he turned the proceedings over to the 509th's S-3 operations officer, Major James Hopkins.[2]

As Hopkins explained, the upcoming mission had many parallels with the Hiroshima mission flown two days earlier. Reconnaissance aircraft would fly out an hour ahead of the strike force to report on weather conditions over the target areas. In this case, *Enola Gay* would head to the primary target, Kokura, while *Laggin' Dragon* would reconnoiter the secondary one, Nagasaki.[3] Reserve strike plane *Full House* would also fly out early, to Iwo Jima, where it would stand by at a hydraulic-lift loading pit identical in structure and function to the two on Tinian. If *Bockscar*—the designated bomb-carrying strike plane—developed mechanical trouble en route to Kokura (or, as the meteorological case might be, Nagasaki), the bomb would be loaded onto *Full House*, which would carry on the mission in *Bockscar*'s stead.

The strike force itself would consist of three aircraft. *Bockscar* would be flown by Tibbets' executive officer, twenty-five-year-old Major Charles Sweeney, a moonfaced Massachusetts Irishman who would also be in overall command of the mission. Sweeney already had one "special mission" under his belt, having participated in the Hiroshima bombing as pilot of *The Great Artiste,* the "instrument plane" that parachute-dropped radiosonde telemetry devices to measure blast force and atmospheric effects over the target.

As it would involve too much time and effort to configure a new plane for this function, *The Great Artiste* would be repeating its instrument plane role for the second strike—this time flown by *Bockscar*'s namesake and normally assigned pilot / aircraft commander, Captain Fred Bock.[4] Rounding out the strike force, the mission's photography plane for recording the atomic explosion with a special "Fastax" high-speed camera would be *Big Stink*, piloted by Major Hopkins. These three B-29s would take off from North Field the next morning at 0300.

In the event of an acceptable Japanese surrender offer being received during the mission's ingress phase, a special coded command to return to Tinian would be radioed to the strike force.

Primary target Kokura, population 130,000,[5] was a former samurai castle outpost on the northern tip of Kyushu. It had grown by leaps and bounds since the Japanese industrial revolution of the early Meiji Period, eventually evolving into one among a contiguous cluster of sprawling factory towns—including Yahata, Tobata, Wakamatsu, and Moji—hugging the shore of the Shimonoseki and Tsushima Straits.[6] It was the location of an important IJA arsenal—a manufacturing and marshaling hub for armored vehicles, weapons, and munitions conveniently situated near some of the country's largest steel mills, which were a ten-minute freight train ride away in Yahata.[7] The arsenal complex itself—which was surrounded by workers' housing—would

FIRST BRIEFING

be the aiming point for the strike plane's bombardier, Captain Kermit Beahan.

Like Hiroshima, Kokura was a key military railhead for men and matériel to shore up defense preparations in Kyushu against the anticipated Allied invasion. As explained by the 509th's S-2 intelligence chief, Lieutenant Colonel Hazen Payette, accurate and intense high-altitude-capable antiaircraft artillery could be expected over this important target. There were also numerous IJA and IJN fighter bases in the area tasked with the air defense of the vital Yahata-Kokura industrial zone and the nearby Shimonoseki Straits—the western gate of Japan's Seto Inland Sea.[8]

Kokura also entailed a bonus target: Its immediate eastern neighbor, Moji, was the site of the southern entrance of the recently completed Kanmon railway tunnel, which linked Kyushu—via the shallow seabed of the Shimonoseki Straits—with the war production and population centers of Honshu. Virtually impervious to conventional bombing, the tunnel was a vital choke point in the entire national rail system; knocking it out would greatly degrade the IJA's lines of communication with a Kyushu battlefront come November 1.[9] General George Marshall, reportedly, had expressed interest in seeing what the nearby detonation of an atomic bomb was going to do to it.[10]

Nagasaki, population 250,000, would be bombed in the event of poor weather and/or visibility conditions over Kokura. In terms of importance to the Japanese order of battle for its upcoming ground war defense of the Home Islands, the northwest Kyushu harbor was less significant than the primary target. But it was home to extensive Mitsubishi Corporation enterprises engaged primarily in shipbuilding and naval munitions production. The city had received a modicum of attention from the XX BC the previous year, as well as a spate of more recent (and, technically, unauthorized) tactical raids, concentrating on Nagasaki harbor.[11] The damage resulting from these attacks, however, was insufficient to disqualify it from becoming a last-minute addition to the approved list of candidate cities for atomic bombings.

According to intelligence reports, the majority of the workers for

Mitsubishi's enterprises in Nagasaki lived in the old downtown districts of the city, where the population density reached thirty-five thousand per square kilometer. If Nagasaki ended up being attacked, this was where Twentieth Air Force HQ wanted the 509th to drop the second combat-deployed atomic bomb—dead-center mass of an approximately eight-square-kilometer area of urban buildup that Committee of Operations Analysis cartographers, over a year earlier, had designated "Nagasaki Incendiary Zone #1."[12] The city's hilly terrain was less than optimal for achieving a wide Hiroshima-style Zone of Total Destruction, but if the second bomb functioned as intended and was at least as powerful as Little Boy had been, blast force and thermal radiation from its airburst would not only completely obliterate downtown Nagasaki but probably also reach clear across the harbor to take out the Mitsubishi shipyards on the far shore.

———

Three days earlier, in this same Quonset hut, an expectant tension had hung over the briefing for the Hiroshima mission. Tibbets and various Manhattan Project experts assured the 393rd Bomb Squadron crews that the top secret bomb they had trained for a year to deploy was possessed of such spectacular destructive power that it was sure to bring the Japanese to their knees, suing for peace.[13] But now—two days after the complete destruction of Hiroshima by one of these bombs—they were going to have to drop another. For the crews, the pre-mission nerves were still there, but the hopes for an early peace—at least as far as they knew—were gone.

Of more immediate concern, they had also lost the element of surprise.

Two days earlier, Tibbett's August 6 strike force had flown over Japanese air defense commands long since inured to the overhead daytime passage of seemingly innocuous small flights of American planes.[14] Now, however, post-Hiroshima, the Japanese high command was fully aware of the devastation capable of being wrought by a three-plane formation of B-29s. As such, Japanese defenders were likely to throw everything they had at a suspected second atomic strike force. For this reason, it was absolutely essential that Sweeney's B-29s avoid detection for as long as possible—preferably until they were nearly on top of their target. Toward this end, the bombers would follow the strictest radio discipline during their ingress to the target, for if Japanese air defense were able to catch an errant radio transmission and use it to triangulate the position of its source, the strike force could be jumped before it reached the Home Islands.[15]

Lieutenant Colonel Payette noted that Nagasaki's harbor area was well fortified with smaller-caliber antiaircraft artillery positions along the wharves and larger-caliber, higher-firing guns in the surrounding high ground. But the city's overall defenses—inclusive of possible fighter response from Ōmura Naval Air Station on the north shore of Ōmura Bay—would be nowhere near as fearsome as what the strike force might face over the primary target.[16] Nevertheless, and again post-Hiroshima, a determined—even suicidal—Japanese fighter defense of the city was still within the realm of possibility.

But even if the strike force did encounter air-to-air opposition over either Nagasaki or Kokura, its crews knew that they had a good fighting chance of evading Japanese fighters. Their specially upgraded "Silverplate" B-29s would be operating near their maximum operational altitude of nine-thousand-plus meters—too high for any known Japanese fighter designs to operate effectively.

Nearly two years earlier, when Tibbets had been working on tactical defensive doctrine for the then new B-29 design, he had consulted with E. J. Workman, a University of New Mexico physics professor. In the course of their research, they discovered that when the bomber was stripped of all of its defensive armament save its tail guns—the same configuration the Silverplate B-29s used—the aircraft, now lighter by thirty-two hundred kilograms, was capable of outmaneuvering even fighters designed to operate at high altitude.[17] When the research team pitted a P-47 Thunderbolt against a B-29 in mock-combat tests, the fighter could stay on its target's tail for only a few seconds before evasive maneuvers by the bomber caused its attacker to stall out and lose so much height that by the time the latter could recover enough altitude to make another pass, the B-29 was long gone and out of danger.

The Republic P-47 had been specifically designed as a high-altitude interceptor and, as such, boasted far superior performance in the rarefied air of this combat environment than the Japanese mainstay Mitsubishi Zero, which had been designed as a nimble, aerobatic, low- to middle-altitude dogfighter. Therefore, in the event of a fighter-interception scenario, the only chance Japanese aircraft would really have to get at the strike force would be if they managed to struggle to altitude beforehand to set up an ambush. Even then, the relatively underpowered Japanese fighters—as per Professor Workman's calculations and demonstrations—would have only one shot before the bombers could brush the Zeros off their tails and leave them in the dust, wheezing for oxygen and losing altitude.

Head-on passes might have been another one-shot option for any Japanese interceptors, but at closing speeds of eight hundred plus kilometers per hour relative to their targets, their firing window would come and go in the blink of an eye. Likewise, kamikaze-style ramming attacks were not beyond the realm of possibility—as the Japanese had already proven repeatedly against conventional XXI BC raids over the Home Islands. However, these would also be constrained by the same fraction-of-a-second window of opportunity that worked against a conventional attack run with guns blazing. In either case, if the fighters missed their first shot, the strike force would be too high, too fast, and too far away to allow for a second. The 509th aircrews would be comforted by these thoughts, although the aircraft commanders would have to remind them that the fighter threat could not be dismissed out of hand.

There was an additional challenge the second mission would have to face that had not been present in the first: the extreme complexity of the weapon *Bockscar* would be carrying—a plutonium-cored device of the type first tested in New Mexico only three weeks earlier.

The simple "gun-barrel"-type firing configuration of the uranium-cored Little Boy Hiroshima bomb had been a sure-thing design; Oppenheimer and his team of scientists had known for years that it

FIRST BRIEFING 147

would work in principle. The only reason it had not been deployed earlier—for example, against Hitler—was because U-235 was devilishly difficult to extract from naturally occurring uranium ore; after nearly three years of around-the-clock refining operations at the Manhattan Project's Oak Ridge facility, only enough of the material for one ready-to-deploy bomb had been collected by August 1945, three months after Germany's surrender.[18]

This serious production obstacle had been known early enough for Manhattan Project planners to undertake a parallel program to produce bomb-ready quantities of Pu-239—a fissile man-made isotope of plutonium. Since 1944, America had been neutron-bombarding common U-238 in nuclear reactors (still referred to as "piles" at the time) at Hanford, Washington, to transform this material into plutonium. The great advantage of Pu-239, then, as the basis of an atomic weapons program was that it could be stockpiled through a straightforward manufacturing process, as opposed to the needle-in-a-haystack refining required for U-235. Toward the desired end of weaponizing plutonium, however, it had one major and, for long wartime years, seemingly insurmountable shortcoming: Its peculiar physical properties prevented it from being used in the gun-barrel-type configuration employed in Little Boy to achieve critical mass—the amount of fissile radioactive material needed to sustain an explosively out-of-control nuclear chain reaction.

A theoretical solution was eventually worked out when it was realized that Pu-239 could be brought to explosive criticality not by slamming two subcritical mass halves of the material together as quickly as possible, as in the U-235 gun-barrel design, but rather by uniformly compressing a perfect sphere of solid plutonium from softball to billiard ball size in an instant.[19] In this compressed state, the individual Pu-239 atoms in the abruptly shrunken sphere would now be close enough to one another for an explosive chain reaction to occur when fission was initiated.

Although the science behind the idea was mathematically elegant and theoretically sound, two daunting obstacles would have to be overcome before the concept could be weaponized. The first of these was finding a way of squeezing a sphere of solid metal into a perfectly uniform sphere of less than one-third of its original volume.

The solution eventually arrived at for achieving this was to embed the Pu-239 core at the center of an encasing sphere of shaped charges that, instead of directing their force out and away from the weapon, as in a conventional bomb design, would direct their force inward toward a central point. However, once the rough strokes of this solution were on the drawing board, a second and far more challenging obstacle arose: If the electrically triggered detonation of the surrounding sphere of shaped charges was not absolutely synchronous and uniform, the Pu-239 would be deformed in the resulting implosion and criticality would not be achieved. The time lag between two electrical triggering signals traveling along wires differing by only a few centimeters in length would be enough to skew the uniformity of the implosion. The result would be a dud that, instead of achieving explosive criticality, would squander its stupendously expensive plutonium in a dirty-bomb-style radioactive cloud that would merely contaminate a few hectares of surrounding countryside.

To achieve the necessary absolute-spherical uniformity of the implosion pressing in on the core, the physics-package heart of the Fat Man Pu-239 bomb required thirty-two separately wired and precisely shaped explosive charges fitted into a spherical configuration perfectly nestled around the plutonium; an electrical firing system with microsecond synchronicity accommodating differences in wiring length from the bomb's electrical firing unit to each explosive charge; the invention of a new type of electrically triggered fuse—the exploding-bridgewire detonator—that could be timed more precisely than standard blasting caps; and the machining of other mechanical components in the weapon to heretofore unknown tolerances.

With everything properly placed and hooked up, the physics package resembled a huge gray soccer ball with separate wires attached to each of the hexagonal- and pentagonal-shaped segments that formed its surface. To complete the weapon for deployment, this wired soccer ball was encased in an egg-shaped, flak- and bulletproof

FIRST BRIEFING

steel outer shell and fitted with a box-kite-shaped tail assembly for aerodynamic ballistic stability during its descent toward its target.

Due to the bomb's exacting preparatory requirements, the Project Alberta technicians at North Field were going to have to load an essentially "live" Fat Man into *Bockscar*, with all wiring connected and electrical systems already powered up.[20] The only step required of the men on the plane to arm the weapon would be to remove two green saltshaker-sized safety plugs from the bomb's outer casing and replace them with their red firing plug counterparts to close the fusing circuitry.[21] To prevent catastrophic mishap, these firing plugs were to be inserted only once the plane had put at least ten minutes of flying time between the bomb and North Field.[22]

Sweeney had been grappling with nerves since Tibbets tapped him for command of the next atomic mission the previous day, and he had barely slept since. Early on the morning of August 8, he ceded victory to his insomnia and decided to pass the time until sunrise watching the 313th BW bombers take off for a mission to Yahata. At one point, he was violently jolted from this groggy monotony when he witnessed one of the overloaded B-29s falter on its takeoff—possibly due to engine failure—then veer off and crash into the ground in a spectacular explosion of napalm.[23] Since witnessing this disaster, he had been tormented by the idea that if *Bockscar* lost an engine on takeoff and augered in, the resulting dirty-bomb explosion of spewed plutonium would probably contaminate the entire northern half of Tinian, including hundreds of B-29s and thousands of Twentieth Air Force personnel. It would also likely take the entire future of the American atomic bomb program along with it.

REPORTS FROM HIROSHIMA

Nagasaki Medical College
3.3 kilometers north of Nigiwai Bridge
Morning of August 8, 1945

SINCE THE LATE 1930s, a Tokyo-centric nexus of seasoned ad men and marketing experts had been assisting the propaganda efforts of the imperial regime. Employing the latest mass communications technologies and Bernaysian media management techniques, they had helped mold and control the worldview of a Japanese populace being groomed for a grueling, long-haul total-war effort.[1]

One vector of these efforts sought to keep the national calendar filled with commemorative events, each aimed at aligning the national zeitgeist with state policy goals. Some of these goals were quite pedestrian and specific, others lofty and symbolic; a given day or week might be devoted to metal drives or improved public hygiene, while others might highlight the importance of sacrifice and fighting spirit in a time of war. In 1933, for example, the Tokyo municipal government began holding an annual citywide air-defense-awareness "blackout week" augmented by department store promotion campaigns featuring model airplane displays and dioramas of home-air-raid-shelter designs; since the passage of the 1937 Air Defense Law, the air-defense-awareness campaign had gone nationwide.[2]

Regardless of theme, these designated awareness days or weeks were coordinated with ambitiously scaled and meticulously choreographed rallies, parades, ceremonies, and other instances of public spectacle and aggressively promoted with great fanfare in radio broadcasts, newsprint, posters, and banners hung from the facades of government buildings.

One regularly scheduled observance, proclaimed in the third year of the Second Sino-Japanese War, was "Rising Asia Service Day" (*Kō'a'hōkōbi*).[3] On these monthly commemoration days, civilians were exhorted to live frugally, emulating the young men fighting in Asia, thereby fostering in the home front populace an indomitable political and, more important, spiritual will to see the war through to the bitter end. Echoing this frugality theme and adding a nativist twist, one concurrent public relations push urged women to switch out their dresses and skirts for *monpe* peasant pants and plain work blouses, as well as to stop wearing Western hairstyles involving any kind of curling or permanent waving. In a similar vein, the nation's white-collar-management types were encouraged to abandon their culturally obsequious devotion to Western-style business suits and don the more down-to-earth, duty-minded, and Asian-modernist *kokumin-fuku* ("national people's clothing")—a dark khaki serge outfit that was a cross between an IJA officer's service dress uniform and a Mao suit. Yet another cultural cleansing campaign sought to root out and replace with new native alternatives the many English loanwords that had crept into the Japanese vernacular since the mid-nineteenth century, though this proved difficult to enforce—even in the military.[4]

On the first morning of each month, beginning on September 1, 1939, NHK would interrupt its regularly scheduled programming to offer special Rising Asia Service Day content.[5] As a way of symbolizing national unity, each month's program was broadcast live from a different prominent venue around the empire. From these locales, a live orchestra—miked and wired for sound—would regale its in-person and radio audiences with a short program of stirring martial music before the content moved on to solemn victory oaths intoned in florid, archaic language; "radio calisthenics" (*rajio taisō*) sessions; and war-related lectures by various military figures or civilian authorities. When listeners were gathered in a group setting, it was customary for the senior person present—company president, neighborhood association leader, teacher/principal, Shintō priest, commander of a local military base—to deliver uplifting and/or moralizing closing remarks at the end of each broadcast.

Starting on January 8, 1942, Rising Asia Service Day was subsumed into a new national monthly calendar event—"Veneration of the Imperial Rescript Day" (*Taishōhōtaibi*). This commemorated the emperor's declaration of war on America and the British Empire, announced immediately after the Japanese attacks on Pearl Harbor, the Philippines, Hong Kong, and Singapore.

Held on the eighth of each month to commemorate the December 8, 1941 (Japan Time), date of that fateful proclamation, these observances followed the same general Rising Asia Service Day format of special radio broadcasts featuring live musical performances, calisthenics programs, speeches, and mass call-and-response intoning of solemn oaths. Listeners were encouraged to pay post-broadcast visits to their local Shintō shrine to pray for victory. Across the country, restaurants and cafés closed up for the day—a reminder to the populace that luxury was an enemy in time of war. Wives and mothers were encouraged to make special, austere boxed *bentō* lunches for their families to foster a sense of solidarity with the nation's frontline fighting men.[6] This last observance, however, assumed a poignant irony from late 1943 on, as the American blockade's slow strangulation of Japan's food supply increasingly saw soldiers at the front (with notable gruesome exceptions) eating better than their family members back in the Home Islands.

On the morning of August 8, 1945, as they did on the eighth of each month, the emperor's loyal subjects gathered for early-morning Veneration of the Imperial Rescript Day ceremonies in workplaces, schools, neighborhood parks, and Shintō shrines all over Japan (perhaps even on the outskirts of Hiroshima).

In Nagasaki, under the shadow of the stately Immaculate Conception (Urakami) Cathedral, the faculty, staff, and students of Nagasaki Medical College gathered on their campus's rugby field, where the morning's ceremony was presided over by the college president,

REPORTS FROM HIROSHIMA

Dr. Tsuno'o Susumu. At the conclusion of the NHK broadcast on this particular day, however, Tsuno'o did not deliver his customary war-effort-cheerleading speech. Instead, he told the assemblage about what he had seen in Hiroshima, some forty hours earlier, as he came back to Nagasaki from official business in Tokyo.

After an apology for his somewhat disheveled appearance—which included a self-deprecating quip about changing into a clean shirt in his office just in time for the ceremony—a noticeably fatigued Tsuno'o began his testimony.[7] When his westbound San'yō Line train had reached the eastern Hiroshima suburb of Kaita'ichi on the afternoon of August 6, there was an announcement that rail service through the city center had been suspended. All passengers headed for points west would have to make their way on foot to the next functioning station to continue their journeys. This would entail following the rail line to Itsuka'ichi, a suburban San'yō Line stop eighteen kilometers away, on the opposite side of the Ōta River Delta.[8]

President Tsuno'o's suitcase-toting trek along the San'yō Line railbed took him across the completely devastated northern half of Hiroshima.[9] Outside of a few empty shells of steel-reinforced concrete buildings, every other man-made structure within view had been knocked flat and its wooden wreckage reduced to ashes. The donjon tower of Hiroshima Castle—the pride of the city's skyline for nearly three hundred fifty years—was now a pile of smoldering kindling.

As for the human toll of the cataclysm, this was, at least for the time being, incalculable. Tsuno'o had seen charred corpses by the thousands—perhaps tens of thousands—covering the blasted ground in all directions and clogging the city's many waterways. And incredibly, according to snippets of witness testimony and rumor Tsuno'o had gleaned along the way, all of this death and devastation had been caused not by a mass incendiary raid but by a single explosion.

Some among the doctor's audience might have had some prior vague awareness that Hiroshima had been attacked on August 6. Perhaps they had seen the August 7 edition of the major national daily *Asahi Shimbun*, which, in a short notice buried amidst the paper's coverage of other B-29 raids around the country,[10] had mentioned "a small flight of aircraft" dropping "incendiary devices" on the city. Some might have even woken up early enough that morning to see the August 8 papers, which carried more detailed information about the scale of the devastation in Hiroshima, including mention of a fiendish, parachute-deployed "new-type bomb" having killed many thousands of civilians.[11]

Still, on some emotional level, those news items were abstractions about things happening far away to other people. But President Tsuno'o emphasized to his audience that they needed to start thinking about something like that happening in Nagasaki today, tomorrow, *soon*. Emphasizing this point, the college president closed his address with an appeal for increased vigilance on campus regarding air defense readiness. Everyone in the assemblage would have already been aware that, during the August 1 raid, several American bombs had hit the campus and its attached hospital, killing three students.[12] There had been no further attacks on the city or the Urakami Valley since then, but it was well within the realm of possibility that the Americans would return to Nagasaki with one of the "new-type" bombs they had used to destroy Hiroshima. If the medical college was going to be in any shape to render first aid on the scale that would be needed in the aftermath of such a catastrophe befalling downtown Nagasaki, its facilities would have to be dispersed to better-sheltered locations as soon as possible. Tsuno'o ended his talk with a request to the staff and students to begin preparations for this dispersal work at once.[13]

One of the hundreds of stunned-silent students who had just listened to President Tsuno'o's sobering warning was Nagasaki native Gunge Yoshio—a twenty-year-old School of Pharmacology sophomore. In a sense, Gunge was present to hear the speech only because of his prodigious test-preparatory cramming as a teenager. If he had not passed the extremely competitive entrance exam to Nagasaki Medical College the year before, he would likely have ended up in some hellhole in Burma—the front to which most IJA draftees and recalled reservists in this corner of Kyushu were sent as members of the Fukuoka-based 56th Infantry Division—and would very possibly no longer be drawing breath.

Like other university-level science, technology, engineering, and medical students around the country, Nagasaki Medical College students were, at least for the time being, exempt from military conscription on account of their anticipated utility for the war effort. Once the Allied invasion of the Home Islands began, Japan was going to experience a drastically expanded need for trained medical personnel; as such, the state considered students like Gunge Yoshio too valuable to be squandered in battle as infantrymen or kamikaze pilots.

Male university students in humanities disciplines had once also originally enjoyed this exemption, but this had changed from October 1943 as mounting casualties in the war forced the military to dip into this previously untouched and class-privileged manpower source, devouring the seed corn of Japanese society's next-generation leaders as they did so. Nearly two years on, some twenty thousand might-have-been future artists, authors, schoolteachers, jurists, and business executives were instead corpses moldering in fetid jungles, lying at the bottom of the ocean, or exploding into molecules against the decks of Allied warships.[14]

It must have comforted Yoshio's father, Masaji, to know that his son would escape such a fate, safe at the medical college while so many other Nagasaki boys were dying every day miserably and far from home. With any luck, the war would end while Yoshio was still a student. Regardless of whether that end would be in Japan's favor or not, he would be alive.

Still, Yoshio's day-to-day was far from carefree. As a civilian trying to get by in late-1945 Japan, he was subjected to the same quality-of-life stressors—most direly, shortages of food and air raid fears—that everyone else on the home front had to endure. Moreover, his medical college studies—and thus his plans for the future—had been completely derailed, and he had no idea when they would get back on track; earlier that year, classroom sessions for the School of Pharmacology had been suspended so that its student body could be mobilized for war plant work. In the case of the school's second-year students, all but nine had been parceled out to the Chisso Minamata chemical plant in nearby Kumamoto Prefecture.[15]

Yoshio was lucky enough to be one of the *nokosare-gumi* (literally, "left behinders"). Instead of toiling over steaming vats of reeking chemicals in Minamata, he and eight other classmates had so far spent the summer contributing to the nation's war effort by inventorying and reordering the bookstacks in the college's reference library.[16]

———

Yoshio's younger brother, sixteen-year-old Gunge Norio, was spending a summer more typical of adolescent Japanese students in 1945. For the past year, since the cessation "for the duration" of his classwork at Nagasaki Prefectural Junior High School, he and the rest of his fourth-grade classmates had been working at the Mitsubishi torpedo plant in Mori-machi.[17] He shared a factory floor with coworkers (including some of the more able-bodied and mentally balanced Australian and Dutch POWs from Fukuoka Camp No. 14); there, steel plating and other parts hot out of Mori-machi's foundry and rolling mill received their initial rough tooling. This work involved drilling rivet holes and removing casting imperfections in these rough pieces before they were gantry-craned over to the Torpedo Finishing Room, where female colleagues would go over them with grinders, sanders, and hand files.

For over a year, Norio had been using a handheld electric drill to make holes at precise spots on steel parts marked with a grease pencil by one of the senior Mitsubishi professionals. The work was monotonous, noisy, and exhausting; at the end of his shift, with his ears ringing, he would need all of his strength to walk home and collapse onto his futon. Things at Mori-machi got easier with the midsummer steel-drought slowdown, but he still had to spend twelve hours a day at the plant; he would have much preferred to be spending that time at home, hanging out with his older brother, Yoshio (whom he idolized), or in school actually learning something more useful for his future than how to drill holes in metal.

For the first eleven months of his Mitsubishi work, Norio had commuted from his birth home, which he shared with Yoshio and his widowed father in Rokasu-machi, an affluent CBD neighborhood stretched out along the southeastern foot of Mount Konpira.[18] The quarter was the location of Nagasaki's most prestigious and well-known Shintō *jinja*, Suwa Shrine, an imposing edifice built by Shogunate authorities atop the ashes of the rousted Portuguese settlement's church district.[19]

The neighborhood was also home to several important bureaucratic facilities, including the official residence of the governor of Nagasaki Prefecture; the sprawling Nagasaki branch of the Bank of Japan;[20] and a heretofore rarely used (outside of drills) bunker complex dug into the slopes of Mount Konpira from where the governor, his chief of police counterpart, and their respective staffs were supposed to direct civil defense operations—in close coordination with Western Army HQ in Fukuoka—in the event of a large-scale air raid.

The Gunges' life in Rokasu-machi came to an end in late July when the civilian residents of the neighborhood were given a week to find alternative lodging. After this grace period, their homes were torn down to clear firebreaks to protect Rokasu-machi's government facilities from incendiary attack. By August, some 7 percent of Nagasaki's population had undergone similar forced displacement, with homeowners given vague promises of future compensation and renters provided with small stipends to help with relocation costs.[21]

As a result of the firebreak-clearance evictions, available housing in the CBD disappeared virtually overnight. The Gunges were in something of a lurch for a couple of nervous days until Masaji was finally able to secure lodging for his sons at the home of a family friend, Shinagawa-sensei, a calligraphy teacher who lived in Shimonishiyama-machi, across the street from his Kenjo workplace. He kindly assented to putting the Gunge boys up on the second floor of his house, near the eastern foot of Mount Konpira. It had been mostly empty since the rest of the teacher's family evacuated the city after the July 29 raid.

The accommodations would suffice for two, but Masaji did not want to put his friend out by crowding his house with a third Gunge mouth to feed. Instead, he picked up stakes and moved into his office at the small artificial sweetener factory he ran in Ōmura. He would drop in to check on the boys whenever he was in Nagasaki on business—which was fairly frequently—but the rest of the time, they would be on their own. He could take some comfort in knowing that Yoshio and Norio were already used to taking care of daily housekeeping chores for themselves, as they had been doing so ever since the untimely death of their mother from stomach cancer two years earlier.

During their time in Shimonishiyama-machi, the Gunge boys barely got to see each other, as Norio had been working all summer on the night shift at Mori-machi. When he would get home, in the wee hours of the morning, Yoshio was usually sound asleep. The only opportunity the brothers—and best friends—had to interact was in the short morning time window between Norio's waking up and Yoshio's leaving to begin another day of "work" at the medical college library.

DIGGING

Fukuro-machi
3.3 kilometers south of Nagasaki Medical College
120 meters north of Nigiwai Bridge
Morning of August 8, 1945

WITH ITS PLETHORA of vertical terrain and clay soil, Nagasaki presented an ideal environment for the tunneling of large-capacity air raid shelters.[1] Beginning in 1944, construction of such facilities occupied a sizable share of local *giyūtai* ("volunteer labor unit") strength.[2]

Neighborhood associations with suitable local terrain, resources, and manpower were urged to construct what were known as *L-ji gata bōkūgō* ("L-shaped air raid shelters"). In the general scheme of this shelter design, an entranceway was dug straight into the face of a vertical terrain feature such as a slope, hillside, cliff face, or embankment. Once the desired penetration depth of the entranceway was reached, and its walls and ceiling were shored up with wood or concrete supports by experienced carpenters, the tunneling work would pivot ninety degrees to the left or right for the excavation of the shelter's main gallery, where evacuees were to sit out a raid. The right-angled configuration of the shelter was designed so that the rear wall of its entranceway would bear the brunt of any nearby bomb impacts,[3] sparing the occupants of the main gallery from direct exposure to blast force and shrapnel/ballistic debris. Neighborhoods without the resources or labor for such involved excavation work simply made use of any empty local lots into which they dug slit-trench-type shelters. These were sometimes bolstered with sandbag walls.

By August 1945, this largely volunteer-performed excavation work had honeycombed the city's ubiquitous hillsides and ridge faces with enough shelters, whether sophisticated or simple in design, to provide an estimated 30 percent of the city's population with protection in an air raid[4]—assuming these evacuees had sufficient warning time to reach their designated shelters in the event of an enemy attack. One nettlesome drawback in Nagasaki's ambitious municipal shelter-digging campaign, which was no fault of its own, was the city's unwieldy military bureaucratic tethering to Western Army HQ in Fukuoka, some eighty kilometers away to the north, which coordinated air defense for all of Kyushu.[5] Under the peculiarities of this arrangement, Nagasaki could sound its sirens only when first cleared to do so by Fukuoka, even when American planes were already flying overhead. Conversely, warning alert sirens sounded across the city at any time of day or night—interrupting war plant operations and ruining sleep—whenever IJA radar installations or observer posts detected enemy air activity anywhere in Western Army's jurisdiction, regardless of its actual distance from Nagasaki.[6] Over time, many in the city began ignoring warning alerts altogether and would respond—grudgingly—only to the more urgent air raid alerts, which signaled that Western Army had determined that enemy aircraft were directly inbound and mere minutes out.

Western Army's compartmentalized decision-making cycle translated to frequent confusion and, far more critically, dangerous time lags on the ground in Nagasaki. In terms of the city's residents needing to know when to run for their designated shelters, a minute of forewarning gained or lost might have made the difference between life and death. This was of particular concern for parts of the city where designated shelters were far away—for example, in districts where tunnel-type shelters were precluded by the lack of suitable surrounding terrain—or where the excavation of slit trenches and outdoor foxholes was complicated by dense urban buildup.

The CBD shopkeepers' district of Fukuro-machi—located almost at the geographical center point of Nagasaki Incendiary Zone #1—was unlucky on both of these counts. As a result, its designated air raid evacuation point—a sandbag-walled, slit-trench-type shelter still under construction on the morning of August 8—was some four hundred meters away, on the northeastern slope of Kazagashira Hill. In order to reach it, Fukuro-machi residents would need at least a five-minute warning—probably more like ten, with mobility challenges for small children and elderly residents and general panicky dithering factored in—before bombs started hitting the city.

———

Three and a half kilometers southeast of where President Tsuno'o was giving his sobering address to the faculty and students of Nagasaki Medical College, thirteen-year-old Fukuro-machi resident Tateno Sueko and her fellow *giyūtai* colleagues had finished their own Veneration of the Imperial Rescript Day assembly and were now excavating their neighborhood's designated air raid shelter at the foot of Kazagashira Hill.

At the shelter site, Sueko's job was to stand by, waiting for diggers—usually able-bodied middle-aged men from the neighborhood—to pass her shovel loads of soil and rock. Sueko would receive this material in a tightly woven burlap sack called a *mokko*. Once her *mokko* was full, she would carry her load away to spill it out onto an ever-growing pile of earth at the edge of the worksite, where another team of neighborhood workers used this material to fill sandbags.

In Nagasaki, as in Hiroshima, girls' school and junior high first-graders were not, as a rule, mobilized for war plant work, and the specifics of the war effort exploitation of this prepubescent labor force were left up to each school. Some schools had on-site work to assign to their first-graders—for example, Junshin frequently had theirs helping the Sisters with the campus truck patch vegetable plots. In the case of Sueko's Keiho Girls' School, the CBD location of which precluded campus space for practical agriculture, any war work contribution their first-graders would make was left up to the students' families—some of whom were simply allowing their daughters to stay at home. Not so, however, for the Tateno family, and Sueko's tender young hands had the work blisters to show for it.

Sueko was the fifth and last child of middle-aged shopkeepers Tateno Seijirō and his wife, Shimi. The Tatenos' middle daughter, Yoshiko, the child nearest in age to Sueko, was fully eight years older than her baby sister. First son, Chūtarō, was sixteen years older. Between these two were second son, Asao (b. 1920), and eldest daughter, Mitsuko (b. 1922).

Sueko's father had undergone apprenticeship as a traditional Japanese confectioner in his native Kumamoto City—across Tachibana Bay, the Shimabara Peninsula, and the Ariake Sea from Nagasaki Prefecture—before moving to Fukuro-machi in the last years of the Meiji Period. After some years of prerequisite toil and saving, he set up his own shop, the Tokuseidō. In time, the enterprise came to specialize in *kasutera*, an eggy sponge cake of Portuguese settlement provenance that had survived the anti-Christian crackdown to become a renowned Nagasaki specialty.

Marriage followed the debut of Seijirō's business. In a typical Japanese shopkeeper's domestic arrangement, the first floor of the house he bought for his new family was given over to his shop and ovens, while he, his wife, and his steadily expanding brood of children occupied the second floor. By 1932, when Sueko appeared on the scene, Seijirō was running one of the premier *kasutera* makers in the city, counting among his corporate customers the headquarters of the IJA Nagasaki garrison.

The shop was also a major tourist draw, including a steady stream of foreign sailors from merchant vessels making ports of call in the harbor dropping in to sample Tokuseidō's renowned sponge cake. Some of Sueko's earliest childhood memories were of her father using his halting self-taught English and body language gestures to communicate with these exotic customers, whose English was more often than not just as challenged as his. On occasion, some sailor would convince the Tatenos to take in his seafaring pet, knowing the animal would never make it through quarantine back in his home port. Although the Tatenos did what they could to foist these Japan-marooned pets upon friends, neighbors, or other customers, supply always outpaced demand; at any given time, the Tokuseidō was hosting a small menagerie of dogs, parrots, and monkeys, providing the shop with a constant ambient soundscape of barks, screeches, and squawks.

Another of Sueko's earliest memories was of the beautiful kimonos her mother would wear in the shop's retail space, while her father and his apprentices ran the *kasutera* production operation in the back. To complete her always stunning ensembles, Shimi would have her hair done in a traditional *yuiwata*—a hairstyle, with origins in Shogunate days, that was already archaic in 1930s Japan and rarely seen outside of traditional geisha districts. The daily preparations of Shimi's *yuiwata* required the services of a professional hairdresser—in this case one of the last in Nagasaki who possessed the ancient knowledge and skills to perform the required elaborate knotting and lacquering work, which could take several hours.[7] Every morning before dawn, when the Tatenos' house would be redolent of the eggy-sweet aroma of baking *kasutera,* the hairdresser would show up to get the glamourous mistress of the Tokuseidō ready in time for the start of business.

As the baby of this happy and prosperous family, Sueko was doted upon by parents and siblings alike. When she began showing an early and enthusiastic aptitude for dancing, her mother enrolled her in training for the traditional Japanese *buyō* form of this art. Mrs. Tateno also began taking her daughter to movie musicals and live dance revues, where Sueko—a talented mimic and natural-born performer—would easily pick up moves and songs, then rush back to the shop afterward to regale family and customers with her newest routines. She also picked up somewhat earthier dance knowledge from various downtown drinking establishments, to which she would accompany her father as a chaperone—the only condition under which Mrs. Tateno would permit her husband to go out carousing with his neighborhood buddies.

But this halcyon period in the family's history came to an end during the late 1930s, beginning with a string of financial calamities that saw the Tokuseidō twice faced with insolvency. In consideration of the family's fiscal straits, elder son, Chūtarō, chose to forgo attending university so that the more academically and intellectually inclined Asao could go in his stead. While his younger brother prepped for his university entrance exams, Chūtarō worked a series of part-time jobs around town to help put food on the family table. Finally, seeking more stable and meaningful employment and aware that the local draft board would get him sooner or later anyway, he joined the IJA. The Second Sino-Japanese War broke out soon after, and he was sent to fight in northern China. When IJA operations spread to Southeast Asia with the onset of the Pacific War in late 1941, Chūtarō—by then a noncommissioned officer—was assigned to a transportation unit in the recently formed 56th Infantry Division.[8]

Asao's acceptance at Osaka Imperial University (Handai) in 1938—a development made possible by Chūtarō's selfless sacrifice—was one of the few bright spots for the Tateno family during this period. This was particularly fortuitous not only because of Handai's elite status and affordable tuition, but also because it meant Asao at least was safe from the grasping hands of the IJA as long as he remained a university student.

Sueko was a nine-year-old third-grader at nearby Shinkōzen Elementary School when Pearl Harbor was attacked and Japan went to war with the United States, Great Britain, and the Netherlands. Like nearly everyone else in the country, she was electrified by the constant stream of radio bulletins in the first months of the conflict, which invariably reported that Japan's series of lightning-fast military and naval triumphs meant that final victory was imminent.[9]

With fighting now ranging from China to the Western Pacific, Southeast Asia, and the Dutch East Indies, Nagasaki became a major embarkation port for IJA troops. Ōhato Wharf, where troopships were loaded, was a march of only a few minutes from Nagasaki Station, the railhead by which units arrived in the city. Whenever a troop train pulled in, housewife members of the Japan Women's Patriotic Association and children from Nagasaki's various elementary schools— including Sueko's Shinkōzen Elementary School—were always on hand to line the entire route from the station to Ōhato, waving little paper Japanese flags and singing patriotic songs as the doomed young men tramped past. One of the martial ballads Sueko and her classmates frequently sang during these Nagasaki Station outings was "Ro'ei no Uta" ("Song of the Field Encampment"), which encouraged its military audience with lyrics that included "You cannot but die with honor, seeing your mother's face in your mind's eye when you hear the bugle call."

Meanwhile, on the Tateno home front, Asao—upon his March 1942 graduation from university—had managed to land a full-time position as an office clerk with a Fukuoka fabric wholesaler. For a year or so, it had looked like the draft board might have forgotten about him, but this illusion was dispelled when the inevitable *akagami* draft notice finally arrived in Fukuro-machi.[10]

Sueko learned of her brother's imminent induction when she arrived home from school one day and her mother was not there, as she always was, to greet her at the front door. With some trepidation, Sueko stepped up into the house, where she heard muffled sobbing coming from a back room. Investigating the source of the sound, she found her mother in a crumpled posture, sitting in front of an open clothes closet with her face in her hands. When Sueko asked what was wrong, Shimi wordlessly held out Asao's pink-colored *akagami*—the meaning of which even a ten-year-old girl was able to grasp in 1943 Japan.

Nevertheless, Asao's luck held out, and his IJA *akagami* did not turn out to be the death sentence it would be for some two million of his peers. Perhaps because of the relatively late point in the war at which he was drafted, he was not posted to a combat theater. Instead, he spent the rest of the war with a Communication Corps unit stationed in the Home Islands, where his duties were apparently leisurely enough for him to meet his future wife at one of his postings.

Chūtarō—true to form as the unluckier of the two Tateno boys—would not have it so easy. In early 1942, his 56th Infantry Division had shipped out from Nagasaki to participate in the IJA campaign for the conquest of British Malaya. Upon the victorious conclusion of this campaign with the British surrender in Singapore, the 56th's next area of operations was the China-Burma-India theater—widely regarded as one of the most miserable fighting environments endured by Japanese soldiers. The division was assigned to the mountainous northern region of Burma, on the southern border of China, where it was tasked with denying the Allies access to the Burma Road as a supply route to aid Chiang Kai-shek's forces.

From mid-1944, the 56th's roadblock also interdicted American supplies to the XX BC base at Chengdu, from which the Twentieth Air Force was launching piecemeal raids against northwest Kyushu—the only part of the Home Islands within striking distance of lightly bomb-loaded B-29s at the extreme limit of their operational range. This denial of the Burma Road route forced the Americans to resort to a stupendously ineffectual and wasteful logistical arrangement by which aviation fuel, bombs, and other matériel for the XX BC were flown "over the hump" of the Himalayas from bases in India. The 56th performed its mission magnificently before it was effectively annihilated by vastly superior Chinese Nationalist forces during the three-month-long Battle of Mount Song during the summer and early autumn of 1944.

Ironically, as the 56th's Burma Road–blocking steadfastness was at least tangentially connected to Twentieth Air Force's eventual decision to abandon XX BC's Chengdu operation in November 1944, Chūtarō and his squad had, in effect, prevented Nagasaki from being firebombed, thus preserving it for atomic-bomb-target candidacy a year later.

But for the time being, once the Allies had B-29s in the Marianas, every city in the Home Islands—including Nagasaki—could be firebombed whenever the Americans saw fit, and there was no longer anything any Japanese infantryman could do to prevent that.

By 1945, things were going from bad to worse for the Tatenos. Sueko's sister Yoshiko had become essentially bedridden with what the family's GP was calling "rheumatism," the only symptom of which was a complete inability of the girl's legs to function. No treatments for the mysterious ailment had been successful so far, and the actual pathology involved was unknown. If the doctor had suspected psychosomatic origins—which, particularly in wartime Japan, would have carried insinuations of malingering—he did not share this theory with his patient's parents.

Adding to the family's woes, the Tokuseidō had finally gone under—a victim of wartime food shortages. With Shimi looking after Yoshiko full-time, Seijirō and eldest daughter, Mitsuko, were now the only able-bodied adults remaining in the family. To keep the household at least marginally solvent, they were left with no other option but to take up war work. Mitsuko worked a *teishintai* job at a nearby munitions plant—possibly Mori-machi—while Seijirō was hired for a low-paying position at Mitsubishi Shipyards. As operations at the latter facility were now at a de facto standstill due to the cessation of the firm's steel supply, Seijirō did not have much to do on the job. The position did, however, come with the arguable side benefit of being privy to relatively reliable scuttlebutt on the factory floor about the true progress of Japan's war—information that was at notable odds with the morale-boosting pabulum the nation was being fed around the clock by its mass media organs. Every night when he returned home from the shipyard, Seijirō would relate to his family what he heard on the job. Although Shimi constantly objected to his sharing this inevitably disheartening information within earshot of their daughters, Seijirō pulled no punches in his resentful laments; the government was lying to its people, and the war was for all intents and purposes already lost.

The sole bright point for the family during this dark period came in March 1945, when Sueko was accepted at Keiho Girls' School, a fairly prestigious private institution within easy walking distance of Fukuro-machi. Nevertheless, she had barely seen the inside of a classroom since her matriculation. With almost the entire faculty doing chaperone work at various area munitions plants, there was virtually no instruction of any kind taking place at Keiho. Sueko was a first-year student there in name only. At present, her full-time occupation—as with millions of other "schoolgirls" across the country—was working as a manual laborer.

NERVES AND GUILT

North Field, Tinian
2000 hours, August 8, 1945

AFTER THEIR BRIEFING, Tibbets took Sweeney and the other key crew members to Fat Man's loading pit, at the northern tip of the 509th CG compound, to observe the bulbous mustard-yellow weapon being hoisted up into *Bockscar's* bomb bay.[1] The boxy tail fin of the device was covered with the graffiti handiwork of the various military personnel and civilian technicians who had lined up outside of Project Alberta's assembly facility earlier that morning to write their grease-penciled signatures—many spiced up with blue-streaked invective directed at the Japanese enemy, including the emperor himself.[2]

As Sweeney watched the loading operation proceed, a Navy admiral he had never seen before sidled up to him.

"Son," the admiral said, "do you know how much that bomb cost?"

"No, sir," Sweeney replied.

"Two billion dollars."

"That's a lot of money, Admiral."

"Do you know how much your airplane costs?"

Having served as a test pilot for the B-29 program since its inception, Sweeney was confident that he knew the answer to this query.

"Slightly over half a million dollars, sir," he said.

"I'd suggest you keep those relative values in mind for this mission," the admiral snarled before stomping away into the milling gawkers, never to be seen again.[3]

Message received loud and clear: *Bockscar* and its crew were expendable.

Until it exploded on time and on target, Fat Man was not.

Sweeney stayed awhile longer watching the action at the loading pit, which would finally wrap up around 2200, when *Bockscar's* bomb bay doors were locked shut. A tractor vehicle then gingerly towed the bomber to the flight line, where it would wait, surrounded by submachine-gun-toting MPs, Fat Man alive and softly humming away in its belly, until the B-29 was boarded by Sweeney and his crew after their final preflight briefing.

For the time being, Sweeney would have to find some way to calm his nerves until he took his seat at the controls of *Bockscar* a few hours later. Perhaps he could try to grab some shut-eye after dinner, but that would probably be impossible. Since Tibbets had given him command of the mission the day before, he had barely slept a wink.

Aside from the anticipated pre-mission jitters, Sweeney also had some unresolved conscience issues to work out—issues he had been quietly wrestling with since the Hiroshima mission. Before Little Boy exploded over its target, the vaunted destructive power of an atomic bomb had existed in a realm of science and dry calculations, punctuated by a bloodless experiment that had lit up a predawn sky and cauterized the sand of a New Mexico desert floor with a patina of green glass. Since Hiroshima, however, the 509th's hands were bloody, and whoever dropped the next bomb would do so knowing what was going to happen to the tens of thousands of human beings unlucky enough to be caught under its fireball.

The day before, when he received his orders, Sweeney had been so rattled by the moral implications of this responsibility that he eventually sought out North Field's Catholic chaplain for counseling.[4] For an hour or so, as the tropical sun slowly sank behind Tinian's swaying palm trees, the two good Catholics mulled over God's Sixth Commandment and just war theory, even bringing Thomas Aquinas into the discussion. As evening fell, they eventually arrived at the conclusion that, since the Japanese had been waging a war of imperialist aggression, they basically deserved everything they had gotten so far and—of more immediate and directly personal relevance to the young bomber pilot—everything they were about to get.

Sweeney had felt a bit better after this clerical heart-to-heart—not, of course, enough to be able to sleep that night, but better. Still, he had some lingering moral trepidation, and his mind wandered back to something he had experienced at the briefing hut earlier that day; while poring over the "litho-mosaic" photo-collage tactical map of Nagasaki, he had been troubled by the likelihood that if an atomic bomb exploded on target over that city's designated aiming point—a bridge over the Nakashima River in the CBD district of Fukuro-machi—the destruction on the ground would exceed even what Hiroshima had suffered two days earlier. At this thought, he found himself silently praying that Fat Man would be dropped on the less densely populated Kokura instead.[5]

While Fat Man was being loaded into *Bockscar*, future Nobel laureate Luis Alvarez and two other young scientists—Philip Morrison and Robert Serber—were in the nearby Project Alberta assembly facilities preparing three radiosonde canisters for deployment over the next day's target.[6] These aluminum-cased cylinders—similar in appearance to old-fashioned fire extinguishers or scuba tanks—were telemetry instruments *The Great Artiste* would drop by parachute—as it had done with three identical devices over Hiroshima—to measure the blast force and other parameters of the atomic explosion.

Earlier that day, the three scientists had been, in Alvarez's words, "discussing the forthcoming mission and wondering what we could do to help shorten the war."[7] During the discussion, Alvarez had recalled that, in their postgraduate student days before the war, they had briefly shared lab facilities with the distinguished Japanese physicist Sagane Ryōkichi, who had been dispatched to UC Berkeley to study cyclotron development with their research boss, Ernest Lawrence.

Alvarez wondered aloud if, by reaching Sagane with some kind of message regarding America's atomic bomb capabilities—the relevant science of which Sagane would readily recognize as valid—the professor might not be able to use his influence and expertise to convince the relevant decision-makers in Tokyo of the dire threat their nation was facing and of the futility of continuing to resist. Toward this end, Alvarez and his colleagues drafted the following letter (in English):

Headquarters
Atomic Bomb Command

August, 1945

To: Prof. R. Sagane
From: Three of your former scientific colleagues during your stay in the United States.

We are sending this as a personal message to urge that you use your influence as a reputable nuclear physicist, to convince the Japanese General Staff of the terrible consequences which will be suffered by your people if you continue in this war.

You have known for several years that an atomic bomb could be built if a nation were willing to pay the enormous cost of preparing the necessary material. Now that you have seen that we have constructed the production plants, there can be no doubt in your mind that all the output of these factories, working 24 hours a day, will be exploded on your homeland.

Within the space of three weeks, we have proof-fired one bomb in the American desert, exploded one in Hiroshima, and fired the third this morning.

We implore you to confirm these facts to your leaders, and to do your utmost to stop the destruction and waste of life which can only result in the total annihilation of all your cities, if continued. As scientists, we deplore the use to which a beautiful discovery has

NERVES AND GUILT

been put, but we can assure you that unless Japan surrenders at once, this rain of atomic bombs will increase manyfold in fury.[8]

After giving the content several revisions, the scientists made three copies of the letter and taped one on the inside surface of each radiosonde, where investigating Japanese authorities would be certain to find them and, it was hoped, relay the message to Professor Sagane.

At or close to that moment, twenty-five hundred kilometers to the northwest, Professor Nishina Yoshio, Japan's leading nuclear physicist and Sagane's research mentor, had just arrived by IJA transport plane at Yoshijima in Hiroshima. He had made this journey as part of a mixed civilian scientist and military investigative team dispatched by Imperial General Headquarters (IGHQ) to make a firsthand assessment as to the nature of the explosion that had just destroyed the city.[9]

Nishina had spent the previous few years trying to develop an atomic bomb for the Japanese military, so he had a better idea than anyone else in the country of what to look for. And judging from what he had seen from the window of the plane flying in, and from what he had seen after a quick circuit of the smoldering outskirts of Hiroshima in an Akatsuki Command truck, Nishina knew that there was only one thing that could have possibly caused such destruction[10] and that the highest civilian authorities should hear the news as soon as possible.[11]

That evening, upon returning to his lodgings—an inn near Akatsuki Command Headquarters—he slipped out of a meeting in which his colleagues were cobbling together a formal report to submit to IGHQ.[12] Locating a miraculously still-functioning telephone, he made a direct call to the office of the prime minister. Reaching Chief Cabinet Secretary Sakomizu Hisatsune, Nishina delivered his assessment of the situation, which was perhaps tinged with a scientist's mixture of pure intellectual admiration, professional envy, and patriotic regret: The Americans now possessed a weapon that the Japanese were—if ever—still years, if not decades, away from developing themselves. Nishina was convinced that Hiroshima had been destroyed by an atomic bomb.[13]

Nagasaki Prefectural Office
Edo-machi, Nagasaki
Evening of August 8

While Alvarez and his colleagues were drafting their peace offering, Charles Sweeney was counting down the hours and minutes to 0030, and Chief Cabinet Secretary Sakomizu Hisatsune was receiving a very unsettling phone call from the outskirts of devastated Hiroshima, a tired fifty-year-old man was sitting alone in his office in Nagasaki.

Earlier in the day, Nagasaki governor Nagano Wakamatsu had received a letter from his adult daughter, who lived in Fukui in northern Japan. In the letter, she informed her father that some 90 percent of her city had been destroyed in a recent (July 19) American incendiary raid that had also killed some thirty-one hundred residents,[14] including Nagano's infant grandchild.

After reading the letter, Nagano had sent the rest of his staff home for the night because he had wanted some time to grieve in peace—something he could not do in front of his subordinates, nor at home in his official residence in Rokasu-machi. It would be unbecoming for the head of the Nagano household—and the governor of Nagasaki Prefecture—to weep in front of others, even his own family members.

Tōdai alumnus Nagano was a onetime high-flying career bureaucrat who, prior to his current posting, had served as director general of the Home Ministry's Air Defense Bureau. In this capacity, he had drafted the guidelines for the stand-your-ground civil defense air raid directive, in force since 1943, by which able-bodied adult civilians were called on to forgo evacuation from cities under air attack and instead stay behind to assist first responders in firefighting efforts.[15] In the immediate aftermath of the Great Tokyo Air Raid of March 9 to

10, 1945, when the Home Ministry was scrambling to find someone or something to blame for the attack's unprecedented death toll of some 100,000, a hasty consensus seems to have been reached that the stand-your-ground civilian firefighting directive was responsible for the tragedy. Nagano's subsequent and swift April 1945 banishment from the half-incinerated capital for a posting to the boondocks of Nagasaki is probably usefully viewed in that light.

Although the stand-your-ground directive had been quickly rescinded in the wake of the Tokyo tragedy—probably saving hundreds of thousands of civilian lives during the American napalm blitz of the nation's cities that followed—Nagano's daughter nevertheless blamed her father's Home Ministry civil defense policy for their own family tragedy.

In the midst of Nagano's dark soul spelunking, the door to his office flew open and an out-of-breath man barged in. It was his friend Nishioka Takejirō, the publisher of the local daily *Nagasaki Nippō*, who had arrived in the city a few minutes ago after a harrowing return from Tokyo. He had rushed straight from the station to the prefectural office because he had to tell his friend about what he had seen in Hiroshima, which had been destroyed by one of the Americans' new-type bombs. Nishioka realized that, in sharing this testimony, he risked arrest by the Kempeitai.[16] But he could worry about that later. Nagasaki was in danger, and the news could not wait another minute.

During his return trip, the westward progress of his train had been halted in the eastern suburbs of Hiroshima. Like Nagasaki Medical College president Tsuno'o, albeit a day later, he had also been forced to walk from there to Itsuka'ichi, on the other side of Hiroshima, to continue his rail journey.

Nagano was aware that Hiroshima had been hit by some kind of special attack. But until now, he had had no idea of the scale of the destruction that had been involved. As he continued listening to the grisly details of Nishioka's testimony, he was gradually overwhelmed by a horrifying certainty: Nagasaki was going to be the next target of the new-type bomb.[17]

After thanking his friend and sending him on his way, Nagano began making phone calls to his various department heads and section chiefs. He was ordering an emergency meeting to be held in his office, starting at 0730.[18] But for now, he wanted to make sure that the local police were up-to-date on the details of the Hiroshima disaster and made aware of the imminent danger facing their own city. Nagano made another series of urgent phone calls, summoning the prefectural chief of police and other key bureaucrats to the governor's office at once. The meeting went late into the night.

Sleep could come later, after the danger had passed.

TAKEOFF

509th Composite Group briefing hut
Tinian Island
0030 hours, August 9, 1945

AS THE FINAL pre-mission briefing drew near, a ritual of sorts—morbidly foreboding to a casual observer but familiar SOP to any combat aviator—played out in several 393rd Bomb Squadron crew barracks. As each crew member filed out of his respective Quonset hut, he placed his wallet in a bag or box by the entrance door. This practice—a hedge against the possibility of the crewman being captured or killed during the mission—served a double purpose. First, it would prevent anything in the wallet of potential intelligence or propaganda value from falling into enemy hands; no one, after all, wanted a grieving mother or sweetheart taunted by personalized on-air condolences from Tokyo Rose. Second, the wallet would provide an intimate item to include in a personal-effects package that would be mailed Stateside to the crewman's next of kin.

With this somber routine completed, each crew group of eleven or twelve men filed off into the illuminated night of an airfield that never slept, making their way to their final pre-mission briefing. If conversation was perhaps less animated than usual during this walk, it was because each man in that moment knew that, in another nine hours or so, he would be helping to kill another Japanese city.

At the briefing hut, the atmosphere was low-key but tense. When

Colonel Tibbets rose to face his now assembled crewmen, the normally taciturn commander chose to open the proceedings with a short speech in which he noted that the plutonium bomb to be used against Kokura or Nagasaki was considerably more powerful than the one that had been dropped on Hiroshima. He also emphasized the crucial importance of demonstrating the successful deployment of the plutonium design, as it was this type that was being hurriedly stockpiled back in the States for upcoming missions against Japan, should they prove necessary.

Before turning the remainder of the briefing over to Hopkins and Payette, Tibbets invited the Project Alberta civilians and military personnel present in the hut to briefly introduce themselves and explain their respective roles as special participants in the upcoming mission.

Strike plane *Bockscar* would be carrying three military representatives of Project Alberta. Navy commander Frederick L. Ashworth's role was explained using the still-exotic job title of "weaponeer."[1] The Annapolis man and former combat aviator had been involved in the technical aspects of the Manhattan Project since its early days. As such, he knew Fat Man inside and out and would be responsible during the mission for maintaining the weapon in good working order until the moment it was dropped over its target.

Accompanying Ashworth would be his "electronic assistant for the weaponeer," USAAF first lieutenant Philip Barnes, who would set up a "black box" monitoring device for Fat Man in *Bockscar*'s forward crew cabin, where he would share desk space with the plane's radio operator, Sergeant Abe Spitzer.[2] From there, Barnes would perform regular status checks on the bomb's power supply and fusing system circuitry, keeping up a running commentary for Ashworth.

USAAF first lieutenant Jacob Beser, who was making his second atomic bombing mission as radar countermeasures officer, would be sharing Staff Sergeant Ed Buckley's radar observer compartment, located aft of *Bockscar*'s bomb bay. Although the technological details of Beser's job were almost as closely guarded as those of the bomb itself, he was able to share a rough-sketch description of his job: During the ingress, he would be using his specialized top secret gear to monitor

TAKEOFF

and jam any Japanese radar signals that might otherwise trigger—inadvertently or deliberately—the final, radar-activated stage of Fat Man's complex fusing circuitry.[3] Nobody, after all—especially Beser and the other occupants of *Bockscar*—wanted the bomb detonating prematurely.

The VIP passengers on instrumentation plane *The Great Artiste* included civilian physicist Lawrence Johnston and Sergeants Jesse Kupferberg and Walter Goodman.[4] They would be in charge of parachute-dropping radiosondes over the target and then monitoring and recording their radio-transmitted telemetry data of Fat Man's explosion for later Manhattan Project analysis.

Also along for the ride would be William Laurence, a *New York Times* science reporter embedded with the Manhattan Project. Originally slated to observe the Hiroshima mission, he had arrived too late on Tinian to do so. Ever since, when not pestering Colonel Tibbets, he had been chewing off the ear of Lieutenant Beser—his Tibbets-assigned babysitter during his Tinian sojourn—in consistently rebuffed and dodged attempts to pry classified technical information out of his harried minder.[5]

Finally, photography plane *Big Stink* would be ferrying the mission's highest-ranking VIP passenger, RAF group captain Leonard Cheshire, a veteran of more than a hundred missions over Germany as a Lancaster bomber pilot. In March 1943, at the age of twenty-five,[6] he had become the youngest group captain in the RAF. After this promotion, he had achieved renown and added more items to his chestful of medals as commander of the No. 617 "Dambusters" Squadron, famed for its exploits in attacking key German dams and hydro-electric installations.[7] At the conclusion of his combat career, he was appointed a member of the British Joint Mission to the United States, where he served first as Prime Minister Churchill's—and now as Prime Minister Attlee's—official observer with the Manhattan Project.[8]

Joining Group Captain Cheshire would be two thirty-six-year-old Los Alamos luminaries, both of whom were participants in the Trinity test detonation of the world's first atomic bomb in New Mexico three weeks earlier. British physicist William Penney, a long-term research colleague of Dr. Oppenheimer, was an expert in blast measurement.[9] American Robert Serber, a UC Berkeley physicist, had been involved in the development of atomic weapons since their conceptual infancy. In this capacity, he had authored an introductory volume on bomb physics that was required (and top secret) reading for all new arrivals at Oppenheimer's Los Alamos brain trust.[10] On the upcoming mission, Serber would be responsible for operating a Fastax camera that would record Fat Man's detonation at some four thousand frames per second.[11] He and Project Alberta colleague Bernard Waldman were the only people on Tinian trained in the operation of this sophisticated piece of equipment,[12] and their presence on the island was essentially the raison d'être for the participation of photography planes in the 509th's strike force formations.

With the introductions out of the way, Major Hopkins and Lieutenant Colonel Payette presented somewhat stripped-down versions of the operational and intelligence briefings they had delivered to the aircraft commanders and other select crew members eight hours earlier. Essential information regarding the primary and secondary targets, expected enemy opposition, navigation waypoints for the ingress-egress routes, and the presence of the various air-sea-rescue resources along the same was provided. Instructions regarding a recall code were also given; that code would be issued by Guam XXI BC HQ in case an acceptable Japanese surrender offer were received during the mission's ingress phase. Radio operators were to keep their ears open for such a signal; if it were received, the strike force would make a U-turn at once and return to base—preferably with Fat Man still on board.[13] In the event that Weaponeer Ashworth determined that the bomb could not be returned safely, he and Major Sweeney were authorized to take the undesirable—and likely career-ruining—precaution of dumping it, unexploded, into the Pacific.

The briefing was also updated with last-minute weather reports by 509th communications officer Captain Edward Lucke[14]—and none of the young captain's news was good. Visibility conditions over the target areas were forecast to be less than ideal and deteriorating rapidly, with a window of minimal bomb-drop criteria likely disappearing by about 1100.[15] The aircrews were also going to have to contend with storms and turbulence for most of the flight out, requiring a higher-than-usual cruising altitude—fifty-five hundred meters versus the SOP twenty-seven hundred meters—in an attempt to fly over the bad weather.[16] Navigators and flight engineers were reminded to take into consideration the increase of fuel consumption this would entail when calculating remaining flight time for their respective aircraft. All were well aware that failing to do so could see those aircraft running out of fuel and ditching into the Pacific instead of making it safely back to Tinian.

Compounding the upcoming mission's weather woes, a developing typhoon system was now threatening Iwo Jima, the strike force's originally planned rally point. This necessitated the designation of a new rally point at Yakushima Island, just off the southern tip of Kyushu and well within Japanese radar coverage. Due to poor visibility conditions expected at this spot, the rendezvous altitude was going to be set at ten thousand meters, in hopes of flying over the cloud cover, instead of the twenty-seven hundred meters used during the Hiroshima mission rendezvous over Iwo Jima.[17] To reduce fuel consumption and stay as close as possible to the designated mission timetable, *Bockscar* was to linger over Yakushima no longer than fifteen minutes, waiting for stragglers. In a worst-case blown rendezvous scenario, *Bockscar* would fly on to the target without the instrumentation and/or photography planes.

Finally, the standard policy on mandatory visual sighting for the bomb run was reemphasized. If visibility conditions over Kokura were unacceptable, the strike force commander should not hesitate to move on to the secondary target of Nagasaki. The inexact method of dropping the bomb with radar aiming would be used only as an absolute last resort and then only over the secondary.

At the close of the formal briefing, Tibbets stood up once again to face the room. Then he said something that must have struck his audience as completely uncharacteristic of their normally unsentimental commander.

"If any of you don't want to go on this mission, where there's no doubt we will be bombing civilians with this new atomic bomb, just say so. If you feel uncomfortable about this, you're free to step down. No action will be taken against you. If that's the way you feel, we'll respect it."[18]

Tibbets had a deep bench of ten other B-29 crews in the 393rd who had been dropping nonnuclear ten-thousand-pound "Pumpkin" bombs on various Japanese targets for the past month.[19] If anyone in the briefing hut—with the exception of Ashworth and Beser—had taken him up on his conscientious objector offer, he could have found a substitute for them. The situation could even have been handled if Sweeney had backed out at the last minute; Tibbets would simply have taken command of the second mission himself.[20] No doubt much to Tibbets' relief, he did not have to make any such decisions: There were no takers of his offer, which might have been made as much to clear his own conscience as it was to assuage his men's.

Finally, Captain William Downey, the 509th's Protestant chaplain, rose to give his benediction for the day's mission. "Almighty God, Father of all mercies," he began, "we pray Thee to be gracious with those who fly this night. Guard and protect those of us who venture out into the darkness of Thy heaven. Uphold them on Thy wings. Keep them safe both in body and soul and bring them back to us. Give to us all courage and strength for the hours that are ahead; give to them rewards according to their efforts. Above all else, our Father, bring peace to Thy world. May we go forward trusting in Thee and knowing we are in Thy presence now and forever. Amen."[21]

With the briefing at an end, the crewmen and their VIP passengers began making their way to the Dogpatch Inn for their preflight breakfast. After their meal, they boarded trucks to the 509th's equipment shed, where they were issued their flight gear, flak suits and helmets, special welder's goggles (eye protection against Fat Man's anticipated intense flash), survival vests and belts, .45 automatic pistol sidearms, and, finally, parachutes. At this juncture, Project Alberta's

TAKEOFF

Dr. Ed Doll—just as he had done at this very spot three days before—handed Lieutenant Beser a slip of paper on which were written the frequencies of the pulsed signals that Fat Man's range-finding radar-fusing system would be bouncing off terra firma during the weapon's descent over the target.[22] Doll reminded the young lieutenant that, if he had to bail out over enemy territory, he was to eat the paper as soon as he touched ground.[23]

Crews and passengers were trucked to the flight line at around 0200,[24] with plenty of time for final preflight checks before the planes would begin taxiing out to the runway. Unlike the morning of the first atomic mission, when the flight line had been packed with throngs of excited onlookers and illuminated with Hollywood-premiere-worthy klieg lights, there were only a few VIPs and Signal Corps still cameramen on hand to observe and record the second.[25]

As the crew members undertook their assigned individual preparatory tasks, weather conditions were steadily worsening. *Laggin' Dragon*, *Enola Gay*, and *Full House* took off, on schedule, at 0230, winging away into an ugly night sky lit up with scattered lightning bolts[26] in the direction of Japan.

In the midst of this activity, Robert Serber realized that he had forgotten to be issued a parachute. As he would not be able to fly on the mission without one, he had no choice but to commandeer a jeep—with Major Hopkins' annoyed permission—to take him back to the equipment shed. If he did not make it back on time, *Big Stink* would leave without him, regardless of the fact that he was the only person ready to fly who knew how to operate the Fastax camera. It was the mission's first snafu.

Some fifteen minutes or so before the scheduled takeoff time of 0300, the crews were aboard the strike force planes. After ground personnel hand-turned the massive propellers a set number of revolutions to circulate oil in and clear debris from the engines, the pilots powered up their planes and the strike force roared to life.

Beser and a few of the VIP passengers were still on the tarmac, busy with final face-to-face consultations or—like the young radar countermeasures officer—simply disinclined to make the effort to climb up into their planes until the last minute. Beser had slept little in the past few days, outside of some decent catnaps stolen in *Enola Gay*'s communication tunnel, which spanned the unpressurized bomb bay and connected the flight deck and the radar observer's compartment, allowing for crew passage (one crawling man at a time) between each.[27] Beser was just about to give up his comfortable seat on the hood of Tibbets' jeep and get to work when *Bockscar*'s props abruptly stopped rotating and its engines shut down.

A few beats later, the plane's crew climbed down the flight deck hatch to mill around on the tarmac. Sweeney and flight engineer Sergeant John Kuharek emerged from the throng and walked over to Tibbets' jeep to confer with their clench-jawed commander.[28] Kuharek had discovered a problem with the plane's fuel system: The pumping mechanism on its six-hundred-gallon reserve tank was not functioning, and there was no time to replace it.[29] Tibbets, in a clearly dismissive tone of voice, tried to convince the flustered and dithering Sweeney that the six hundred gallons in the reserve tank were there only to add forward ballast to the special Silverplate B-29s; *Bockscar* would be OK to fly to "the empire" and back without needing to tap into it.

Still, Sweeney was not persuaded. Eventually Ashworth and navigator Captain James Van Pelt came out to join the conference. As more minutes ticked away and more lightning cracked along the horizon of Tinian's northern offing, the animated discussion went back and forth, punctuated by dramatic finger stabs at Van Pelt's navigation map. At one point, an exasperated Tibbets pulled Sweeney out of clear earshot of the jeep-side conference, although Beser could still catch the agitated tone of the conversation—entreaty and dressing-down in equal measure—between commander and XO. When the pair returned to join the group, Sweeney informed everyone that everything was all right.

The mission had just weathered its second snafu (or its third, if counting the last-minute rallying point switch from Iwo Jima to Yakushima), and it was now going on an hour behind schedule, with the weather window over Kokura rapidly closing.[30] They were out of time.

When the now chuted-up Dr. Robert Serber finally found Colonel Tibbets at the 509th's radio shack, *Big Stink*—the strike force's "Tail-End Charlie"—was already thirty minutes gone, flying away into the stormy skies to the north.[31] After consultation between the civilian physicist, Tibbets, and Brigadier General Thomas Farrell—deputy commander of the Manhattan Project—it was decided that the mission's strict-radio-silence parameter could be waived just this once; if Serber could go on air to explain to someone on board Hopkins' plane how to operate the sophisticated Fastax, then *Big Stink*'s mission might still be salvaged. But before Serber could deliver his technical lecture broadcast, Tibbets and Farrell took the opportunity to give Major Hopkins a piece of their mind about his performance on the mission so far. It would not be the operation officer's last screwup.

INGRESS

Fifty-five hundred meters above the Central Pacific
Twenty-two hundred kilometers south-southwest of Kokura
0500 Tinian Time / 0400 Japan Time

THE STRIKE FORCE was now at the cruising altitude of fifty-five hundred meters it would take most of the way to the rallying point.[1] As the planes at last emerged from the worst of the storm system they had been battling since taking off from Tinian, their crews and passengers were enjoying a far smoother ride[2] in shirtsleeve comfort, separated from the outside temperature of minus thirty-three degrees Celsius by their pressurized cabins and a few thin millimeters of aluminum airframe skin.[3]

As Yakushima was still four hours away, many were also enjoying some pre-mission downtime. Going "by the book," such crew members should have been wide-eyed and alert, manning anti-collision watch—either under the domed glass-house-like flight deck and nose of the plane, behind one of the porthole-like apertures in the fuselage, or, for Sergeant Albert "Pappy" Dehart, from the plexiglass cage of his isolated tail gunner turret. But this morning, no one on the strike force planes looked askance when many of their colleagues instead took the opportunity of this lull to catch some shut-eye. Even Major Sweeney joined in on the slumber party; turning *Bockscar*'s controls over to his copilots—First Lieutenant Charles Albury and Second Lieutenant Fred Olivi—the mission commander climbed up into the front end of the plane's communication tunnel to stretch out for a nap.[4] At the opposite end of this tunnel, First Lieutenant Beser was doing the same. His special skills and top secret radio-signal-jamming equipment would not be needed until the strike force approached Japanese airspace and radar coverage.[5]

For First Lieutenant Barnes, however, there would be no sleeping on the job. He had been busy since takeoff and would not be able to relax for the next five or six hours, until the moment Fat Man went into free fall over the target. In the meantime, he kept a vigilant eye on his Black Box, with which he conducted regular circuit tests, checking for any electrical blip or hiccup from the armed atomic bomb quietly humming away in *Bockscar's* bomb bay.

One plane back in the formation, in *The Great Artiste*, William Laurence passed the time in his bombardier's station perch. While jotting notes and gazing out into the slowly brightening gloom of a morning twilight sky, he noticed Saint Elmo's fire beginning to form around the tips of the plane's propellers. As Laurence watched, the luminous plasma slowly spread from the engine nacelles to crawl along the forward edges of the wings before reaching the aluminum framework of the B-29's canopy.

As the self-made and self-titled science correspondent for *The New York Times*, Laurence knew that this eerily beautiful phenomenon was of electromagnetic origin. And as a Manhattan Project–embedded journalist, he was privy to enough classified information to know that Fat Man used an electrical fusing system. At the intersection of these two areas of knowledge, an unwelcome train of thought began to form: Assuming that the other strike force planes were similarly aglow with Saint Elmo's fire, what would happen if a tendril of it wormed its way into *Bockscar's* bomb bay and thence into Fat Man's complex and sensitive circuitry? When the nervous passenger voiced these concerns to the flight deck, Captain Bock reassured him that there was nothing to worry about—bomber crews saw Saint Elmo's fire all the time during missions,[6] and it never caused any problems.

This information put Laurence's mind at ease somewhat. But

unbeknownst to him—and to anyone else in the strike force except Sweeney, Ashworth, and Barnes—a far more serious electromagnetic drama had just played out on *Bockscar* while he was enjoying (and then fretting over) the light show.

About ten minutes out of Tinian, while *Bockscar* was still unpressurized and flying at low altitude, Ashworth had performed the final stage of arming Fat Man. To access the weapon, he had first had to open the pressure bulkhead next to the radio operator's desk.[7] After negotiating a short ladder to descend into the bomb bay, he replaced the two green "safety" plugs in Fat Man's bulletproof-steel outer casing with red plugs, completing the device's fusing circuitry and activating the firing system to "ready" status. The bomb was now fully armed, waiting for the physical action of the final drop to begin the initiation sequence of its multilayered, redundant fusing protocols.

Returning to the flight deck, Ashworth reported the bomb's state of readiness to Sweeney, who in turn ordered Spitzer to send a brief coded signal to Tinian to that effect. Barring a "Mayday" call from the strike force in the event of an emergency or an "aborted" message for a weapon malfunction, this "bomb armed" signal was supposed to be *Bockscar*'s only divergence from radio silence[8] until a later report of the successful deployment of the bomb.

At his station, Barnes returned to his watch over the Black Box to ensure that everything had gone all right with the arming procedure. When (redundant second) copilot Olivi nonchalantly asked Barnes what Ashworth had been doing in the bomb bay, he replied that the weaponeer had just armed Fat Man. Then he added that if *Bockscar*'s altitude dipped below fifteen hundred meters with the device still aboard, it would automatically detonate.[9] Olivi instantly regretted having given voice to his curiosity.[10]

Although Fat Man's nuclear core achieved an explosive fast chain reaction using a method entirely different from the one used in Little Boy, the two bomb designs were quite similar in terms of their multilayered fail-safe fusing redundancy and the basic initiation sequence of their respective firing systems: Upon final drop over the target, a tether wire linking Fat Man with *Bockscar* would pull loose, setting in motion a bank of timer clocks in the bomb that would then begin counting down forty-three seconds—the time the device would take falling from ten thousand meters to reach its designated "Air Zero" burst altitude of five hundred meters.

Fifteen seconds into Fat Man's descent, a signal from the clocks would power up nine onboard barometric sensors. When any three of these sensors detected an appropriate altitude, they would in turn initiate the final stage of the firing system—four radar fuses whose antennae would then start pinging pulsed radio signals (the frequencies of which were Beser's primary concern during the mission) off of the rapidly approaching terra firma below. When any two of these antennae agreed that an altitude of five hundred meters had been reached, they would send a detonation signal to the explosive charges surrounding the bomb's plutonium core, crushing this softball-sized sphere to billiard ball size and triggering a "fast" critical mass chain reaction.

The timer clocks were the fail-safe if the barometric or radar fusing failed to function en route to Air Zero; if the clocks had not otherwise been already vaporized by Fat Man's explosion by this point, they would send the final overriding detonation signal once they counted down to zero seconds.

As a final meta-fail-safe for the timers, Fat Man had also been equipped with mounting points for contact fuses that would detonate the bomb if and when it smashed into the ground. However, as these fuses posed the risk of being set off by a lucky enemy bullet or flak shrapnel hit, they were not mounted on Fat Man for the Nagasaki mission. Ultimately, success or failure would all come down to the reliability of the timer clocks.[11]

When the strike force had still been festooned with Saint Elmo's fire, Barnes had performed another of his regular circuit tests on Fat Man's firing system. This time, however, the test illuminated a small white light on the Black Box, indicating that Fat Man's circuitry was now fully closed and its firing system active. Barnes anxiously shook awake a catnapping Ashworth to report this development.[12] Quickly assessing the unsettling implications of the erratic signal lamp, weaponeer and assistant concurred that, for all they knew, the fail-safe timer clocks in the firing system had just commenced their forty-three-second countdown to detonation.

The situation—including the possibility of imminent explosion—was immediately reported to Sweeney, who now faced a potentially life-and-death command decision. Accepting the weaponeer team's assessment of the risk involved, he could: (1) drop the malfunctioning Fat Man at once before whatever remained of its detonation count-down ran down and hope that the strike force could outrun the sub-sequent explosion; or (2) tell Ashworth and Barnes to do what they could to try to fix the situation.[13] Sweeney opted for the latter, and the weaponeer team went into action, poring over schematics charts while Barnes removed the outer case of the Black Box and began pok-ing around in its innards. As the end of a possible timer-clock-detonation countdown came and went, Barnes continued his probing and wire tugging until he eventually found the problem: Some fool in the Project Alberta assembly shed back on Tinian had reversed the assigned settings of two dials in the Black Box.[14] When Barnes cor-rected this error, the white indicator light went dark.[15] All systems normal. Crisis averted.

Bockscar's crew was none the worse for not knowing that Ash-worth and Barnes might have just saved their lives, nor that their mis-sion commander—with a different dice roll—could have ended them. As for Sweeney himself, his gamble not to ditch the bomb had almost certainly saved his Air Force career. But it had also sealed the fates of tens of thousands of people, either in Kokura or Nagasaki, who were now doomed not to live out the morning.

═════

Nagata-chō, Tokyo
Two thousand kilometers northwest of Bockscar's current position

At his official residence, Foreign Minister Tōgō Shigenori received a phone call from the radio room of the Foreign Ministry a few hours before dawn: Radio Moscow was reporting that the Soviet Union had declared war on Japan; crack armored spearheads of the Red Army—including many veteran units of the apocalyptically decisive Battle of Berlin—were now pouring over the border into Manchuria[16] and facing weak resistance. Tōgō then rushed to Nagata-chō to bear the bad news to his boss, Prime Minister Suzuki Kantarō, and share with him his opinion that the Manchuria development meant that the war was, for all intents and purposes, over.

Seventy-seven-year-old Suzuki Kantarō was born the son of a Kansai regional administrator, but politics had never really been in his blood—an irony he must have appreciated with some chagrin during the tumultuous summer of 1945. His professional life had begun in the IJN with his graduation from the naval academy at Etajima in 1887.[17] After his commissioning, he went on to become a leading expert in torpedo tactics, covering himself in glory as one of the great heroes of the decisive Battle of Tsushima Strait during the Russo-Japanese War.

After retiring from the IJN in 1929 at the rank of full admiral, Suzuki remained in public service as a loyal chamberlain and trusted senior advisor for Emperor Hirohito. In this role, he earned respect in Palace circles for his ever-levelheaded counsel and for his wariness of the Imperial Way fanaticism then beginning to take hold in the country; in February 1936, the latter stance had seen him targeted by fanatic IJA officers during their failed coup attempt.[18] Nine years later, he still carried one of his would-be assassin's bullets in his body.[19]

In April 1945, Suzuki was recalled from semiretirement by direct imperial command to replace his headstrong but bumbling predecessor, IJA general Koiso Kuniaki. Koiso's unpublicized mission—at least as the emperor and his closest advisors interpreted it—had been to bring the war to an unsatisfactory but at least bearable negotiated conclusion. In a best-case scenario, this would entail something along the lines of Germany's nominally national-sovereignty-preserving Treaty of Versailles surrender after World War One. Whoever held the premiership at war's end would have to see that this was accomplished without Japan suffering post–World War One Germany's fate of monarchy-toppling domestic turmoil. In this regard, he would have to take particular care to prevent a Communist or Socialist revolution among a disaffected, defeat-embittered, and half-starved populace—the postwar scenario that most terrified the emperor, his advisors, and the military. The Japanese media had quite openly reported the grisly post-defeat fates of Mussolini and Hitler, and no one—at least no one who was Japanese—wanted such an ignominious end to befall the emperor.

For his part, Koiso wanted to ensure that Japan would be able to approach any armistice negotiating table with its head held high. As he saw it, Japan would be able to do this only by bloodying the Allies' noses with a spectacular Japanese victory in some decisive final battle. However, during his ten-month-long pursuit of this elusive victory, he had merely overseen another string of catastrophes: While Japan lost the Philippines, Okinawa, thousands of aircraft, and nearly the entirety of its surface fleet, half a million civilians had died under Curtis LeMay's incendiaries. And so far, the best idea the armed services had come up with to deal with the situation was to formalize kamikaze suicide tactics[20] and exhort the populace to glorious, national-honor-preserving mass self-immolation in the event of an Allied invasion.

After the debacle of the Koiso Cabinet, the task had fallen to the superannuated Suzuki to bring the conflict to a speedy end, aligning the IJA and IJN with the updated bottom-line war aim of preserving as much as possible of the Japanese state as it went down in now inevitable defeat. But in his pursuit of these goals, he was trapped between a rock and a hard place: an increasingly untenable war situation, on one hand—underscored by the horrific recent destruction of Hiroshima—and on the other, a potential coup d'état if the rank and file of the armed services caught wind of his peace overtures.

The political tightrope Suzuki was constantly forced to walk to avoid national disaster (and another attempt on his life) might have also led to the occasional lapse of judgment and slip of the tongue.

INGRESS

Some twelve days earlier, when a press conference reporter asked him for an official government stance regarding the Allies' then recently announced Potsdam Declaration, Suzuki had given the one-word response of *"Mokusatsu"*—a slippery term to translate into English, possibly meaning "I refuse to even dignify that query with a response" in a haughtily dismissive context or simply "No comment" in another.[21] Suzuki's statement made headlines around the world, and when the news reached Washington, *mokusatsu* was interpreted as carrying the "haughtily dismissive" nuance, implying that the Japanese had no intention of surrendering (at least unconditionally)—an interpretation that no doubt eased the American decision to begin dropping atomic bombs on Japan.[22]

Meanwhile, beyond media scrutiny, Suzuki's efforts at bringing the war to an end were being stymied, primarily by the IJA's representatives in the Supreme War Council—army minister General Anami Korechika and IJA chief of staff General Umezu Yoshijirō. So far, at least, the two generals were refusing even to contemplate accepting the Potsdam Declaration surrender terms, no matter what the Allies dropped on the nation's cities or how many civilians perished in the flames. Making matters worse, they had also managed to win IJN chief of staff Admiral Toyoda Soemu over to their side, therein deadlocking the council's ability to bring the war to a conclusion. As long as both sides stuck to their respective stances, the only means of breaking the stalemate would be through beseeching the emperor for direct intervention in the matter. But no one on the council was ready to make that unprecedented request—at least not yet.

Until a few hours earlier, Suzuki had had what he believed was an ace up his sleeve: Since the previous May—while completely ignorant of Stalin's secret Yalta Conference promise to enter the war against Japan three months after Germany's surrender—he had had his foreign minister, Tōgō Shigenori, send out top secret feelers to the yet officially Japan-neutral Soviet Union for help in securing a negotiated settlement of the war with the Western Allies.[23] Tōgō had even recruited the services of the old Fukuokan charmer Hirota Kōki, brought back from retirement to work back-channel negotiations with the Soviet ambassador to Japan, Jacob Malik, in a series of secret meetings at a resort hotel in Hakone.[24]

In the meantime, and operating under the disastrously mistaken assumption that their rear flank was protected by the 1941 Soviet-Japanese Neutrality Pact, the Japanese military had been busily preparing to make their Alamo stand in the Home Islands themselves, intending to bleed an Allied invasion dry enough to compel the Americans and British to grant generous surrender terms for Japan.[25] Toward this end, they had been siphoning off men and matériel from the Kwantung Army in Manchuria—most critically, its tanks and anti-tank artillery—to shore up defenses along the anticipated first Allied landing beaches in Kyushu.[26] Thus stripped of the primary means by which it might have better resisted the crack Soviet armored units[27] now being thrown against it, the woefully depleted Kwantung Army was crumbling quickly.[28]

If the Soviets managed to push all the way to the Sea of Japan in northern China and the Korean Peninsula—which all signs indicated was now a near certainty—it would not matter if the Americans were fought to a bloody standstill in Kyushu. The Soviets would have a staging-area springboard for launching an invasion of the Home Islands and rolling through the sparsely guarded northern and western approaches to Tokyo—a contingency for which the IJA had made no actual physical defensive preparations and for which it did not even have a formal plan.[29] In other words, having failed to avail themselves of the vital mid-twentieth-century wisdom that one should never trust a treaty signed with Stalin (or, for that matter, with Hitler), Japan's military leaders had bet the farm on marshaling all of their forces to meet the anticipated American and British invasion landings in Kyushu and on the Pacific Kantō coast. And now they were caught with their pants down.

At 0700, when Tibbets' weather planes were entering the final leg of their respective reconnaissance flights to Kokura and Nagasaki, Suzuki visited the Imperial Palace to tell His Majesty the bad Soviet news. Over several hours of consultation, Suzuki shared his opinion that the war was effectively over and advised that there was no choice but to accept the terms of the Potsdam Declaration and hope for the best. The emperor concurred and ordered Suzuki to work out the specific details on how this was to be done.

In compliance with His Majesty's wishes, Suzuki ordered Secretary Sakomizu to make arrangements with his IJA, IJN, and Foreign Ministry counterparts for a meeting of the Supreme War Council to start at 1030.[30] Perhaps now, with the recent catastrophe in Hiroshima and the nightmare scenario of Soviet entry into the war about to come to pass, Anami, Umezu, and Toyoda would at last come to their senses and agree to a surrender.

Approximately one hour into—and some fifteen hundred kilometers southeast of—Suzuki's somber conference with the emperor, Sergeant Spitzer picked up the weather reports from *Enola Gay* and *Laggin' Dragon* on *Bockscar*'s radio: hazy clouds and partial sunshine over Kokura and Nagasaki—not ideal for a visually sighted drop, but not bad enough to abort the mission.[31] Fifteen meters aft of Spitzer's radio desk, in the radar observer's compartment of *Bockscar*, First Lieutenant Beser prepared for a repeat of his Hiroshima mission duties— readying his ECM radar-jamming equipment and checking the radio gear he would use to detect scrambling / intercept direction activity at Japanese fighter bases once the strike force entered Home Island airspace. As he did so, the strike force continued on its northwesterly heading, slowly climbing to the ten-thousand-meter altitude it would be flying over the rallying point, and thence through the bomb run and egress from Japanese airspace.

An hour later, *Bockscar* reached Yakushima and turned into a holding pattern over the island.[32] Captain Bock had *The Great Artiste* on-site, on time, and at the correct altitude just as *Bockscar* was completing its first circuit. Going by the order and intervals in which the bombers had taken off from North Field, Major Hopkins should have shown up a minute or two later. When that time window came and went, however, *Big Stink* was nowhere to be seen; unbeknownst to the rest of the strike force, Hopkins had, in fact, already arrived at Yakushima—but at an altitude three thousand meters higher than the other two planes.[33] In the sun-glared, particulate-hazed air of a Japanese summer morning (even at that altitude), this was a distance that utterly precluded mutual visual identification—especially when considering that the respective pilots of either element of the divided strike force would have been swiveling their heads around on a horizontal plane instead of a vertical arc as they searched in vain for their missing counterpart(s).

At several junctures in the two briefings Sweeney had attended for Special Mission #16, Tibbets had emphasized that the strike plane was to wait over the rallying point no longer than fifteen minutes and that if one or both of the other two planes failed to show up within this time span, *Bockscar* was to proceed to the target(s) alone. This directive, however, was not followed. Instead, Sweeney kept the two-plane formation circling over Yakushima, waiting in vain for Hopkins to appear. After some forty-five minutes, the exasperated mission commander finally waggled *Bockscar*'s wings—the signal for *The Great Artiste* to follow him—and pushed on to Kokura without *Big Stink*.[34]

The mission was now nearly two hours behind schedule, and as flight engineer Kuharek would soon inform his pilot, *Bockscar* was in the early stages of a burgeoning crisis: Over Yakushima, it had just burned through forty-five minutes' worth of fuel that it could not spare.

A PEACEFUL THURSDAY MORNING

Former Daiwa Textile plant
North Ujina, Hiroshima
Two hundred fifty kilometers east-northeast of Nagasaki
3.7 kilometers southeast of Hiroshima Ground Zero (GZ)
August 9, 1945

IN HIS KHAKI SERGE *kokuminfuku* uniform and the white *hachimaki* headband of a Yamato stalwart, the short, bespectacled fifty-four-year-old Professor Nishina Yoshio must have looked less like Japan's preeminent nuclear physicist and more like a rural school principal presiding over a patriotic rally. His appearance would have been even more at odds considering that he was at present collecting evidence to support his initial informed gut-reaction theory—already shared with the prime minister's office the previous evening—that the Americans had destroyed Hiroshima with an atomic bomb. But he was going to need more quantitative empirical observations to put into the report his survey team would eventually submit to Imperial General Headquarters.

In lieu of Geiger–Müller tubes or other specialized detection equipment the team did not possess, Nishina had to come up with another method of acquiring incontrovertible evidence that physical matter in Hiroshima had been exposed to an extremely high dose of radiation delivered in an extremely short span of time. Toward this end, he asked the Akatsuki Maritime Command—the local IJA organization in charge of Hiroshima rescue and recovery—to provide his team with the bodies of bomb victims on which to perform autopsies. Specifically, he needed the bodies of people who had succumbed not to burns, blast force, or impact with ballistic objects but rather who had been killed at a molecular level—the genetic material in their cells shredded by the shower of gamma rays and neutrons that he knew, at least theoretically, would have been released by the detonation of an atomic fission weapon.

Among the at least 100,000 corpses strewn across Hiroshima at that moment and awaiting cremation, there would have been any number—perhaps even thousands—of bodies that fit the esteemed physicist's needs. However, to avoid any jurisdictional (and ethical) issues that would have been involved in using civilian victims for this purpose without the permission of next of kin, the Akatsuki Command instead relied on a supply of bodies of individuals over whom the emperor's military had incontestable authority. This morning, the outwardly unblemished remains of IJA soldiers collected for Professor Nishina's autopsy requirements were lined up in the first aid room at the Daiwa Textile factory—the facility Akatsuki Command had requisitioned to serve as the headquarters for its training division.[1]

For the first autopsy, an Army doctor named Kosaka made an incision into the abdominal section of the body of a young soldier. Without further ado, Nishina reached into the opened body cavity and held up a lump of internal organs that was closer in consistency to gelatin than it was to normal flesh.

"Does everyone see this?" Nishina asked the gathering of civilian scientists and military observers. "Make no mistake . . . This is internal organ destruction caused by an atomic bomb."[2]

For Nishina, this was the most convincing piece of evidence he had found so far to confirm his theory about what had destroyed Hiroshima. The following day, he and his colleagues would make their formal written report to that effect to Imperial General Headquarters.[3]

A PEACEFUL THURSDAY MORNING

Nagasaki Prefectural Office
Edo-machi
Four hundred sixty meters west of Nigiwai Bridge

Two hundred fifty kilometers west of Professor Nishina's grim autopsy session, Governor Nagano was preparing for the morning's upcoming emergency meeting to discuss the civil defense implications of the American new-type bomb. At 0748, warning alert sirens began wailing across the CBD.[4] Two minutes later, when the sirens were upgraded to an air raid alert, Nagano instructed his secretary to contact the relevant department heads, police, and fire officials to inform them that the venue for the meeting would be changed to the prefectural civil defense bunker in Rokasu-machi.[5] There would be fewer distractions there, and the governor was going to want everyone's full attention when he announced a decision he should have made weeks if not months earlier: He was going to order the immediate evacuation from the city of all members of the civilian population who were not otherwise directly engaged in essential war work.[6] At least if he could help it, no one else's grandchild was going to die on his watch because of a decision he made—or failed to make in time.

Nagasaki Appellate Court chief judge's official residence
Katsuyama-machi
Seven hundred meters northwest of Nigiwai Bridge

Ishida Masako woke up with the toothache that had been bothering her all summer. She had been meaning to see a dentist at some point, but her hectic daily schedule at Ōhashi—inclusive of her three hours of commuting every day—had so far precluded the luxury of receiving professional dental care.[7] Judge Ishida—perhaps getting tired of hearing his daughter complaining about the ailment or, perhaps, having discussed the Hiroshima news with his daughter the night before and now harboring some unvoiced premonition of catastrophe—told Masako that he wanted her to take the day off from work to go get the tooth looked at. Besides, the household would be busy today, making the move to the new Nagasaki Appellate Court chief judge's official residence, a few blocks over in Yaoya-machi; perhaps his daughter could lend a hand with that after her dentist visit.[8]

Masako, however, was having none of it. With the nation fighting for its very existence, it would have been untoward for an employee in a vital war plant—especially the daughter of such an important and highly visible public official—to take off from work on account of a little toothache. The judge relented in the face of his daughter's determination, perhaps more than a little proud of her patriotic pluck.

Masako readied her work outfit while the three adult women of the house—Hayashi-sensei and her mother and the Ishidas' young live-in maid, Yamaguchi Shige—went about their preparations for the day, beginning with breakfast. As Masako had started on her job too late to receive one of the smart khaki Mitsubishi work suits the company had issued its earlier-mobilized students, she had to make do with her school's designated war labor outfit instead—her Kenjo uniform blouse with "KENJO"-emblazoned armband, a Rising Sun headband, and a pair of *monpe*. She was particularly attached to the latter item of clothing, which she had fashioned from a set of pajamas her father had had tailor-made at a fancy Tokyo department store before the war.[9] The expensive fabric's bold—bordering on gaudy—particolor pattern of black, white, and light blue stripes was a reflection, in a sense, of its previous wearer's personality, and it was a favorable contrast with the khaki or gray everyone else wore at the plant.

Masako made it to Ōhashi on time, as usual, for the plant's daily *chōrei* morning assembly. At 0748, warning alert sirens began to sound while she was formed up in ranks with the other workers to listen to someone's speech or perhaps to sing patriotic songs. As this less urgent of the two varieties of air defense alarms was always ignored at the plant as a rule, the assembly was still in formation when, two minutes later, the sirens sounded an air raid alert. Unlike the warning alert, this alarm could not be ignored—at least not legally; the work-

A PEACEFUL THURSDAY MORNING

ers broke ranks and evacuated in orderly fashion to company shelters in the hills about five hundred meters east of the plant, where they would remain until the all clear was sounded.

In almost all respects, Masako—true to her breeding—was the very model of a modest and gracious *ojōsan*. Still, because she was the proud daughter of a VIP, it was not beyond her to brag from time to time about her beloved, doting, and very important father. On the way back to her workstation after the 0830 all clear, Masako indulged this innocent conceit by regaling some of her Kenjo coworkers with a claim about her father's apparently magical ability to protect himself and his family from American bombs. According to her, the Ishidas had escaped unscathed countless raids on Tokyo—including a huge one in March that had burned her father's workplace to the ground. But the clincher of the "magically lucky" story was in its punch line: If her father's scheduled posting to Hiroshima had not ended up being canceled by the Ministry of Justice the year before, Masako and her father would have been living in the middle of the city when it was destroyed by the American's new-type bomb three days earlier.[10] Masako's friends agreed that this was indeed luck bordering on the supernatural, and the girls chattered happily on their way back to what they probably expected would be another slow day of late-war doldrums at the Ōhashi plant.

Mitsubishi Steel and Arms Works

Mori-machi

2.2 kilometers northwest of Nigiwai Bridge

Kiridōshi Michiko was late for work again—and this morning by over an hour. Although this was a not-infrequent occurrence during her tenure as a Mitsubishi employee, she had never received so much as a sharp word from her supervisor over these infractions. But today, at least, she could legitimately blame her lateness on unforeseen circumstances beyond her control: Her overcrowded streetcar had jumped its rails, as it was wont to do from time to time, while attempting to negotiate the big turn the Number One Line took on its approach to the Dejima stop. As a result, she had had to walk the last two kilometers of the way to work—a trek that was, in turn, disrupted by her having to shelter in place during the morning's air raid alert.

In this slow season at the plant, any out-of-the-ordinary event that disrupted the day-to-day monotony was always fodder for factory-floor gossip among the chatty girls of the parts-polishing work team. When Michiko finally strolled onto the floor to take a seat at her worktable, she was immediately informed that she had missed an interesting sight that morning: A dashing, high-ranking Kempeitai officer on horseback had posted himself by the main entrance to the plant, exhorting the day shift workers passing by to "fight until the end, even if you are a girl. . . . Kill at least one enemy soldier before you die!"[11]

Never a fan of this kind of rhetoric—with which she and the rest of the country had been bombarded for years—Michiko inwardly bristled at the anecdote before the running dialogue changed tack to rumors about the new-type bomb the Americans had just dropped on Hiroshima. Michiko reported reading in the newspaper that people wearing white clothes had survived the blast. Another girl said she heard that they would be all right as long as they were not directly exposed to the flash of intense light from the bomb, so if that happened while they were at work, their factory building would probably protect them. Both of these theories were, in fact, at least partially correct; however, the new-type-bomb threat they did not yet know about—and against which the flimsy sheet metal and asbestos roof of their building would offer no protection whatsover—was the genetic-material-destroying shower of gamma rays and neutrons the weapon would release at the instant of its detonation.

As the stream of lively chitchat bounced to the next topic, Michiko gradually tuned it out and settled into her work: what was looking to be yet another boring morning of polishing and repolishing already finished and gleaming torpedo parts. Lunch break—which she would share, as usual, with her best buddy, Honda Sawa—could not come soon enough.

A PEACEFUL THURSDAY MORNING

Junshin Girls' School
Ieno-machi
4.4 kilometers north of Nigiwai Bridge

Sister Itonaga Yoshi, like the other novices in the Junshin order, was an early riser. And this morning, she had already been up and about when the Fat Man strike force crews were still performing their pre-mission aircraft checks on the Tinian flight line.

First, she had attended Matins prayers in the school chapel, then helped her novice colleagues prepare breakfast for six-hundred-odd diners—a task that had to be accomplished by the time Junshin's students returned to campus from their daily morning mass at Urakami Cathedral. The students would take their meal in their respective homeroom classrooms, while the Sisters and novices would eat in their designated dining hall.

After breakfast, Mother Ezumi rose to address the room, as she did most mornings. But today, she had something special to talk about: her concerns over newspaper reports she had seen regarding a new-type bomb the Americans had used to destroy Hiroshima.[12] As there was a danger that the Americans might use one of these on Nagasaki, she wanted to keep as many of Junshin's students as possible away from the city. Although the war effort could not spare the second-, third-, and fourth-year girls working across the street at Ōhashi or at any of the other nearby Mitsubishi facilities where they toiled, there was no reason for the first-year girls to be in the open and exposed every day, working on the athletic ground truck patches. Toward this end, starting today, she was going to order the first-year commuters to stay home until further notice.

As for the first-year boarders, Mother Ezumi wanted six of the younger Sisters to march them to a privately owned pine forest deep in the mountains in Mitsuyama, 4.4 kilometers northwest of the campus.[13] An illustrious old *kakure Kirishitan* family—the Takamis—was letting Junshin use this land to collect pine sap for donation to government authorities, after which it would be distilled into fuel for warplanes. This was a very common patriotic project for volunteer laborers in late-war Japan—especially among those either too old or too young to perform more demanding and exacting full-time war plant work. Although the "fuel" resulting from this collection-and-distillation process was poor in quality and tended to rapidly clog precious aircraft engines, it was increasingly relied upon by Japanese military aviation, which was now almost literally flying on fumes since the near-complete strangulation of its overseas petroleum supply routes by the Allied blockade.[14] And poor, engine-damaging quality or not, the ersatz aviation fuel had to work only once to get a kamikaze plane up and away to hit one of the enemy warships now lazing about in the offing around the Home Islands, often close enough to be spotted from shore with the naked eye.

After Mother Ezumi read off their names, the Sisters in the pine sap detail were sent on their way to load a wheelbarrow up with tapping implements and buckets, collect their student charges, and march off to Mitsuyama.[15] Mother Ezumi then called out the names of four other Sisters who would remain on the campus with the junior novices as a faculty skeleton crew, with the former attending to school administration and the latter engaged in their customary truck patch tilling.

The other Sisters and senior novices—including Sister Yoshi— would go out on their usual factory chaperone duties with their student groups after the dismissal of the *chōrei* assembly. The five-hundred-or-so-strong Ōhashi detachment was supervised by Sister Christina Tagawa Tadako, and it was always a stirring sight—and sound—when the popular young Sister marched her girls through the school gate and across the Nagayo Road to their workplace, her bell-like voice ringing high and clear over everyone else's as the group sang some patriotic ballad or another.[16]

Although the much smaller Michino'o/Togitsu metal foundry detachments could not compete with the Ōhashi unit in terms of sheer noise and numbers, these girls were in high spirits this fine and yet-too-hot hot morning. Today it was Sister Yoshi's turn to escort them to their respective work floors. To enjoy this pleasant weather while it lasted, Sister Yoshi decided to forgo the usual dusty Urakami Valley main drag, the Togitsu Road, and instead head the group north along back streets and bucolic farm lanes to reach the foundries.

Back at the Junshin campus, the junior novices were still cleaning up after breakfast when sirens for a warning alert—quickly upgraded to an air raid alert—began echoing throughout the valley. Mother Ezumi, as she always did upon hearing air raid alarms, rushed to secure Junshin's most sacred icon—a crucifix bestowed upon the order by Bishop Hayasaka. Once she took this down from her office wall, she cradled the precious item while assuming a crouch in a smaller slit trench beside the main building entrance. As per Junshin SOP, everyone else made for the larger trenches on the school's athletic ground. There, Sister Hatanaka Yoshino, one of the novices, watched as Sister Clara—the order's normally drill-sergeant-strict novitiate mistress—mumbled prayers and nervously thumbed her rosary.[17]

With the morning's drama apparently coming to an end with the 0830 all clear, the campus returned to its normal workaday routine. In the dining hall, the novices finished their interrupted breakfast cleanup, then headed out to the truck patches for another day of pulling radishes and weeds. In her office, Mother Ezumi returned the Founder's Crucifix to its spot of honor on the wall—right next to the Kempeitai-imposed *kamidana* installation; then she went back to the politically tricky business of running a Catholic parochial school in a Shintō country at war with—and more recently being bombed by—other Christians.

Fukuro-machi
One hundred twenty meters north of Nigiwai Bridge

Tateno Sueko woke up at her usual 0630. After participating in the semi-mandatory daily morning ritual of radio gymnastics with the other members of the Fukuro-machi neighborhood association, she marched off with her volunteer work team to begin another day of drudgery at the shelter-digging site in Togiya-machi.

Work had been underway for less than an hour when the 0748 warning alert sounded. At this signal, Sueko and the other underage members of the work team took shelter in the same hole they were helping to dig. Two minutes later, they were joined by their adult colleagues. Work resumed after the 0830 all clear, and Sueko returned to her regular slog of toting excavated soil to the sandbag-filling team on the edge of the worksite.

Shimonishiyama-machi
1.4 kilometers from Nigiwai Bridge

On a normal day in their second-story boarding room, the Gunge brothers would have enjoyed only a few minutes of each other's fully conscious company in the brief time window they had together. But this morning, an air raid alert had sounded just as Yoshio was about to leave, so he was able to spend some unscheduled and rare downtime with his younger brother.

The brothers leisurely chatted for the next forty minutes, until the all clear sounded at 0830. At this, Yoshio set off to begin his half-kilometer walk to the Suwa Shrine streetcar stop while Norio watched from a window to give his brother his customary wave at the front gate. When Yoshio was still a few steps from reaching the street, he stopped in his tracks, turned around, and called up to his brother.

"Hey, I forgot my fountain pen. . . . Could you bring it down for me?"

Ever the obedient younger brother, Norio did as requested and handed over the pen.

When Yoshio reached the gate, he turned around and, smiling warmly, gave his brother one final wave.

"CAN ANY OTHER GODDAMNED THING GO WRONG?"

Yahata Steel Works
8.5 kilometers west of Kokura aiming point
0930 local time

SIRENS WERE SOUNDING an air raid alert across Yahata for the second time in twenty-two hours. Following instructions from his supervisor, sixteen-year-old Miyashiro Satoru bounded up to the roof of his workplace to set alight a row of coal tar barrels.

Once the barrels reached full blaze, these crude but effective smoke screen generators belched thick black plumes up into an already overcast sky still hazy from the previous day's B-29 raid on the city. Borne on the morning's prevailing winds, the smoke spread quickly over the Yahata plant. Soon it was cloaking the skies to the east in murk as far as Miyashiro could see.[1]

Himeshima Island
Designated initial point for Kokura bomb run
Seventy-five kilometers east-southeast of target

At approximately 0915 local time, *Bockscar* and *The Great Artiste* banked left from their northerly ingress course to enter their westerly bomb run on Kokura Arsenal. At their assigned airspeed of three hundred kilometers per hour, the target was fifteen minutes away.

Ten minutes out, *Bockscar* bombardier Captain Beahan could already see, from his plexiglass-encased vantage point in *Bockscar*'s nose, that the target area "was completely covered by clouds and industrial haze," and this was duly reported to Sweeney.[2] Nevertheless, the bomb run continued on course. Visibility might improve with proximity to the target, and if Beahan could find even the smallest hole in the smoke and clouds over his aiming point, the Manhattan Project was about to claim its second Japanese city.

Beahan flipped a switch and *Bockscar*'s pneumatically operated bomb bay doors snapped open.[3] When he reported this had been done, the rest of the crew donned their welder's goggles[4]—while Beahan, without goggles, crouched behind his Norden bombsight. If he located the AP in the bombsight's crosshairs, he would flip an initiating switch, and Sergeant Spitzer would begin broadcasting a sixty-seconds-to-drop signal tone to *The Great Artiste* that would continue humming in the headsets of all crew members in the strike force until the instant that Fat Man fell free from *Bockscar*. The signal would also be monitored on radio sets 2,500 kilometers away, at 509th CG HQ on Tinian, and at General LeMay's XXI BC HQ on Guam.

The purpose of the drop signal was to let the instrumentation plane know when to deploy its radiosondes and go into its 155-degree escape turn—a maneuver that would be mirrored by *Bockscar*, heading in the opposite direction to avoid the possibility of collision. If the turns were performed properly and with sufficient dive-assisted airspeed, the planes would be far enough way to escape the worst of the blast effect when Fat Man detonated after its forty-three-second, 9,500-meter free fall plummet toward the target.

Although the crew had been able to make out certain landscape features in Kokura—even individual streets and parks—earlier in the bomb run, Beahan's AP remained shrouded in murk and clouds.[5] Repeating his assessment that a visual drop was impossible, the bombardier snapped the bomb bay doors shut and Spitzer canceled the drop signal tone.

Sweeney flipped his coms switch to "intercom," barked, "No drop! Repeat, no drop!" and banked *Bockscar* back toward the IP.[6] From

"CAN ANY OTHER GODDAMNED THING GO WRONG?"

there, he would take the two-plane attack formation on a second bomb run, this time from a slightly different angle, in hopes that this might give Beahan a better chance for a clear shot at the arsenal.

As Sweeney powered the plane through a wide, wheeling turn, tail gunner Dehart got on the intercom to shout, "Flak! Wide but altitude is perfect."[7] The special high-firing antiaircraft artillery protecting Kokura had opened up with its first salvo.[8]

As the formation bore in for its second go at the arsenal, the flak batteries—ten kilometers straight down from their high-speed-moving targets—began improving their aim, and *Bockscar* was buffeted by several near misses. In an attempt to throw off the flak gunners' accuracy and the airburst height-fusing of their shells, Sweeney pulled up on his controls to give his plane another 330 meters of altitude. But the experienced Kokura gunners were quick on the ball, and they shifted fire to match Sweeney's maneuver.

Dehart broke in on the intercom again, his voice now carrying a panicky edge.

"This damn flak is right on our tail and getting closer."

"Forget it, Pappy," Sweeney said, using the tail gunner's nickname. "We're on a bomb run."[9]

While Sweeney's sangfroid routine was apparently convincing—an admirable skill in any leader—it was for nought. Halfway through the bomb run, Beahan reported once again that he could not make out Kokura Arsenal.

At this point, flight engineer Kuharek warned Sweeney that as a result of their spending too much time lingering over Yakushima and flying back and forth over Kokura, *Bockscar*'s fuel situation was rapidly deteriorating—a problem compounded by the continued inaccessibility of the contents of the reserve tank. *Bockscar* was no longer capable of making it back to Tinian and would have to land at Iwo or, if things got much worse, the much closer Okinawa. Despite this burgeoning crisis, Sweeney was determined to take one more shot at the primary. After a quick flight deck conference with Ashworth, he swung *Bockscar* back toward the IP.[10]

As the flak continued to fine-tune its range on the formation,

Beser called in to report that the strike force might soon have company: His equipment was picking up radio signal patterns consistent with Japanese air controllers scrambling fighter interceptors.[11] If the Japanese planes were older Zeros, the high-flying Americans probably did not have much to worry about. But if they were newer, high-powered designs—such as the Mitsubishi Raiden or Kawanishi Shidenkai—things could get dicey within the next ten minutes or so. It was not a scenario the crew would relish, flying on a B-29 stripped of all of its defensive armament save the tail guns, not to mention carrying an armed atomic bomb.

While Beser and Pappy Dehart kept tabs on this developing situation, navigator Van Pelt and radar operator Buckley were getting a good, clear radar picture of the aiming point—data that could be used if Beahan came up empty again and Sweeney and Ashworth opted at the last second to forgo the visual-only directive[12] and drop by radar.

In the end, though, mission commander and weaponeer nixed the radar option; after Beahan's third and last "No drop!" pronouncement, Sweeney pointed *Bockscar* west to fly on to the secondary target—fuel willing. As the strike force left Kokura, Dehart got on the intercom to report Japanese fighters emerging from the clouds below.[13] Their appearance—and the strike force's departure—was heralded with a few final desultory puffs of flak.

The people of Kokura—and the rest of the world—would not know for another ten years how close their city had come to going down in history as Hiroshima's partner in atomic obliteration.

As *Bockscar* winged away from the abandoned primary target, Sweeney noticed that *The Great Artiste* was not in its assigned formation spot off his right wing. Assuming he was addressing the crew over the intercom, he called out, "Where's Bock?" A beat or two later, a familiar and, under the circumstances, decidedly unwelcome Texas-accented voice crackled in his headset: *"Chuck? Is that you, Chuck? Where the* hayl *are you?"*[14]

Unbeknownst to Sweeney, his elbow had bumped into his coms switch at some point—perhaps as he was pulling *Bockscar* around to exit the target area—and this had changed the switch's setting from "intercom" to "radio transmit." And now Hopkins, the 509th's lost ops boss, was compounding Sweeney's radio silence breach by letting any enemy listening post with a signal direction finder know that there was an at least two-plane American formation flown by highly agitated pilots trying to find their bearings somewhere over northern Kyushu.

Chagrined as much by his own carelessness as he was at Hopkins', Sweeney ignored the Texan and, setting his coms switch back to "intercom," calmly requested Van Pelt to give him the heading for Nagasaki.[15] The mission was now nearly two and a half hours behind schedule, and *Bockscar* would soon be flying on fumes.

His anger briefly returning, Sweeney turned to copilot Albury and exclaimed, "Can any other goddamned thing go wrong?"[16]

The flight logs of the principal crew members involved in piloting or navigation on Special Mission #16 have been missing since the end of the war.[17] This means it is impossible to ascertain the exact flight path taken by the Fat Man strike force from Kokura to Nagasaki. The best that can be done toward tracing the most likely route is to piece together vague hints from crew member (and passenger) testimony—most of them recorded decades after the fact—and cross-reference these with contemporary Japanese military records.

In postwar memoirs, Albury recalls turning south and away from Ashiya[18]—west of Yawata—after more Japanese aircraft were detected scrambling from an air base there. Aside from that location, however, no other verifiable geographical place-names appear in any American testimony until the strike force is closing in on its target.[19] In William Laurence's *New York Times* account of the mission, published three weeks after the war ended, he recalls the strike force flying "southward down the channel"—probably the Ariake Sea—before turning left and heading due west into the Nagasaki bomb run.

Japanese air observer reports from the ground support this theorized south-then-west ingress dogleg. At 1053 local time, a

Japanese air defense post in Kumamoto spotted "a" B-29 (singular) far to the north of the city and headed west.[20] Some minutes later, another observation post reported "several" B-29s over the Shimabara Peninsula "presently headed in the direction of Nagasaki."[21] Since, by strict stipulation of Twentieth Air Force Field Order Number 17, there were to be no B-29s anywhere near the primary and secondary target areas on that morning, it seems almost certain that these were sightings of the Fat Man strike force headed due—or close to due—west.

Tracing a straight line through these two recorded Kumamoto and Shimabara locations and extending it through to Nagasaki suggests that, after the strike force flew some hundred fifty kilometers—thirty minutes of flying time—due south from Ashiya, it began its bomb run some twenty to thirty kilometers short (perhaps as a fuel-saving measure) of its original assigned Nagasaki IP of Uki, south of Kumamoto City.[22]

Be that as it may, what *is* conclusively known about the status of the mission at that point is that, as the two-plane formation entered the final approach to the secondary target, tempers were flaring again on the flight deck of *Bockscar*; by all visual indications thus far, the Nagasaki environs were socked in by something on the order of eight- or nine-tenths cloud cover.[23] Visibility—at least from the vantage point of the plane—was so bad, in fact, that the flight crew members had to rely on radar just to get their bearings on the city, let alone the AP.[24]

The tension was ramped up when Kuharek reported that the plane had only fifteen hundred gallons of fuel left—about three hours of flight time—in its accessible main wing tanks.[25] According to Van Pelt's updated navigation calculations, this meant that *Bockscar* now had only enough fuel for one bomb run on the designated Nagasaki AP—the Nigiwai Bridge in the city's CBD.[26] Moreover, the plane was no longer capable of making it to Iwo Jima, in which case Sweeney would have to opt for Okinawa or, barring that, have no choice but to ditch *Bockscar* in the East China Sea and hope that the air-sea-rescue teams were on the ball. Moreover, the fuel situation would be even more dire if Beahan once again missed his aiming point and the no-radar-drop directive was followed to the letter, forcing Sweeney to attempt to ferry the extra five tons of an undropped Fat Man to a friendly airbase.[27]

As Bockscar continued on its radar-guided bomb run, Beahan looked in vain for the Nigiwai Bridge.[28] The haze over downtown Nagasaki was too thick, and not even the bombardier's renowned eagle eyes could make out anything on the ground. In the meantime, he—and the Norden—was losing nearly a football field's worth of ground distance to the AP with each passing second.

From the mission commander's standpoint, a radar drop would have been the least of three evils if the other two were: (1) trying to return to Okinawa with an atomic bomb on board; or (2) ditching the bomb unexploded in the East China Sea. As the first option was too dangerous—and the second too career-endingly wasteful—to even contemplate, Sweeney decided that there was no choice but to drop the bomb on Nagasaki by whatever means available.

On the flight deck, Sweeney and Ashworth anxiously debated making a radar-aimed drop on the downtown area, with the mission commander assuring his weaponeer counterpart that he would "take full responsibility for this."[29] With the seconds ticking down to a go/no-go on the radar drop, the weaponeer finally relinquished his earlier stubborn opposition, now agreeing that they had no choice but to use this aiming method if Beahan could not visually locate the AP. Meanwhile, Van Pelt and Buckley had already worked out a good radar target solution; over the intercom, they "talked in" the necessary data for Beahan to input into the Norden, which was now flying the plane via autopilot.[30]

One minute out, Beahan opened the bomb bay doors and initiated the drop sequence. At the sound of Spitzer's drop tone signal, the goggles-donning routine was carried out for the fourth time this morning.

Perhaps half a minute later, Beahan shouted out, "I've got it! I've got it!"

Sweeney replied, "You own it."[31]

Overriding the previous drop sequence, Beahan manually reoriented *Bockscar* a few degrees to the left toward some industrial infrastructure—possibly, if not likely, the towering red-and-white smokestacks of the medical college's waste incinerators—that he had spotted poking up through the cloud cover over the Urakami Valley. Working furiously to reset the Norden for a drastically shortened drop sequence, he fixed its reticle crosshairs on a racetrack by the Urakami River roughly halfway between two Mitsubishi munitions plants. Shouting, "Thirty seconds away!" he flipped the "drop" switch.[32]

Spitzer's drop tone signal began sounding again in the headsets of everyone on board *Bockscar* and *The Great Artiste*.[33] Thirty seconds later, it cut off and *Bockscar*, now five tons lighter, leapt upward.

"Bombs away!" Beahan shouted.

A beat later, he corrected himself. "*Bomb* away!"[34]

Fat Man was in free fall, hurtling earthward toward the heart of the Urakami Valley.

DETONATION

Shimonishiyama-machi
2.9 kilometers southeast of Beahan's ad hoc aiming point

GUNGE NORIO HAD been alone in the house most of the morning since his brother, Yoshio, and their landlord, Shinagawa-sensei, had both left for their respective workplaces. In the meantime, he had been passing the hours before the 1500 start of his evening-night double shift at the Mori-machi plant reading books and thumbing through old magazines on a perch on a northwest-facing windowsill. He had taken off his shirt in hopes of catching the last few wafts of cooler night air floating down the wooded slopes of Mount Konpira behind his house, but it was an endeavor doomed to end in failure: The morning sun was beginning to heat things up, and the second floor of Shinagawa-sensei's house had already become its usual sweatbox.

Around 1100, Norio heard B-29 engines high up but almost directly overhead—the same sound he had heard over the city a few hours ago. But this time, there were no sirens—not even for a warning alert. Still, there seemed little cause for concern. The thrum of American airplanes had long since become an integral part of the soundscape of normal daily life for him, just as it had for everyone else in Nagasaki and in every other city in the Home Islands by the summer of 1945.

Norio casually craned his neck out the window to scan the neighborhood's narrow view of the sky for any sign of the bombers but found none. He gave the planes no more thought—until the steady drone of the far-off B-29 engines abruptly shifted into an angry, metallic, Dopplering growl. Fearful that his neighborhood was about to be dive-bombed, Norio instinctively turned his face away from the window and was just about to hop down from the sill when the brightest light he had ever seen froze him to the spot. In the next instant, it felt like someone had just pressed a laundry steam iron onto his bare back. He did not have time to work up a scream before the house rocked with a tremendous gust that sent him and everything in his room tumbling through the air.

Suwano-machi shelter dig site
3.6 kilometers southeast of Beahan's ad hoc AP

Tateno Sueko had been working at the shelter dig without interruption since the 0830 all clear. It had been cooler then, under a cloudier sky. But now the morning haze was clearing, and the temperature was rising.[1] Sueko had another hour of *mokko* sack toting—back and forth between the shelter ditch and the sandbag-filling team—before the noon break, when she would be able to run home to grab a bite and refill her canteen. Hopefully, today's break would not be interrupted by another air raid alert, as had happened the previous day.

Her train of thought was broken by the sound of multiple engines droning far off overhead. At this, she lay down her *mokko* and searched the sky for the usual high-flying silvery (and sometimes contrail-streaming) suspects, but today she saw nothing.

She remarked to an older coworker, "Sounds like airplanes . . ."[2]

As the last syllable passed her lips, there was a dazzling flash of white light. At this, she immediately threw herself facedown into the shelter ditch and—assuming the anti-concussion posture she had been trained to use since toddlerhood—opened her mouth wide, placed her thumbs in her ears, and covered her eyes with her fingers.

About ten seconds later, a blast of hot wind hit her like a giant slap, lifting her off the ground and flinging her into the far wall of the ditch. The physical pain of the "slap" subsided quickly, but Sueko's fear did not. When she opened her eyes for the first time since the flash, the sky overhead—which had been bright a few seconds before—had turned twilight dark. As she lay trembling in fear and shock, trying in vain to make sense of what had just happened, an older man leapt into the ditch and shouted, "They've just bombed Fukuro-machi!"

Unsteadily, Sueko rose to her feet. Visions of her family members' faces flashed through her mind. She wondered if she was going to be able to make it back to her house—and, if she could, what she would find when she got there.

Junshin Girls' School
Ieno-machi
1.4 kilometers north of Beahan's ad hoc aiming point

Sister Hatanaka was preparing the altar in the school chapel as the hour approached for the morning's Eucharistic Adoration—one of the contemplative exercises in the order's daily officium schedule.[3] After setting out the ciborium, the chalice-like container for the Eucharist communion wafers, she lit a candle signaling the arrival in the chapel of Christ's corporeal presence.

Good Catholics that they were, the Junshin Sisters were firm believers in literal transubstantiation; true to their creed and vows, they would protect the Eucharist contained in the ciborium with their lives if circumstances so dictated. Such a contingency aside, the Sisters' normal daily interaction with the ciborium was limited to using it during the Adoration sessions as a kind of meditative-prayer mandala. Of not-insignificant benefit in summertime Nagasaki, these ciborium-focused daily prayers also allowed the Sisters to enjoy a respite from the blazing sun outdoors for an hour or so.

At the appointed time, those novices who were able to get away from their manual labor tasks—either in the dining hall kitchen or out on the truck patches—filed into the chapel, blessing themselves with holy water as they entered; then they joined the senior Sisters in the pews. Once Sister Hatanaka was satisfied that everyone who was going to show up was present, she began the Adoration session by making the sign of the cross. This gesture was mirrored by the assembly.

At the moment Sister Hatanaka brought her hands together in prayer, an intense light shone through the chapel's stained glass windows. Acting by pure reflex, she grabbed up the ciborium, covered it with its special gold brocade cloth, and had just brought it to her chest in a protective embrace when the windows blew in.[4]

———

Five kilometers north-northwest of Junshin, Sister Yoshi was in the second-floor office of the Togitsu branch of Sonoda Foundries writing a prayer to recite with her students to celebrate the upcoming August 15 anniversary of the Assumption of Mary when the walls turned a blinding white.[5] Simultaneously, she felt an unfamiliar heat on her back penetrating right through her work clothes. Turning to look out the south-facing window, she saw a large ball of pulsing, smoke-trailing fire silently rising above Mount Konpira. Overcoming the urge to stand in place and watch this uncanny false sunrise, she grabbed up her things and ran into the next room, where the Junshin detachment girls were working. The moment she closed the door behind her, the whole building wobbled under an abrupt inrush of air— more freak wind gust than explosion—and its windows shattered.

After a few dumbstruck seconds, Sister Yoshi was snapped back into situational awareness by the screams and cries of the children in the building.[6] After taking a quick accounting of her charges on the second floor, she herded them downstairs, where she made sure everyone—including the first-floor workers—got out of the building and down into the nearby slit trenches they had been digging all summer. Some of the Junshin girls started praying aloud.

DETONATION

Mitsubishi Shipyards Ōhashi plant
Ieno-machi
1.4 kilometers from Beahan's ad hoc aiming point

A few minutes before 1100, the loudspeaker system in the Main Torpedo Assembly Building crackled with a local air defense bulletin: "Large enemy aircraft have been spotted near Isahaya, headed west."[7] But no one on the factory floor, including Ishida Masako, paid much attention to the seemingly routine bogey warning.

At her worktable in the waterproofing section, Masako was beginning to feel hungry. Wondering how long she was going to have to wait until lunchtime, she glanced up at a wall clock. At that instant, the factory floor was bathed in a heat-emitting pinkish-yellow glow. Instinctively realizing that there was something "off" about this light, she shut her eyes tight and hit the floor between two large blocks of heavy machinery as her brain raced to interpret what was happening. She had just enough time to come up with a theory that one of the plant's torpedoes must have exploded before the factory ceiling and all of its girders and gantries came crashing down. In the next instant, a hot gust of wind blew her a few meters across the floor. She came to a stop when she felt something hard and heavy fall onto and pin her leg. Then she passed out.

When she came to, the air was dark with airborne dust—much of it no doubt asbestos from the roofing material—and permeated with the hot, ferrous odor of blood. Freeing her leg, she stood up and, through her confusion and shock, attempted to make some kind of sense out of her current situation.

Like anyone else in the building who survived the ceiling collapse, Masako had been able to do so because she had hit the floor between sturdy objects—big machine stands, worktables, and the like—that had taken the brunt of the impact of the falling girders and roofing material. But despite this initial stroke of luck, she was far from being out of danger; she began to feel pain from her leg now, although she did not yet feel any from whatever it was that was dripping down her arm. She glanced at the front of her Kenjo uniform blouse and it was soaked in blood, looking like someone had upended a bottle of red ink onto it.[8]

Nearby, one of the full-time Mitsubishi employees was tearing off strips of blackout curtain and handing these out as bandaging material. Masako had just received one for herself when she saw the first tongues of flame begin to lick up and out from under the wreckage. This prompted a round of loud masculine voices yelling, "Fire!" and ordering the female workers to evacuate the building. These voices of authority were quickly drowned out as the scene descended into general screaming chaos and the air filled with smoke, dust, darting flames, and the thunderous clap-clomping of hundreds of *geta*-shod feet frantically scrambling over piles of wreckage.[9]

The fires began closing in from all directions. In the shattered, now fiercely burning Main Torpedo Assembly Building, hundreds still trapped under the wreckage shouted for help; shortly, these voices would change to screams as they were steadily enveloped by the encroaching flames. Masako was in danger of becoming one of them if she did not start moving, but for the moment, she was still frozen in place with shock and indecision.

Mitsubishi Steel and Arms Works

Mori-machi

1.3 kilometers from Beahan's ad hoc aiming point

At 1102, Michiko and several other girls were sitting around a table filing small metal parts when there was a sudden flash of intense light. At first, Michiko wondered if one of the overhead gantry cranes had broken down again, as these frequently did, always emitting showers of arcing bright sparks whenever this happened.

Like many who survived the bomb at close range, Michiko did not hear any explosion. Michiko would not hear anything until a few sec-

DETONATION

onds later, when sound-carrying air rushed back in to fill the dome of blast-voided atmospheric vacuum over Urakami. When this happened, the first things Michiko heard—just before she passed out—were screams and the sounds of girders, roofing material, and toppling machinery crashing down all around her.[10] Instinctively, she hit the floor, but when she finally came to—whether seconds or minutes later—she found herself in a pocket of space formed by fallen roofing material bridging two large pieces of machinery she had fallen between. This configuration had prevented any of the falling wreckage from directly impacting her body, and the only physical injury she had suffered—probably from flying glass shrapnel—was a small cut on her arm. Nevertheless, she was trapped.

Michiko's workplace—the torpedo finishing section—was the closest facility in the Mori-machi compound to GZ. Bereft of the shielding benefits of any intervening substantial structures or defilade-providing terrain, the lightly constructed, hangar-like building caught the blast from Fat Man's nearby twenty-kiloton detonation full on, and it went down like a house of cards. If it had been made of more substantial steel-reinforced concrete or brick, the collapse of its roof under Fat Man's supersonic downward shock wave would have showered the factory floor below with masonry missiles—ballistic chunks and bits of all sizes—against which tables and machinery would have offered little in the way of shelter. In fact, many of the workers in the older buildings in the Mori-machi compound were killed or horribly mangled on account of this difference in building materials.[11]

Still in shock, Michiko somehow managed to extricate herself from her wreckage trap and get out of the ruined building, the contents of which—and the people trapped within—were also beginning to burn. Looking about to get her bearings, she found that at least momentarily she was unable to do so; this was due not only to the smoky false twilight now blotting out the sun but also because all of the buildings in the Mori-machi compound that had been there a minute or two earlier no longer existed.

Prefectural civil defense HQ bunker
Rokasu-machi
2.7 kilometers south-southeast of Beahan's ad hoc AP

Governor Nagano's air-raid-alert-delayed meeting was finally underway.[12] Addressing his assembled department heads as well as police and fire officials, he had started off the meeting with its most urgent agenda item—his decision to order the immediate evacuation from Nagasaki City of all schoolchildren and other civilian residents who were not directly engaged in war production work.[13] While most other municipalities in the country (including Hiroshima) had already undertaken such evacuation efforts earlier that summer, following the lead of Tokyo and the other major metropolises on Honshu, Nagasaki's response had been sluggish and piecemeal in comparison.[14] Nagano was of the opinion that this was unacceptable, particularly considering what had just happened in Hiroshima. Once he was sure he had everyone on board with his decision, the meeting moved on to a discussion of ongoing firebreak-clearing work and provisions for residents who had lost their homes as a result of their associated evictions.[15]

In the midst of this discussion, a clerk entered the meeting room and informed the governor that Mayor Ko'ura Sōhei of Sasebo was waiting outside[16] with an urgent matter to discuss. After Ko'ura was shown in, he immediately blurted out, "Something really terrible has happened to Hiroshima."[17]

"Wait a moment," the governor said. "Where did you come about this information?"

"I heard it directly from the commander of the Sasebo Naval Garrison," Ko'ura replied.

"Well, that is very timely news," Nagano said, "because we just happen to be holding a meeting to discuss that very subject. Please tell us exactly what the garrison commander told you."

At that moment, the lights in the bunker flickered out.

"Are there any candles in here?" Nagano asked the room.

DETONATION

"There are," responded Special High Police Chief Nakamura.

As soon as he said this, the lights flickered back on. Then the bunker echoed with a deep, rolling boom. Nagano's first thought was that a conventional bomb had landed nearby. Chief Nakamura ran outside of the bunker to take a look, but when he returned, he reported that he could see no sign of any nearby explosion. Someone offered that perhaps the Americans were going after the shipyard again, but Nakamura did not think so. He had been told by a group of workmen who had been outside on the street that there had been an intense flash of light seemingly emanating from behind Mount Konpira, followed by the sound of a loud explosion.[18]

"Perhaps it is one of those new-type bombs we were discussing last night," Nakamura said.

"That can't be right," Nagano replied. "Those things are supposed to wipe out everyone and everything in sight, but you are saying there are people standing around outside talking. . . ."[19]

At 1102 local time, Fat Man exploded at an altitude of five hundred meters over a tennis court in Matsuyama-chō, two hundred meters east of the racetrack Beahan had used as his aiming point.[20] For approximately eight seconds after detonation, everything (and everyone) out to about a kilometer and a half from the bomb's fireball was bathed in thermal radiation to a temperature of some four thousand degrees Celsius, which was hot enough to melt the surface of ceramic roof tiles.[21]

Once Fat Man's shock wave reached the ground at the full range of its destruction, nearly every man-made structure—including some eighteen thousand homes—was flattened[22] across an oblong Zone of Total Destruction (ZTD) of 6.7 square kilometers.[23] Channeled and contained by the contours of the terrain, the ZTD extended from Nagasaki Station in the south to Ieno-machi in the north, running the breadth of the valley in between.[24] If Nagasaki—like Hiroshima—had been built on flat terrain better suited for maximizing the blast damage of an atomic bomb, its ZTD would have been five times larger, no doubt also encompassing the entirety of the downtown area, with a commensurate increase in death toll that could very well have surpassed Hiroshima's total (by year's end) of 140,000. Instead, the most densely populated part of the city—the CBD—had been saved by the shadow of Mount Konpira[25] from the worst of Fat Man's blast force, direct line-of-sight thermal rays, and prompt gamma and neutron radiation. But even with the defilade protection provided to so much of the city by its terrain, Fat Man's triple-lethality repertoire of blast effects, thermal burns, and acute radiation syndrome (ARS) would still kill some 74,000 of Nagasaki's 250,000 residents (again, by year's end) and wound another 75,000.[26]

———

The strike force planes' post-drop escape maneuvers had taken them some eleven kilometers away from Urakami, headed east-northeast, by the time Fat Man detonated,[27] "illuminating the entire sky all around" with "a bluish-green light."[28] After the flash and despite the already dire and steadily worsening fuel situation, Sweeney wheeled *Bockscar* around to make one final pass over the city to assess and photograph the mission's handiwork, albeit not with Serber's fancy Fastax camera.

Bockscar's crew had taken off their flash goggles by this point and many were now staring out of apertures on the left side of the fuselage at the roiling column of multicolored smoke rocketing up from the floor of the Urakami Valley.[29] The smoke had already nearly reached the strike force's altitude when its planes were buffeted by the first and strongest of three rapid-succession shock waves—one stemming directly from the blast and the other two from its reflection off of Nagasaki's convoluted topography.[30]

After the fleeting interruption of the aftershock rattlings, crew members of the two strike force planes resumed their observation of the continuing ascent of the uncanny smoke column, which was still a few minutes and a few thousand meters away from assuming its

iconic mushroom cloud configuration. From *Bockscar*'s cockpit, Sweeney saw "a vertical column, boiling and bubbling up in those rainbow
hues—purples, oranges, reds—colors whose brilliance I had seen only
once before and would never see again. The cloud was rising faster
than at Hiroshima. It seemed more intense, angrier. It was a mesmer-
izing sight, at once breathtaking and ominous."[31]

From his bombardier's station perch on *The Great Artiste*, *New
York Times* reporter William Laurence saw "a meteor coming from the
earth instead of from outer space, becoming ever more alive as it
climbed skyward. . . . It was no longer smoke, or dust, or even a cloud
of fire. It was a living thing, a new species of being, born right before
our incredulous eyes. . . . [I]t was a living totem pole, carved with many
grotesque masks grimacing at the earth."[32]

After the strike force's single circuit of the target area, Sweeney
straightened *Bockscar* up to head due south for Okinawa. Then he ordered Spitzer to radio the bombing results report:

> *Bombed Nagasaki 090158Z visually. No opposition. Results
> technically successful. Visible effects about equal to Hiroshima.
> Proceeding to Okinawa. Fuel problem.*[33]

PART FOUR

DEATH VALLEY

A SEA OF FIRE

Mori-machi
1.4 kilometers south of GZ

AFTER EMERGING FROM the collapsed torpedo finishing section building, Kiridōshi Michiko stumbled along with the flow of fleeing workers heading toward the main Mori-machi gate. At one point in this exodus, however, she found her forward progress blocked by a man who was charred completely black from head to toe. The man was staggering around the same spot in a tight circle, mumbling incoherently to himself. From his burns and what was left of his work outfit, he appeared to have been a full-time Mitsubishi professional caught outdoors by whatever had just destroyed the Urakami Valley.

Frozen in place by a mixture of horror, disgust, and pity, Michiko wondered if she should help the man—which none of the people streaming past seemed inclined to do—or simply join the rest of the hell-bent fleeing crowd to make good her own escape. After a few long seconds, she was relieved of the burden of this decision when she heard a girl's voice emerging from the chaos behind her and calling her name. It was her best Kenjo friend and coworker, Honda Sawa, returning the shoulder-strapped emergency bag Michiko had left on the factory floor during her initial panicked escape from the collapsed building. Apparently, the normally rather meek and withdrawn Sawa had made her way from her own ruined workstation—in the plant manager's office loft—through the flames and stampeding crowds in the ruined factory to look for Michiko. Upon reaching the polishing section's workstation, she found no trace of her friend except for her abandoned first aid shoulder bag, which Sawa-san had had the presence of mind to take with her when she finally made her own exit from the wreckage. Michiko would never know whether Sawa-san had done this with the intent of returning it to its owner or perhaps, in a sadder scenario, giving it to a bereaved Kiridōshi family as a personal effect.

At the moment, Michiko's most pressing consideration was to get Sawa up to speed on her charred man conundrum. After a brief discussion, the girls shouldered the grievously injured Mitsubishi man—one under each of his arms—and led him toward the factory gate. From there, they took him across Togitsu Road[1] to the closest Morimachi employees' air raid evacuation point. This was a large-capacity tunnel-type shelter dug into an embankment-cut cliff face where the Togitsu Road curled around the southwest base of Mount Konpira.

The shelter was packed with evacuees and screaming or moaning victims. It was also permeated with a stomach-wrenching stench of vomit and burned flesh. Amidst this reeking pandemonium, the less injured were trying to care for the worse off, many of whom were badly burned and—like the man the girls were carrying—clearly close to death.

The prostrate forms of the dying covered the floor of the shelter wall to wall. Adding an unwelcome brass section to this symphony of misery, a group of patriotic stalwarts in the back of the tunnel was loudly chanting the Imperial Rescript to Soldiers and Sailors. Even though, like everyone else in the country, Michiko had long ago memorized the rescript word for word—thanks to countless schoolyard *chōrei* recitations since childhood—the thought of joining the present chorus never entered her mind.

With some effort, the girls managed to find space on the shelter floor to lay down their ailing charge. They stayed by the Mitsubishi man's side for ten or so completely wordless and excruciatingly long minutes. Finally, the sights, sounds, and smells of the shelter proved more than they could stand, and they took their leave.

After stepping over bodies to reach the shelter entrance, the girls were crestfallen to see that the Togitsu Road—the southbound first leg of their usual route to reach their homes in the eastern CBD—was completely impassable in that direction. Hundreds of houses and other structures had tumbled down the lower western slopes of Mount Konpira. On the level ground below, the tangled, burning debris from this man-made landslide was piled so deep that it was impossible to see the roadway anymore. Nothing—not only streetcars and other vehicles, but foot traffic[2] as well—was going to get through that mess.

Still with no grasp of the geographical extent of the devastation caused by the explosion, the girls briefly considered a marathon hike in the opposite direction: up the Togitsu Road, then around the northern foot of Konpira and down through Nishiyama to reach the CBD. But they had second thoughts when they noted the southbound crowds they would have to fight their way through to take that route. And once they caught sight of the towering and billowing cloud of smoke rising in the twilight-dark sky to the north, the Konpira-circumnavigation idea was dismissed out of hand. As they soon came to understand, there was only one way out of their present predicament; if they could not go around Mount Konpira, they were going to have to go over it.

Grabbing onto the scrub tree branches and bush clumps ringing the shelter entrance, the girls began to slowly pull themselves up. During the ascent, Michiko was grateful for the sturdy, brand-new *geta* that she had recently received through the neighborhood association rationing system. They would serve her well over the next twenty hours.[3]

Before long, the girls reached the first substantial patch of level land during their climb—the cemetery of Shotokuji Temple. Like the rest of Konpira they had seen so far, this spot was also a mess, although it was not quite as piled with house wreckage as everywhere else. Still, it was a sorry sight. The temple building itself was a shambles, and all of the headstones in the cemetery had been toppled to point away from the explosion and toward the CBD to the southeast.

While the girls rested up for their next round of climbing, Michiko passed the time looking at the headstones, noting the names and dates written on each. As she did so, she began to wonder if she was going to survive this day. Continuing this memento mori–triggered train of thought, she imagined a tombstone reading, "Kiridōshi Michiko, August 9, Aged 15."[4]

The appearance of new tongues of fire in the rubble around the cemetery prompted the girls to realize that their present sanctuary was only temporary; they were going to have to hurry to reach higher ground. Unfortunately, every potential ascent route was covered in multilayered piles of house wreckage, and much of this was beginning to burn. Taking what appeared to be the path of least resistance, the girls resumed their ascent; hand in hand and choking on smoke, they picked their way over the smoldering debris, carefully placing each step to avoid a fall that might send either—or both—of them tumbling into some deep wreckage crevice or patch of fire. As they climbed, Michiko briefly wondered how many trapped people she and Sawa were stepping over to save their own lives. She quickly flushed this thought from her mind to focus on the matter of her own survival.

Not long after they had negotiated the worst of the debris field behind the cemetery, the girls encountered a bare-breasted woman and two naked young boys—perhaps four and six years old—squatting in the rubble. They were the first living people Michiko and Sawa-san had seen on Konpira so far.

The woman had a large, gaping wound in her chest. She was immobilized and clearly did not have much longer to live. With what might have literally been her last words, she pleaded with Michiko and Sawa to take her boys to safety. Perhaps with thoughts of the man they had abandoned back at the shelter still on their minds, the girls required no further entreaties from the mother to take on these new charges. Piggybacking one shell-shock-silenced boy apiece, they continued their wordless trek, leaving the dying mother to her fate.

The trek became much easier when they found a long and relatively debris-free concrete staircase curving up the mountain. The foursome took this up to its last flight, which opened out onto a level clearing where a group of people—including some soldiers and Caucasian POWs (Sawa-san believed they were Australians from Mori-machi)—was clustered around a water well. A *keibōdan* air warden who was presiding over the scene caught sight of the girls and approached them to inquire about the children they were carrying. After listening to the girls' explanation of the situation, he offered to take the boys off their hands and urged Michiko and Sawa-san to keep going.

The girls did as they were told, following a winding footpath to the upper reaches of Konpira. There they found a ginger patch that offered a spectacular vista of the surrounding area, including their own home neighborhoods. They decided that they would wait there until someone told them it was safe to come down off the mountain. As they settled in, Michiko began rummaging around in her bag. Almost as an afterthought, she pulled out and donned her padded cotton *bōkūzukin* air raid hood. In the bag she also found a covered lunch tin of boiled beans her mother had placed in there that morning. Eating these one at a time with her fingers, she sat with Sawa-san, silently watching the fires far below slowly spread from Urakami to the CBD.

<hr>

Katsuyama-machi kansha
Three kilometers southeast of GZ

The Ishida household was moving out of the old *kansha* to a new one a few blocks west in Yaoya-machi. Helping the judge that morning with the heavy lifting were several of his clerks—playing hooky from the courthouse for their boss' moving day—and the household's young live-in maid, Shige-san.

Work had been underway for several hours when a flash briefly lit up the sky. Perhaps ten seconds or so later, a tremendous boom echoed across the CBD. Simultaneously, the Katsuyama-chō house wobbled once, violently, knocking the judge off his feet. As he lay prone on the floor surrounded by a pile of loose items that had fallen on him from a nearby shelf, his first thought was not of a bomb; rather, he experienced a flashback to a personal (and national) trauma he and millions of other Japanese had experienced some twenty-two years earlier[5]—the Great Kantō Earthquake, which had leveled and burned most of Tokyo and Yokohama to the ground.

With some help from Shige-san—who had also sustained some cuts and bruises from her own fall—the judge was able to get back on his feet and go outside to try to figure out what had just happened. By now he was beginning to suspect that some kind of bomb had impacted nearby. But when he looked at the *kansha*, he saw that it had suffered nothing more than some loosened roof tiles and cracked windows. Moreover, he saw no evidence of destroyed houses, smoke, or fire in the surrounding neighborhood; nor did he hear any of the anguished screams one would have expected in a bombing scenario. Instead, he heard only the hushed whispers of stunned people milling around in the street; most of them were looking up, toward the north. Turning around to look for himself, the judge saw a huge column of smoke rising up from behind Suwa Shrine and the green mass of Konpira and slowly drifting toward Nishiyama.

When someone on the street mentioned the phrase "new-type bomb," the judge at last began to make sense of the situation. But his immediate concern was not about his daughter in Ōhashi but rather about his duty. After instructing Shige-san and his clerks to watch over the house and coordinate with any authorities who might arrive on the scene, he set off on foot to the west—now nursing what he recognized was a lightly sprained ankle—to check if the courthouse had suffered any damage.[6]

Mitsubishi Shipyards Ōhashi plant
Ieno-machi
1.4 kilometers north of GZ

Ishida Masako was initially at a complete loss as to how to get out of the burning ruins of the main torpedo assembly building. None of her

A SEA OF FIRE 235

Kenjo classmates were anywhere to be seen, and she did not begin moving until she attached herself to a mixed group of three Keiho girls and about an equal number of adult *jokō* female workers led by a woman named Ōta-san.[7]

For long minutes, Masako's group ran this way and that in the fire-orange murk, only to find each potential escape route blocked by either flames or debris. Their progress was also impeded by the twisted corrugated sheet metal they were forced to clamber over. As Masako soon realized, *geta* were singularly unsuited for this uneven, slippery surface, and she fell flat on her face numerous times during the escape scramble.

Adding to the mood of panic and futility, the air was filled with the screams and weeping of yet-ambulatory survivors and the pathetic mewling of dying girls trapped under tangles of roof girders or overturned piles of ruined machinery. Moreover, secondary explosions from acetylene tanks and the like were sporadically popping off, punctuating and temporarily amplifying the general pandemonium.

At long last, the intrepid Ōta-san found an opening that led to the athletic ground north of the main torpedo assembly building—the place where the Ōhashi workers gathered for their *chōrei* assemblies every morning. The roughly soccer-pitch-sized space was surrounded by other plant facilities that were now also ablaze, throwing up towering walls of smoke and flame. But it would at least provide the group with temporary sanctuary until they figured out their next move. In the meantime, the athletic ground was steadily filling up with others who had been lucky enough to find their way there. Many of these survivors were unable to walk and had been carried out by coworkers. Few if any were carried out of danger for a second time when steadily swelling fires rendered the athletic ground untenable and those who could still walk ran for their lives.

At some point, someone among the hundreds—if not thousands—assembled on the athletic ground shouted out that everyone should head for the Nagasaki Teachers College campus northeast of the plant, assuming (incorrectly) that only the Ōhashi plant had been hit and that the college would offer a safer sanctuary. Compelled by this thin straw of hope and acting under the irresistible psychological imperative of crowds in duress, the panicking survivors needed no more impetus to begin a stampede toward the Nagayo Road, oblivious to the reality that this route was going to lead them right into yet another wall of smoke and flame. As others around her began running, Masako joined them—this time without a moment of indecision—though she felt heartsick about the victims being left behind on the ground.

Chaos ensued when the crowd reached the east side of the field and found their way blocked by fire. But Masako—at last beginning to find her survival instincts and keeping her head while all around her lost theirs—caught sight of a small gap in the flames; it was the Nagayo Road gate to the factory. Masako called this out to Ōta-san and anyone within earshot who had the presence of mind not to be screaming.

As Masako and Ōta-san made their way through the gate, they came upon a horribly burned horse. Spooked by the flames and clearly in agony from its injuries, the crazed animal—instead of running away from the fire, as it could have easily done—merely circled about back and forth in front of the gate, perhaps waiting for a master who would never return.

Just east of the compound, what had been Junshin Girls' School's spread of lovely green farm patches not ten minutes before was now a singed, smoldering mat of dead brown stalks. Corpses were strewn about on the road as far as the eye could see, and houses were on fire all the way to the horizon. The air stank of blood and scorched flesh. Masako and Ōta-san—who were on their own now, having lost the other members of their group in the athletic field panic—walked out onto the burned field to figure out where to go next.

During this pause in their flight, they encountered a specter so surreal that Masako at first thought she was hallucinating: It was a man standing straight and motionless like a scarecrow. Masako looked at him a little closer, and she caught some movement. Her line of sight traced this to the man's hand, which held a raw eggplant he was methodically nibbling. Looking a little higher, she saw that half of the man's cranium had been blown off. It would be only when she recalled this long-blocked memory decades later that she paused to contemplate how such a thing might have been physiologically possible. In the moment, though, she merely shuddered in horror and looked away, back toward Ōhashi, which with everything around it and all the way up into the ridges and foothills on both sides of the valley seemed to be aflame and belching smoke. For the first time since all of the commotion had started, Masako began to worry about her father and wondered if the devastation had reached all the way to Katsuyama-machi.

Masako and Ōta-san could not remain on the field any longer. All of the structures up and down the Nagayo Road—including Junshin Girls' School—were on fire, so the only way out appeared to be to cut east across the rest of Junshin's athletic ground. However, this route soon threw up another obstacle: the Urakami River. Normally this would not have been a particularly daunting barrier—the river was so shallow at this point that it could have been easily waded across. However, at the moment, it was filled with burned, lacerated, and mostly naked bodies—victims, many of them scorched bald, whose dying act had been to jump into the water in a desperate attempt to soothe the pain of their injuries. Swallowing their horror and disgust, Masako and Ōta-san stepped down into the corpse-clogged water and began wading. During their crossing, Masako lost one of her *geta*, while Ōta-san lost both of hers. Neither was enthusiastic about putting their hands down into the water to try to fish them out, so they kept going.

Coming up on the opposite bank, the pair found their easterly progress blocked by burning house wreckage, so they had no choice but to take a farmer's path south through more singed fields and past more burning structures and dead bodies. The ground under their bare feet (or foot, in Masako's case) was hot and strewn with torn metal bits and broken glass, so as they walked, they kept their eyes out for salvageable footwear. Finding none, Masako picked up a shred of reed matting and wrapped it around her bare foot. The solution worked for only a short while before disintegrating, so she gave up on the idea of trying this again, and in the meantime, in lieu of hobbling along on one *geta*, she went barefoot instead. She made sure to hold on to the remaining *geta*, however, against the possibility that it would come in handy later. (It would not, as she would later lose it in the crush of fleeing crowds on Togitsu Road.)

The twosome's southerly progress stopped when they reached the collapsed railway crossing at Ōhashi Bridge. As they stood around trying to figure out their next move, Masako heard a man's voice behind her.

"Hey, you two," the man said, "where are you coming from? The weapons plant?"[8]

The women answered in the affirmative, and the man told them that things were worse—much worse—to the south, so their best bet would be to keep following the tracks north to Michino'o, where an aid station had been set up near the railroad underpass. At this, Masako, Ōta-san, and the helpful man joined the throngs of people heading north on the Togitsu Road, paralleling the Kokutetsu tracks.

Takami family pine grove

Mitsuyama-machi

5.3 kilometers northeast of GZ

The members of the morning's Junshin pine-sap detachment had been at work on Mitsuyama Hill for about two hours and were about to break for lunch when they heard the faint sound of aircraft engines far overhead.[9] As this sound droned on high and distant, a flash emanating from the southwest briefly lit up the sky. As no sound immediately followed this heat lightning–like illumination, the Sisters and their first-year charges thought no more of it and went back to their work. But when a tremendous boom shook the air some ten seconds later, everyone ran into the nearest tree line to take cover, assuming that Mitsuyama was under attack. Meanwhile, a plume of smoke from the southwest gradually crept into the sky over their position, casting the pine grove under a pall of gloom.

The work detail members came out from under their cover only some minutes after they heard the last of the aircraft sounds fade off in the distance. As they emerged back into the clearing, an intense squall began. But mixed in with the falling raindrops were leaves of singed paper. A Sister picked one of these pieces of paper up—it was company letterhead from some factory. Then she picked up others and, to her astonishment, saw that they were pages from Bibles and hymnbooks. In that instant, she knew that something terrible had happened in Urakami. Everyone put all of their tree-tapping tools into the wheelbarrow with their uneaten *bentō* lunches, and the detachment set off down the hill posthaste to head back to Junshin and do whatever they could to help.

As the group wended their way down Nagayo Road, they passed ever-increasing numbers of horribly injured people going in the opposite direction, away from Urakami. From time to time, when they came across someone who looked like they might still be in mental and physical condition to speak, the Sisters would ask them if they knew what had happened to Junshin. Each one of them who answered affirmatively used the same term to describe the shattered school and grounds they had seen there: *hi no umi* ("a sea of fire").[10]

THE NAGASAKI CABLE

Prefectural civil defense HQ bunker
Rokasu-machi
2.7 kilometers south-southeast of GZ

AFTER EYEWITNESS REPORTS about parachute-dropped bombs and spreading fires began coming in from police and other authorities in districts surrounding the Urakami Valley (but ominously not from *in* the valley), Governor Nagano stepped outside of the Rokasu-machi bunker to look at the massive smoke column rising up from behind Mount Konpira.[1] Upon seeing this, he concluded that two bombs had been dropped on the northern end of his prefectural capital. He then returned to the bunker (which would have been equipped with a backup electrical generator), where he drafted and ordered the transmission of a report to his higher-ups (both civilian and military) in Fukuoka.

Concurrently, Nagano directed the prefectural chief of police to mobilize his sixty-odd-man-strong *keibitai* guard rescue unit, which was headquartered directly across the street from the Rokasu-machi civil defense bunker. Nagasaki's *keibitai* members had all been present on-site as a result of the morning's earlier warning and air raid alerts and they had sustained neither casualties nor damage to their HQ building from the explosion.[2]

As the prefectural *keibitai* was the only intact civilian first-responder organization in the city by this point, its members were immediately dispatched to the Urakami Valley to assist in rescue and information-gathering efforts. Finding their initial attempted foray into the ZTD blocked by the hopelessly debris-clogged (and burning) Togitsu Road, they were forced to double back and begin climbing up the southern slopes of Konpira to make any headway. The shattered victims they began encountering there put paid to Governor Nagano's overly optimistic report about the extent of the city's damage and death toll, and runners were sent back to the civil defense bunker to report as much.

=====

Imperial Library annex
Chiyoda Ward, Tokyo
Nine hundred forty-five kilometers east-northeast of GZ

Approximately half an hour before Fat Man detonated over the Urakami Valley, the Supreme War Council was called to order in what one witness described as an atmosphere of "impatience, frenzy, and bewilderment."[3] The venue for the meeting was a dank underground conference room in the euphemistically named *Obunko fuzoku ko* ("Imperial Library annex"), which in terms of function was actually the Imperial Palace's main bomb shelter. The sole agenda item for the morning was a continuation of the council's ongoing debate over whether or not to accept the Allies' terms of "unconditional" surrender laid out in the Potsdam Declaration. Whichever way that decision went—either for acceptance and surrender or for rejection and continuation of the war—the council's political tradition demanded that it be unanimous.[4] Even though the emperor had made clear his desire to see the war end as soon as possible,[5] the council seemed no closer to a decision on the matter than it had been when the Potsdam news first broke two weeks earlier.

His Majesty's patience was beginning to wear thin. The previous day—when the dream of Soviet diplomatic salvation was still alive—the emperor's wish for immediate peace had been imparted in this very room during a private imperial audience with Foreign Minister

Tōgō Shigenori. On that occasion, it had fallen upon Tōgō to be the first person to inform the emperor that American claims about possessing atomic bombs appeared to be true and that President Truman's promise to continue dropping them until Japan surrendered was not an empty threat. As Tōgō later recalled of the discussion that followed, "The Emperor... warned that since we could no longer continue the struggle, now that a weapon of this devastating power was used against us, *we should not let slip the opportunity* [to secure immediate peace] by engaging in attempts to gain more favorable conditions"[6] (italics the author's). The new-type bomb from the emperor's perspective, then, was not an empty threat on the Allies' part but rather a chance to secure the end to the war he had long sought but had until that moment not openly demanded because he had not possessed the political capital to do so.

Nobody on the council was prepared to deny the emperor's wish for peace out of hand. Nor could any—even the fight-to-the-finish, diehard War Minister Anami—deny that Japan's prospects for the continuing war effort were exceedingly grim, not only in light of the American atomic threat but also, as of ten hours ago, the Soviet Union's entry into the war. In the meantime, the Supreme War Council was doing exactly what His Majesty had feared: endangering the peace process by bickering over surrender conditions while his loyal soldiers and civilian subjects were suffering and dying with each debate-squandered minute.

At risk of oversimplification, the sticking point that had so far prevented the council from accepting the Potsdam conditions came down to a matter of bitterly contested rival definitions of "Japan."[7] More specifically and rephrased as a philosophical proposition, the matter of contention was how much the holy national body of the *Kokutai* might lose in a surrender scenario, through either voluntary or forced amputation, and still survive in recognizable and valid form, both politically and, of vital importance, *spiritually.* In short, the question was: Could the *Kokutai*—again, depending on one's definition of the same—survive the surrender scenario outlined in the Potsdam Declaration? If the answer was yes, then the surrender could be accepted; if it was no, then the Allies would have to amend the declaration to meet Japanese demands. Barring that, the war would continue, with Japan now forced to wage it against three global superpowers, one of which possessed an atomic arsenal.

The one bottom-line, sine qua non *Kokutai* definition term upon which all council members—as well as Hirohito himself—were in agreement was that a Japan without an emperor was utterly unthinkable, and any suggestion to the contrary was utterly unconscionable.[8] From this perspective, "the honorable death of the hundred million" (i.e., the annihilation of the Japanese race) would have been preferable to being forced to live in the spiritual and cultural wasteland that would result from a surrender scenario involving the abolition of the imperial throne or even, gods forbid, having the emperor put on trial (and possibly executed) as a war criminal.[9]

Nevertheless, the council's "peace faction"—Foreign Minister Tōgō, Navy Minister Admiral Yonai Mitsumasa, and a frequently waffling Prime Minister Suzuki—harbored concerns that a prolongation of the war would result in the very *Kokutai* collapse that continued resistance was supposed to prevent. In their opinion, the sum pressures of more American atomic bombs, impending Anglo-American (and likely Soviet from the north) ground invasions, the growing threat of mass starvation from the Allied blockade, compounded by a poor rice harvest forecast for that year and general overall war-weariness, would combine to create a perfect storm of political and social chaos that could very well end either in a military coup or, even worse, a Communist revolution[10] that would succeed in destroying the *Kokutai* from within before a single Allied soldier ever set foot on Home Island soil. In light of these clear and present dangers, the peace faction held that the Potsdam Declaration should be accepted immediately, in accordance with the imperial wish and, again, with the line-in-the-sand proviso of Hirohito remaining on the throne.[11]

The council's "war faction"—War Minister Anami, Army Chief of Staff Umezu, and Navy Chief of Staff Toyoda—were also wary of the same likelihood of political and social chaos. From their perspective, however, this scenario would come to pass not because of a continuation of the war but rather as the result of a too-hasty ending of the same. In their opinion, Japan's valiant military and loyal populace would never accept the indelible scar on national honor, the loss of territory, and the humiliation of occupation that would result from an acceptance of the Potsdam terms as they were. Instead, the war faction proposed that Japan keep fighting until those terms were modified to include: (1) no Allied occupation; (2) military and naval demobilization carried out by the IJA and IJN themselves; and (3) Japanese adjudication of "war crimes" (in the unlikely event that any were deemed worthy of prosecution).[12]

If the Allies rejected these conditions, then the war would go on. In that scenario, invading enemy ground troops would be met with such fierce and bloody resistance by both Japanese military personnel and civilians—acting as one single unified national defense force—that Allied leadership would be forced to the negotiation table. Anami and his confederates were under no illusion, nor did they claim, that this would not involve grievous Japanese bloodshed and widespread destruction across the Home Islands. But they appeared sincere in their belief that this sacrifice was necessary and that ultimately it had a good chance of success.

In the context of the war faction's attempts to downplay the elephant in the bunker conference room—the atomic bomb menace—Anami brought up the subject of an American fighter pilot, one First Lieutenant Marcus McDilda, who had been shot down over Osaka Bay the previous day.[13] Under initial questioning by the Osaka Kempeitai, this prisoner revealed to his interrogators that Hiroshima had, indeed, been destroyed by an "atomic" bomb; that America had a stockpile of an additional hundred such weapons; and that the next target for one of them, "in the next few days," would be either Tokyo or Kyoto.[14] These astounding revelations were dutifully reported to superiors in Tokyo, and McDilda was immediately flown to the capital to undergo more intensive questioning by seasoned interrogation

THE NAGASAKI CABLE 245

professionals at Kempeitai National HQ.[15] Once there, the prisoner did not take long to admit that his Osaka testimony had been a complete fabrication, created to avoid execution by his captors. This raised the obvious possibility that the Americans were merely bluffing.

Running with his colleague's rhetorical momentum, Admiral Toyoda raised the possibility that the Americans actually had a much smaller atomic arsenal than was feared and thus would be incapable of a sustained bombing campaign using these weapons.[16] For all anyone knew—and if developing such a weapon was as fiendishly difficult and ruinously expensive as Professor Nishina and other scientists suggested—the atomic bomb dropped on Hiroshima might have even been a one-off.

In the midst of this pitch for continuing the war, a runner came into the conference room with a copy of a report that had just been wired to Western Army HQ by Nagasaki Prefectural Governor Nagano Wakamatsu; the report read:

> *Item One: At 1053 today, two enemy B-29s approached from the direction of Amagusa, Kumamoto Prefecture, to the north, then crossed Tachibana Bay and western Shimabara Peninsula to enter Nagasaki airspace. At 1102, two parachute-deployed new-type bombs were dropped.*
>
> *Item Two: These bombs would seem to be smaller versions of the type dropped on Hiroshima. Although considerable casualties are expected, overall damage is expected to be much smaller compared with the damage sustained by Hiroshima, with much lower numbers of deaths and destroyed.*
>
> *Addendum: There have been no casualties among executive members of the Prefectural Office.[17]*

Although this report would appear to have taken the wind out of the war faction's downplaying of the American atomic threat, Nagano's initial claims of the merely modest damage caused by the Nagasaki "bombs" might also have had the effect of blunting the shock effect of the attack. In any case, the respective positions of the two factions were not budged by the news, and the council remained deadlocked. With no progress in sight, Suzuki adjourned the meeting and scheduled another for his full Cabinet (inclusive of War Minister Anami and Navy Minister Yonai) to be held at his official residence from 1430.[18]

IN KONPIRA'S SHADOW

East China Sea
Three hundred kilometers south-southwest of GZ

AN HOUR INTO the egress from the target area, William Laurence could still see the twenty-kilometer-high mushroom cloud over Nagasaki.[1] In the other direction, four hundred fifty kilometers of open water separated *The Great Artiste* and the fuel-starved *Bockscar* from Yontan, Okinawa—the location of the nearest friendly runway long enough to accommodate B-29s.

But it was beginning to look like Major Sweeney might not get a chance to use that runway; flight engineer Kuharek had just announced that there were only three hundred gallons of accessible fuel left on the plane,[2] and quick calculations said that the engines were going to run dry anywhere from seventy-five to one hundred kilometers short of Yontan. After receiving this report, Sweeney told radio operator Spitzer to begin hailing air-sea-rescue channels.[3]

As Sweeney later recalled of his thoughts at the time: "We were going into the ocean. It was only a matter of when, not if. This prospect didn't disturb me that much. We'd get a little wet, wait for a Flying Dumbo or a friendly destroyer to pick us up, and we'd be home free. I didn't like the idea of losing my airplane, but at least I'd get the crew home safely."[4]

In the midst of these sobering reflections, Sweeney's mind

wandered to Stateside days when he and Colonel Tibbets had been working on the development team for the B-29 design.[5] During that time, Tibbets had told him about an experimental technique called "flying on the step"[6] that could be used for extending the range of a high-flying aircraft in a fuel emergency. The method involved throttling back on the engines to save fuel while simultaneously putting the aircraft into a shallow dive to pick up a little airspeed before leveling off and flying straight under normal power again. Once air resistance had eaten up the energy gained in the dive, the pilot would repeat the procedure, sacrificing another "step" of altitude, and so on. With a lot of skill and a little luck, a pilot using this technique could get a plane to its destination before running out of altitude and/or fuel—at least according to theory. It was now up to Sweeney to find out if it worked in practice.

Bockscar's situation was far from enviable, but neither was it hopeless. Sweeney, despite his lack of combat seasoning, had a reputation in USAAF bomber circles as a "hot stick." His ability had gotten him recruited to become a flying instructor right out of flight school, and it was the primary reason he had been chosen for the B-29 development program—an experience that gave him hands-on working knowledge of the B-29 that was probably second only to Tibbets'.

Also working in their favor, *Bockscar*'s current altitude of nine thousand meters gave Sweeney's step technique some breathing room—perhaps even enough to coax out of the fuel tanks the extra twenty minutes or so of powered flight they would need to reach Yontan.

Still, nothing on the mission had gone right so far, and in a "When it rains, it pours" sense, few on board could have been optimistic about their luck changing now.

Second Lieutenant Olivi—*Bockscar*'s superfluous third pilot—had spent most of the mission doing his best to stay out of everyone else's way.[7] But his perch on the flight deck had provided him with a front-row seat to all of the day's drama. And fortunately for the cause of history, the young Chicagoan had a keen eye, a good memory, and nothing much else to do but watch and listen.

For the past hour, Olivi had used his advantageous vantage point to follow the running back-and-forth commentary between pilot, flight engineer, and navigator as they gamed Tibbets' step trick—reading aloud from their respective charts and gauges, weighing the distance to Yontan against the remaining fuel in the plane's nearly bone-dry fuel tanks. And what Olivi heard was not encouraging.

"For the first time in my brief flying career," he later recalled, "I tightened up my 'Mae West' life preserver jacket, wondering if it would work. I also started to rehearse in my mind our 'ditching' procedures if we ended up in the ocean[8] that was gradually getting closer and closer as we neared Okinawa."

Fifteen minutes out of Yontan, Sweeney had Spitzer patch him through to the control tower frequency so he could begin calling in Maydays for *Bockscar*'s imminent emergency landing. But he got no response.[9] Spitzer attempted alternate channels on his radio gear, but nothing seemed to be getting through. Meanwhile, the young major caught sight of land and, far off in the hazy distance, Yontan, which appeared to be swarming with aircraft taking off, landing, and circuiting the field in holding patterns.[10]

Kuharek called out, "Major, all gauges read empty,"[11] just as the right outboard engine gave a final gasp and died. Sweeney used the pitch control setting on the dead engine's propeller to "feather" its four blades to reduce their drag, rotating them so that their leading edges cut directly into the airstream. Like any qualified B-29 pilot, he had no serious problems keeping the plane flying straight and level on three engines, but if he lost another, things could get very hairy very quickly—particularly if it was on the same wing and especially if this occurred during their landing approach. To mitigate the risk of a catastrophic stall and/or an uncontrollable yawing of the airframe in such a scenario, Sweeney would have to bring *Bockscar* in "hot"—that is, well above the suggested maximum safe landing speed for a B-29. There would be no wave-offs or holding patterns, no waiting for clearance to land—only one shot at getting *Bockscar* on the ground, hopefully with its six hundred gallons of useless aviation fuel unexploded.

After a final, unanswered Mayday call to the Yontan tower,

250   NAGASAKI

Sweeney barked orders to Van Pelt and Olivi to "[f]ire every goddamn flare we have on board!"

"Which ones?" Olivi asked.

This was not an unreasonable query, as the flares were color-coded (against the event of an incoming aircraft's radio being inoperable)[12] to signal specific emergency messages to a control tower—e.g., one color was for "dead and wounded on board," another for "aircraft out of fuel" or "prepare for crash," etc.

"Every goddamn flare we have!" Sweeney answered. "Do it now!"

In their current situation, the color distinctions of the flares were unimportant. The only thing that mattered now was that everyone on the ground and in the air over Yontan should see *Bockscar* barreling in, lit up like a Christmas tree, and get the hell out of the way.

Olivi and Van Pelt did as they were told, sending up round after round through the flight deck's special Very pistol firing port. Before they had finished, the fuselage was filled with so much smoke that First Lieutenant Beser and the other men in the rear compartments became concerned that the plane was on fire.[13]

This final attempt at communicating *Bockscar*'s desperate situation to its intended audience seems to have done the trick, as various airborne aircraft began veering off from their landing approaches to clear the way for the ailing B-29.[14] Gingerly threading this traffic needle and praying that he wouldn't lose any more engines,[15] Sweeney put the plane into its final descent.

He brought *Bockscar* in so fast and hard that the plane bounced ten meters or more back into the air the first time the wheels hit the ground. At the moment the plane returned to terra firma, the other outboard engine seized up and died. Sweeney stomped hard on the brakes and threw the propellers on his two remaining good engines into reverse. He just missed plowing into a tight row of parked B-24s before *Bockscar* finally rolled to a stop.

The Great Artiste came in shortly after, landing without incident.[16]

Apparently, every emergency scenario signaled by the color-coded flares activated its corresponding crash squad on the base into its designated response. As pilot and crew caught their breath and began coming down from their adrenaline spikes, a convoy of every category of emergency vehicle—fire trucks, wreckers, ambulances—sped out to meet Yontan's mystery visitors.

A few seconds later, someone on the tarmac popped *Bockscar*'s nose landing gear hatch and poked his head up into the flight deck. It was a medic.

"Where's the dead and wounded?" the medic asked.

Sweeney wearily hiked a thumb over a shoulder, pointing off to the north toward Nagasaki.

"Back there," he said.

Shimonishiyama-machi

2.9 kilometers southeast of GZ

On any other sunny August morning, the slope of Konpira abutting Shinagawa-sensei's house would have been alive with a jungle-worthy cacophony of birdcalls and the incessant ambient buzz of teeming insect life. But not on this one. When Norio regained consciousness after the explosion, absolute silence hung over everything. The disk of the sun had turned a dark rusty gray. A strange rain with huge greasy black raindrops began falling, as did variously sized chips and shards and fragments of wood and other materials.[17] It was as if the whole world had died, and for a few panicked moments Norio wondered if he might be dead, too. But as the sense-dulling numbness of his initial shock wore off, the first stabs of physical pain told him that he was still alive. And the source of his most insistent pain was his back.

On the Urakami side of Mount Konpira, the thermal rays directly emanating from Fat Man's fireball had inflicted third- and fourth-degree burns on people—particularly on their bare skin—if they had been unlucky enough to be caught out of doors or sitting in or near open windows when the bomb detonated. The roof-tile-boiling intensity of this heat charred flesh all the way down to musculature and tendons within seconds, instantly igniting human beings, wooden houses and telephone poles, trees, and any other organic matter across the valley.

The areas of central Nagasaki fortunate enough to be in Konpira's bomb shadow, however, were shielded from the full fury of Fat Man's fireball. But they did not escape completely unscathed. During the eight or so seconds of its existence, the fireball had created the atmospheric equivalent of an air fryer centered over Ground Zero. In the brief span of its functionality, this "air fryer" had been hot enough to cause second-degree burns—like sunburn penetrating to the dermis and requiring medical attention—to exposed flesh. More than three kilometers away, it had seared the inside of Tateno Sueko's mouth in the second or two between her seeing the flash and then hitting the ground facedown in response. A kilometer closer, it had scalded the skin on Norio's back as he sat in his open window. Unlike the direct thermal energy that ravaged Urakami, however, this heat phenomenon did not set anything—or anyone—on fire. Mercifully, for those caught underneath this dome, this giant convection oven was quickly blown away when the tremendous energy of Fat Man's shock wave briefly displaced the superheated atmosphere over the target. When air rushed back in to fill the resulting vacuum, the scalding heat was gone.

In Norio's case, this same atmospheric displacement also contributed a secondary tier—after the back scalding—to his pain portfolio. When this mass of speeding air impacted with his house, knocking its frame a few degrees off-kilter and upheaving all of its loose items, tatami matting, and floorboards, it also transformed all of the glass in the structure into vitreous shrapnel. The resulting ballistic swarm of shattered glass had pockmarked the left side of Norio's body from his waist to his head with tiny but nevertheless profusely bleeding puncture wounds.

As he assessed the damage to his body and tried to shrug off the last of his shock, Norio became aware of the first ambient sounds in his heretofore deathly silent environment; he took a look out the now glassless and frameless window and traced the sound to the hushed murmuring of neighbors milling around in the street, probably wondering—as he was—if a bomb had just fallen on or near their houses. Although he was eager to find out what had just happened, he did not know anyone in the neighborhood yet—other than Shinagawa-sensei—and now did not seem like an optimal time to be making self-introductions. In the end, his social reticence getting the better of his curiosity, he just stayed in his wrecked room, doing what he could about his injuries and sweeping up broken glass.

He finally left the empty house around 1400 to begin his commute walk to Mori-machi. Once he rounded the southern slope of Konpira to head west into the CBD, he noticed the smoke still hanging over Urakami and surmised that the morning's air-heating and glass-shattering disturbance on his side of the mountain had occurred with unimaginable ferocity on the other. Still, he continued on until his forward progress was halted by first responders directing traffic away from the area.[18] He was told that fires from the Urakami Valley—which was now utterly inaccessible—were beginning to penetrate the CBD[19] and that he should go back whence he came. Taking the harried authority figures at their word, Norio obediently turned around and walked back to Shimonishiyama-machi. He had yet to start thinking much about Yoshio at this point, beyond wondering what his older brother—who tended to be a bit of a neat freak—was going to say tonight about the condition of their room.

Later that afternoon, a billy-goat-bearded fifty-something white man in Christian monk's garb called at the front door of Shinagawa-sensei's house, asking for water. After gulping down the contents of the cup he was given, he thanked Norio for the drink, said in very broken Japanese, "Ima, Nagasaki wa, taihen desu" ("Now, Nagasaki, it's terrible"), and went on his way. Years after the fact, Norio identified the man as Brother Zeno Zebrowski, a Franciscan friar who went on to some measure of fame caring for war orphans in postwar Japan.[20]

When Shinagawa-sensei came home that evening, he informed his boarder that the downtown district was rapidly filling up with horribly burned and dying people. Everything east from the station and up to Shinkōzen Elementary School was on fire, and the prefectural office and Nagasaki Appellate Courthouse had already succumbed to the flames. Hearing this, Norio finally began to get a grasp of the destruction the mysterious foreign caller had been trying to describe. It was only then that Norio at last found the presence of mind to begin worrying about Yoshio.

When evening descended on the burning city, Norio and Shinagawa-sensei sat in silence in the blackout-darkened house, gazing out at the pulsating red skies to the west silhouetting Konpira while they awaited Yoshio's return.

Fukuro-machi

3.4 kilometers southeast of GZ

After shaking off the dust and shock of the blast, Tateno Sueko abandoned the shelter dig site and ran off in search of her loved ones. When she reached Fukuro-machi, its residents were in a panic. Some were running around screaming and crying or barking unheeded orders. Others just stood in place, slack-jawed and stunned. No houses had escaped damage, with most at least knocked crooked on their foundations and some partially collapsed. Underfoot, the streets were glittering with glass fragments and crunchy with broken roof tiles and other light debris. But as in Shimonishiyama-machi and most of the rest of the CBD in Konpira's shadow, nothing was on fire—at least not yet.

Instead of going home, Sueko first headed for her family's preferred air raid evacuation point—a private bomb shelter owned by the neighborhood general practitioner, Dr. Takao, who always allowed the Tatenos to use it during air raid alerts. After pushing and dodging her way through the madding crowds in the streets to reach the clinic, Sueko found her mother and sisters, Mitsuko and Yoshiko, huddled together in Dr. Takao's shelter, apparently unharmed. Sueko promptly burst into wailing tears of relief and joy, which were soon echoed by her loved ones. As she was informed in the torrent of words and emotions of the moment, the family had experienced a miracle in the midst of Nagasaki's disaster: When the wind gust and its accompanying boom hit the neighborhood, Yoshiko had practically leapt out of her sickbed, and now she was walking normally again. Apparently, the psychological shock of the explosion had shaken her system loose of whatever neuralgic condition it was that had been binding her legs into immobility over the past year. An added bit of good fortune for the family was that Mitsuko had just happened to come home early from work that morning.[21]

A short time later, Sueko's theretofore missing father showed up at the shelter. The tears of relief and joy that ensued were so rapturously shed that no one bothered to ask where he had been when the explosion occurred or why his head was bandaged.[22]

The injury story might have emerged at some point if the reunion had not been interrupted; a uniformed first responder poked his head into the shelter and ordered its inhabitants to evacuate immediately to the prefectural office, as fires from the west were now threatening Fukuro-machi.

Thinking to grab what belongings they might yet save from the encroaching blaze, the Tatenos—following the letter rather than the spirit of the first responder's order—made a quick detour to their house, only to find it a shambles. The roof had been completely blown off, and the rest of the house was crooked and leaning, looking as if it might topple over at any moment. Judging that it was too dangerous to venture inside, they abandoned the idea of fetching any precious and/or sentimental items[23] and went on their way, headed south.

For the first leg of their evacuation, the Tatenos crossed the Tokiwa Bridge over the Nakashima River, intending to stop over for a spell in Kōtaiji—one of a strip of historic Buddhist temples built in the seventeenth century along the northwest foot of Kazagashira Hill. During their walk to Kōtaiji, they were caught in a brief but intense rain squall.[24] It was only decades later, as she and her family members fell victim to one mysterious health issue after another, that Sueko wondered whether the squall might have been radioactive-fallout-contaminated "black" rain.

By the time the Tatenos reached Kōtaiji—perhaps two hours or so after the explosion—its main hall and grounds were overflowing with people. The air over the space reeked of scorched flesh and hummed with a low, moaning drone of suffering randomly shattered by screams. The evacuees primarily consisted of panicked residents fleeing CBD neighborhoods ahead of the arrival of the afternoon's expected conflagrations. But from the seriousness of some injuries, it was apparent that they also included many broken ZTD survivors who must have made superhuman efforts to reach this far south before their strength gave out and they collapsed.

The lucky died quickly. The severe-burn cases were the most pitiable, and Sueko was unable to look at them. Many of these victims— who would be dead soon, anyway—were even begging passersby to kill them on the spot to put them out of their agony. Sueko's ears would be filled with their screams for the next three days and sleepless nights.

From their vantage point on the temple grounds, the Tatenos watched as fires from Urakami curled around the southern foot of Konpira, spreading and growing in intensity as they began to reach the high-density areas of the CBD. One of the most prominent blazes in their field of vision was rapidly consuming the prefectural office. Weeping at the sight of fires closer at hand spreading to Fukuromachi, Sueko and her family members knew that their house would soon be no more.

FALSE TWILIGHT INTO NIGHT

Sonoda foundry
Togitsu
6.2 kilometers north-northwest of GZ

WHEN THEY WERE still huddling in their slit trench, some of the Jun-shin girls, following Sister Itonaga Yoshi's lead, had worked their rosaries while murmuring Hail Marys. A few of the more composed theorized aloud that something terrible had just happened in the Urakami Valley and expressed concern about their classmates at the Michino'o foundry.[1] Most of the girls, however, cowered in wordless terror.

But when they eventually emerged from their trench, each person had the same reaction—freezing in place—when they caught their first sight of the smoke cloud climbing into the southern sky. For long minutes, the girls, their chaperone, and the Sonoda full-timers stood and stared at this billowing apparition in a tight, silent huddle, the only sound over the scene a brown noise rumble of far-off chaos rolling up the valley.

Someone eventually broke the spell of stunned silence with sniffles and sobs. And in the infectious mammalian nature of such things, everyone else—even the Sonoda blacksmiths—soon joined in.

Sister Yoshi indulged her own cathartic tears until her sense of duty nudged her back into action. She could work through her own emotions later, when she next had the luxury of time for prayer and meditation—whenever that might be. For now, she had to take care of the girls that were with her at the moment, and she had another ten more girls to look after in Michino'o—half again as close to whatever that mushroom-shaped cloud was.

After some negotiations with the regular foundry employees, it was agreed that the Junshin students and the children from other schools would shelter at the house of the foundry owner—Sonoda-san—until the situation to the south stabilized. Sister Yoshi or someone else from Junshin would come and get their girls later.

With this responsibility dispatched, Sister Yoshi had one more chore before she could set out for Michino'o. A student who had been cut on the face by flying glass did not want to go to Sonoda-san's house; she wanted to go home to her mother. Luckily, the girl's home was nearby, and after Sister Yoshi dropped her off there, she pushed on to the other Sonoda foundry.[2]

At the start of her 2.5-kilometer southbound trek, Sister Yoshi noted only light damage—broken windows and the like—in the landscape she traversed. And while the people she passed were clearly agitated as they milled about in front of their still largely intact houses and wondered what had just happened, nobody was visibly injured.

But this would change with time and Sister Yoshi's proximity to the smoke and fires in the south. As she progressed deeper into the Urakami Valley, signs of destruction, both structural and human, became incrementally—then steadily—more conspicuous.

When Sister Yoshi finally reached Michino'o, she steeled herself for the worst when she saw that the flimsy sheet metal Sonoda foundry building had completely collapsed. Miraculously, though, none of her students had been injured. And their subsequent evacuation—again, to Sonoda-san's house—had been arranged without complication, with the sole exception of yet another student—Arima Setsuko—who adamantly insisted on being taken home.[3] As the girl lived in Sumiyoshi-machi, which was on the Togitsu Road route from Michino'o to Junshin, Sister Yoshi agreed to this request, and the two set off together for their respective destinations.

The roadway the pair traversed was strewn with broken glass and debris and thick with burned and bleeding people limping and staggering in the opposite direction. Tongues of orange flame—bright under the afternoon's false twilight—flickered and darted out of piles of wooden house wreckage.

Around Michino'o Station, an aid facility had been hastily established by a mixed ad hoc group of first responders. The density and urgency of victim traffic here approached panicked-mob levels. For perhaps a hundred meters or more, the embankment and the station side of the rails were lined with bodies, living and dead, laid out on tatami frames, corrugated metal sheets, wooden boards, or any other plank-like material that could be used in place of nonexistent stretchers.

Reaching Sumiyoshi-machi a kilometer later, Sister Yoshi was relieved to find the Arima house still standing and family members present to welcome their daughter home. Thus disencumbered from her last student charge, Sister Yoshi trudged on alone in her sensible schoolmarm lace-up half boots—year-round regulation footwear for the order—walking against the flow of soot- and blood-streaked people fleeing the fires of the valley.

Increasingly conspicuous in this stream of human suffering were the severe-burn victims, most of whom were completely naked. In a brief flash of stomach-lurching visual association, the outer layers of skin hanging off of their salmon-pink dermis in translucent sheets and strips reminded Sister Yoshi of the peeling, shredded skin of blanched tomatoes. The only way she could keep moving—and keep her breakfast down—was by elevating her line of sight over the heads of these woeful passersby to avoid looking at them or at the bodies lining the sides of the thoroughfare. But averting her gaze from the gore on the ground involved some sacrifice in ambulatory stability. More than once, she tripped over and, to her utter disgust and horror, fell onto piles of bloody, lymph-slimy corpses.[4]

To stave off her growing nausea and anxiety, which threatened to render her legs useless, she attempted to rationalize what she was seeing—to come up with some explanation for what could possibly have created so much human devastation so quickly. For some reason,

Mother Ezumi's dining hall talk that morning about the Americans' new-type bomb never came to mind. Instead, the theory Sister Yoshi came up with on the fly was that a giant vat of boiling water or a tank of some caustic chemical at Ōhashi must have burst, ruining all of these people in an instant and sending up that giant cloud of smoke that still hung over the valley hours after the explosion. Because she was faced with the urgent emotional exigency of needing to believe that her post-catastrophe world still made sense, it did not matter to her in that moment whether her theory was correct or not—just that she had one.

Throughout her trek through this valley of death, Sister Yoshi also called on a second battery of worldview defense for succor and strength: her Catholic faith. Since leaving Arima Setsuko in Sumiyoshi-machi, she had been reciting prayers aloud while she thumbed the rosary beads wrapped around her right hand—something she would have never dreamed of doing in public, out and about among her infidel compatriots, under any other circumstances.

But her faith would receive a body blow—on top of all the other indignities she had already experienced on this horrible day—when she rounded a bend in the road and caught sight of Urakami Cathedral off in the distance. When Fat Man detonated, a mere 760-odd meters away, parish priest Father Nishida Saburō, fellow cleric Father Tamaya Fusakichi, and ten Urakami parishioners had been inside the church preparing special Assumption of Mary services for August 15[5]—the most important summer event on the Catholic calendar. Pastors and flock were most likely killed instantly by the bomb's shock wave and concussion, then buried—and subsequently consumed by flames—under brick rubble and shattered wooden support beams.

For the next thirteen years, the jagged silhouette of the ruined cathedral—visible for kilometers around—would stand sentinel on its rocky knoll in Moto'o-machi, simultaneously a stark memorial of August 9, 1945, and, as many of Urakami's surviving faithful would come to see it, an unwelcome visual prompt for theological implications that few were yet prepared to consider.[6] For the time being, though, the burning ruins of the cathedral would help Sister Yoshi find her bearings in an otherwise featureless and colorless moonscape where the surface of what had once been roads was difficult to distinguish from the smoke- and flame-belching piles of what had once been houses and storefronts.

As she entered the final leg of her long march to Junshin, she was approached by a kindly middle-aged man who said that he was trying to get home to Tateyama on the southern slope of Konpira, but that he would be happy to escort her as far as Ieno-machi.[7] She welcomed his offer and fell in step behind him, her formerly waning confidence to push on now revived. With her escort running interference ahead of her, Sister Yoshi—by simply focusing on the small of the man's back and matching his steps—could keep moving while avoiding having to look at all of the horrors on the ground.

The two parted ways when they reached the Ieno-machi stretch of the Togitsu Road. From there, Sister Yoshi took a shortcut east through a relatively wreckage-free municipal cemetery, then skirted the northern edge of the Ōhashi compound. The teeming, moaning crowds back on Togitsu Road, only a few hundred meters to the west, were now just a bad memory. All around her was deadly silent, save for the continuous crackling of flames from the still-burning factory ruins.

Finally reaching Nagayo Road, she clambered over a blast-twisted fence to enter the Junshin campus.[8] The afternoon's false twilight, compounded by the smoky air blowing over from the torpedo plant, made it very difficult for her to see very far ahead, and it was only after a few moments of orientation effort that she could determine that she was standing on Junshin's northern athletic ground. Then, through the murk, she thought that she could make out the black-cloaked figure of one of her seniors, Sister Nakashima Mitsuno, standing alone and motionless on the riverbank edge of the campus. But when she got closer, she saw that it was only the burned trunk[9] of a blast-decapitated tree.

Reorienting herself to the southwest and stepping gingerly, she set off across the field in the direction of the main campus buildings. The first one she got close enough to see was—or had been—the

Sisters' dining hall / kitchen, which was now a completely collapsed pile of smoldering rubble and debris. Pushing on, she encountered the first living person she had seen after parting with the man on the Togitsu Road: It was one of her order's seniors, Sister Fukahori Fujiko, who emerged from a slit trench protectively clutching a jar of pickled plums she had salvaged from the collapsed kitchen. After the two shared a quick crying jag, Sister Fukahori proceeded to fill her junior sister in on everything the latter had missed on campus during her trek from Togitsu and Michino'o.[10]

First, as far as anyone could tell and compared to what seemed to be going on outside of it, it appeared that the campus had gotten off relatively lightly in terms of casualties, particularly in consideration of the complete destruction of its facilities. The worst case Sister Fukahori knew of at the moment was Sister Ōsako, who had been caught in the open by the explosion while she was working one of the truck patches; her burns were horrendous, and her survival seemed doubtful. . . .

Many of the novices were displaying real bravery and fortitude—qualities no one would have suspected they possessed before today. Among their number, Sister Hatanaka had been exemplary, proving to be a dynamo of initiative and decisive action in the wake of the catastrophe; after extricating herself from the school chapel—and saving the sacred ciborium—she had helped pull out from under the rubble of the collapsed kitchen some other novices, dusty and contused but alive. . . .[11]

The members of the Mitsuyama pine sap detail had been the first off-campus Junshin personnel who made it back to the school after the explosion. They were all uninjured, but one of the first-year boarders was missing. She was supposed to have gone to Mitsuyama with the others that morning, but she had taken ill and stayed behind in the campus student dormitory. This structure had subsequently burned to the ground, and its debris was still aflame, so no one had been able to go into the wreckage to look for her.

But so far the day's biggest drama, after the explosion itself, had been the discovery of the theretofore missing Mother Ezumi in the wreckage of the main classroom and administrative building. Initially trapped under a collapsed firewall, she had been extricated just as fires from the building's burning wooden debris were closing in on her. She was alive and conscious but still in shock, unable to walk and nursing a broken jaw. Some of the Sisters were now taking care of her in Junshin's more substantial air raid shelter, which was dug into the riverbank edge of the campus.[12] This was now the de facto new headquarters of the school, and it would remain so for close to a week, until some students' fathers helped to erect some tents and built shacks out of wood and sheet metal wreckage for the Sisters on the athletic ground. The Junshin Sisters would still be inhabiting the shacks four years later, when the rebuilding of the Ieno-machi school finally got underway.

Aside from the chaos and trauma of the devastated campus and the ongoing care for the wounded therein, the greatest source of dread in the Junshin community at the moment was the as-yet-unknown status of all but a handful of the five-hundred-odd students who had been working across the street at Ōhashi that morning. When the returned Mitsuyama group chaperones and several other Sisters from the campus had gone across Nagayo Road to look for the Junshin girls, they had found a gravely wounded Sister Christina. Despite her injuries, she refused entreaties to return to Junshin to receive aid, insisting instead that she would stay in the ruined factory to help with the search for her girls.

Over the next few days, Junshin activity would be monopolized by the ongoing search for the girls at Ōhashi and the other nearby Mitsubishi facilities and by providing care for the survivors the Sisters found. In the meantime, later on the afternoon of August 9, Sister Christina was seen helping her injured students get onto a relief train ferrying bomb victims to the IJN hospital in Isahaya, nearly thirty kilometers away.

Later that evening, the order would suffer its first bomb fatality when Sister Ōsako—whose last words were "Jesus, Mary, and Joseph, help us in our hour of need. . . ."[13]—succumbed to her burns and, in all likelihood, also undiagnosed ARS. The Junshin Sisters cremated her on the athletic ground that night, singing hymns in a circle around her funeral pyre.

———

Michino'o Station

3.5 kilometers north-northwest of GZ

It is quite likely that on the afternoon of August 9, Sister Itonaga Yoshi and Ishida Masako passed each other on the Togitsu Road somewhere between Michino'o and Ieno-machi. It is less certain, however, whether Masako was still standing when this conjunction occurred. The answer, one way or the other, would require chronologically precise timelines of Sister Yoshi's and Masako's respective movements on that day—data that, unfortunately, does not exist.

What is known about Masako's movements is that, by the early afternoon, she and Ōta-san—her stalwart *jokō* evacuation companion—had spent nearly two hours essentially circumnavigating the Ōhashi compound, completing this giant circle after determining (or, rather, being told) that they should take the Togitsu Road north to seek aid and refuge at Michino'o.

Midway through their Ieno-machi circumnavigation, when the twosome encountered the anonymous gallant who convinced them to head north, Masako had lost her remaining *geta* in the crowd crush at Ōhashi Bridge and was now barefoot. Although the past five months of her *geta*-shod Nagasaki existence had toughened her feet up considerably since her shoe-shod Tokyo tenderfoot days, her bare soles were still having a rough time with the painfully hot glass- and debris-strewn ground. Still, this was the least of her problems at the moment; her various wounds were still bleeding profusely, and she was feeling increasingly drained by bone-deep exhaustion. Like her schoolmate Kiridōshi Michiko 2.5 kilometers away on Mount Konpira, she was beginning to wonder if this was going to be the last day of her life.

As Masako headed north, it seemed to her as if the whole world were on fire. This impression had really been driven home for her when she passed the west side of the Ōhashi plant, the only still recognizable features of which were its oddly unmarred smokestacks poking up from what looked like endless, undulating rows of collapsed roller-coaster tracks—all that was left of the light steel framework of the plant's gargantuan main factory floors. Adding to the surrealism of the scene, random secondary explosions still rumbled deep within this wreckage, each sending up new geysers of fire. Although these were most likely caused by rupturing gas tanks, Masako's gentleman escort shared his theory that these were time-delayed bombs—like the ones the Americans had dropped on the waterfront the week before—used to discourage firefighters and other first responders from approaching the area.[14] In any case, Masako was relieved to put the blazing scene behind her and to see that, as the trio drew closer to Michino'o, the fires on either side of the Togitsu Road began to diminish in scale and intensity.

Michino'o Station was a scene of bedlam. As the trio neared the aid station, the northerly flow of the crowd suddenly reversed. There was some kind of panic up ahead, and people were shouting to run for the hillsides. Instinctively, as she had been doing all day, Masako followed the crowd—running as fast as her exhausted body and injured legs could carry her—until word spread that it had all been a false alarm. At this, she went with the flow of the now listlessly shuffling crowd back to the Kokutetsu railbed, but she was now alone. Somewhere back in the false-alarm commotion, she had lost Ōta-san and their gentleman escort, and she would never see either again.

The railbed and embankment area in front of the station were lined with hundreds—perhaps even thousands—of victims no longer able to stand. Some were laid out on mats and planks, others directly on the ballast gravel and weeds. The living emitted a ceaseless drone of moaning, amidst which a single word could be distinguished, repeated over and over: *"Mizu . . . Mizu . . ."* ("Water . . . Water . . .").

For the many among these prone bodies who were already dead, the day's agony was over. They would lie in place until someone came along and cremated them. Among the standing—either the thousands of walking wounded attempting to get aid or the dozens of first responders attempting to give it to them—Masako did not see a single individual who was not bloodied, scorched, limping, or otherwise injured in some way.

She had initially approached the aid station in hopes of getting someone to look at her injuries, but—judging from the number of other people waiting for the same thing—she believed that might take hours yet. As her bone-deep exhaustion steadily hammered away at her now rapidly ebbing adrenaline-fueled fight-or-flight energy, she decided to rest for a while until the aid station crowd thinned out a bit. She lay down in the weeds amidst the dead and dying lined up along the railbed embankment. It was the first time she had been off her feet since she and Ōta-san had briefly sat on the scorched Junshin farm field, right after escaping from Ōhashi. That was at least three or four hours before.

No sooner had she begun to feel a little—a very little—of her energy coming back than someone yelled out, "Enemy plane!" Along with all of the other yet-ambulant people in her vicinity, she jumped into a nearby ditch and went into the customary open-shelter crouch, with clasped hands protecting the back of her down-turned head. She kept this posture while the plane—no doubt trying to get photos of the ruined city to take back to its base—circled around for a bit before flying off. As its engines faded off into the distance, someone spoke to her.

"Hey, your head is really bleeding badly," the person said. "You'd better get to the aid station over there."[15]

Reflexively, Masako's hand went to her head. When she brought the hand back down, it was bloody. The wound that had soaked the front of her school blouse had not been in her neck, after all. Thinking it better now to heed her informant's advice, she stood up and, resigning herself to a long wait, was prepared to shuffle off to the aid station when the day's second Good Samaritan—an apparently uninjured man who would shortly introduce himself as Taira—made his appearance.

Masako initially thought Taira-san might be a fellow Ōhashi employee, but she never asked and was never told. Whoever he was, he exuded competence, confidence, and authority, and Masako was grateful to have him as a protector.

"Say, you're really hurt badly, aren't you . . . ?" Taira-san said. "Come with me."[16]

Taira-san escorted Masako to the aid station. While he had her wait outside, he pushed through the crowd and went inside for a minute before coming back with a futon mattress. He laid this out for her by the embankment. After reaching into his pocket to produce a little Mercurochrome and hydrogen peroxide, which he announced—perhaps with a little pride—were the last drops of either substance that had been left at the aid station, he used these ointments and a bit of bandage to dress her head and leg wounds.

Just then another American plane flew over. Taira-san and Masako took cover under a tree and returned to the futon after the intruder had gone. Taira-san produced a folding *sensu* fan from a pocket and began slowly fanning Masako with it. In an offhand flashbulb memory of the day Masako-san would carry for the rest of her life, she noted—and later remembered with a sense of irony—that Taira-san's *sensu* was inscribed on its slats with the ideograms "*Kami*" and "*Kaze.*"

As the adrenaline spurt from the latest American flyover waned, the pain from her various wounds came back hard; these ailments were now joined by a new one—a cut on the bottom of her left foot, probably from broken glass. She began fretting about getting to see a real doctor and about the status of her father in Katsuyama-machi. When she shared these concerns with Taira-san, he reassured her that everything was going to be all right. He would get word to the judge as soon as possible and tell him that his daughter was alive. In the meantime, he would get her to a safer place where someone could take better care of her wounds.

By way of some information whose source he did not elaborate, Taira-san was privy to prior knowledge about a relief train from

Isahaya that was due to pull into Michino'o. This was going to pick up wounded, go as far as the damaged rails would allow to Ōhashi to pick up more victims, then double back up the tracks to take them to the naval hospital in Isahaya. (N.B.: There was no station in Ōhashi, and the eponymous railroad bridge leading south had collapsed.) He promised Masako that he would be sure she got on that train.

Around this time, a shivering, completely naked, and badly burned boy of about thirteen shuffled past them. Perhaps catching a look of pity in Masako's face, Taira-san stopped the boy, who identified himself as Fukahori, a first-year student at Nagasaki Commercial School. Then Taira-san told the boy about the relief train and urged him to ride it with them to Isahaya.

When the train finally pulled in around sunset, the ambient moaning hanging over the embankment rose in pitch. Those victims who could still move did so en masse, lurching toward the open doors of the passenger cars. Taira-san muscled his young charges through the crowd, ensuring the threesome got on board.

The cars were soon crammed with victims, many clearly on the cusp of death and, as Masako-san would later realize, in the final throes of ARS. When the train lurched forward and got underway, some of the passengers began vomiting a milky yellow and foul-smelling liquid. The sickened people were soon joined by others, then by almost everyone in the car, the floor of which quickly became slick with their upchuck. Masako was soon overcome with nausea herself but managed to keep the contents of her stomach down by opening a window and sticking her head out into the moving evening air.

As the train rolled to a stop on an Ieno-machi siding next to Ōhashi, Masako could see from her car window that the entire area was still on fire, the flames now reaching up into the house-wreckage-piled ridges on either side of the valley. When the train doors opened, first responders (including Junshin's Sister Christina) loaded more wounded—many screaming in pain—onto the already packed cars. Soon there was barely enough room to breathe, let alone stand.

In the crush aboard the train, Taira-san collared an enlisted IJN medic and exchanged a few terse words with him. Now pointing to the medic—whom the children would call and thereafter know only as Kaigun-san ("Mr. Navy")—Taira-san instructed Masako and Fukahori-kun to stick with the young man whatever happened and to do everything he told them to do.[17] As he hopped off the train, Taira-san promised to find Judge Ishida in Katsuyama-machi and Fukahori's family in Akuno'ura and tell them that their children were alive and receiving care. Masako would never see him again.

When the train started off again to begin its long, slow, backward haul to Isahaya, Kaigun-san told his young charges that, because of the huge number of far more seriously wounded people that would be going to the IJN hospital, the prospects of getting any decent medical care there were not good. Instead, he said that their best bet would be to get off the train when it stopped at Michino'o again and go with him to the Mitsubishi tunnels in Sumiyoshi-machi, where they would at least be able to pass the night with a ceiling over their heads and, if they were lucky, receive some kind of first aid. In the meantime, Kaigun-san promised, he would do what he could for them with what he could scrounge up in the way of medical supplies in Sumiyoshi.

THE LONGEST NIGHT

Yontan, Okinawa
Seven hundred forty kilometers southwest of GZ
Afternoon of August 9, 1945

THE REST OF the strike force had been compelled to wait nearly four hours for the *Big Stink* to show up[1] so that the three planes could fly back to North Field together. While the other crew members and passengers used this downtime to enjoy the base's amenities,[2] Sweeney and Fred Bock found themselves guests at the Yontan headquarters of Eighth Air Force commander General James Doolittle.[3]

Until now, Doolittle's knowledge about Tinian's 509th Composite Group had been strictly need to know—a restriction that applied even to the main Allied Pacific Theater commanders, Douglas MacArthur and Chester Nimitz, and to the 509th's Tinian landlord, Curtis LeMay. For his part, Doolittle was aware that the operational prerogatives of this security-shrouded organization compelled him to order his aircraft to avoid certain parts of the Japanese Home Islands. And like MacArthur, Nimitz, LeMay, and almost everyone else on the planet outside of Tinian, Los Alamos and the other Manhattan Project sites, and Washington, he had probably never even heard the term "atomic bomb" used until President Truman had used it three days before in his official White House statement about the Hiroshima mission. But now, as his guests regaled him with broad-brush accounts of what had transpired during their mission that morning,

Doolittle was one of the few people outside of the Pentagon-Tinian command nexus who knew that one of these atomic bombs had just been dropped on Nagasaki. The rest of the world would have to wait until the following morning to hear this news.

The 509th men in Doolittle's office were frank in their self-assessment that the mission had been far from "textbook" in its execution. Bock, for example, pointed out that the bomb had missed the designated Nagasaki AP—dead center of the downtown area—by some three kilometers. Hearing this, Doolittle was gracious enough to note that this was perhaps for the best, as untold civilian lives had no doubt been spared as a result. He added that the strike force members could also take some consolation in knowing that the bomb seemed to have detonated over some important Mitsubishi factories, at least according to the map, so no one could say the mission was a complete wash.[4] Still, Doolittle's consolations, taken together, were far from a ringing endorsement for the mishap-plagued Nagasaki run.

After *Big Stink*'s landing and refueling brought the Yontan layover to a close, the reunited strike force headed back to Tinian with *Bockscar*[5] leading the way, wheels up at 1730. During the five-hour flight, there was none of the excitement and sense of accomplishment aboard *Bockscar* that had prevailed on *Enola Gay*'s triumphant return flight the previous Monday.[6] To pass the time and break up the silence, Sweeney had Spitzer patch the Armed Forces Radio signal over the intercom, expecting to hear electrifying news of the second atomic bombing bringing the war to an end. But the only war news the crew heard between the musical interludes was about the invasion of Manchuria[7] early that morning that had just kicked off the Soviets' entry into the conflict. The machinations of officially encouraged public amnesia about the embarrassing Nagasaki mission, perhaps, were already underway—at least until the War Department could come up with a more compelling narrative about it.

Around 2230 local time, *Bockscar* touched down in Tinian. When the plane rolled to a stop and the exhausted crew members dropped down through the hatches to the North Field tarmac, there was none of the hail-the-conquering-heroes hoopla and medal pinning that had welcomed Tibbets and his men back to this very spot three days earlier. Instead, only a handful of "very subdued" high-ranking officers, the planes' ground crews, and a lone Signal Corps photographer were there to meet them.[8]

Sweeney was the last man out of the plane, and when his boots touched macadam, he was greeted by Tibbets' voice.

"Pretty rough, Chuck?"

"Pretty rough, boss," Sweeney replied.

After the crew posed next to the plane for the de rigueur photo op, they and the VIPs were trucked to the intelligence (S-2) Quonset hut for post-mission debriefing interviews.[9] While the assemblage awaited the arrival of the S-2 people, one of the VIPs on hand—Pentagon observer Rear Admiral William Purnell—recounted a Tinian episode from earlier in the day: In yet another one of Hopkins' radio-silence violations during the ingress—in this case, during the botched strike force rendezvous over Yakushima—the major had queried, "Has Sweeney aborted?" This message, however, was garbled in transmission, emerging from the console speakers in the 509th's radio room as "Sweeney . . . aborted . . ." Upon hearing this, Brigadier General Thomas Farrell—Leslie Groves's Manhattan Project representative on Tinian—ran outside of the headquarters Quonset and vomited.[10] No one at headquarters would know with certainty that the mission had not been canceled until Spitzer's first transmission about the Nagasaki drop came in some three hours later.

Purnell had perhaps shared this anecdote in an effort to cut the glum tension that hung over the gathering. But instead of imparting levity to the proceedings, its more likely effect was to inform Sweeney and his men—including Hopkins, now present and accounted for—that yet another entry would have to be chalked up on the mission's already lengthy list of snafus. Likewise, Purnell's echoing of Doolittle's earlier observation regarding the missing of the downtown Nagasaki AP as having been a humanitarian blessing in disguise probably also missed its mark. Whether the admiral's comments were well intended or not, the strike force crews did not need to be reminded that they had screwed up that day; they would be hearing plenty enough

THE LONGEST NIGHT 273

about it when the formal S-2 interrogations began in a few more minutes. And Sweeney—deservedly or not—would get the worst of it; from this night on, whispered intimations (and later public accusations) of poor judgment and other leadership failings on his part during the mission would dog him not only for the rest of his military career, but for the rest of his life.[11]

After the interrogation sessions, the crews went off to chow and thence—for those who still had some surplus physical energy—a little post-meal alcoholic carousing, inclusive of belated celebrations for Kermit Beahan; while standing on the flight line after the mission, *Bockscar*'s bombardier—much to the amusement of his colleagues—had suddenly remembered that today was his twenty-seventh birthday.[12] Luckily for the birthday boy and his fellow merrymakers, the "O club" was up to the occasion that night, with a well-stocked bar, and the drinking went on until the wee hours of the morning.

A few hours later, Tibbets received a message from General LeMay: He had decided that it was time to introduce the 509th Composite Group's heroes to the world. Toward this end, a press conference was going to be held the following day at his Tumon Bay headquarters for the benefit of the many journalists who were flocking to the Marianas for leads on the story of the century—the atomic bombings of Hiroshima and Nagasaki. Tibbets was to bring along the other commissioned officer members of the *Enola Gay* crew. From the *Bockscar* crew, however, only Sweeney was summoned.[13]

When Tibbets and his officers arrived at Tumon Bay, they went directly to LeMay's office, where the general briefed them on what kinds of questions they could and could not field at the press conference. As things turned out, the ever-security-conscious XXI BC commander's concerns about any accidental divulging of sensitive information to the Fourth Estate proved to be unfounded: The print and radio reporters in the conference room were primarily interested in feel-good human-interest fluff, and they lobbed to Tibbets and his officers mostly softball questions about their hometowns and the like.

At the conclusion of the hour-long presser, LeMay cleared the room of everyone but his two strike force commanders. Momentarily, the purpose of this post-event three-man conference became clear: It was the first time LeMay had been face-to-face with Sweeney since the Nagasaki mission, and he wanted to take this opportunity to share his opinion of that mission with the young major in person.

Wearing his usual deadpan poker face, LeMay looked Sweeney in the eye and said, "You fucked up, didn't you, Chuck."[14]

Imperial Library Annex
Chiyoda Ward, Tokyo
Nine hundred forty-five kilometers east-northeast of GZ
2330 hours, August 9, 1945

While the Nagasaki strike force crews were still in the midst of their post-mission debriefing interviews on Tinian, the "library annex" underground-bunker complex at the Imperial Palace compound was hosting yet another conference to discuss the matter of whether or not to accept the surrender stipulations as laid out in the Potsdam Declaration—and if so, how.

After the Supreme War Council session held in the bunker that morning, there had been two Cabinet meetings convened at the *kantei*—the prime minister's official residence in Nagata-chō—to discuss the same matter. But thanks to the obstinacy of War Minister Anami, these had also ended in the same frustrating stalemate. Despite Foreign Minister Tōgō's best efforts to convince Anami otherwise, the latter was still refusing to accept the Potsdam Declaration unless that document were amended to include the provisos he and the other members of the Supreme War Council had demanded that morning[15] (in addition to the imperial-sovereignty-guarantee condition, for which agreement was unanimous): Japanese self-disarmament; Japanese-adjudicated "war crimes" prosecution; and no Allied occupation of the Home Islands.

Of the day's two full Cabinet sessions, the atmosphere of the second—lasting from 1800 to 2100—had been particularly vituperative.[16] Following Suzuki's formal commencement of the meeting, For-

THE LONGEST NIGHT

eign Minister Tōgō was the first to have the floor—an opportunity he used to fire a bombshell at Anami: In Tōgō's opinion—delivered in a notable divergence from his usual diplomatic tone—there was no chance of convincing the Allies to accept the war faction's "three additional conditions."[17] To insist on them would only prolong the war and subject the nation to more suffering and destruction.

Anami responded with fury to Tōgō's challenge, declaring, "The appearance of the atomic bomb does not spell the end of war. . . . We are confident about a decisive homeland battle against American forces."[18] Although he admitted that "given the atomic bomb and the Soviet entry, there is no chance of winning on the basis of mathematical calculation," he still insisted that "there will be some chance as long as we keep on fighting for the honor of the Yamato race. . . . If we go on like this and surrender, the Yamato race would be as good as dead spiritually."[19]

Coming to Tōgō's defense, Navy Minister Yonai attacked the irrationality of Anami's position; in support of his argument, he counted off items from the long and uninterrupted list of decisive military defeats Japan had suffered since the fall of Saipan. To this, Anami countered that this time would be different, as none of those previous battles had taken place in the Home Islands, where numerous advantages not enjoyed in previous campaigns would favor Japan's cause. Supply lines, for example, would be exclusively overland and thus invulnerable to the Allied naval blockade. Formidable IJA forces were being marshaled in Kyushu, preparing to meet the Allies' anticipated invasion there. Moreover, the entire eighty-million-strong civilian population could be mobilized—using whatever implements at hand they might wield as weapons—for last-ditch, house-to-house resistance to the death against the invaders. As such, he was confident that Japan could inflict enough casualties on the Allies to force them to the negotiating table to accept the multi-conditioned compromise peace the war faction desired.[20]

The debate continued back and forth like this on the same tiresome seesaw until Suzuki finally called for the day's third vote on the Potsdam Declaration. After the tally, nine of the members present supported Tōgō's proposal for "unconditional" acceptance (again, with the exception of the imperial-sovereignty condition); three (Anami himself and two others) supported the war minister's proposal to continue fighting toward a negotiated peace; and an additional three favored a position somewhere between those two positions.[21]

Although at first glance it would appear that Tōgō's proposal had prevailed, due to its winning an overwhelming majority of the votes, Anami had an ace up his sleeve. Half a century earlier, when the Meiji Constitution was being drafted, the leaders of the emperor's new military had insisted upon the inclusion in that document of the so-called *tōsuiken* ("prerogative of supreme command") clause, which codified direct and ultimate authority over the nation's military as belonging solely to the emperor, proscribing any civilian oversight of military (and naval)[22] affairs outside of a narrowly defined and perennially bitterly contested purview of budgetary control.

A later interpretation of the *tōsuiken* clause served as the legal basis of a 1936 law (enacted during the premiership of Hirota Kōki) requiring that war and Navy ministers be active-duty generals and admirals,[23] respectively. This was significant because, in effect, the law gave the services the ability to blackmail prime ministerial Cabinets by withdrawing their war or Navy minister, via resignation, and then withholding a replacement—a quorum requirement for a Cabinet to legally exist as such—until the sitting prime minister bent to their will or, in lieu of that, was himself forced to resign[24] and dissolve his Cabinet. In such a scenario, a new prime minister would have to be appointed (by the emperor and his privy council advisors) and a new Cabinet formed—a time-consuming and politically fraught process, even in peacetime, that could bring the government to a standstill for days or even weeks. Because of the nation's current straits—with two atom-bombed cities and the Soviet juggernaut rolling down from the north—this was time Japan did not have.

With his back thus up against a wall—and the nation's survival in the balance—Suzuki had no choice but to play a hand he had avoided resorting to until now. After adjourning this Cabinet–Supreme War

THE LONGEST NIGHT

Council meeting, he and Tōgo maneuvered behind the backs (and over the heads) of the war faction and their supporters, negotiating directly with the imperial household to ensure that a fourth August 9 conference on the Potsdam matter would be convened and, of critical importance to Suzuki's plan, upgraded to a *gozen kaigi*—"a meeting held in the august presence" of Emperor Hirohito. The *tōsuiken* sword, in this case, would cut both ways; if the emperor decided in favor of immediate acceptance of the (slightly modified) Potsdam Declaration, then Anami, Umezu, and Toyoda—as professional military men sworn to loyalty to the emperor and, moreover, subject to His Majesty's direct authority—would have no choice but to bow to the imperial will. It would be game, set, and match for the peace faction.

Suzuki's maneuvers to hold a fourth meeting—with imperial blessing—were successful. At 2330, a *gozen kaigi* was convened in the bunker, presided over, at the emperor's pleasure, by his prime minister. In attendance (in addition to Suzuki and the emperor) were the full prime ministerial Cabinet; the other uniformed members of the Supreme War Council; Chief Cabinet Secretary Sakomizu; the president of the privy council, Baron Hiranuma Ki'ichirō;[25] and numerous military and bureaucratic aides.

At the opening of the meeting, the Potsdam Declaration was read aloud for the emperor, after which Foreign Minister Tōgō, as was the prerogative of his office, gave his ministry's interpretation of the document's meaning and portent and offered his opinion regarding the desirability of its acceptance. This was followed by the sharing of opinions by other attendees, for and against the same. After three hours of discussion, debate, and the occasional outburst of indignant pontification, the conference was brought to a head when Suzuki made his decisive move. Rising to address the meeting, the seventy-seven-year-old premier said:

> We have discussed this question for a long time and everyone has expressed his own opinion sincerely without any conclusion being reached. The situation is urgent, so any delay in coming to a

decision should not be tolerated. I am therefore proposing to ask the Emperor his own wish and to decide the conference's conclusion on that basis. His wish should settle the issue, and the Government should follow it.[26]

Anami, Umezu, and Toyoda must have been absolutely floored by this turn of events—not only because they perceived what it would mean for the war, but also because they realized that they had just been checkmated by an old fox. But the emperor had known this was coming and had prepared for it. Speaking from a dais-elevated chair backed by a gold-leafed folding screen, the forty-four-year-old emperor replied:

I agree with the first opinion as expressed by the foreign minister. I think I should tell the reasons why I have decided so. Thinking about the world situation and the internal Japanese situation [i.e., fear of military rebellion and/or Socialist revolution], to continue the war means nothing but the destruction of the whole nation. My ancestors and I have always wished to put forward the Nation's welfare and international world peace as our prime concern. To continue the war now means that cruelty and bloodshed will still continue in the world and that the Japanese Nation will suffer severe damage. So, to stop the war on this occasion is the only way to save the Nation from destruction and to restore peace in the world. Looking back at what our military headquarters have done, it is apparent that their performance has fallen far short of the plans expressed. I don't think this discrepancy can he corrected in the future. But when I think about my obedient soldiers abroad and of those who died or were wounded in battle, about those who have lost their property or lives by bombing in the homeland, when I think of all those sacrifices, I cannot help but feel sad. I decided that this war should be stopped, however, in spite of this sentiment and for more important considerations.[27]

THE LONGEST NIGHT   279

After a few seconds of stunned silence, one of the ministers or military officers in attendance—and soon all of them—began weeping, some sobbing loudly. Several tumbled out of their chairs, fell to their knees, and pressed their foreheads against the floor—a gesture of ultimate supplication and self-debasement in Japanese culture.[28]

Over the sounds of middle-aged and elderly male weeping—and probably fighting back tears of his own—Prime Minister Suzuki bowed deeply to the emperor to acknowledge the imperial will, then turned to face his peers.

"The Imperial decision has been expressed," he said. "This should be the conclusion of the conference."[29]

Following the emperor's departure from the bunker, the Cabinet remained behind to attend to the formality of officially ratifying His Majesty's stated wishes.[30]

At 0900 that morning, Tōgō would cable the neutral Swiss and Swedish governments with details of the Japanese government's decision to accept the Potsdam Declaration, dependent on inclusion of a new condition acknowledging the post-surrender continuance of the emperor's sovereignty.[31] The Swiss were asked to relay this information to Washington through the American embassy in Bern, while the Swedes would inform the British, Soviet, and Chinese embassies in Stockholm. But in the end, the Allied decision on whether to accept this Japanese offer of a slightly less-than-unconditional surrender would ultimately come down to Harry Truman and his White House advisors.

======

Nagasaki Appellate Court chief judge's kansha *(new)*
Yaoya-machi
2.9 kilometers southeast of GZ

The Nagasaki Prefectural Office (*kenchō*) in Edo-machi was designed by Yamada Shichigorō (1871–1945), an acolyte of Tatsuno Kingo (1854–1919)—doyen of Meiji Era institutional architecture. The ornate two-story redbrick building was topped by a high-angled mansard roof

280   NAGASAKI

with porthole windows and onion-domed turrets.[32] These latter items added an exotic flair to the structure, whose overall style—which might be described as Versailles meets Addams Family—already bordered on the anachronistic when the prefectural office was opened to the public in 1911. Stately edifice or eccentric eyesore, the *kenchō* had been a showpiece on the harborside skyline and an object of pride and reverence for local residents ever since.

At 1102 on August 9, while Governor Nagano had been away from his office and holed up in the prefectural civil defense bunker a little over one kilometer to the northeast, the *kenchō* was situated in such a way that the tip of its high gabled roof poked over the edge of Konpira's bomb shadow when Fat Man detonated five hundred meters up and 3.3 kilometers away to the north. Although much of the energy of the bomb's line-of-sight thermal rays had already been dissipated by atmospheric humidity and dust by the time they reached Edo-machi, they were still hot enough to start something smoldering under the green oxidized-copper sheeting that covered the roof.[33]

Immediately after the explosion, the staff on duty at the *kenchō* had been too preoccupied by the blast wind damage to the building— mostly in the form of blown-in windows—to notice anything in the way of a developing fire situation. The first sign of trouble was not detected until 1230, when a passerby on the street below spotted a thin spiral of white smoke curling up from one of the small onion domes on the *kenchō* roof.[34] A fire truck was eventually borrowed from the ongoing battle against the conflagration then creeping down the Togitsu Road, but by the time it showed up at the *kenchō*, the flames there—concurrently being watched by Kiridōshi Michiko and Honda Sawa from atop Konpira—were already out of control.

Closer to hand, the prefectural office blaze, in combination with the early afternoon's prevailing westerly winds, was showering the appellate courthouse in nearby Banzai-machi with flurries of sparks and embers. The primarily wooden courthouse had already suffered heavy structural damage from Fat Man's earlier atmospheric displacement over the city. This included catastrophic ceiling collapses on the second floor of the building, including in Judge Ishida's chambers.[35] Had he been on duty that morning instead of taking the day off to move into his new official residence in Yaoya-machi, there is little doubt he would have been killed by falling debris.

Although a midafternoon shift in the direction of the prevailing winds ended up saving city hall and the rest of the CBD east of nearby Shinkōzen Elementary School, it had come too late to save the courthouse.[36] After one of his clerks ran to Yaoya-machi to tell him the news, Judge Ishida returned with the man to Banzai-machi.[37] Taking charge of the hectic situation there and keeping up a brave face in front of his subordinates would help him for the time avoid collapsing under the psychological strain of his growing worries over his missing daughter. But this demon would be waiting for him when he returned to the Yaoya-machi residence at sunset.

That night, the sporadic appearance of American aircraft over the city had driven the judge and those household members still present—Hayashi-sensei and her mother and Shige the maid—into the cramped and humid confines of the kansha's backyard underground bomb shelter. During the long hours while sleep proved evasive for him, he attempted to keep at bay his gnawing and growing fears that Masako had been killed by entertaining happy memories of his favorite child. One of these reminiscences was of how he used to hear the happy voices of Masako and her Kenjo classmates when they would come down the street at night after their Ōhashi shifts, singing some patriotic song or another.[38] Sleep eventually arrived for the judge, but it did not last long. He was awakened in tears by a nightmare in which he was cradling the lifeless body of his daughter. He looked at his watch. It was 0305.[39]

THE DAY AFTER

Sumiyoshi tunnel complex
2.3 kilometers north-northwest of GZ
Night of August 9 to 10, 1945

KAIGUN-SAN HAD DONE his best to make his young charges comfortable, with the far worse-off Fukahori-kun taking up most of his attention. But the young Navy medic did not have much to work with, either in terms of supplies or facilities. The tunnel he had chosen for a shelter spot was crowded and damp, and it reeked of the victims' vomit, blood, and the now all-too-familiar and distinctive stench of burned skin. It was also unlit, with the exception of a single candle around which a Korean-speaking family with small children huddled near the tunnel entrance.

The young Navy medic decided to set Ishida Masako and Fukahori-kun up next to the Korean group. At least here they would have a little light, and he would do what he could to keep them dry. Finding some wooden pallets, he laid these on top of the tunnel's single-track mine cart rails to keep the children off of the puddled and effluvia-slick floor. But he could do nothing to protect them from the water condensation constantly dripping from the tunnel's ceiling. Throughout the night, Masako was pestered by water drops hitting her body, especially her face and head, and she shivered with cold each time this happened.[1]

Fukahori-kun was also experiencing cold—probably due to his extensive burns and nakedness—and he constantly complained about this in between his plaintive and repeated cries for his mother. Finally, the generous (and likely also exasperated) Kaigun-san literally gave the boy the shirt off his back to use as a blanket.[2] Despite this kindness, which was soon augmented by a sheet of tatami matting the medic found outside near the tunnel entrance, the shivering Fukahori-kun could find no relief. Seeking body warmth—and likely a measure of solace—from his palette mate, he spooned up alongside Masako, who shuddered in revulsion at the sensation of the boy's burned, lymph-slimy skin brushing against her bare arms.

As Masako had not suffered any burn injuries herself, she did not experience the infamous unslakable thirst that plagued so many hibakusha in Japan's two atomic-bombed cities. Fukahori-kun, however, was not so fortunate. Like nearly every other burn victim in Nagasaki still drawing breath that night, he was incessantly complaining about thirst—so pitiably that the Korean family (most likely from one of the nearby *hanba* workers' hamlets in Sumiyoshi-machi) eventually gave him a drink from their water kettle. Not five minutes later, he begged for and received more water, albeit it over the objections of some of the Japanese people sheltering in the tunnel who intoned the old IJA field manual saw about how giving water to injured people would cause them to die. Probably figuring that the poor boy was going to die, anyway, and perhaps motivated as much by wanting to keep him quiet as they were by merciful generosity, the Koreans indulged his demands until Fukahori-kun drained the last drop from the kettle—an act that resulted in a sharp but indecipherable rebuke from the group's mother figure. No one in this part of the tunnel would receive any more water until daybreak.

In the meantime, Kaigun-san had managed to scrounge up some hardtack crackers, which he distributed to his "patients." Masako was grateful for the gesture, but when she took her first bite of one of the crackers, she was overcome with nausea and had to give up on eating any more. She did not know it at the time—and would not have understood the ailment even if it had been explained to her—but she was suffering from the early stages of the ARS that would steadily worsen and come close to killing her over the next month.

———

Tateyama-machi, near the summit of Mount Konpira
Two kilometers southeast of GZ
Dawn, August 10, 1945

By the time the sky began to brighten in the east, Kiridōshi Michiko and Honda Sawa had been sheltering in place in their ginger patch sanctuary for over twelve hours, since being told to do so by a passing soldier the previous afternoon.[3] Although the fires the soldier had warned them of had never come close to the girls' position, they had been plagued by a litany of other stressors during the sleepless sojourn they had just passed on Mount Konpira.

Several times during the night, the girls had been startled by the appearance of American planes flying over the city, dropping illumination flares. Whenever this happened, Sawa would panic, fearing that another attack was in progress—a belief (and a reaction) no doubt simultaneously shared by many of the other thousands of survivors in the city below. Seasoned Tokyo air raid veteran Michiko, however, knew that these were just reconnaissance planes dropping flares for nighttime photography, and despite sharing this hard-won knowledge with her companion, Sawa would still scamper into a nearby clump of bushes each time she heard a plane overhead.

The girls were also drenched several times by sudden squalls of what Michiko would only later realize was probably "black" rain seeded by all of the radioactive-fallout-poisoned dust and other debris that had been carried up into the atmosphere by the towering smoke column[4] that had risen over the Urakami Valley after the previous morning's explosion. Adding to the atmosphere of general dread and misery, the deep, agonized lowing of some large animal—most likely a farmer's cow—echoed up from the slope below throughout the night.

During their time on the mountain, the girls had enjoyed a peerless vantage point from which to track the development of the fires in the city. And as the Nagasaki-savvy Sawa had pointed out early on in their fire watch, it appeared that the flames were not going to reach their respective neighborhoods in the eastern Nakashima Valley. Several times the previous night, the girls had discussed climbing back down the mountain and going home—where their loved ones were no doubt worried sick about them—but they were loath to disobey the soldier who had told them to stay put.

The next morning, the sleep-deprived girls were ready to make their move. Contrary to their earlier fears, no authority figures stopped them during their descent from the mountain and passage through the surprisingly lightly damaged neighborhoods on the lee side of Mount Konpira, and the girls reached Nakagawa-machi without further incident. When the joyously relieved (and half-angry) Kiridōshi family rushed the *genkan* entranceway to welcome Michiko home, pecking-order protocol dictated that her politically powerless mother—as the lowest-ranking adult in the household—should allow her mother-in-law and husband to hug the girl before she did. Meanwhile, as this ritual played out, Michiko's sisters, Teruko and Yasuko—unable to wait their turn for a hug—ran outside of the house to scream and bawl away their pent-up anxiety and false-alarm grief of the past twenty hours.

Following the drama of the *genkan* homecoming, Michiko gave a brief rundown of her current physical condition and an account of what had happened since the explosion. Hearing that the girls (as with everyone else in the household) had not slept at all the previous night, Michiko's mother insisted that Sawa-san rest up for a while with Michiko before getting back to her own family (despite the certainty that they were as anxious about their daughter as the Kiridōshis had been about their own). The matter settled, Michiko's mother laid out futon mattresses on a tatami floor still twinkling here and there with bits of shattered window glass, which the family would still be finding in the house months later. The girls were sound asleep as soon as their heads hit their pillows.

Shimonishiyama-machi
2.9 kilometers southeast of GZ
Morning of August 10, 1945

Gunge Norio had sat up most of the previous night waiting for his older brother, Yoshio, to come home. That night had now melted away with the sunrise of a new day, but Yoshio had yet to appear. Norio's initial response to the ball of hot dread getting steadily heavier in the pit of his stomach was to sit in place and just hope everything would be resolved on its own. But eventually the waiting became unbearable, and he decided to walk the 4.5 kilometers to Nagasaki Medical College to look for his brother.

Throwing on some clothes, he left the house to begin his trek. But he was hardly halfway through the CBD before he found his way blocked by fires. These were still so bad that he could hardly get close to Nagasaki Station, let alone negotiate the Togitsu Road curve around the base of Mount Konpira to try to make it up into Urakami. Returning to Shimonishiyama-machi deterred but not yet defeated, he came to the same conclusion that Kiridōshi Michiko and Honda Sawa had reached the previous day: If he could not walk around Konpira, he would have to climb over it.

At this point, Norio still had no idea of the enormity of the calamity that had befallen the city on the other side of the mountain. He did not even bother to bring his water canteen with him. As he began making his way up the slope behind his house, he passed increasing numbers of staggering, scorched, and bloodied figures coming down in the opposite direction. The tree foliage and undergrowth he was walking through were still perfectly green and unmolested and, as such, incompatible with the obviously burned people he was passing. He could not fathom what kind of catastrophe could have possi-

THE DAY AFTER

bly caused all of this carnage, and he would get a firm idea of its scale only once he crested the mountain.

When he did so, he was beyond stunned by what he saw. Nothing. The valley was a beige-colored wasteland as far as he could see. And farther down the western slope, where the pretty white buildings of the medical college should have been, there were only shattered, blackened concrete shells poking up here and there out of fields of smoldering wooden wreckage.

The trauma he experienced in this moment—as he realized that his brother was probably somewhere down there in those smoking ruins—was so rapid and so intense that he barely had time to register horror and grief before he felt himself washed over by a wave of complete, dead numbness. In lieu of attempting to process the unthinkable, Norio's sixteen-year-old brain instead opted to shut down everything but the simple animal level of functioning the boy required to keep moving.[5] In this zombie-like dazed state, he headed down the slope toward what was left of the medical college.

When he reached the main hospital wing, the magnificent institution he remembered visiting as a small boy was now completely hollowed out. Inside the building, everything was charred black, including the bodies he found there. Outside of the scorched husks of what had been the campus' sturdier concrete structures, the ground underneath Norio's feet was a carpet of gray rubble and bones. Surveying this scene, he decided to try to identify some of these human remains as Yoshio's. Over the next few hours, as each foray into the rubble came up empty, he began to feel not disillusioned but rather hopeful that Yoshio had survived and was perhaps in an aid station somewhere. As he prepared to give up for the day and head back to Shimonishiyama-machi, he caught sight of a single singed book page on the ground. Picking it up, Norio saw that it was from a German medical manual, and it was imprinted with a red Nagasaki Medical College Library seal. On an impulse, he decided to bring it home with him.

This is Gunge Norio's last memory of August 10, 1945.

NAGASAKI

Sumiyoshi tunnel complex
2.3 kilometers north-northwest of GZ
Morning of August 10, 1945

Ishida Masako had passed a rough night. But poor Fukahori-kun's had been much worse, and by the light of daybreak, it was clear to see that he did not have much longer to live. Since then, in his sporadic moments of semi-lucidity, he had begged to be taken to the naval hospital in Isahaya. But Masako was in no condition to help, and Kaigun-san was busy with other duties, though he had found time at one point to bring his young charges a breakfast of small lumps of mixed rice and barley wrapped in newsprint. Masako nibbled at this meager repast hesitantly, but Fukahori-kun took a large bite and immediately began vomiting violently, further draining his already near-desiccated body of precious water. Memories of the pity, helplessness, and guilt Masako felt watching this scene would haunt her for the rest of her life.

Later that morning, from her vantage point near the tunnel entrance, Masako could see Kaigun-san—who was just out of earshot—trying to stop southbound passersby on the Togitsu Road, but they all brushed away his entreaties before moving on. Then she saw one of the pedestrians on the road—a youngish man who looked like some kind of civil servant—stop and have with Kaigun-san a discussion more substantial than the quick dismissals everyone else had given him so far. During this exchange, Masako was able to make out the young man's mention of a new-type bomb.[6] At last, she had a name for the monster responsible for all of this hell.

The young men came over to Masako, and the civilian introduced himself—namelessly—as a prefectural office employee.

"Rather than trying to go to Isahaya," the *kenchō* man continued, "you should go home as soon as possible. Think of how worried your family must be about you. The prefectural office and the courthouse and the area around them burned down, but Katsuyama-machi is OK. I can take you as far as the Inasa Bridge."[7]

THE DAY AFTER

Masako eagerly assented to the escort offer, but before the pair set out on their journey, the *kenchō* man found some pieces of burlap on the ground and bound this material around each of Masako's feet with metal wire. The new footwear was uncomfortable, but because of the condition of the road surface Masako knew she was about to start walking over, it was certainly preferable to the alternative of having to go barefoot again.

As she left, Masako thanked Kaigun-san for his help and said goodbye to Fukahori-kun and the other people near the tunnel entrance, apologizing—in the manner dictated by Japanese etiquette—for her impertinence for leaving before they did.

South of Sumiyoshi, everything was either still aflame or at least smoldering. The Togitsu Road became impassable past Ōhashi—clogged with wreckage and bodies—compelling Masako and the *kenchō* man to follow the Kokutetsu railbed instead. The ground under Masako's feet here was still hot—even through her wire-tied burlap foot sacks—and covered everywhere with razor-sharp shards of window glass. Several times during their journey, when the ground ruined the footwear Masako was wearing, the *kenchō* man had to fashion new pairs for her out of found materials. At one point he also gave Masako a piece of wood for a crutch. She used this to limp along, favoring her injured leg, which was starting to throb with pain again.

The farther south they proceeded, the more gruesome the scenery became. Masako consciously tried not to step on any prostrate bodies—dead or not—but she encountered many situations when she had no choice but to do just that in order to keep moving forward. This was especially true in Mori-machi, which seemed to be the worst part of the ZTD in terms of overall devastation. Much of this detritus had been houses—and their occupants—on the western side of Konpira twenty-four hours earlier; after being smashed by Fat Man's shock wave, whole neighborhoods had slid down the steep western slope of the mountain to bury the roadway below, adding to the carnage and debris from the nearby Mitsubishi plant compound. Everywhere Masako looked, she saw carbonized corpses. Completely depleted of the water that had made up 70 percent of the mass of their living bodies, adults had shrunk to the size of children and children to the size of dolls. Incredibly, there were still some survivors strewn about here and there on the ground, mixed in amidst all of this death. Invariably moaning for water, some were so badly burned, it was impossible to tell if they were male or female—they had been reduced to animated lumps of scorched fat and protein. The smell of these victims—both living and dead—hung over everything. There was no getting away from this stench, which forced Masako into constant struggles with nausea she did not always win.

The way forward at last began to clear once Masako and the *kenchō* man entered the long turn around the southwest foot of Konpira. There, emergency work crews of *keibitai*, Kawanami shipyard personnel, and Allied POWs were in the process of opening a two-meter-wide footpath—walled in on both sides by palisades of debris and bodies—down the middle of this stretch of the Togitsu Road.[8]

Before taking his leave at the Inasa Bridge, the *kenchō* man changed Masako's foot wrappings one final time and replaced her crutch with a new length of wood. Then he called out to passersby to see if anyone was going as far as Nagasaki Station and eventually found a man who agreed to escort Masako there.[9]

After parting with the anonymous Good Samaritan, Masako entered the last leg of her journey. Under normal circumstances, walking from the station (which was now a charred skeleton of twisted girders) to her home neighborhood would have been a nice, easy fifteen-minute stroll past Nishizaka and up a shallow slope leading to Katsuyama-machi. But on this day, in her sleep-deprived, injured, and—as she would later find out—irradiated condition, those fifteen minutes might as well have been fifteen hours. Sporadically dusted by drifts of spark flurries from nearby blazes, she hobbled along alone on her makeshift crutch, passing the ruins of the Naka-machi Catholic Church on the way. Each step forward required a concerted, conscious

THE DAY AFTER 291

effort to make—with her legs feeling like the useless, floppy rubber appendages one has in nightmares when being pursued by a monster.[10] All the while she had to resist the urge to surrender to her exhaustion and frustration—to just lie down on the ground and go to sleep. But over the past twenty-four hours she had already seen too many people do that and they ended up never getting up again. She kept moving.

After what seemed like hours, Masako's spirit picked up when she caught sight of the tiled roof of Katsuyama Elementary School over the rise of the slope. It was not much longer now. But when she reached the *kansha* in Katsuyama-machi, she was disheartened to find it empty. Then, remembering the previous day's scheduled move into new lodgings, she doubled back to nearby Yaoya-machi. When she arrived at the new *kansha's* front gate, she saw a note scribbled in chalk on one of its wooden posts:

Masako: I'm OK. Come to the Appellate Court ruins after the fires die down. [August] 10th.[11]

Just then the front door opened. Masako and Hayashi-sensei caught sight of each other simultaneously and both burst into tears. Once the tears had subsided, Hayashi-sensei bade Masako to enter the house with the burlap wrappings still on her feet, as the floors inside were covered with broken glass. Then she swept a space on the floor and put out a row of *zabuton* seat cushions for Masako to lie down on.

All of Masako's exhaustion seemed to sweep over her at once, and she was hit by heavy waves of nausea. But she managed to keep from vomiting while Hayashi-sensei helped her change into clean clothes and dressed her young charge's cuts and other injuries with Mercurochrome and gauze bandages. As she did so, she filled Masako in on the status of the household and the whereabouts of its members. Shige, their maid, had gone home—with the judge's blessings and severance pay—to the nearby village of Mogi-machi that morning.[12] The judge himself, as per his gatepost note, was supervising recovery activities at the ruins of his courthouse.

In the midst of this conversation, Masako heard her father's voice as he entered the *genkan* vestibule of the house. Copious tears of joy were shed over the ensuing miraculous reunion, and Masako was elated at the thought that her waking nightmare was at last over. But in fact, another one had already begun.

PART FIVE

AFTERMATH

RUINS

Tera-machi
3.6 kilometers southeast of GZ

IN THE IMMEDIATE aftermath of the bombing, Kōtaiji Temple was strictly standing room only, and it remained so throughout the following night. The next morning, once it became clear that the worst of the downtown fires had largely subsided, many among the crowd of evacuees at the temple began trailing off to their home neighborhoods. The Tatenos, however, were not among them. They were already aware that they had no home to which to return. And after having been on their feet for almost twenty-four hours by this point, they were too exhausted to even contemplate walking.

Seizing the opportunity presented by the thinning of the temple crowds, Mr. Tateno was at last able to stake out enough space on the ground for his family to sit down. But whatever meager succor this new arrangement provided was merely physical; it offered no relief from the incessant, insistent cacophony of suffering still hanging over the temple—the screams of the wounded, the moans and sporadic retching of the dying, and the anguished cries of the newly bereaved.

Things took a slight turn for the better on the evening of August 11 when a detachment of military men arrived in Tera-machi to distribute *onigiri* rice balls to survivors. As a megaphone-wielding officer informed the crowd, this emergency ration was strictly limited to one *onigiri* per person per day. Still, it was the first food any of the Tatenos had seen since the morning of the bombing, so they were thankful to have anything at all. Unfortunately for Sueko, the scorched mouth and tonsils she had suffered on August 9 meant it would be a couple of days yet before she could manage to swallow solid food.

As August 12 dawned, the Kōtaiji crowds had further thinned, but the grounds and temple buildings were still full of prostrate victims—alternately moaning and screaming—as well as piles of rapidly putrefying and fly-blown corpses awaiting disposal. Having just passed their third consecutive sleepless night in this hellscape, the Tatenos resolved that they had had enough. After packing up the few belongings they had managed to bring with them, they set off to take their chances back in the ashes of Fukuro-machi. If they were going to be miserable, at least they could be so on familiar ground.

It came as no surprise to anyone in the family that the charred ruin of their house was utterly uninhabitable, but the sight of it was a sad disappointment nevertheless. Moving on to their evacuation plan B, the Tatenos pitched camp on the relatively uncluttered grounds of Dr. Takao's clinic, where they proceeded to erect a lean-to made out of a couple of propped-up sheets of corrugated metal. Insofar as their new home provided the family with an ostensible "roof" over their heads, it was a vast improvement over what they had left behind in Kōtaiji. Moreover, the site came with the amenity of a broken main that provided the Tatenos and the other survivors sheltering nearby with a limitless supply of (presumably) potable water—a resource that helped keep their stomachs full in between the once-a-day, one-to-a-person Army rice ball rations, which were barely sufficient to stave off starvation.

The next morning, Mr. Tateno mentioned that, back in the days when the IJA Nagasaki garrison was still one of the Tokuseidō's best customers, he had had frequent occasion to see the inside of a storehouse full of canned goods at the local Kempeitai headquarters near Nagasaki Station. Although this area had been swept by the fires of August 9 to 10, there was still a possibility that some of those cans had survived the conflagration. After a quick family conference, during which the risk of being caught looting was likely called into consideration, Mr. Tateno and his eldest daughter, Mitsuko, set out to see what they could rescue from the ruins of the burned Army storehouse. They returned to Fukuro-machi with a handful of cans, which were no doubt appreciated back at the lean-to. But from a cost-benefit standpoint, going back to the storehouse on another food raid would not have merited the danger of getting arrested or worse, a distinct possibility now that the authorities were beginning to restore some semblance of order in the CBD. And in any case, there was no use going back there, the family reasoned, as the storehouse ruins had probably already been picked clean by other scavengers.

One aspect of public order that Nagasaki authorities were having a much harder time getting under control was the matter of body recovery and disposal. Days after the bombing, there were still tens of thousands of corpses strewn across the city, not only in the ZTD but in the CBD as well. The unsatisfactory resolution of this issue would go on to become one of the widest disparities between the respective post-bombing experiences of Nagasaki and its sister in atomic tragedy, Hiroshima.

In the aftermath of the latter city's destruction, the recovery and disposal of bodies was handled with quite remarkable efficiency, given the circumstances.[1] Favoring these efforts was Hiroshima's flat topography—the very characteristic that had made the city an ideal target for an atomic bomb—as well as its robust transportation network of waterways and wide (and relatively easily rubble-cleared) thoroughfares.

These accidental advantages of geography and infrastructure allowed for the timely recovery and transportation of corpses to large field crematories located at key points around the city. These were operated around the clock for several weeks and kept supplied throughout with pyre fuel of diesel oil and wood transported by military trucks and flatboats. Within a month after the bombing, these operations had managed to cremate (and carefully tally) probably close to 100,000 of Hiroshima's eventual (by the end of 1945) 140,000 bomb fatalities.[2]

The manpower and logistical support indispensable for this operation were available because of the fortuitous proximity to Hiroshima's ZTD of two major military commands that had survived Little Boy's fury more or less intact. These were the IJN arsenal at nearby Kure and, far more significant, the IJA Akatsuki Maritime Command. Headquartered in nearby Hiroshima harbor—some five kilometers over flat terrain from the hypocenter—the Akatsuki organization was able to dispatch several thousand troops into the ZTD within hours of the explosion to fight fires, rescue survivors, clear vital roadways, and, finally, do most of the heavy lifting for the systematic large-scale cremation of the city's dead.

In Nagasaki's case, however, the nearest large military commands still in functioning condition after the bombing were IJN facilities in Ōmura and Isahaya—both some twenty-five kilometers away—and Sasebo Naval Arsenal some fifty-five kilometers distant.[3] To reach the ZTD, first responders from these bases had to battle their way through the rubble-clogged Togitsu Road—either down through the deep belts of mountain ranges north of the city or up from the essentially undamaged harbor. Only after these arduous and time-consuming journeys were these elements able to link up with whatever manpower Governor Nagano and Mayor Okada Jukichi managed to rally locally, augmented by volunteers coming into the city from the surrounding countryside.[4]

But large numbers of first responders did not materialize, and despite the best efforts of those who did show up, they were simply not equal to the enormity of Nagasaki's body-recovery task, the difficulty of which was exponentially complicated by the topographical treachery of the Urakami Valley and the mountains of smoldering debris under which that terrain (and tens of thousands of bodies) had been buried by Fat Man's blast. Because almost the entirety of the ZTD was completely inaccessible to vehicles, first responders had no choice but to climb up into the bombed-out areas in two-man stretcher teams, then bring bodies down one at a time to cremate on wreckage-cleared level ground on the valley floor.[5] Battling heat, lung-ravaging smoke, stomach-turning stench, and—more than anything else—gravity, stretcher teams working the steeper areas of the ZTD could barely maintain a turnaround of one recovered body per hour. As these hours became days, the public health threat of hot-weather-accelerated decomposition of unrecovered bodies quickly outpaced the ability of these first responders to deal with the situation. As a result, many victims ended up being simply left in place[6] and covered over with debris and soil. The entire Urakami Valley reeked of their decaying remains for months afterward.

In the end, the Japanese funerary dignity of proper cremation was afforded to only a fraction of Nagasaki's bomb fatalities by September 1945.[7] In fairness to these overwhelmed cremation efforts, nobody knows how many victims were simply blown to bits and, as such, impossible to recover. The augmented power of the plutonium Fat Man bomb dropped on the city—some 40 percent greater than Hiroshima's Little Boy—resulted in a ZTD that, due to the force- and heat-channeling properties of Urakami's topography, was only one-fourth the area of Hiroshima's.[8] The sheer devastation and extreme lethality of the Urakami ZTD can be appreciated by considering that, while the Little Boy device dropped on Hiroshima had detonated over a densely populated city center, Fat Man had exploded over suburbs, industrial parks, and farms. If the latter had detonated over the Nigiwai Bridge as originally intended, there is little doubt that—as Major Sweeney's superiors postulated—Nagasaki's death toll would have easily exceeded Hiroshima's.

In sharp contrast again to Hiroshima's case, the majority of Nagasaki's cremations were carried out not by official first responders but rather—and out of necessity—by private citizens. These were generally surviving family members conducting their grim rites of parental, filial, or fraternal duty on any open ground they could find and using whatever pyre fuel (mostly scrap wood scrounged from wreckage piles) was at hand.[9] Many such cremations were performed on-site in the ZTD by lone household survivors—often working fathers— who had been away from the Urakami Valley on the morning of the bombing, then had returned to their destroyed homes to find their families wiped out. Others were attended to by people from surrounding areas who went into the ZTD to find the corpses of loved ones who had been caught by the explosion and/or fires in Urakami workplaces and schools. Many cremations were also carried out in the CBD for loved ones carried from the ZTD back to their homes, as well as for victims who had miraculously made it home to the CBD from Urakami on their own, only to later succumb to their injuries and/or ARS. For weeks after the bombing, right up to the arrival of the first Allied occupation forces in the city,[10] the ubiquity and volume of these privately conducted cremations meant that there was no escape from the stench of burning corpses anywhere in Nagasaki.

Unfortunately for the Tatenos, the grounds of the Takao Clinic were among the few open spaces in densely populated Fukuro-machi suitable for burning bodies. Depending on the quality of the pyre preparation and the availability of fuel, the thorough incineration of a single body could take hours. This meant that there were cremations going on around the clock only meters away from Sueko and her family, even while they ate and slept.

In addition to the hideous sights and unbearable smells involved, another traumatic aspect of these rituals was their sounds: the crackling and sizzling of burning flesh; the sobbing and sometimes wailing of the bereaved; the clunking of bones in the metal buckets survivors brought to carry away the remains of loved ones. Sueko would later describe that latter sound using the Japanese onomatopoeic expression *karan-karan* to emulate the tinny rattling of dice tumbling in a metal can. The compounded psychological effect of these various visual, olfactory, and audial stressors soon had the Tatenos wondering aloud how long they would be able to remain in Dr. Takao's garden before losing their minds.

They might have been comforted if they had known that they would not have to endure this hell for much longer. At noon on August 15, a radio announcement by the emperor—and a terrifying rumor that began making the rounds in Fukuro-machi immediately following His Majesty's message—was going to give the Tatenos all the excuse they needed to escape to the countryside. In the meantime, though, they lived each minute of their new lives in Nagasaki's ruins under the assumption that the war was going to continue and that they would be expected to participate in the fighting—and give their lives if necessary—when enemy troops invaded the Home Islands. This was an assumption—and a resignation—that the Tatenos concurrently shared with eighty million compatriots, with the exception of a small elite circle of Tokyo decision-makers.

Ruins of Junshin Girls' School
Ieno-machi
1.3 kilometers northeast of GZ

Once Sister Itonaga Yoshi and her colleagues weathered the initial shock and horror of August 9, they adapted to the routine and rhythm of the grim reality of their new lives with remarkable speed. From there on out, the sole focus of the Sisters' attention and efforts, day and night, was the rescue and recovery of the students who had been working at Ōhashi and the other Mitsubishi facilities nearby when the new-type bomb detonated over the Urakami Valley.

This work became more systematic after a wounded student had staggered up to the school ruins on the morning of August 10. She had been one of the Ōhashi girls and had just passed the night with some Junshin students and coworkers in the Sumiyoshi tunnels. Since she was the least seriously injured of the girls in the tunnel, the others had asked her to go down to Ieno-machi to check on the school and report back. Upon hearing this, Sister Yoshi and a team of other novices carried the girl piggyback to Sumiyoshi, then put her and the rest of the Junshin girls in her group on the next relief train headed for Isahaya. Encouraged by this confirmation of Junshin survivors from the Mitsubishi plant, Sister Yoshi and three colleagues who had been with the Mitsuyama pine sap group—Sisters Urata, Nagatani, and Kataoka—spent the rest of August 10 scouring Ieno-machi, Ōhashi, and neighboring Nishi-machi for students.[11]

The foursome had barely begun making their way along the banks of the corpse-clogged Urakami when they started finding

Junshin girls. When they came across any who were still able to walk, they told them to head back to the school campus. Whenever they came upon a girl immobilized by her injuries, passing first responders were flagged down until one could be found who was willing to take the girl to the aid station[12] that had been set up in the ruins of Ōhashi.

Continuing their search of the river area, the team was approaching the Iwaya Bridge when they were hailed by a man who recognized them as Junshin Sisters, despite their khaki "civilian"-work-clothes mufti. After identifying himself as a neighborhood resident, the man led the Sisters to the bodies of three girls carefully laid out side by side on the riverbank. Incongruously, the corpses were dressed in cheerful summer *yukata* kimonos. As the man explained, he had found the girls—horribly injured but still alive—on the riverbank the previous afternoon and suspected that they might be Junshin students.[13]

The girls' clothes had been either burned or blasted off of their bodies, and the man had felt pity for their nakedness. Wanting to give them some dignity in what were clearly their last moments, he recovered three *yukata* from the wreckage of his nearby home and brought the garments back to the spot to clothe the dying girls, whom Sister Yoshi identified as second-year Junshin students who had been dispatched to the Mitsubishi facilities at the campus of the nearby school for the deaf and blind only a few days before. The man emphasized that he had wanted to stay to do what he could for the girls, but as he had injured family members of his own, he had returned to his house to care for the latter instead. By the time he came back to the riverbank spot the next morning, the three girls were dead.

As heart-wrenching as this scene was for the Sisters, it did little to prepare them for the situation they would encounter in the Ōhashi compound, where hundreds of their students had burned to death trapped under collapsed girders and toppled industrial machinery. Once the extent of this carnage was reported back at Junshin, any Sisters who were not directly involved with caring for Mother Ezumi and/or holding down the fort at the school to deal with the authorities and panicking parents were mobilized to help out in the ruined factory complex. Working alongside the plant's surviving professionals—who were soon joined by Mitsubishi colleagues coming up from the Akuno'ura shipyard with desperately needed supplies—the Sisters spent most of their waking hours over the next week enduring the stench and gore on the site as they looked for Junshin girls, dead or alive.

When survivors were discovered in the wreckage—or when they found their way back to the ruined campus—the Sisters would put them on the relief trains to Isahaya, where Sister Christina Tagawa, the sole surviving Ōhashi chaperone, had set up a special wardroom in an elementary school near the IJN hospital.[14] Despite her own grave injuries and steadily worsening ARS, Sister Christina—later joined by other Sisters—cared for Junshin students and dealt with parents who had managed the arduous journey to Isahaya to see after their daughters. If one of the Navy doctors on-site ascertained that a girl was sufficiently out of danger and up to the journey, she was allowed to go home. If not, the family members would stay to help care for the girl, who would inevitably be severely ill with ARS in addition to the burns and other external physical injuries she would have suffered in the explosion and collapse of the factory buildings. The luckiest girls recovered—some taking weeks to do so—and got to go home. But all too often, the Junshin girls in this makeshift wardroom would slowly and painfully succumb to the horrible ravages of ARS—hair loss, bleeding gums, incessant nausea and diarrhea—presenting their loved ones with the grim decision of either carrying their daughters' bodies home for funeral arrangements or cremating them on-site and receiving a can or box of their bones and ashes.

At Junshin, the cremation of students' bodies from the Ōhashi plant on the campus athletic ground began on August 11 and continued around the clock for the next week.[15] For the rest of her life, Sister Yoshi would be haunted by the memory of saying evening Vespers and eating meals by the firelight of these pyres while their unforgettable smell wafted by on the breeze.

The Junshin Sisters were assisted in the cremation work by Mitsubishi men, who in addition to being instrumental in keeping the school supplied with lumber for pyre fuel also provided the Sisters with purpose-built wooden ossuary boxes for the students' remains. After each girl was cremated, her bones and ashes would be collected from the smoldering pyre and placed in one of these containers, inscribed with the girl's name. This was then stored with others in Junshin's dugout bomb shelter and eventually handed over to the girl's bereaved family members. Often, parents would show up at the school and find out that their girls were dead only when they were handed boxes of their daughters' remains. But as traumatizing as these transactions were, it was almost worse when the Sisters had to tell parents that their daughters had disappeared without a trace. Sometimes the staff at the temporary city hall was able to provide information on girls who had been taken to faraway aid stations or who had died and been cremated elsewhere. But some girls were simply never seen again, and only years after the war were they declared legally deceased (thus qualifying their families for government survivor benefits).

Every night, the novices would take turns sleeping in the bomb shelter with the stored ossuary boxes so that the spirits of the dead girls would not become scared and lonely while they waited to be returned to their families. When not sleeping with the ossuary boxes, Itonaga and the other Sisters slept in tents—borrowed from Nagasaki Commercial School (Fukahori-kun's alma mater)—which were set up on top of the Junshin ruins with help from adult males from the surrounding area, including some fathers of Junshin students.[16]

Imperial Library annex
1000 hours, August 14, 1945

The American response to the single-condition imperial peace offer of August 10 had arrived on August 12,[17] precipitating another flurry of urgent Cabinet meetings over the next forty-eight hours to interpret its nuances. A discerning reading of the American response—and the one favored by Foreign Minister Tōgō and the rest of the peace faction—was that "it implicitly recognized the Emperor's position by prescribing that his power must be subject to the orders of the Allied supreme commander."[18] But Anami and the other two members of the war faction, taking the contents of the American message at face value, saw it as a reiterated demand for "unconditional" surrender—a demand that later appeared to be emphasized explosively by the August 14 resumption of conventional B-29 raids on the Home Islands, which had seen a five-day moratorium after the Nagasaki bombing.[19]

The peace and war factions' conflicting interpretations of American intentions resulted in another Cabinet impasse regarding acceptance of the Potsdam Declaration, once again compelling Prime Minister Suzuki to go over their heads by inviting direct intervention by the emperor to resolve the matter. Toward this end, another *gozen kaigi* was scheduled for 1000 on August 14.[20]

At the appointed hour, the same participants who had attended the August 9 to 10 *gozen kaigi* once again assembled in the library annex bomb shelter under the Imperial Palace compound.[21] Once the meeting commenced, the floor was left open for discussion, with the range of opinions expressed breaking down upon all-too-familiar and opposing lines. Anami, Umezu, and Toyoda maintained that the American response was insufficiently specific regarding the preservation of the emperor's sovereign prerogative. Predictably, they pushed for a continuation of fighting until this matter was resolved to their satisfaction. Tōgō countered this with the peace faction opinion that the response did in fact safeguard the emperor's fate and position and that it constituted an invitation—carefully couched to save American face—for His Majesty to cooperate with the Allied authorities in the smooth transition of Japan from wartime to peacetime status.[22]

Once again, the buck would stop with the only person in Japan capable of breaking this impasse. Addressing the assembly, the emperor said, "It seems to me that there is no other opinion to support your [the military's] side. I shall explain mine. I hope all of you will agree with my opinion. My opinion is the same as the one I expressed the other night. The American answer seems to me acceptable."[23]

The emperor closed his remarks with a request for the immediate drafting of an imperial rescript "to stop the war" (as opposed to "to surrender"). Then he would take the unprecedented action of addressing the nation directly, via radio broadcast, to read the contents of the document.[24]

The conference was adjourned, and while Prime Minister Suzuki attended to the prerequisite Cabinet rubber-stamping of His Majesty's decision, Sakomizu got busy seeing to the drafting of the surrender rescript and coordinating the necessary recording and broadcasting arrangements with NHK.[25] Later that afternoon, the Foreign Ministry would send the following communiqué to the Allied powers, once again making use of the Swiss government as a go-between:

> *With reference to the Japanese Government's note of August 10 regarding their acceptance of the provisions of the Potsdam declaration and the reply of the Governments of the United States, Great Britain, the Soviet Union, and China sent by American Secretary of State Byrnes under the date of August 11, the Japanese Government have the honor to communicate to the Governments of the four powers as follows:*
>
> *1. His Majesty the Emperor has issued an Imperial rescript regarding Japan's acceptance of the provisions of the Potsdam declaration.*
>
> *2. His Majesty the Emperor is prepared to authorize and ensure the signature of his Government and the Imperial General Headquarters of the necessary terms for carrying out the provisions of the Potsdam declaration. His Majesty is also prepared to issue his commands to all the military, naval, and air authorities of Japan and all the forces under their control wherever located to cease active operations, to surrender arms and to issue such other orders as may be required by the Supreme Commander of the Allied Forces for the execution of the abovementioned terms.*[26]

News of the U.S. government's receipt of this note was officially announced by President Truman at a White House press conference at 1900 EST on August 14.[27] In Japan, where it was 0600 on August 15, anyone illegally listening to American radio broadcasts would have known that the war was over. But aside from these radio scofflaws and a tight-lipped group of top-level decision-makers, bureaucrats, and NHK engineers in Tokyo who were aware of what had just happened, the rest of the emperor's loyal subjects woke up that morning in a nation still at war and wondered when the time would come for them to make the ultimate sacrifice.

AUGUST 15

Fukuro-machi

3.3 kilometers south-southeast of GZ

ON THE MORNING of August 15, an official government request began making the rounds in the pyre-smoke-reeking and blowfly-buzzing precincts of Fukuro-machi: Every loyal subject in the empire was expected to be standing in front of the nearest radio at noon. They were going to be listening to something only a handful of Japanese had ever heard: Emperor Hirohito's speaking voice.

A little before the scheduled broadcast time, Sueko saw several adults fussing over a radio cabinet they were trying to set up in the street in front of the Takao Clinic. Soon, a small group of neighborhood residents had formed up facing the radio, many standing at a military position of attention. After Sueko heard a crackly instrumental rendition of the national anthem emitted from the radio speaker, a high and warbling male voice began intoning strange words that sounded like some kind of archaic Japanese and were completely indecipherable to the thirteen-year-old. The cryptic message lasted about five minutes, and upon its conclusion, some of the adults in front of the radio began to weep. Others appeared stunned or merely confused.

Eventually, a vernacular interpretation of His Majesty's message reached the Tatenos' lean-to: Japan had lost the war because the dastardly Americans were beginning to use some terrible new weapon, and his loyal subjects were being asked to "endure the unendurable" as they toiled to rebuild the country. Hearing this, Sueko was overcome with a powerful mixture of regret and sadness over the defeat. She also felt—very much to her shame— relief that she was going to survive. As she began to bawl, her mother stroked her back, softly saying, "The war is over. . . . Thank goodness . . ."[1]

A few minutes later, the neighborhood's pensive post-surrender mood was exploded by a Kempeitai man with a megaphone shouting that the war was not over and that the radio broadcast the nation had just heard was an enemy trick. Everyone pretended not to pay any attention to him, and it is unlikely that anyone believed what he was saying. Nevertheless, another locally generated bit of fake news would shortly sweep across the neighborhood, and this time it would be believed by many—including the Tatenos.

By the late summer of 1945, Japan had been involved in some form of military intervention on the Asian continent since the IJA's seizure of Manchuria nearly fifteen years earlier, and it had been waging total war against China for more than half of that time span. Although many of the veterans of this chain of ongoing conflicts were still in His Majesty's uniform—either as military professionals (like Sueko's brother Chūtarō) or as reservist "retreads" recalled to service after Pearl Harbor—millions of others had since returned to civilian life.[2] Among this latter category of combat veteran, enough of them had come home with war stories about what they had done—or at least seen—in China for their family members, coworkers, and neighbors to have a fairly graphic idea of the kind of treatment vanquished civilians could expect when conquerors showed up on their doorsteps. Moreover, scare-messaging along these lines had been employed by the Japanese media, particularly since the fall of Saipan the previous year, in its exhortations to the nation's civilians to continue to support the war effort on the home front.[3]

The population of Nagasaki, then, was in this sense already psychologically primed for panic when, on the early afternoon of August 15, a rumor began going around that American occupation troops were on the way and that when they arrived, they were going to rape and probably murder all of the women and girls in the city as punishment for Japan not having surrendered sooner.

When this disturbing bit of scuttlebutt reached Fukuro-machi, Mr. and Mrs. Tateno—as the parents of three daughters—were understandably alarmed. A tense family conference to discuss how best to safeguard the Tateno girls followed. It was quickly determined that they had to get out of Nagasaki immediately. Mrs. Tateno suggested that they go to her family home in the village of Mieda-machi, which was about twenty kilometers away to the northwest and small and insignificant enough that any American marauders might end up overlooking it.

In preparation for the move, Mrs. Tateno used her husband's steel helmet as a pot to boil up the last of their emergency stash of uncooked rice, producing just enough for each member of the family to receive a single *onigiri*. Barring some foodstuff windfall on the way, these rations would have to suffice for their long road march to Mieda-machi. After saying goodbye to their neighbors, the Tatenos bowed in gratitude to the lean-to that had sheltered them for four days; some other refugee group would no doubt move into it as soon as it was vacated.[4]

The Tatenos left Fukuro-machi in the late afternoon, turned onto the now partially cleared Togitsu Road at Nishizaka, and headed north, not knowing when—or if—it would ever be safe to return to Nagasaki. They also had no idea that what they were about to expose themselves to in the air and under their feet during their four-hour trek through the Urakami Valley would be far more hazardous than anything they might have faced had they chosen to remain in Fukuro-machi.

As they entered the southern end of the ZTD around Mori-machi, Sueko found it impossible to picture this landscape of blasted and burned ruins as having once been inhabited by human beings. It looked more like a giant gravel pit that stretched to the horizon and up and away into the hillsides in every direction, pocked here and there by lumps of black stuff and the occasional burned-out streetcar

AUGUST 15

or automobile skeleton. Even though it had been nearly a week since the bombing, corpses were still mixed in with all of the rubble and wreckage piles lining both sides of the road. These bodies were in varying stages of incineration and dismemberment, and they varied in terms of their recognizability as having once been human beings. But all were tented over with blowflies and their voracious maggot offspring, and all emitted the same nauseating stench of putrefaction. As the family walked on, Sueko's dry heaves became so bad that, in desperation, she hit on the idea of simply holding her breath and taking little sips of air through her mouth whenever she would start to feel dizzy. With time, though, she gradually became accustomed—or, perhaps more accurately, benumbed—to the smell of death.

At dusk, the number of fellow pedestrians on the road dropped off sharply. An unnerving stillness set in over the valley; it was broken only by the rhythmic clip-clop shuffle of the Tatenos' *geta*, by an occasional unidentifiable pop or hiss bubbling up from the ground, or by a sudden sob from some family group clustered around the glowing pyre of a loved one out in the rubble field.

With a pale half-moon providing the only illumination of the road ahead, each step the Tatenos took on its uneven surface ran the risk of a twisted ankle or a spill. Putting her faith in her father's surefootedness, Sueko held on tightly to his hand as the family marched on through the pitch-black night.

After a few hours, the Tatenos reached Michino'o, where an acquaintance of her father owned one of the most renowned sake breweries in Nagasaki. Mr. Tateno got permission from the owner for the family to rest for a while under the eaves of the undamaged building before the next leg of their journey. Sitting on some matting provided by the sake master, the Tatenos ate the *onigiri* they had made in Fukuro-machi with the last of their rice. Sueko, however—recalling the sights and sounds (and smells) she had just experienced in the ZTD—had difficulty eating even her single rice ball.

After their humble repast, the Tatenos stretched out on the matting and were able to get a few hours of sleep. Once they roused, they continued their northbound moonlit trek, during which they met several other groups of girls who reported that they were also fleeing the imminent arrival of the feared American troops.

Around noon the next day, the Tatenos reached the village of Kyōdomari, about 3.5 kilometers from Sueko's maternal grandfather's place in Mieda-machi. Everyone in the family was black, head to foot, from the journey, stained and streaked with sweat, road dust, and soot. By this point, Sueko and her sisters were staggering from the heat of the day's blazing sun and the accumulated physical and mental exhaustion of their journey. Sensing his daughters' flagging enthusiasm, Mr. Tateno attempted to buck up their spirits by telling them they had only a little farther to go. Hearing this, Sueko chimed in, "Right! Nobody wants to get caught by the Americans! March on!"[5]

They stopped to take one final rest and eat some remaining *onigiri* crumbs before pushing on for the last leg to Mieda-machi. As soon as they reached her grandfather's house, Sueko sat down on the tatami floor and promptly toppled over, dead asleep. When she woke up, it was dusk.

Kiridōshi home

Nakagawa-machi

Kiridōshi Michiko had suffered only a minor contusion on her left arm in the factory collapse and had received no burns during her escape through its wreckage. Over the following days, however, her family's initial optimism about her apparently miraculous survival began to wane when she complained of a feeling of listlessness and exhaustion that she could not seem to shake, no matter how long she rested. She was also suffering from chronic, nonstop diarrhea. For the time being, the only plan of action her mother could come up with to help her daughter was to let her continue to rest at home as long as she wanted.

On August 15, Michiko was listening to the radio when the surrender announcement was broadcast. As she later recalled of her feelings at the time, she did not experience any grief or despair at the news that Japan had been defeated—only a sense of relief and liberation. She had never believed in the war and had harbored sharp cynicism and loathing (that she was careful not to express outside of the house) toward the constant messaging about fighting on to the end and being prepared to die for the great imperial cause with which she and her compatriots had been bombarded by the media and authority figures in her daily environment.

A few hours after the broadcast, a Kempeitai truck rigged with a loudspeaker drove through Nakagawa-machi screaming that the surrender broadcast was an enemy ruse. Hearing this, however, Michiko did not bat an eye. This announcement was only so much meaningless noise, as had been the case a few days earlier when that same truck had been blaring messages telling everyone to prepare to die in the final battle for the Home Islands and exhorting women to kill themselves in lieu of suffering the dishonor and horror of being taken alive by the Americans.

For Michiko, all of that was behind her now—ancient history. There would be no more panicked running to shelters every time an airplane flew over; no more having to comply with blackout regulations by keeping the windows closed and the curtains drawn in the middle of summer; no more drudgery and morning assembly slogan-chanting sessions at the munitions plant. It was time for Michiko to get on with her life again.

Not everyone in her family, however, had such a sanguine view of these developments. When Mr. Kiridōshi returned home that night, he expressed concern over a rumor he had heard at his workplace about what the Americans were going to do to the women of the city once the occupation began. As telephone service in the CBD had been restored that day,[6] Michiko's father was able to begin making calls of inquiry about possible evacuation sites. He finally managed to find an available place in Toisu, a Tachibana Bay fishing hamlet some sixteen kilometers east of the city. For the time being, the plan was that he and Grandmother Kiridōshi would hold down the fort in Nakagawa-machi, waiting for the American occupiers to reveal their intentions in the city, while his wife and three daughters went to ground in Toisu until it was safe for them to come home.

Michiko, as was always the case in family discussions, was unabashed in expressing her opinion about the plan. For one thing, there was no train line along the coast of Tachibana Bay nor any bus service, so the Kiridōshi women were going to have to cover the sixteen kilometers to Toisu on foot. As Michiko pointed out, in her present weakened condition, she had barely been able to walk two kilometers at a go when her sister Yasuko had taken her to see the medics at the Shinkōzen Elementary School aid station. Moreover, there were too many unknowns involved in the plan. The women did not know anyone in Toisu. They did not know if the shack was really going to be habitable or not. They had no idea of what they were going to eat when they got there nor whom they would be able to turn to for help if anyone got sick or if Michiko's condition worsened. Michiko thought the whole evacuation idea was a ridiculous overreaction on her father's part and told him as much, adding that she was not in the slightest bit worried about what the Americans might do when they arrived in Nagasaki. The media, after all, had been lying about everything else during the war, so why believe them now?

In the end, however, Michiko's father had the final say (no doubt with some coercive backing from Grandmother Kiridōshi). The Toisu party set out on foot the next morning toting water canteens, a few days' worth of food, and bedding rolls.

Shimonishiyama-machi
2.9 kilometers southeast of GZ

Gunge Norio never heard any rumors about impending American atrocities, nor did he hear any surrender broadcast. He was still in such a profound state of mental fugue over his missing brother, Yoshio, that he would not even realize the war was over until American Marines arrived in the city in mid-September.

On August 9, his father had been away on a business trip in Karatsu, near Fukuoka. Although he did not hear the initial emergency broadcast out of Kumamoto that morning, he had heard on a regular radio news broadcast about a new-type bomb having been dropped on Nagasaki. But the news program's description of what had happened—read from an IJA-censor-authored script no doubt—was so vague and the announcer's tone of voice so dispassionate that Mr. Gunge assumed there was no urgent need to check on his boys. He would keep to the original schedule of his business trip. After paying a visit to his old friend at Kyushu Imperial University in Fukuoka, he would catch a train from that city to arrive in Nagasaki on the tenth.

The trip from Fukuoka—which under normal conditions would have taken not more than a few hours to reach Nagasaki—ended up taking nearly two days due to repeated American strafing attacks on the train as well as on various railway facilities along the line. As Mr. Gunge had not heard during his journey anything particularly terrible about what had happened to Nagasaki, he began to worry in earnest about the possible fate of his sons only when the train entered the void of the Urakami Valley on the night of the twelfth. When he eventually reached their boardinghouse in Shimonishiyama—after having walked through the half-burned CBD to get there—he was understandably elated to find his younger son still alive. But this emotion quickly segued into grief when Norio related to him that he had not seen Yoshio since before the explosion of the new-type bomb and that he had been visiting the shattered campus of the medical college every day since to look for his brother's body.

Despite the ravages that the harrowing and sleepless train trip from Fukuoka must have taken on his middle-aged body, Mr. Gunge insisted the next morning that Norio take him to the medical college to look for Yoshio. Norio would never forget the twosome's somber, wordless ascent up and over Konpira that morning, nor their grim survey of human remains throughout the ruins of the campus. During the latter activity, Mr. Gunge would pick up various burned skulls from the ground and turn them around in his hands, desperately looking them over for any familiar jawline or cheekbone angle that might tell him he was holding his firstborn's head. As he did so, he asked Norio for his assessment as well, but they never made a convincing find.

Father and younger son repeated this expedition the next day—the fourteenth—but again to no avail. When Mr. Gunge returned to his factory in Ōmura on the morning of the fifteenth, leaving Norio to his own devices, he did so as a grief-broken man, and so he would remain for the rest of his life.

Tokusanji Temple

Tagami Village

5.7 kilometers southwest of GZ

As with her Kenjo schoolmate Kiridōshi Michiko, Ishida Masako's physical condition had steadily worsened since she arrived home on the morning of August 10. Although Masako, as the daughter of the third most important man in the city (after Governor Nagano and Mayor Okada), had access to far better medical attention than most bomb survivors, the doctors in Nagasaki were at a loss as to what to make of the steadily worsening malaise and other mysterious symptoms—severe gastrointestinal distress, strange purple spots (petechiae from subcutaneous hemorrhaging) on the skin, etc.—they were seeing in survivors who had emerged from the August 9 catastrophe otherwise visibly unscathed (or, like Masako, only slightly injured). As such, with no one knowing what they were dealing with, aside from a vague idea that it had something to do with special properties of the new-type bomb, the doctors could offer Masako little more in the way of care than to urge her to keep rested and hydrated and to try to get some sustenance into herself that she might manage to keep down.

In the meantime, Judge Ishida was also on pins and needles about the American planes sporadically flying over the city since the bombing. Although these had not dropped any more bombs, their appearance was still unnerving. As a result, the judge insisted that Masako stay in the *kansha*'s fetid and sweltering backyard bomb shelter full-time instead of having to be carried back and forth to and from the house each time there was an enemy aircraft alert—a task that would have been particularly difficult for Hayashi-sensei if she had had to handle it by herself when the judge was out.

On the morning of August 11, a prosecutor from Fukuoka District Court arrived in Nagasaki on an official fact-finding mission to check on the status of the appellate court.[7] When he came by the Yaoya-machi *kansha* to pay his respects and saw the conditions the judge's daughter had to endure in the backyard bomb shelter, he suggested that the judge evacuate with his household to the Nagasaki Youth Association retreat facility at Tokusanji Temple in Tagami, a hamlet deep in the mountains southwest of the CBD.[8] Various other families associated with the appellate court had already done so, and the mountain air would be good for the ailing girl.

The judge agreed with this suggestion, and that evening, his chief secretary sent the appellate court's official (and, miraculously, still functioning) motorcar around to the *kansha* to drive the judge, Masako, Hayashi-sensei, and her mother the three or so kilometers up into the mountains to Tagami. When they arrived at Tokusanji, the temple's abbot insisted that the judge's party forgo the spartan youth association retreat facilities and instead stay in an eight-tatami-mat room he had reserved for them in the rear of the main temple building.[9] The judge was thankful for this special treatment, as it would give Masako a nice, quiet place to rest away from the hubbub of daily activity at the retreat facility as well as in the surrounding mountains, which were full of evacuees from the city sleeping rough in the woods.

Despite the Ishidas' comparatively well-appointed lodgings, Masako's condition—which no one yet realized was ARS—continued to worsen. She was running a continuous high fever that left her half delirious and suffering with unremitting headaches and nausea. She was barely able to hold down water or green tea and as often as not she would regurgitate the *umeboshi* pickled plums and rice that were the only foodstuffs she could countenance putting in her mouth at the time. When her suffering was particularly bad, she would sometimes express a wish that she would just hurry up and die already so she could be reunited with her mother.

For several days, one of the city's harried (and few surviving) doctors made house calls at the temple, but he quickly concluded that if Masako were to have any chance of recovery, she would have to receive care in a proper medical facility. The temple abbot was able to suggest the services of a neighborhood doctor named Sugiyama Shigeo, who had a very well-equipped, modern private clinic located down the mountain a ways.[10] For the next two weeks, on his way to work at the courthouse ruins every morning, the judge would piggyback Masako down the twisting mountain paths from Tokusanji to receive treatment from Dr. Sugiyama, and Hayashi-sensei would carry her back up to the temple in the afternoon.

On the morning of August 15, Masako—who had yet to begin receiving her treatment at the Sugiyama clinic—was lying on her futon on the floor of the Ishidas' temple room when a clerk from the appellate court arrived with a handwritten note from the judge instructing Masako and the Hayashis to try to get to a working radio by noon to hear an important announcement from the emperor.[11] Masako asked the clerk if he had any idea what this was all about. He replied that he did not but reported that he had seen something odd on his way to Tagami that morning: a lone and apparently half-grief-mad soldier standing on a promontory in the CBD screaming something about unconditional surrender. Masako found this impossible to believe and said as much.[12]

Masako was unable to get out of her futon at noon, but Hayashi-sensei managed to hear the broadcast somewhere else on the temple grounds. When she returned to the room, she reported that the broadcast's static was so bad that no one within earshot of the radio had been able to tell exactly what His Majesty was saying, but that apparently there was to be a cessation of hostilities, and this would explain why no one had heard any planes flying overhead that day. Masako still refused to believe that Japan would do anything so craven as to surrender to the dastardly enemy who had just done such a terrible thing to Nagasaki. It was not until the judge returned to the temple that night to report that this was, in fact, the case that Masako knew that the war was over and that Japan had been defeated.[13] And no one knew what would happen next.

LEARNING TO LOVE COCA-COLA

Fukuoka

September 1945

BY AUGUST 29, Masako's condition appeared to have recovered sufficiently for Judge Ishida to move his household back into the Yaoyamachi *kansha*. The next day, Masako was even feeling fine enough to accompany her father to Nagasaki Station when her paternal aunt Chiyoko arrived from Fukuoka for a visit.[1] But two days later, her condition took a sudden turn for the worse; specifically, her post-bombing malaise and vertigo had returned with a vengeance. After a doctor ran some tests on her blood, he found that Masako was suffering from leukopenia—a catastrophically low white blood cell count.

Where a normal, healthy person's white blood cell count would have been in the six thousand to eight thousand range, Masako's was only eighteen hundred fifty.[2] What was occurring in hibakusha cases like Masako's was that, in a mechanism that would be understood by nuclear medicine researchers in later decades, the DNA in their heavily and rapidly irradiated bone marrow—the blood factories of the human body—was so damaged that it was no longer able to sustain cell mitosis sufficient to carry out this function. And while doctors in 1945 Nagasaki (and Hiroshima) might not yet have been aware of what exactly was happening at the cellular—or, more specifically, the molecular—level in the crashing-white-blood-cell-count patients

LEARNING TO LOVE COCA-COLA 321

they examined, they were already familiar enough with the syndrome to recognize it as a telltale symptom of what they had come to refer to as *genbaku byō* ("atom bomb disease").[3] They also knew that if a hibakusha's white blood cell count did not recover soon, such a patient would inevitably die—either after the *genbaku byō* metastasized into its far grimmer and agonizing advanced stages or, for arguably luckier victims, when they succumbed to common infections, such as colds and the like, that the white-blood-cell-based immune system of a healthy body would normally shrug off with ease.

After consultation with Masako's doctor, Judge Ishida decided that it would better for his daughter to get away from the miasma still hanging over Nagasaki (and whatever pathogens it carried) and into an environment with cleaner air. Aunt Chiyoko agreed to take the ailing girl with her back to Fukuoka, where she could convalesce in a mountain lodge the Ishida family owned in a small hamlet near the city. Meanwhile, the judge would stay behind in Nagasaki, attending to duties that would shortly involve close coordination with the soon-to-arrive American occupation troops. He would visit his daughter in Fukuoka when he could.

On September 20, the Ishida family—no doubt making use of its considerable local influence—was able to secure for Masako the almost unheard-of early-postwar luxury of a private room at the Sawada Clinic of Kyushu Imperial University Hospital in Fukuoka.[4] There, Masako would receive the best medical treatment available in the region, under the direct care of the clinic's eponymous chief surgeon as her personal attending physician. Aside from her daily regimen of painful liver hormone injections and regular blood transfusions (provided by a Fukuoka relative), Masako's extended stay at the clinic was relatively pleasant and made immeasurably more so by the steady stream of extended Ishida family visitors, who inevitably came bearing sweets and other hard-to-come-by delicacies to augment the girl's otherwise bland diet of hospital food.

Although Masako made promising progress, she was far from full recovery, and her hospital stay stretched from days to weeks, and eventually to months. As a way for her to pass the time, her brother,

Jō'ichi—always a reliable idea man—suggested that she write about her atomic bombing experience for his handwritten newsletter, the *Ishida Times*, which he had been editing and mailing out (always in a single handwritten edition) for circulation among the extended Ishida family since his precocious childhood.

At first Masako was resistant to this suggestion, pleading a lack of writing talent on her part and declaring—somewhat more reasonably—that she had no desire to revisit those traumatic memories. But Jō'ichi was persistent, and he was eventually able to win her over by appealing to her sense of family obligation: Her Ishida relatives were concerned about her, and it was Masako's duty to let them know what had happened to her, that she was receiving good care, and that she was going to be all right.

She began writing that October, eventually taking nearly two months to complete her "bomb memoirs," which Jō'ichi serialized over eight consecutive editions of the *Ishida Times* under the banner headline *"Masako Taorezu"* ("Masako Is Still Standing").[5]

Nagasaki

One month after the surrender

From one perspective, the American-led Allied occupation of Japan was a humanitarian exercise in nation rebuilding carried out at great expense by gracious victors on behalf of a vanquished foe. From another, it was an exercise in geostrategic realpolitik, the grand objectives of which were securing a permanent base for the projection of American power in the far western Pacific and permanently hobbling Japan's ability to ever again pose a threat—military or otherwise—to a world order[6] mirroring the values, prioritizing the prerogatives, and operating to the advantage of the West.

In real time, the major goals of the occupation's initial phase were of an urgent search-and-secure nature similar in this regard to American efforts in Iraq in 2003 and 2004. These early objectives included the dissolution of the IJA and IJN as functioning military organizations; the rapid return of their rank and file to civilian status and peaceful economic activity; the seizure and dismantling of Japanese military facilities and weaponry (with particular emphasis on harbor fortifications and kamikaze-warfare capability); the securing of key transportation hubs and (intact) infrastructure; the capture of high-profile military and political figures for later war crimes prosecution; and finally, of utmost urgency and priority, POW rescue and repatriation. Despite the high priority given that last goal, however, there was a lag of up to several weeks between the heavily media-publicized initial liberations of POW camps in the Tokyo-Yokohama area at the end of August and those in more far-flung regions of the Home Islands.[7] The last POWs on Kyushu—inclusive of Nagasaki—were not liberated until September 22.[8]

The second phase of occupation military operations—which lasted from roughly January 1946 until the restoration of Japanese national sovereignty in April 1952—constituted a long-term hearts-and-minds campaign to remake Japan into an ostensibly "democratic," pacifist, and docile partner vis-à-vis American geostrategic interests. Toward this end, the MacArthur-led occupation overturned—or at least attempted to overturn—every social, political, ideological, legal, religious, and pedagogical aspect of Japanese life deemed complicit in the militaristic misadventures of Japan's Imperial Era.[9]

During the occupation's initial search-and-secure phase, primary responsibility for the demilitarization of Kyushu was assigned to the Marine Corps. Within this jurisdiction, the Nagasaki region was to be the bailiwick of the 2nd Marine Division—a unit of combat-hardened veterans who had served from Guadalcanal all the way up through the Okinawa campaign. Preparation and arrangements for the arrival of the main force were coordinated with local Japanese authorities (including Judge Ishida) and overseen by a Marine Corps advance party that arrived by aircraft at Ōmura on September 16.[10] Soon after, a special Marine detachment from two Navy cruisers—*Biloxi* and *Wichita*—made their way ashore to secure Allied prisoners at Mori-Machi's Fukuoka Camp No. 14 and other POW facilities in the city.[11]

The main Nagasaki occupation force consisted of the 2nd and 6th Marine Regiments, sailing from Saipan. On September 23, these units made landfall at Ōhato Wharf in the CBD and the Mitsubishi shipyards on the opposite shore of the harbor "in full combat kit with fixed bayonets and full magazines."[12] The first-day objectives of the main occupation force were to secure the CBD and harbor area and to "cordon off" the ZTD, not only as a safety precaution but also to discourage any Marine Corps souvenir hunters who might be tempted to enter the zone before the assigned units,[13] thereby contaminating the area's forensic value for follow-up surveys by American scientists eager to research Fat Man's effects on the city.

When the 2nd Marine Division landed in Nagasaki, Ishida Masako had already been in Fukuoka for nearly three weeks, Kiridōshi Michiko and Tateno Sueko were gone to ground in their respective fishing village evacuation hideaways, and Gunge Norio was still spending most of his time in his boardinghouse room on the eastern edge of the CBD. Therefore, it is likely that Sister Itonaga Yoshi was the first of this volume's five primary research informants to lay eyes on—and certainly the first to come face-to-face with—Marines from the 2nd Division.

A week or so earlier, around the time the Marine advance party landed at Ōmura, a local priest—Father Yamakawa—had been hearing confessions for the Junshin Sisters in the campus dugout shelter when one of his penitents offhandedly mentioned hearing that the Americans had arrived in the city. Hearing this, the priest stopped everything he was doing and ran off to share the news with Mother Ezumi, who was at the time convalescing with the Takami family at their spacious home in Mitsuyama.[14] Upon receiving this report, Mother Ezumi sent word back to Junshin instructing the Sisters still on the campus to dirty their appearance as much as possible to discourage the Americans from taking any interest in them as females. Although Mother Ezumi's advice was appreciated by the Sisters, it was—in their opinion—completely unnecessary because of what they looked like after five weeks of living in tents, still spending the better part of each day searching for the bodies of Junshin girls in the Ōhashi ruins and assisting the Mitsubishi men in cremating these bodies on the school grounds. And though they tried to bathe—when they could—in the still corpse-strewn Urakami River, no amount of scrubbing seemed to be able to remove the soot that had long since stained their skin from head to toe.

On or about September 23, the tail end of the low-pressure front that had spawned the Makurazaki Typhoon a week earlier was still dumping large amounts of rain on the Nagasaki area[15]—so much so that the Junshin Sisters on the campus had no choice but to suspend their work and hunker down for the day in their tent. At one point, the Sisters heard male voices nearby speaking in a foreign language. Peeking out from behind the tent's flap entrance, Sister Yoshi spotted three large figures in unfamiliar military uniforms poking around the perimeter of the gray ash field that was once the school's athletic ground. Then, to her alarm, the poncho-draped figures took notice of the tent and began to walk toward it. After reporting what she had just seen to the other occupants of the tent, Sister Yoshi quickly shut the tent flap. The Sisters trembled in place until the flap opened and the Americans stuck their heads in to look around. After a few seconds, one of the soldiers said something that sounded like a question, but it was delivered in a stream of rapid-fire words none of the Sisters could understand. Receiving no response, the soldier then pointed to a crucifix displayed in the tent and asked another question. This time, however, the Sisters were able to catch the word "Catholic" in the soldier's utterance, and upon doing so, they nodded and repeated, *"Katoriku."* At this, the soldiers nodded, smiled briefly, and walked back off into the rain.

Tateno Sueko's radiation-exposure symptoms began to appear in earnest during the family's Mieda-machi evacuation. In addition to her steadily worsening gastrointestinal issues and general malaise, she was also the target of vicious teasing by local children who began calling her "Demon Claw" because of the crusty bloom of blistery red warts that had erupted around her fingers and toes. She also suffered from chronic insomnia, spurred by her constant fear that she was going to end up like the many people in the city she had watched die during the days after the bombing even though they had seemingly escaped initial injury. With this thought preying on her mind, Sueko became obsessed with the idea that toxic smoke from cremated corpses had soaked into every pore of her body and was now slowly killing her.

Every night when Sueko bathed, she frantically checked her body for signs of the telltale purple petechiae that signaled imminent death for hibakusha. Using soap and a *tawashi* bristle brush—an implement normally used for laundry or kitchen cleaning—she scrubbed at her skin until it bled. Yet no matter how often or hard she washed herself, she could not get over the idea that the American bomb—and the six days she had spent around burning corpses—had fatally contaminated her body.

Toward the end of September, word reached the Tatenos that the Konpira-shielded and thus relatively undamaged Keiho Girls' School would shortly resume class sessions. Emboldened by this news and eager to escape her tormentors and crushing boredom in Mieda-machi, Sueko encouraged her family to make the move back into the city—no matter what it still smelled like. This wish was indulged forthwith, and after bidding farewell to their Mieda-machi relatives, the family returned to Nagasaki to live with Tateno cousins in Higashi'uwa-machi, just north of Ishida Masako's neighborhood of Yaoya-machi.

Although Sueko was happy to be returning to some semblance of her pre-bomb life—her bodily ailments and unsightly hands and feet notwithstanding—she was crushed and guilt stricken to learn how many of her first-year classmates had been killed by the bomb in their Urakami homes and the higher-grade girls in the Mori-machi and Ōhashi plants. Many of the factory girls were said to have disappeared without a trace—either destroyed immediately by the explosion or anonymously cremated on-site by Mitsubishi employees in the days and weeks after August 9. Sueko was confronted simultaneously with both the unthinkable scale and the intimate tragedy of this loss on her first day back at school when she saw all of the empty desks in her homeroom.

Salient in her memories of this period was the first time she saw American Marines, who at that point in the occupation were still carrying rifles with fixed bayonets. Her first impression of the foreigners, with their big bodies and red faces, was that they reminded her of the *aka oni* ("red demons") in Japanese fairy tales.

Her sole direct interaction with Nagasaki's Marine occupiers—which did nothing for her initial unfavorable impression of them—came one day when a squad of them, in full combat gear, conducted a house-by-house search of Higashi'uwa-machi, apparently looking for weapons and other contraband. When the Marines reached Sueko's house, they barged into it with their boots still on—an unconscionable breach of etiquette that happens in Japan only when police officers are raiding a criminal's abode—and then started poking around at the ceiling with their bayonets, listening for the tell-tale clunking of hard objects against the other side of its wooden slats. When the Marines found nothing, the search moved to the second floor, which was given a thorough tossing, resulting in a mess of emptied and dumped drawers and overturned cabinets. Returning to the first floor, the Marines began saying something in English to the Tateno women. They soon augmented these utterances with drinking gestures made with hands holding imaginary cups or bottles. Quickly ascertaining that the Americans were asking not for water but for alcohol, Mrs. Tateno was able to communicate (truthfully or not) that there were no such beverages in the house. Visibly vexed, the Americans filed out wordlessly before proceeding to ransack the next house over.

The other children in Higashi'uwa-machi were also initially terrified of the Americans, and when a Marine Corps jeep would roll through the neighborhood, they would call out, *"Aka oni! Aka oni!"* before running away to hide. Eventually, though, after their initial early shock and fear wore off, the neighborhood children started swarming the Marines and asking them for chocolate and chewing gum whenever they appeared—especially the ones in jeeps. Mrs. Tateno, however, was having none of this, declaring it "a shameful way to behave, seeing how we are defeated." She strictly forbade her children to partake of any candy or other food the Americans were giving away for the asking.

This no-food-from-the-Americans rule, however, did not apply to Mr. Tateno. As a means of supplementing his family's income, Mr. Tateno began doing part-time interpreting work for the occupation forces. Using the rudimentary but still serviceable self-taught English skills he had honed before the war, he worked first for the Marine garrison, then later for the U.S. Army Nagasaki Military Government Team (NMGT), the city's long-term occupation administrative organ. In the cases of both employers, he was more often than not paid in food for his services. On one memorable occasion, he brought back a box of several off-white and, to contemporary Japanese olfactory sensitivities, rather off-smelling blocks of what the Tatenos initially thought were bars of soap. As the Tatenos discovered after unsuccessfully attempting to use this unusual substance for bathing, it turned to be cheese—a food that few Japanese at the time had ever seen.

Far more welcome in the household were the chocolate and chewing gum Mr. Tateno often brought home after his interpreter gigs. Sueko's first encounter with Coca-Cola, however, was a less happy experience. She thought it tasted like cough syrup, and the feeling of its carbonated bubbles in her mouth and throat was utterly alien and unpleasant. But as with so many other cultural artifacts the occupation introduced into / imposed upon the lived environment of postwar Japanese, the beverage was something that she eventually came to adore and continues to do so to this day.

Nakagawa-machi

Autumn 1945

The Nagasaki CBD the Kiridōshi girls returned to after their Toisu evacuation sojourn was barely recognizable from the one they had left. Their schools had reopened. The cinemas had already started showing movies again. And, most alien of all, the CBD was awash in

Americans walking arm in arm with young local womenfolk or careening around town in jeeps, tossing gum and chocolate to children on the street. Although Mr. and Mrs. Kiridōshi had forbidden their daughters from accepting these candy gifts, Michiko's sister Teruko frequently disobeyed this parental command when out of sight of their house. At the time, she thought she had never eaten anything so delicious in her life.[16]

Another big change—albeit a temporary one—for the Kiridōshi household was the miraculous return from Manchuria of the girls' maternal uncle, Tetsurō. When the war veteran showed up at the Nakagawa-machi house that autumn, he was essentially cap in hand and for all intents and purposes jobless and homeless. The Kiridōshis offered to let him stay with them until he could get back on his feet again, and the haggard war veteran accepted the invitation.

During his stay, Tetsurō regaled his relatives with the saga of his harrowing escape from the continent. As he told it, the command structure of his unit had disintegrated under the initial impact of the tidal wave of Soviet armor that rolled over their front lines on the morning of August 9. During the ensuing rout, high-ranking officers and their entourages—including the local Kempeitai—skedaddled away by any available railway transportation, stranding their respective commands to fend for themselves. Moving quickly, Tetsurō and a group of his comrades jumped onto one of the last IJA trucks leaving the area and rode standing room only in the truck bed. Staying barely one step ahead of the advancing Soviet tanks, the truck eventually reached a port in Korea in which Tetsurō was able to board a ship and make good his escape to Japan. Those IJA soldiers who were neither so quick nor so lucky found themselves prisoners in Stalin's Siberian gulags for the next several years.

Meanwhile, on the Nakagawa-machi front, Michiko was undergoing a development of ARS symptoms and pathology very similar to those concurrently afflicting her Kenjo schoolmate and Mitsubishi colleague Ishida Masako, who had been exposed to Fat Man's radiation at almost exactly the same distance and separated from the bomb's shower of neutrons and gamma rays by the same flimsy factory roofing material. At first, neither Michiko nor her family members—whose own mild post-bombing symptoms (diarrhea, etc.) had already cleared up—had any idea of what was wrong with her. Michiko's parents, who did not know what radiation was or what it was capable of doing to human bodies, ascribed to lazy malingering their daughter's frequent absences from Kenjo classes and overall listlessness.

It was not until Michiko's father began taking her for regular visits to the large and now well-supplied aid station at Shinkōzen Elementary School—which had taken over the role of the city's main medical care facility from the destroyed Nagasaki Medical College—that the Kiridōshis learned about the so-called *genbaku byō*, in this case after tests were conducted on Michiko's blood. In test results revealing pathology even more dire than Ishida Masako's, Michiko's white blood cell count was found to have dropped to thirteen hundred. If, as United States Strategic Bombing Survey (USSBS) researchers later stated, "the degree of leukopenia was probably the most accurate index of the amount of radiation a person received," then it was clear that Michiko had been catastrophically exposed.[17] Out of earshot of his patient, the attending physician (probably a Kyushu University med student) told Mr. Kiridōshi that Michiko probably did not have much longer to live.

After this revelation—which would not be divulged to Michiko until decades later—her parents became much more doting toward their chronically exhausted daughter, often buying treats just for her on the black market in an attempt to lift her spirits and get her to eat something she would not just throw right back up again. Family members also took turns taking Michiko to Shinkōzen for iron supplement pills and vitamin B shots.

In his desperation to help his ailing daughter, Mr. Kiridōshi—who had been privy to spurious rumors that bull's blood was supposed to be good for *genbaku byō* sufferers—was able to secure a quantity of the substance, which would have been exceedingly exotic and proportionately expensive in early postwar Japan. Gagging through the effort, Michiko did her best to swallow and keep down the muddy, awful-tasting stuff, and although she never thought it was doing her any actual good, she was grateful to her father for having made the effort of acquiring it, and she now credits her father's and the rest of her family members' love and support for getting her through this difficult time.

Although the adolescent Kiridōshi Michiko survived her encounter with Fat Man—perhaps miraculously—the adult Kano Michiko-san never fully recovered, with lingering malaise being the most salient symptom of the physiological damage she sustained from radiation exposure. Another symptom she had to deal with after the bombing was chronic nausea and lack of appetite. When she and the family accompanied Mr. Kiridōshi for another bank managerial transfer—this time to the still war-ruined Kumamoto—she used to wrap the food from her uneaten meals in newspaper and distribute it to the war-orphaned street urchins and beggars who congregated around the entrance to the local train station.[18]

When the family was still in Kumamoto, Michiko—despite her lingering malaise—was able to begin studying for university entrance exams while working in her father's bank to save money for tuition.[19] In 1950, she matriculated at the elite Keio University, where she majored in Western history; fortunately, her father's final job transfer had at last returned the Kiridōshis to Tokyo, allowing the still frail Michiko to commute to school from home.

Now far removed—at least geographically—from Nagasaki, Michiko was gradually able to push her atomic trauma from her mind and get on with her new life. After graduation from Keio in 1954, she became a history and social studies teacher in Tokyo-metropolitan-area *tokujisei* (part-time evening) schools until her retirement in 1983 to take up writing full-time and follow her newfound passion of Basque studies.

When the Fukushima nuclear plant disaster occurred in March 2011, the Nagasaki trauma she had long believed she had conquered came back with a vengeance. For the first time in decades—since her pregnancy with her son, Risaku—she began to worry again about what Fat Man had done to her own body and possibly to that of her only child, and she wondered when it was going to finally kill her. As a way of working through this psychological turmoil, she learned how to use a computer and began writing a blog about her Nagasaki experiences, tying these to her unfailingly acid observations of how the Japanese state and the Japanese people have failed to learn from the errors of World War Two. It was through this blog that she became close friends with Hiroshima survivor Seki Chieko, and it was through this connection that I would eventually make the acquaintance of Kano Michiko.

In addition to her blog activities (which ended in 2019), Kano-san has authored numerous books over the years, including well-regarded works on Basque culture and the Spanish Civil War. With Seki Chieko, she coauthored and published a compilation of their correspondence titled *Hiroshima-Nagasaki kara sengo minshushugi wo ikiru* (*Life in Postwar Democracy After Hiroshima and Nagasaki*) (2012). Her last major work, coauthored with her son, Kiridōshi Risaku, was *Jūgosai no hibakusha: Rekishi wo kesanai tame ni* (*A Hibakusha at Fifteen: That History Shall Not Be Erased*) (2015).

I have read and reread *Jūgosai no hibakusha* numerous times since Kano-san gave me a copy in 2017, and it was a major source for the present volume. Out of the many moving passages in the book, my favorite is contained in the afterword, written by her son. In it, Risaku-san recalls taking his mother to see *Haha to kuraseba* (2015),[20] a then newly released family drama about postwar Nagasaki in which one of the lead characters is a former war-mobilized girls' school student survivor of the destruction of the Mitsubishi Mori-machi plant.

In the passage, Risaku-san describes the powerful—almost alchemical—cathartic effect the film had on his mother, and he marvels at the fact that it was only during the long discussion the two had after viewing it that his mother was able to shed tears over the atomic bombing in front of her son for the first time—something she had never come close to doing even during the months the two spent together compiling the material for *Jūgosai no hibakusha*.[21]

As of the writing of this book, Kano Michiko-san, now age ninety-six, resides full-time in her Odawara assisted-living home. Although her mind has been gradually shutting down in recent years, as Risaku-san has reported to me, I was blessed to have encountered it when her memory was still rich and fruitful, and my research has benefited enormously from the window unto now vanished worlds it provided me. I can only hope that I have done her testimony justice and that others will benefit from it as I have.

RENDEZVOUS IN KŌENJI

Suginami Ward, Tokyo
June 2018

ON THIS SUNNY Thursday afternoon, I have taken the JR Chūō Line to Kōenji, in western Tokyo's Suginami Ward, to meet with today's interview subject: Nagasaki native Tateno Sueko. I am about half an hour early, so I decide to do a quick lap around the neighborhood to see how much it has changed since the last time I was here—thirty years, twenty kilograms, and several centimeters of hairline ago.

In 1988—the last full year of the Shōwa Period—Kōenji was a semi-suburban bedroom community for train schleppers working or studying in downtown Tokyo. Its Chūō Line train station was surrounded by a few blocks of twisting alleyways lined with funky bars that were venues for a small but vigorous local rock and blues scene. But beyond this narrow ring of electrically amplified subculture, the rest of Kōenji was more of the same soot-streaked low-rise Shōwa apartment blocks and wooden single-family residences you would have typically seen as far out into the Kantō Plain or up into the Saitama hinterlands as you could go before you started hitting industrial parks and rice paddies. These days, Kōenji's live music scene is still hopping, but the sky over the station is a lot smaller than it used to be, hemmed in by taller and glassier office and apartment buildings.

As the rendezvous hour approaches, I position myself near today's appointed meeting spot at the south entrance of the station. A few minutes later, an elderly but bell-clear female voice sounds somewhere off to my right.

"Sumimasen . . . Shefutaru-sensei de gozaimasu deshō ka?" ("Excuse me, are you Professor Sheftall?")

The voice belongs to Tateno Sueko—a white-haired, bespectacled, and strikingly handsome octogenarian. She is even tinier than is typical for a Japanese woman of her generation, but she offsets the effect of her small size with the straight posture of a West Point cadet and the confident charisma of someone who clearly enjoyed great beauty in her youth. The vestiges of this beauty are still easy to detect in her face, hiding in plain sight just beneath a thin patina of senescence, and a vigorous athleticism I imagine she also enjoyed in her youth is still there in the smooth grace and agility with which she carries herself. Although she is eighty-six years old, she moves with the quickness and ease of a fit sixty-year-old.

Aware as I am that most Japanese women of Tateno-san's generation have never been comfortable with the gendered and culturally alien ritual of the handshake, I forgo extending my hand. Instead, we go through a quick round of bowing while we recite the stock first-greeting utterances demanded by Japanese etiquette.

With these formalities out of the way, we proceed to the day's interview venue—the nearby Suginami Ward Kōenji Welfare Office. When we arrive at this unmistakably 1980s Bubble Economy Era facility, Tateno-san checks in with the receptionist, who hands over the key to the rec room we will use for our session. There, Tateno-san informs a lively group of elderly Ping-Pong players that the time limit on their reservation for the room has expired and politely but firmly sees to their eviction. After a modicum of grumbling from the evictees, the large, sunny room is all ours. Tateno-san and I pull out some folding chairs from a stack against the wall and use one of the Ping-Pong tables for our workspace. I unshoulder and open my architect's blueprint tube case and extract from it a highly detailed, poster-sized 1946 USSBS map depicting Nagasaki in early August 1945.

I extend a magnifying glass to Tateno-san and indicate that she is free to use this for the map while she provides her narration about prewar and wartime life in the city. However, she waves this off with an apology.

"Sorry to make you carry that all the way here, but I've never been able to use these things," she says, making a dismissive brush-away hand gesture at the map, "even when my eyesight was better."

"That's OK," I say. "I'll be using it, anyway, to find places you mention in your talk."

After ten or twenty more minutes of ice-breaking chitchat, we move on to weightier matters. When the conversation comes around to the role of fate in atomic bombing experiences—a guilt-fraught topic with which any living hibakusha is intimately and often painfully familiar—she muses on the facts that the original Nagasaki aiming point for Fat Man was the Nigiwai Bridge and that if the bomb had been dropped as planned, her mother, her sisters, and she would have been killed within seconds of its detonation.

Continuing with the topic of fate and survival, Tateno-san brings up the subject of her elder brother Chūtarō. Although she claims he was the luckiest of all of the Tatenos—because he was the only member of his Transportation Corps platoon to survive the 56th Infantry Division's yearslong ordeal of slaughter, disease, and starvation in the Burmese jungles—he was never comfortable being told as much. When he came home from the war in 1946—shortly before his mother's premature death from slow-onset ARS-exacerbated heart disease—Master Sergeant Tateno did so with nothing but the tattered uniform on his back, a stubborn case of malaria, a woeful thousand-yard stare, and a small cotton sack of tagged human pinkie fingers in varying stages of mummification.

These last items were not grisly war trophies. Rather, the amputated digits had belonged to the dead soldiers in his platoon. The jungle combat environment and lack of logistical support Tateno and his men endured during the last year or so of the war had precluded the proper cremation and return home of remains to next of kin—normally a solemnly observed tradition that was supposed to be the right and privilege of the emperor's soldiers. In lieu of this, Tateno believed that it was his duty as the ranking sergeant of his platoon to return at least some part of the sons, husbands, or fathers to loved ones back in Japan. Toward this end, he had removed a pinkie finger from each of his soldiers upon their deaths, caused by wounds, disease, or starvation, and carefully recorded their home addresses.

After Sergeant Tateno's return to Nagasaki and securing of employment at Mitsubishi Electric Corporation in Akuno'ura, he spent several years' worth of Sundays traveling by train to various points in northwest Kyushu to return each pinkie to each bereaved family. This labor of love and old-school Japanese honor was never forgotten—as Tateno-san informs me with palpable pride—and when Chūtaro died at seventy-six in 1992, he received a Buddhist temple send-off worthy of a famous politician or movie star, with hundreds of Mitsubishi employees, Nagasaki *shitamachi* residents, and surviving family members of his old platoon mates in attendance.

———

Not long after the qualified joy of Chūtarō's homecoming, the Tateno household was rocked by Mrs. Tateno's death at the age of fifty-two. The family would always blame this calamity on her exposure to what they and many other Nagasakians called the "atom bomb poison": on August 9, when the flash and wind blast of Fat Man's detonation had caught her outdoors (as it had Sueko); during the family's Nagasaki exodus through the ZTD on August 15; and during the intervening six days they had all been breathing in the smoke and stench of Fukuromachi's main cremation pit at the Takao Clinic.

These forensic matters aside, in practical terms of household management, the most significant consequence of Mrs. Tateno's premature death was that responsibility for the constant daily care required for the badly ailing Sueko now fell squarely on the shoulders of her sisters. Although the Tateno's youngest daughter never developed the dreaded petechiae, nor lost any substantial amount of hair, her ARS symptoms fell just short of that level of severity. For example, as her radiation-compromised immune system left her wide-open and vulnerable to any cold virus or other germ with which she came into contact, she was constantly running fevers that left her too nauseated to eat and too weary to go to school. Often, she was too weak to walk to the first aid station at Shinkōzen or even to doctors' clinics in the immediate neighborhood. Instead, doctors would make frequent house calls to the Tatenos' temporary home in Higashi'uwa-machi.

Sueko eventually had her tonsils removed, and this helped to ameliorate the throat problems she had been dealing with since the day of the explosion. But as the household entered 1947—and various neighbors, including young adults and children, were still dying from the atom bomb disease, often without prior symptoms—Sueko still suffered frequent but sporadic bouts of nausea, diarrhea, and other gastrointestinal issues, in addition to her omnipresent malaise / lack of energy. Out of earshot, her family members discussed—and steeled themselves for—the seeming likelihood that she did not have much longer to live.

Luckily for all concerned, premonitions of Sueko's imminent demise proved unfounded, and in spite of her chronic ailments, Sueko graduated (or perhaps more accurately, she was allowed to graduate) from Keiho Girls' School on time in 1948. After this, she matriculated at Tamaki Vocational College, also in the CBD, where she majored in home economics. In the meantime—and despite her lingering but gradually waning ARS symptoms—she returned to her war-interrupted passion of traditional Japanese *buyō* dance. In October 1949, when NMGT commander Lieutenant Colonel Victor Delnore authorized the revival of the "Nagasaki Kunchi"—a nominally Shintō CBD festival that, like its sponsoring institution, Suwa Shrine, had its roots in the Shogunate's crackdown on Christianity in the city—Sueko, as one of the stars of the event, had her photograph prominently featured in local papers under the headline *"O-Kunchi Musume"* ("The Darling of the Kunchi Festival"). She would eventually go on to receive teacher's qualification in the *hanayanagi ryū* school of *buyō*, and as of 2018, she was still teaching part-time in the Tokyo area, where she has lived since 1965.

When Tateno-san became pregnant with her first daughter in 1962, many Nagasaki doctors, including Sueko's gynecologist, continued the early postwar practice of discouraging hibakusha from having children, warning them (without clinically substantiated evidence) of the danger of birth defects (euphemized as "difficulties") arising from their 1945 radiation exposure. Tateno-san did not listen to the doctors then, and she now has two middle-aged daughters to show for it. Unfortunately, when those daughters were adolescents in the 1980s, there were yet doctors—including in Tokyo—who were scaring hibakusha and their children with stories about the potential risks of atomic bomb genetic damage (again, without clinically substantiated evidence). But unlike their mother, the girls took these stories to heart and, compounded by a modicum of bullying about radiation they received as grade and junior high schoolers, they never had children. Since the daughters' subsequent graduation from university and commencing of careers, the three Tateno women have lived within a stone's throw of one another in Tokyo's Suginami Ward.

Hearing about her daughters' bullying in real time was part of Tateno-san's motivation to become involved in Kōyūkai—the Suginami Ward branch of the Nihon Hidankyō (the Japan Confederation of A- and H-Bomb Sufferers Organizations) in the 1970s. She has remained active in this group ever since, albeit in a diminished capacity since hitting her eighties.

As it has been since she first joined, the primary activity of the Kōyūkai is not peace activism but rather to check in regularly with known hibakusha in Suginami Ward (regardless of whether or not they are Kōyūkai members themselves), see how they are doing, and help coordinate medical care and government financial assistance for the ailing and infirm. Tateno-san and the more active members of the Kōyūkai used to attend to this business in person, going door-to-door to visit hibakusha residents in the ward, but since the 1990s or so, as the years have taken their toll on energy levels and knee and ankle joints, they have been conducting this activity primarily by telephone and newsletters.

Although Kōyūkai membership peaked at about eight hundred in the 1970s, it nearly went under just a decade later. One dissolution threat in the 1980s was the advanced senescence and mortality of the first-generation leaders who founded the organization as 1950s adults; a second was the various midlife career and family demands of younger charter rank-and-file members, many of whom left the Tokyo metropolitan area after retirement to return to provincial hometowns. But the organization averted extinction when younger-generation hibakusha like Tateno-san stepped up—with varying degrees of enthusiasm—to take the reins. The Kōyūkai has been muddling along ever since, with Tateno-san and the other board members meeting once a month in the same venue where she and I are having our interview.

Since the 1955 dedication of Nagasaki Peace Park, city-hall-administered memorial ceremonies have been held at the facility every August 9. Tateno-san, however, has never participated in any of these events—even though she was still living in Nagasaki for the first ten of them. Over the years, she came up with various rationalizations for not going—it was always too hot, or she was busy with child-rearing, or she was getting too old—but more recently, she has come to realize that the real reason she has never gone back is that she dreads having to set foot in Urakami again. There are too many ghosts under the asphalt there.

Hearing this, I experience anew a rush of sympathy for what Tateno-san has gone through—not only in 1945 but ever since. I am overwhelmed with humility and gratitude at the thought that she has been willing to share her stories with someone who looks (or looked, before I turned into *Chimes at Midnight*–era Orson Welles) like the people who once came close to killing her with an atomic bomb.

This thought naturally leads me to the question I invariably get around to sooner or later whenever I interview hibakusha.

"Do you have any hatred—or at least resentment—against Americans because of what happened?"

Tateno-san says that she does not, though she regrets that we invented the atomic bomb in the first place, and she is ever impatient—Obama's 2009 nuclear disarmament speech in Prague notwithstanding—that we are not doing more to help rid the world of them.

"Thanks to America, though," she adds with a somewhat sardonic laugh, "Japan has become so peace addled [*heiwa boke*] that we don't even have to think about war anymore."

We talk a bit more about *heiwa boke* and its ramifications, one of which is that young Japanese today seem particularly disinterested (unless for the wrong nationalistic reasons) in the twentieth-century events that led to this syndrome of mass historical amnesia. And if being historically forewarned is to be politically forearmed, I cannot help but think that these blissfully ignorant younger generations will be mere helpless, apathetic onlookers—neither pro nor con—if the Japanese state decides someday to acquire nuclear weapons. This is a scenario conservative politicians in Japan have been discussing with increasing candor of late as the reliability of Japan's traditional post-war protector on the other side of the Pacific comes into question.

Tateno-san acknowledges this point. But she insists that the thought of Japan one day building "those mass murder devices" makes her physically ill. I have little doubt that most hibakusha feel the same way, though I am not so sure about their grandchildren.

The conversation returns to the subject of health—specifically, to the lingering effects of Fat Man on her own. Tateno-san recites for me a litany of physical ailments that she is convinced are bomb related. To these she adds the psychological stress caused by wondering when Fat Man's radiation will finally get around to killing her. She has endured it since 1945—and it has been trans-generationally transmitted to her daughters.

Still, she does not claim to be a completely innocent victim. If she had been just a year older, she would have been making weapons in one of the Mitsubishi plants, and as it was, she supported the war wholeheartedly—just like everyone else around her did (or at least pretended to do in front of others). She recounts the story of how she and her classmates used to send soldiers off to the front, waving paper *Hinomaru* flags and singing war songs. She serenades me with a few bars of *"Ro'ei no Uta"* ("Song of the Field Encampment").

"That war really messed up my life," she says at the end of her performance, and she gives that sardonic little chuckle again—this time unsmilingly.

DR. NAGAI'S FOOTPRINTS

Urakami
November 23, 1945

THREE AND A HALF MONTHS after Fat Man wiped out some two-thirds of Urakami's Catholic community, Sister Itonaga Yoshi, her Junshin colleagues, and about three hundred other members of the district's surviving faithful gathered for a memorial mass before the jagged ruins of their beloved cathedral.[1] The congregants, holding small wooden crucifixes and many also holding boxes containing their dead family members' ashes, sang hymns between prayers and liturgy presided over by Bishop Uragawa Kazusaburō of Sendai, one of the many clergy members from other regions of Japan who had come to Nagasaki to help rebuild Urakami's shattered Catholic community.[2] But the dramatic climax of the event was a eulogy delivered by Dr. Nagai Takashi, a former IJA doctor and now Nagasaki Medical College faculty member who had lost his wife, Midori—the daughter of an old *kakure Kirishitan* family—in the bombing.

Nagai was already well on his way to becoming a local legend by this point, primarily due to the heroically selfless contributions he had made to first aid efforts in the initial days and weeks after the bombing, despite his own grievous wounds. But what he was about to say would catapult him, over the remaining five years of his life, to a stature approaching sainthood.

DR. NAGAI'S FOOTPRINTS

Nagai's eulogy saw the public debut of what would come to be known as his *hansai setsu* ("burnt offering theory") of Urakami's atomic destruction. Addressing the congregation, Nagai summarized its basic theological gist in the following passage:

> *[Has not Urakami's Catholic community been c]hosen from among the world as a flock of pure lambs that should be offered on the altar of the Lord? Alas, the great burnt offering that was offered up before this cathedral on August ninth and duly ended the darkness of the great world war and shined the light of peace! Even in the nadir of sadness, we reverently viewed this as something beautiful, something pure, and something sacred. . . . [T]he church of Urakami was placed on the altar of sacrifice as atonement for the sin of humanity that was the world war. It was chosen as a pure lamb, slaughtered, and burned.[3]*

Lay Catholic (and adult convert) Nagai was not a trained theologian, nor does it appear that he consulted with one before taking the *hansai setsu* public.[4] He just came up with it on his own.

In historical and psychological context, the *hansai setsu* can be looked at as a form of a theological Hail Mary pass to answer a question—namely, "How could God allow something like this to happen?"—that, as it must have preyed on many a Catholic mind in Urakami during that bleak season, clearly preyed on Nagai's own. The *hansai setsu* denied possible answers to that question such as "Because He is a sadist," "Because He doesn't care," or, most frightening of all for a believer, "Because He doesn't exist," insisting instead that the atomic destruction of Urakami had occurred as part of some grand divine design and, as such, did not have to be considered a "tragedy" at all.

Although the *hansai setsu* raised many an eyebrow in real time, as it continues to do so today, it made Nagai a household name in Japan almost overnight, with his story carried in newspapers first domestically, then around the world.[5] His message of forgiveness and redemption, immeasurably burnished by the optics of the messenger's hibakusha credibility and inspiring personal backstory, won the doctor admiration from non-Christian compatriots and former foes alike, the latter approval evidenced by the cash donations earmarked for Urakami[6] reconstruction that shortly began to pour into the district from American Catholics. That money went on to help rebuild Junshin Girls' School, for example, and eventually Immaculate Conception Cathedral itself.

Some three and a half years later, after a lengthy back-and-forth with Allied censors, Nagai was allowed to publish his volume of hibakusha memoirs, *Nagasaki no Kane* (*The Bells of Nagasaki*), on the proviso that it include an appendix of photographs of wartime atrocities committed by the Japanese military in the Philippines.[7] Irrespective of this photographic contribution to the volume, *Nagasaki no Kane* became a runaway bestseller in Japan, as well as an overseas royalties generator in translation.[8] In the wake of this success, and before succumbing to radiation-induced leukemia in 1951, Nagai authored a slew of additional memoirs, essay collections, and other bestsellers, always donating his earnings to various Urakami causes.

As the old saw goes, victory in battle usually goes to whoever shows up on the field "the firstest with the mostest"—a nugget of homespun wisdom that applies not only to warfare but to the domination of information spheres as well. In the case of the early postwar hibakusha discourse, Nagai not only arrived on the scene as the firstest with the mostest, but he essentially had the entirety of the field to himself (with the lesser and far briefer exception of a Nagasaki survivor named Ishida Masako—more on this shortly). Significantly, and for reasons whose complexity is beyond the limits of this volume to address in the detail it deserves, no Hiroshima equivalent to Nagai appeared—or, rather, was allowed to appear—for the remaining three years of the occupation. As a consequence, at the national level, this gave Nagasaki a relative salience over Hiroshima in Japanese public awareness during this brief but important period.

Nagasaki's dominance of atomic bomb discourse, however, basically ended with the occupation as the city was pushed out of the spotlight by the flood of more strident Hiroshima content, which, when it arrived in bookstores and cinemas, was more attuned to the zeitgeist of 1950s Japan. At the local Nagasaki level, Nagai's works and legacy had the lasting effect—whether intentional or not—of skewing the public narrative of the city's atomic bombing experience by making Christians and Christianity the central elements of its plot. This development would lead to the diminishment of non-Christian Nagasaki hibakusha voices for decades to come,[9] and it is still resented to this day.

———

Junshin Middle and High School for Girls
Bunkyō-machi (formerly Ieno-machi), Nagasaki
August 9, 2018

For the first time since I have begun my hibakusha research, I am going to be missing the annual Nagasaki Peace Park memorial ceremony. But I will be sure to make next year's event, and in the meantime, I am availing myself of a precious fieldwork opportunity made possible by the good offices of the Catholic Archdiocese of Nagasaki: Today I will be attending the annual August 9 memorial mass at Junshin Girls' School.

Junshin occupies the exact same plot of land that its first incarnation did when it was destroyed by Fat Man, and its cream-colored campus buildings, with their tastefully understated ecclesiastical motifs, clearly share architectural DNA passed down from their atom-bombed predecessors. Just inside and to the right of the main Bunkyōdōri (formerly Nagayo Road) gate, one can find a handsome bronze bust of Bishop Hayasaka Kyūnosuke—the charter benefactor of the Junshin Sisters order. At the north, or opposite, side of the gate, there is a beautiful white marble statue of the Virgin Mary standing on a tall granite pedestal. As I would later learn, the statue was built with donations to the school from American Catholics, and it was erected on the very spot where Mother Ezumi used to see her students off to their ordnance plant worksites every morning.[10]

When I inspect this serenely imposing icon more closely, it does not take long to find the footprints of Nagai Takashi's *hansai setsu* all over it. On the front of the statue's pedestal are two bronze plaques. These are arranged vertically and are inscribed in the Japanese textual tradition of vertical script. The upper plaque reads: "Holy Mother of Mercy" (*Jihi no seibo*).

The lower plaque features the following lines from *"Hansai no Uta"* ("Song of the *Hansai*"), which Dr. Nagai wrote for the first postwar Junshin graduation ceremony, held at the temporary Junshin campus at Ōmura Airfield in March 1946:

> *In the flames of burnt sacrifice,*
> *The girls of white lilies*
> *Rose up to the bosom of the Lord,*
> *Singing the glories of peace.*
> *Nagai Takashi, MD*

On the rear of the pedestal are two more plaques, again arranged vertically; the upper plaque is devoted to a summary of the "state of the *hansei setsu* narrative" in 1949, the year of Junshin's return to the Ieno-machi campus and, as already noted, the year of the first publication of Nagai's *The Bells of Nagasaki*:

> *Two hundred and four young schoolgirls, daughters of the Virgin Mary,*
> *were mobilized to work at factories, where they prayed and toiled for*
> *their country. Because of the atomic bomb, they died pure and*
> *beautiful deaths while singing out hymns to the Virgin.*
> *Our Heavenly Father, who is just and merciful, accepted this sacrifice*
> *and brought peace on the Feast of the Assumption of*
> *the Blessed Virgin on 15 August 1945.*
> *This statue of the Virgin Mary was erected to commemorate the 400th*
> *anniversary of the arrival of the Gospel in Japan,[11] and some mortal*
> *remains [of Junshin bomb victims] have been placed under her feet.[12]*
> *"May Junshin alumni always remember with fondness their alma mater,*
> *And pray for the mercy of Our Lady to be bestowed upon our country,*

*That the people of Japan will soon be bathed in
Her light of justice and truth."*
30 May 1949
Tanka *poem by Dr Nagai Takashi, calligraphy by Matsuoka Kunikazu.
Nagasaki Junshin High School for Girls, August 9, 1945*[13]

Under this, the second plaque carries a roster of the Junshin Sisters, lay faculty members, and students killed by the bomb.

While I am studying this list for familiar surnames, a firm and mature female voice calls out, *"Ohayo gozaimasu,"* in my general direction. The voice belongs to a diminutive middle-aged Junshin Sister who ushers me into the school's administrative office. There, I am given a brief audience with the principal—an older Junshin Sister— before I am shown to the school chapel. I take a seat a respectful distance from the altar and the front pew, which is occupied by three superannuated Junshin Sisters. I do not know it at the time but one of these Sisters is Itonaga Yoshi—or, as she has been known since taking her religious name concurrently with final lifetime vows in 1955, Sister Ursula Itonaga Yoshi.[14]

While more congregants file in, a student dressed in the school's white-and-blue summer uniform serenades the gathering with hymnal organ music. This is soon joined by singing from the students seated in the rear half of the chapel and the balcony. I get a quick rash of goose bumps on my forearms when I realize that Junshin students probably sang these same hymns in this very spot (albeit in a no-longer-extant building) during the war.

When the chapel is full, the day's formal Catholic mass begins. We rise for prayers at several points between speeches delivered by students and bereaved Junshin family members. After this, the presiding priest gives communion to the queued-up faithful—among whom are a couple of elderly congregants, but only about twenty or so out of the several hundred Junshin students in the chapel at the moment.

Looking at this, I wonder what Mother Ezumi would have thought if she could see her Junshin successors' rather anemic proselytization accomplishments among the school's current student body. I am pretty sure, though, that the Junshin founder—at least after 1937 or so—would regard more generously the dramatic climax of the mass, when the communion wafer ciborium is removed from the altar and replaced with a propped-up picture frame containing, behind glass, two age-browned and soot-stained cotton Junshin armbands that were worn by students killed at Ōhashi. When this switch is made, an old man—probably a brother of a Junshin victim—approaches the framed armbands and bows deeply before these historical (and literally religious) relics. Some more words I cannot quite make out are intoned before a student and more Junshin bereaved—some young enough to be second- or even third-generation mourners—lay flowers on the altar.

At the conclusion of the ceremony, the other special guests and I are given a lunch held in our honor at the campus cafeteria, where we are welcomed by several speakers and entertained by the school's merrily thumping brass band. After the event, I thank my hosts and hightail it to be on time for the afternoon's Nagasaki Medical College memorial ceremony, where Gunge Norio is once again the featured lecturer. On my way out of the Junshin gate, I note that the framed armbands have in the meantime been moved out of the chapel and placed on the pedestal of the Holy Mother of Mercy statue directly underneath the plaque with the *Hansai no Uta* verse.

NEGOTIATED MEMORY

Megumi no Oka Nagasaki Genbaku Home
Mitsuyama-machi
August 10, 2018

IT IS THE morning after the Junshin Girls' School ceremony. A research colleague, Dr. Tomonaga Masao, has been kind enough to pick me up at my hotel—the Hotel Washington in Nagasaki's Chinatown—to drive me to an institution with which he has been affiliated since he was a young physician in the 1970s: the Megumi no Oka (Hill of Blessings) Nagasaki Genbaku Home. This is an assisted-living facility for Nagasaki hibakusha administered by Junshin Sisters and built on land donated to the Archdiocese of Nagasaki by the locally illustrious Takami family. The home occupies essentially the same top spot— deep in the belt of lush green mountain ridges northeast of the city— where the members of the Junshin pine-sap-collection detail saw singed hymnal and prayer book pages fall from the sky on the morning of the atomic bombing.

When we arrive, we are met at the entrance of the main hall (*honkan*) by two Sisters to whom Dr. Tomonaga hands me off while he goes up into the wards to do his weekly rounds for Megumi no Oka's residents. In the meantime, the Sisters give me a brief tour of the facility, which is so quiet that the predominant sounds are the grinding buzz of cicadas in the lushly wooded hillocks and dales of the

Takamis' mountain and the short, rapid-footstep *squeak squeak* of the Sisters' sensible rubber-soled sandals.

As we walk down a long corridor, we pass various peace-themed paintings, sculptures, macramé hangings, and the like—some clearly the work of professionals, others not. The likely provenance of this latter category is soon self-evident when we stop briefly to look inside a rec room, which with its arts-and-crafts tables and drawings on the walls brings to mind a kindergarten classroom with higher chairs.

We pass the cafeteria, where a small cluster of residents—some in wheelchairs—encircles a young Junshin Sister who looks as if she is just out of her novitiate. She is leading the group in some kind of reflex-exercising hand-gesturing game. A male participant seems to have made an error, and the comically exaggerated groan he emits at this is greeted with a round of mostly female cackling. The young Sister indulges the disruption for a few beats before restoring order to begin a new round.

When we reach the small conference room where I will be conducting this morning's hibakusha interview, the elder of the two Sisters escorting me helps set up my table and engages me in innocuously interrogative small talk about my background and research while the younger one goes off to bring around my interview subject. A few minutes later, I am introduced to Sister Ursula Itonaga Yoshi, age ninety-five.

When we sit down, settle in, and regard each other across the table, I am struck by the round circle of Sister Yoshi's ancient face, which looks like it has been hewn from hand-worn alabaster. Set against the black backdrop of her veil, it seems almost disembodied and floating in space. For the next two hours, I will watch this face as its owner tells me about the day the bomb fell.

We reach the end of Sister Yoshi's harrowing August 9 testimony, and the conversation segues into what she witnessed during Junshin Girls' School's long and arduous postwar resurrection. Sister Yoshi recounts the hard first few months after the war, when the physically ailing and emotionally broken Mother Ezumi was convalescing at the

Takamis' home here in Mitsuyama, where she spent some time under the care of Dr. Nagai Takashi.

At the time, Mother Ezumi often spoke about what she saw as her sole personal responsibility for the two hundred students her school had lost at Ōhashi. In particularly despondent moments, she even opined that it would have been a fitting fate for her if she had eventually been assassinated by one of those students' grief-crazed parents.

Mother Ezumi had also convinced herself that, on an institutional level, the only proper act of contrition for the surviving Sisters would have been for them to hold one final, grand prayer-and-memorial ceremony for their dead girls, then shut down their educational program forever. But then more and more people started to make pilgrimages to Mitsuyama to console the ailing Mother Superior, including many bereaved parents of Junshin girls who implored Mother Ezumi to rebuild the school so that their daughters' deaths would not be in vain. As Sister Yoshi recalls, some of these guardians even thanked Mother Ezumi for providing their daughters with the opportunity to die such magnificent deaths for God and emperor.

Prefectural education board members soon joined these parents in the soft-pressure campaign to nudge Mother Ezumi back onto her feet to rebuild the school. After Mother Ezumi finally acquiesced to the idea, one of the senior Junshin members—Sister Nagatani Martina (who would become Mother Superior of the order after Ezumi's death in 1980)—was singularly instrumental in getting things moving. Most days during the early stages of the project, Sister Martina—usually with Sister Yoshi in tow as her assistant—would make the long trek to downtown Nagasaki on foot to file the prerequisite application paperwork with the prefectural government and negotiate directly with the Americans toward securing the necessary logistical support.

A major breakthrough was achieved when Colonel Delnore's NMGT gave Junshin permission to set up a temporary campus at Ōmura. The land occupied by the IJN base had reverted to prefectural property after the war, so the requisite real estate transaction was relatively straightforward—and free of charge. The school resumed classes there in the middle of the autumn semester, using old barracks buildings for classrooms and dormitories. Faculty and students did their best to ignore the constant sonic interruptions of Marine Corps and U.S. Army planes using the airfield.

Three and a half years later, Junshin's phoenix finally rose from the ashes of Ieno-machi when its new campus was opened on the grounds of the old school. The climax of the dedication festivities was the unveiling of the beautiful white marble Holy Mother of Mercy—containing its small ossuary of students' and Sisters' remains at her feet—on the same spot by the main gate that it occupies today.

Sister Yoshi devoted her long life to the order that completely circumscribed her lived environment for more than eighty years. During her career, she served as its novitiate mistress before assuming her last post as chairperson of the Junshin school system. She retired from full-time duties in 2009, at the age of eighty-six, and died just two months short of her ninety-ninth birthday in September 2022.[1] She was the last member of the order who had experienced the atom bombing of Nagasaki as a Junshin Sister.

Bunkyō Ward, Tokyo

May 2019

My graduate student and I have entered the final phase of our interview with Ishida Masako at her small but comfortable Tokyo apartment. We start talking about postwar Nagasaki.

After her long convalescence in Fukuoka, Masako returned to the city to find that her father's official judicial status had miraculously survived the defeat that saw so many of his peers purged from office by the country's new occupation masters. And not only had he survived but—and no doubt due to his resourcefulness, natural extroversion, and mastery of English—his standing in the community seemed to be even more elevated than it had been during the war, so much so that other movers and shakers in the city eventually began jokingly (or possibly a little resentfully) referring to him as "the Mayor."[2] True to form, upon the arrival of the NMGT, Judge Ishida made fast friends with its commander, Colonel Delnore. This connection would end up putting into motion a chain of events that would alter the course of Masako's life.

About a year after Masako's return to Nagasaki, where she had resumed her studies at Kenjo, her father broached the idea of compiling for commercial publication the *Masako Taorezu* memoir articles she had written while in Kyushu Imperial University Hospital. Masako was initially aghast at the suggestion, but Judge Ishida was insistent, telling his daughter to look beyond her own personal circumstances and think about the contributions that *Masako Taorezu* could make toward encouraging Japanese peace and warning the world about the horrors of the atomic bomb. Eventually, after Jō'ichi began adding pressure as well, Masako relented.

Jō'ichi—corresponding from Tōdai, where he was following in his father's footsteps at the Faculty of Law—assisted with the editorial and compilation work for the manuscript, which included a long commentary by the judge. When the manuscript was completed in March 1947, Judge Ishida submitted it to the NMGT, whose chief censor, Captain Irvin W. Rogers, approved of the work as "a vivid personal experience of the atomic bombing of Nagasaki."[3] In the package prepared for final submission from the NMGT to the Kyushu District Civil Censorship Detachment (CCD) office in Fukuoka, Colonel Delnore added a personal endorsement that included the following comments:

> [The work] show[s] the reactions of the members of one small family in the holocaust; [it] show[s] the heartbreak and the pain. . . . For us to properly realize the significance of the atomic bomb, to experience vicariously the feelings that so many thousands of Japanese people experienced is desirable in these propitious times.[4]

At the end of the first round of negotiations with Fukuoka, in which the judge had augmented the case for publication with a petition from leading Nagasaki citizens supporting Masako's book, the Kyushu CCD detachment denied approval of the work, stating that it "would disturb public tranquility in Japan and that it implies the bombing was a crime against humanity," but the CCD also suggested that the text might be approved sometime in the future when it posed less danger of "tear[ing] open war scars and rekindl[ing] animosity."[5]

Nevertheless, Judge Ishida continued to lobby for publication, even making a pilgrimage to Urakami—with a hesitant Masako in tow—to enlist the support of the already famous (but now seriously ailing) Dr. Nagai. The following day, after the press got ahold of the story, a group of reporters and cameramen convinced the judge and Masako to return to Dr. Nagai's one-room Urakami shack to reenact their original visit for a photo op and a human-interest story. Once the flashbulbs started popping, Masako was so nervous that she could barely utter a word, only nodding and interjecting with the occasional *"hai"* while Nagai—by then a seasoned veteran of media attention— lectured her on the importance of sharing Nagasaki's story with the world.

After her March 1948 graduation from Kenjo—where her class year group had been nearly halved in size by Fat Man—Masako, despite knowing little English, was able to secure a coveted post as a librarian with the Civil Information and Education Section (CIE) office of the NMGT. It can be assumed—though not known with certainty— that this demonstrated cooperation with occupation goals on Masako's part might have greased the wheels in Fukuoka toward approval for publication, but in any case, this was finally granted. After the removal of a few problematic passages from the resubmitted manuscript—including references to the bitterness 1945 Masako felt toward the Americans and a remark toward the end of the book about her belief that her life had been spared so she could once again be of service to the emperor someday—*Masako Taorezu* went to the presses at Nagasaki's Fujin Taimuzu Sha (Women's Times) in February 1949 with an initial run of two thousand copies.[6] Several months later, the book was picked up by a Tokyo publisher and marketed nationally.

Masako was excruciatingly self-conscious about her newfound

fame, which she had never wanted and, moreover, felt she did not deserve. Whenever she was out and about in public, she was constantly convinced that people recognized her in the streets, and in this paranoid state, she was sure that they were giving her dirty looks. After a few weeks of this, she just wanted to shrink away and disappear.

Although Masako was grateful for all that her father and relatives had done for her after the bombing, she also felt profoundly guilty about it. She was fully aware that, during her hospital stay, she had been pampered to a degree that precious few other survivors had had the wherewithal and means to enjoy. To make things worse, she was beginning to hear rumors that there were people in the city who were also aware and bitterly resentful of this care and that they were going around saying that she did not have the right to represent the city's survivors. In their eyes, Masako was disqualified from calling herself a hibakusha, not only because she had gotten this special medical treatment but also because she had not suffered any scarring or permanent injury nor lost any loved ones. Masako probably imagined a lot more of this negative scrutiny than actually existed, but in her fragile state, it seemed all too real and threatening at the time.

When the Ishidas relocated to Kyoto, Masako was able to secure employment once again as a librarian with the CIE office, working for the Americans until the end of the occupation. In 1953, Jō'ichi arranged for her to go on a date with his old friend Yanagawa Toshikazu. The boys had known each other since elementary school in Tokyo, had come up through junior high and the Tōdai Faculty of Law together, and were now working at the Ministry of Justice in Tokyo. Yanagawa was quiet and scholarly—very different from Jō'ichi, whose extroverted temperament and wide range of interests resembled those of their father—but Masako was impressed by the dedication the young man had shown in braving a seven-hour train trip to come to see her in Kyoto.

Toshikazu had to endure the trip only a few times after that; the couple was married on Valentine's Day 1954, and Masako dutifully accompanied her husband from one judicial posting to another until his retirement in 1987. On the occasion of one of the many overseas business trips on which she accompanied her husband, she was amazed to find an original first-printing edition of *Masako Taorezu* in the Library of Congress in Washington, DC.

Masako's renown as Nagasaki's second-most-famous hibakusha faded quickly after she left the city, and *Masako Taorezu* went out of print for the next forty-two years. By the time the Yanagawas and their two children relocated to Tokyo in the 1960s, she had returned to a state of almost complete anonymity. Family friends, the members of her local Nihon Hidankyō branch, and a handful of neighbors knew about her past, but those few exceptions aside, Ishida Masako and *Masako Taorezu* had long since become little more than footnotes in the history of atomic bomb memory.

Masako's comfortable and near-total anonymity came to an end, however, in 1985, when a neighbor—an editor for the major women's monthly *Kurashi no Techō*—coaxed her into giving an interview about her Nagasaki experiences. This was published in the magazine, along with a portion of *Masako Taorezu* up to the point where she returns to the Yaoya-machi *kansha* on the morning after the bombing to reunite with her father. This exposure—and a 1991 reprint of *Masako Taorezu*—garnered her a degree of renewed attention from the press, but by the time this was happening, Ishida Masako was merely one among the many hundreds or even thousands of hibakusha who had taken their stories public since the end of the occupation, and her fame never came close to the levels she had known from 1949 to 1951.

Around the time of the 2009 Prague speech that won President Obama that year's Nobel Peace Prize, and with renewed resolve after the Fukushima nuclear plant meltdown in 2011, Masako—in spite of her lifelong phobia of public speaking—began giving lectures about the dangers of nuclear weapons to Tokyo-area schoolchildren, university students, and senior citizens' groups. She was greatly encouraged in these efforts by Hayashi Kyōko—a Kenjo classmate who had also survived the destruction of the Mitsubishi Ōhashi plant and gone on to win the prestigious Akutagawa Prize for her own hibakusha memoir, *Matsuri no Ba* (1975).

Masako—Yanagawa-san—had at long last come to accept that her hibakusha experience was a central part of her identity. Over the final years of her life, Masako stood unbroken, overcoming her fears and reticence to share her story with others in the cause of peace.

THE OTHER SIDE OF KONPIRA

IN OCTOBER 1945, an American combat engineer battalion bulldozed and steamrollered the ruins of the already Fat Man–obliterated riverside slum neighborhood of Komaba into an airstrip that the GIs soon dubbed "Atomic Field." Also crushed under the earthmoving equipment were the unrecovered remains of hundreds of Komaba's residents and unlucky August 9 Togitsu Road wayfarers and streetcar passengers still strewn on top of, inside, and under the debris. Apparently, the Americans either did not care or did not know—because no one from city hall or the police department had bothered to tell them—that they were plowing under and paving over what was in effect a mass grave site.[1] In Komaba's final consignment to oblivion, its name was officially retired from city maps and administrative rolls in 1961, and the geographical area it constituted was amalgamated into present-day Matsuyama-machi. A 1960s-era municipal sports complex consisting of athletic fields and an Olympic-sized indoor swimming pool now stands on the site.

I have long felt that in many ways Komaba's fate was symbolic of the amnesiac quality with which Nagasaki—compared with Hiroshima—approaches its engagement (or lack thereof) with atom-bomb-memory commemoration in the city's public space. This tendency can be traced, I believe, to the circumstances of Urakami's destruction on August 9, 1945.

In a phenomenon I discuss at length in *Hiroshima: The Last Witnesses* (2024), perhaps as many as half of Hiroshima's victims were commuters—bureaucratic officials and other white-collar employees, students mobilized to clear firebreaks in downtown districts, etc.—from outside of the city. When these tens of thousands of commuters were wiped out en masse by an atomic bomb that detonated directly over dead-center mass of Hiroshima's CBD, this catastrophe instantly created a commensurate number of bereaved surviving families living in the undamaged suburbs and rural outskirts of the city. In the early postwar years, even while Hiroshima was still under Allied occupation, this community of bereaved households coalesced into a powerful pressure group that was able to push local (and eventually national) authorities into prominently commemorating the deaths of Little Boy victims in Hiroshima public space.

In the case of Nagasaki, however, this demographic phenomenon was reversed: With the notable exceptions of those at Nagasaki Medical College and the Mitsubishi ordnance plants, the overwhelming majority of that city's atomic bomb victims were not people who had traveled *to* Urakami on the morning of the bombing but rather the families that commuters left at home in the district. This dynamic meant that in many cases the only surviving members of Urakami households were fathers, husbands, or sons who had been away from the valley—at work in the CBD or away on military service—when their homes and families there were wiped out. When these young or middle-aged males underwent the emotionally shattering experience of returning to post-bombing Urakami only to find no trace whatsoever of their loved ones, they no longer had any reason to stay in the area—and it is not difficult to imagine that they had many compelling reasons to leave it far behind.

Due to the uniquely discourse-stifling circumstances of this demographic dynamic, as well as to the outsized early influence of Nagai and the *hansai setsu*, Nagasaki would never see the coalescing of a community of *secular* atomic-bomb-memory activists comparable in any way—certainly not in terms of size and political influence—to the one that quickly formed in Hiroshima. This is not to suggest, however, that there were not people in Urakami who tried to form such a community outside of Dr. Nagai's Catholic purview—just that they were very few in number.

Two such non-Christian Nagasaki memory activists were bereaved Urakami fathers Sugimoto Kamekichi and Takigawa Masaru, whose August 9 morning commutes had spared their own lives from the cataclysm that wiped out their households. In 1946, perhaps after reading or hearing about preparations for a similar event in Hiroshima and perhaps even wanting to push back a bit at the rapidly spreading influence of the *hansai setsu*, Sugimoto and Takigawa began petitioning local government officials to issue the required public assembly permit for—and if possible help sponsor—a memorial ceremony in the vicinity of the atomic hypocenter on the occasion of the upcoming first anniversary of the bombing.[2]

From the start, Nagasaki City Hall expressed trepidation about the risk of offending the sensitivities of NMGT, and it attempted to extricate itself from any entanglement in the matter on the pretext that atom-bomb-related matters were in any case under the jurisdiction of Nagasaki Prefecture. Next visiting the prefectural offices—whose bureaucrats were similarly averse to involvement—Sugimoto and Takigawa were promptly rebuffed and sent back to city hall. Exasperated by this Kafkaesque red-tape runaround, the bereaved fathers were finally driven to the desperate measure of taking their case straight to the NMGT office in Shindaiku-machi, where a lowly lieutenant handled their case and signed off on their proposal without argument or further ado. Nagasaki officials, scrambling to save jurisdictional face as well as loath to countermand the will of one of General MacArthur's local representatives—even if that representative was barely old enough to shave—had no choice but to sign off on the proposal, and they threw in a very modest amount of funding as an added gesture.[3]

The first-anniversary Nagasaki Ground Zero memorial ceremony was a far cry from Hiroshima's major event, which three days earlier had drawn a crowd of thousands, including numerous representatives of the Japanese and international press.[4] In contrast, Nagasaki's ceremony—or what would perhaps be more accurately called Sugimoto and Takigawa's ceremony—ended up drawing approximately a hundred mourners and a few Buddhist monks to chant sutras in a drizzling rain.[5]

Over coming years, local government officials keeping a competitive eye on doings in Hiroshima eventually began displaying more enthusiasm about the annual August 9 commemorative events—especially after the National Diet's passage of the 1949 Atom-bombed Cities Reconstruction Law meant there would be plentiful funding coming in for such purposes. Nevertheless, intent as always on avoiding any possibility of controversy or friction, local Japanese politicians and bureaucrats insisted on referring to these events throughout the rest of the occupation period not as "memorial ceremonies" for the bomb victims but rather as "culture festivals"[6] that just happened to be held on August 9.

In the meantime, Nagasaki was still without an official municipal ossuary or even a centralized temporary collection point for the unclaimed remains of bomb victims, and it would not have one until 1959—some thirteen years later than Hiroshima, which essentially built its Peace Park around its own, providing its bereaved citizens (and visitors to the city) with a memory space that would go on to assume a dominant symbolic and defining permanent role in that city's atomic narrative.

There are myriad reasons why it has been the name of Hiroshima—and not that of Nagasaki—that has since gone on to become synonymous in global awareness with the horror and moral turpitude of nuclear warfare.[7] The extreme difficulties Nagasaki faced in terms of body recovery after the bombing is one of them. So is the absence in Nagasaki of a robust memory activist community of bereaved but intact households and the related lack of conspicuous bomb memory sites in CBD public space. And finally, so is city hall's hand-wringing during the critical early postwar period regarding how—and, perhaps just as important, where—the bombing should be memorialized.

One legacy of this history is that in contrast with Hiroshima, atomic bomb memory in Nagasaki is separated—one could almost say "quarantined"—from the mainstream environment of the city's lived experience. This separation is so effective that today tourists, residents, and investors who prefer to visit, live, or do business in the city without being constantly reminded of its atom-bombed past can do so quite easily as long as they avoid what is in effect and function a municipal atomic-memory-containment zone in Urakami.

This zone consists of the Nagasaki Atomic Bomb Museum, a hypocenter marker, and, straddling these two sites, Nagasaki Peace Park, which occupies a patch of land about the size of two football fields on the pre-bombing site of Nagasaki Prefectural Prison—a small, leveled hill some two hundred meters north of Ground Zero. The hilltop park is set far back from Togitsu Road (which is now a busy six-lane stretch of National Highway 206), and its primary access point is a tandem series of long escalators leading up from the street below. The entrance to these escalators is so inconspicuous that motorists and pedestrians oblivious to street signage could easily pass it by without knowing it was there (something that, in fact, happened to me the first time I visited the city).

Built using funding from the 1949 Atom-bombed Cities Reconstruction Law, the park is dominated by sculptor Kitamura Seibō's Peace God colossus, which was unveiled on the occasion of the park's opening in 1955. The rest of the small park is crowded with almost the entirety of Nagasaki's public-space atom-bomb-related cenotaphs and other memorials, a surprising number of which were donated by Communist Bloc countries in the 1970s and 1980s.

Overall, the impression that the commemorative space gives is that the city chose long ago not to make its atomic trauma the central element of its reconstructed postwar identity. One reason for this, as already discussed, is the grim body-recovery backstory. An-

THE OTHER SIDE OF KONPIRA

other, perhaps, is an acknowledgment of Hiroshima's overwhelming dominance of atomic-bomb-memory discourse since the end of the occupation. The simplest explanation, however, may be that the prerogative of being able to downplay the legacy of the bombing is a reflection of the vast and permanent power disparity between the CBD—which, by a fluke, survived Fat Man's wrath relatively unscathed—and the industrial, agricultural, and historically suspect *Kirishitan* communities of the Urakami Valley, which came close to being wiped out. From this perspective, inhabitants of the city's political, economic, and cultural center of gravity in the CBD can, when they choose to do so, regard the events of August 9, 1945, as something that happened not to the *real* Nagasaki but rather to *those people* on the other side of Konpira. Hiroshima—which was destroyed from its center out—has never enjoyed the luxury of such a choice.

Matsuyama-machi

August 9, 2017

I am attending my second city-hall-administered memorial ceremony at Nagasaki Peace Park. Thanks to the hospitality of Tōyūkai, the Tokyo regional organization of the Nihon Hidankyō, I have a much better seat than I did last year. I am only about ten rows back from the ceremonial stage, which is centered on a black granite cenotaph at the foot of the Peace God statue. Flanking the cenotaph on both sides are two large depictions of origami cranes—originally atom-bomb-memory iconography of Hiroshima provenance; all of this is surrounded and fronted by abundant floral arrangements. Finally, up front and center—with the dramatic black box of the cenotaph as its backdrop—is a dais from which Prime Minister Abe Shinzō is scheduled to speak later.

There ensues about an hour or so of choral interludes, followed by speeches by hibakusha, foreign diplomats, various political dignitaries, and Nagasaki mayor Ta'ue Tomihisa. After the mayor's address, it is time for the symbolic climax of each year's ceremony, when cages are opened to release hundreds of "peace doves" (pigeons) to fly over the venue and, it is hoped, eventually away to freedom. But some of the birds are uncooperative—or just unambitious—and after a bit of desultory flapping, they take up perches on top of the giant origami cranes, other backdrops, and, naturally, the Peace God's head.

Throughout all of this, Prime Minister Abe has been sitting off to the side, with eyes closed and a mildly irritated facial expression. After the "dove" release, he mounts the dais and begins to read from his prepared script. Listening to his speech, I am nearly certain that he is delivering—pretty much word for word—not only the same boilerplate pabulum he read in Hiroshima three days earlier but also in both venues last year. As he drones through his speech with an obvious—almost defiant—lack of enthusiasm, there are a few catcalls from way in the back in the cheap seats, probably from the Japanese Communist Party protest squad I always see at these events.

At the close of the ceremony, I part from my Tōyūkai companions and set off for the day's next appointment. One of my research colleagues, Research Center for Nuclear Weapons Abolition (RECNA) professor emerita Mine Mariko, has invited me to attend that afternoon's annual Nagasaki Medical College memorial ceremony and symposium at the Nagasaki University School of Medicine—which occupies the same campus (with new buildings, obviously) as its institutional predecessor. This year's featured lecture will be by a hibakusha named Gunge Norio, and Mine-sensei has assured me that this is someone whose testimony I need to hear.

The event venue is in the campus' main auditorium, and when I arrive, nearly every seat has already been taken. After grabbing a spot in the nosebleed seats, I survey the audience, which is much younger overall than the one I just left in Peace Park. There are some superannuated attendees in the front row who appear old enough to have memories of or at least direct personal connection to the atomic bombing, but the other 80 to 90 percent of the crowd are clearly School of Medicine people—faculty doctors and nurses and students.

When it is time for his lecture, eighty-eight-year-old Gunge-san

THE OTHER SIDE OF KONPIRA 365

mounts the stage with a studied, slow solemnity that belies his more than passing resemblance to 1970s TV advertisement fixture Frank Perdue. During his brief self-introduction, he explains his family's proud connection and undying gratitude to Nagasaki Medical College, which gave his brother, Yoshio, such a rich educational environment in the last year and a half of his life. Left in the immediate wake of that observation is something unsaid but still clearly expressed; the audience is to meditate on the wonderful life that promising young man would have gone on to lead had it not been cut short so brutally.

Gunge-san's monologue then moves on to his memories of August 9, which are also his last ones of his brother. His voice begins to quaver when he reaches the story about the forgotten fountain pen and Yoshio's final smiling wave at the front gate of their boarding-house. It takes a tough man to make a tender story out of such tragedy and horror, but Gunge has pulled it off. When he finishes his talk, there is not a dry eye—including my own—in the auditorium.

After the lecture and ceremony, I tag along to an informal late luncheon session for attendees held at the nearby campus cafeteria. There I wait for an opening and allow a respectable amount of time to pass before I approach Gunge-san. When I finally do, we exchange business cards, and I explain that I have been researching the hibakusha and the atomic bombings since Obama's visit to Hiroshima. Gunge-san unhesitatingly agrees to my request for a formal interview, and after some mutual schedule consultation, we agree on a date. I will go to his home in Kumamoto City, Kumamoto Prefecture, in December.

Kumamoto City

December 2017

Gunge-san and I are in the living room of the well-appointed Western-style house where he has lived with his wife since the late 1980s, when he took up a position as a lecturer at a local private college. Mrs. Gunge makes a brief appearance to formally welcome me and thank me for the Nagasaki *kasutera* cake I have brought as a gift. She then retreats to another room to watch TV, and we will not see her again until it is time for me to leave; while the house's architecture may be Western modern, the social dynamic playing out under its roof is definitely traditional Japanese.

For the next few hours, Gunge-san shares with me his testimony about his life before, during, and shortly after August 9, 1945. During our dialogue, he pulls out an album of various maps and photos of old, pre-bombing Nagasaki and Urakami, pointing out spots of both historical and personal significance. Included in the album is the last photo ever taken of Yoshio—a formally posed shot of him as a nineteen-year-old pharmacology student, proud and resplendent in the military-style button-down tunic of his medical college uniform. As Gunge-san shares some more fond anecdotes about Yoshio, his hands begin to shake and his voice segues into that same quavering timbre I heard at his lecture four months earlier. But this time, he holds nothing back. Now, through sobs, he talks about the pain of losing a sibling and says that no one can ever understand that unless they have experienced it themselves. I tell him that I know exactly what that feels like—and then I start to lose it, too. Doing something I have never done with a hibakusha before, I put a hand around Gunge-san's shoulder, and the two of us hold that pose for what is probably only thirty seconds or so but feels much longer.

When we recover our composure, I ask him to tell me about his life in Nagasaki during the occupation.

After his emotionally broken father went back to his starch plant in Ōmura, sixteen-year-old Norio had to fend for himself in Shimonishiyama-machi. While Norio's natural inclination might have been to spend more downtime working through his grief over his brother, the need for food eventually prodded him to go out of the house to look for it. And in the grim and lean autumn of 1945, the only people in Nagasaki who had a surplus supply of that otherwise scarce commodity were the Americans.

Like many other Nagasaki students his age, Norio eventually

ended up working for the occupation forces—in his case, as a member of a team of boys cleaning barracks first for the Marines, then for the NMGT troops. He and the other boys were paid for their labor with boxes of C rations, which the boys found luxurious and delicious beyond belief. To their initial astonishment, the C rations even came with dessert—something none of the boys could have imagined Japanese soldiers in the field ever seeing. In wistful observations of the kind commonly made by Japanese in the early postwar period, the boys opined that their country must have been crazy, going to war with a people so prosperous, they could provide their combat soldiers with dessert.

While Norio felt some natural resentment toward the Americans because of what had happened to his family, he never harbored any hatred for them. Like the vast majority of his countrymen at the time, he found that the best way to get through his day-to-day interactions with the foreign occupiers was just to keep his head down, follow orders, and do his job.

In the meantime, Norio tried to deal with the loss of his brother as best he could, with these efforts occasionally falling back on fantasy and denial as last-ditch psychological defense measures. For at least ten years after the bombing, for example, Norio frequently experienced a "tingling" anticipatory feeling that his brother was going to suddenly show up at his door one day. Yoshio's body, after all, had never been found; therefore the eventual occurrence of such a miracle, though highly unlikely, was not entirely beyond the realm of possibility. That possibility—however slight—presented a straw that Norio could not always resist grabbing when the alternative was unthinkable.

After their initial search forays together into the ruins of Nagasaki Medical College, Norio's father never mentioned Yoshio's name again in his surviving son's presence. But when father and son began living together again in 1946—while Norio worked by day and crammed for entrance exams by night—he sometimes heard his father, in the early hours of the morning, softly talking to Yoshio's photo on the family *butsudan* Buddhist prayer altar in their living room.

When Norio heard this, he knew that his father's sadness and regret over the fate of his firstborn son were never far from his mind. Gunge-san believes it cast a pall over his father's life for the rest of his days, until he died at the age of seventy-one in 1958.

After Norio's graduation from the elite Kyushu University, where he followed in his father's footsteps to prepare for a research career as a zymologist specializing in yeast fermentation, he worked for a large food corporation in the Tokyo-Yokohama area until his retirement and move to Kumamoto. Throughout his time in the Kantō region, he never told his employers, colleagues, or other acquaintances that he was a hibakusha, and he never talked about his Nagasaki experiences with his wife or children until he was well into his seventies. In fact, Gunge-san confesses, he never even told his future wife during their 1950s Tokyo courtship that he had survived an atomic bombing. Even now he is still uncomfortable discussing his hibakusha experience in person with his children and grandchildren, preferring instead to express his memories and feelings on the subject to them in the form of letters and, more recently, emails.

Gunge-san started talking about his hibakusha experiences in public only in the early 2010s, after he received an initial invitation to do so from Yoshio's old alma mater. On the occasions of Q and A sessions after his public talks, he often receives audience comments to the effect that he must be thankful for Mount Konpira having saved his life by shielding him from the full measure of Fat Man's lethality. To such comments, he always responds that contrary to what someone hearing his hibakusha testimony might think, he actually wishes that the mountain had not existed, as without the massive blast- and heat-baffle functions it ended up performing—out of sheer geological coincidence—Fat Man's detonation would not have been concentrated on Urakami with such horribly destructive intensity, and Yoshio might just have managed to survive.

Whenever he returns to Nagasaki, whether to speak at Nagasaki University or to attend reunions at his old junior high school, Gunge-san always feels a tightness in his chest when he walks through Urakami and thinks of all the bones that are under the ground there.

Like me when I am there, he wonders how many of the people residing there now are aware of what (or whom) they are living atop.

In August 2005, when he still had just enough physical vigor left for such exertions, Gunge-san decided to retrace the steps of his Konpira ascent of the morning of August 10, 1945, when he had set out on his first foray to look for Yoshio. Pushing his seventy-six-year-old body through the heat, humidity, and steep angle of the climb, he traversed the same bamboo- and tall-tree-wooded lee-side slope where he had once passed shattered and scorched people.

When Norio had crested Konpira's summit in 1945, the ridge and the blast-side slope of the mountain had been completely denuded of trees and any other foliage. From this artificially blast-cleared vantage point, Norio had been able to see the entire length of the gray-and-brown moonscape that was Urakami, and he had looked down in dumbfounded horror onto the disintegrated buildings of Yoshio's college. But now, standing on the exact same spot exactly sixty years later, Gunge-san could not see the valley. He could not even see the nearest building of the School of Medicine only a few hundred meters away. There were too many trees.

EPILOGUE

Shizuoka University
Hamamatsu Campus
October 11, 2024

IT IS A Friday evening, and I am at my desk, working on one of the chapters in this book, when an iMessage banner notification pops up in the upper-right corner of my desktop screen. It is from my wife, Keiko. The Norwegian Nobel Committee in Oslo has just announced that it is going to award the 2024 Peace Prize to Nihon Hidankyō.

My initial reaction is similar to that of a New York Mets or Chicago Cubs fan who has just heard that their team has won the World Series. With hands shaking from the emotion of the moment, I type a few search terms into Google and shortly find the Nobel Prize Organisation press release, the meat of which is contained in the following passages:

> In awarding this year's Nobel Peace Prize to Nihon Hidankyo, the Norwegian Nobel Committee wishes to honour all survivors who, despite physical suffering and painful memories, have chosen to use their costly experience to cultivate hope and engagement for peace.
>
> Nihon Hidankyo has provided thousands of witness accounts, issued resolutions and public appeals, and sent annual delegations to the United Nations and a variety of peace conferences to remind the world of the pressing need for nuclear disarmament.

EPILOGUE

> One day, the Hibakusha will no longer be among us as witnesses to history. But with a strong culture of remembrance and continued commitment, new generations in Japan are carrying forward the experience and the message of the witnesses. They are inspiring and educating people around the world. In this way they are helping to maintain the nuclear taboo—a precondition of a peaceful future for humanity.[1]

Wonderful words, I think, and a wonderful honor for my friends in the Hidankyō. But then reality sets in: With the post–World War Two international order on the verge of collapse, liberal democracy in retreat around the world, and toxic narcissists seizing the reins of power in one nuclear-armed country after another, will this Peace Prize really change anything? Will it even change anything *in Japan*?

There is a certain stripe of Japanese nationalist that has never approved of the old-school postwar narrative wherein the atom-bombed legacy of Hiroshima and Nagasaki is something to be passed down from generation to generation as an eternal—if not actually sacred—reminder of the importance of peace. Though admitting as much in public would be the political equivalent of mugging Rosa Parks or torching the Shroud of Turin, many influential Japanese of this inclination—such as the many national legislators and public intellectuals belonging to the Nippon Kaigi political pressure group—do not see the memorialization of Japan's atom-bombed cities as embodying noble Japanese aspirations for world peace. Rather, they see it as a monument of Japanese shame and unbearably long decades of American-enforced national weakness, and in their heart of hearts, they would be unlikely to shed a tear seeing the Hiroshima Peace Park and its Nagasaki counterpart—the twin meccas of canonized Japanese pacifism—bulldozed into parking lots.

To unpack this a bit, it is important to peer, for a moment, into the mindset of this breed of postwar Japanese nationalist. The most prominent and defining feature of their psychic landscape is a worldview slashed gut to gills with a jagged dark belief that Japan was essentially emasculated as a result of its defeat and occupation in 1945.[2] From this perspective, Japan's current (and largely American-authored) constitution, which—at least by its letter—prohibits the use of military force by the Japanese state as an instrument of national policy, is regarded as the ultimate manifestation of this humiliation. As such, the abandonment of this document and its replacement with something closer to the Meiji Constitution invalidated by Japan's defeat has been an openly pursued, multigenerational goal of postwar nationalists practically from the day the Allied occupation ended in 1952.

In this context, the atomic bombings are resented not so much because they happened—killing 200,000-odd countrymen and permanently scarring hundreds of thousands more—but rather because of the deep taproots of pacifist sentiment their traumatic legacy keeps planted, fertilized, and watered in Japanese consciousness, therein blunting the political appeal of conservative messaging about tossing the postwar constitution. As such, hardcore nationalists regard atomic bomb memories—the very thing the Peace Parks were built to preserve—as the obstacle nonpareil to their ultimate goal of remasculinizing and remilitarizing Japanese culture. In the worldview of these "patriots," it will be only when the shame of 1945 has been erased and expunged from the national soul that Japan can ever hope to become a "beautiful country" again.[3]

But these Japanese are not the only forces in the world who are invested in tweaking the narrative (or, as the case may be, preserving an alternate narrative) of what happened to the people of Hiroshima and Nagasaki in 1945.

Eight years ago, when my wife first suggested that I make a field trip to observe Obama's May 2016 visit to Hiroshima, I can remember muttering, "That's all we need this year . . . another *Enola Gay* thing. . . ."

The "*Enola Gay* thing" I was referring to was a particularly nasty excrescence of partisan ugliness that rocked American public discourse in the mid-1990s, in the process nearly destroying the Smithsonian Institution. The point of contention was a proposed exhibit of the epoch-making eponymous B-29 at the National Air and Space Museum (NASM), one of the Smithsonian branches on the National

Mall. The 1995 opening for the exhibit was scheduled to coincide with the fiftieth anniversary of the end of World War Two.

What began in 1993 as a largely internal debate among curators and administrators over details of the museum exhibit evolved by 1994 into a national donnybrook over the right of government-funded scholars to engage in the critical reinterpretation of national historical canon for public consumption.[4] Ultimately, the conflict expanded into a boundary dispute over the cultural influence of knowledge experts in American public life as a whole and, as such, is rightly regarded as one of the battle-line-defining rounds of the culture war that has been roiling American society and politics in one form or another since the Reagan Era.[5]

The controversy's storm clouds had begun to gather after it was revealed that the exhibit of *Enola Gay*'s newly restored fuselage (the only portion of the massive B-29's airframe that would fit in the NASM's National Mall facility) would also devote gallery space to explorations of the bomber's influence and symbolic importance in the larger contexts of World War Two, the Cold War, and the birth of the Nuclear Age.[6] Most controversially, as it turned out, these supplementary displays were to also include a special corner for atomic-bombed artifacts and hibakusha photos from the Hiroshima Peace Museum and the Nagasaki Atomic Bomb Museum, whose loan the NASM had secured after painstaking negotiations with then Hiroshima mayor Hiraoka Takashi and Nagasaki mayor Motoshima Hitoshi.[7]

After these details began circulating outside of the NASM, American veterans' organizations went into full torches-and-pitchforks mode—with the charge initially led by the magazine of the Air Force Association.[8] Predictably, much of the rhetorical ammunition unleashed in the opening salvos fired against the proposed exhibit script recruited vintage wartime grievances and whataboutisms about Pearl Harbor and Japanese mistreatment of POWs. For critics, it did not matter that the NASM's exhibit script also included explorations of these very topics; their objections were raised not in the interest of historical balance and perspective but rather to reinforce decades-old excuses for why the American public should not be obligated to face up to what American atomic bombs had done to human beings in Hiroshima and Nagasaki.

Many angles of critical attack also relied on late-1940s-era bomb-justifying casualty-projection figures (for both sides) for an invasion of the Japanese Home Islands that *Enola Gay* (and, less convincingly, *Bockscar*) ostensibly rendered unnecessary—a line of argument that has always encompassed the backhanded suggestion that the Japanese should be grateful for the bombs, all things said and done.[9] Of course, casualty-figure hypotheticals for an invasion that never happened are perfectly valid (and even academically worthwhile) topics for what-if history roundtables, but they were non sequiturs in this case as arguments against an exhibit that, again, had already stated in its script its intention in the interest of fairness and perspective to devote display space to that very topic.[10]

Behind all of this rhetorical jockeying, it was clear from the start that there was more potent emotional rocket fuel driving the opposition. This was evidenced in the critics' vehement insistence that the NASM's "pull[ing] heartstrings by portraying Hiroshima's devastation" was tantamount to taxpayer-funded defamation of the nation's World War Two heroes.[11] Imagery of incinerated women and children apparently was an unhappy fit with the sacred iconography of America's last "good war."

From this perspective, the NASM's curators were undermining a cherished narrative in which the atomic bombs had ridden in like the cavalry in the final act of the war to keep the world safe for democracy—end of story. Because of the role this narrative had long played in preventing the horror of the bombs from tainting American honor (and haunting American nightmares), no holds were barred in the subsequent effort to see that the NASM exhibit was strangled in the crib.[12]

Museum director Martin Harwit and his tweedy colleagues at the NASM never stood a chance against the tsunami of righteous, magenta-faced rage that hit them when politicians like Newt Gingrich and public opinion influencers like George Will and Rush Limbaugh jumped in on the conservative gang tackle.[13] As the tide of

EPILOGUE   375

public sentiment turned decisively against the proposed exhibit, both sides of the DC aisle saw the position of defending the NASM as a clear-cut political loser. House members and senators either threw in with the critics or avoided the issue altogether.[14] Nor was any help for the museum forthcoming from President Bill Clinton, who had a re-election campaign coming up and was no doubt loath to alienate the seven or eight million "Greatest Generation" Americans still living (and voting) at the time.[15]

The Republican Party's resounding victory in the November 1994 midterms hammered the final nail into the exhibit's coffin.[16] With the specter of vindictive congressional budget cuts now hanging over the Smithsonian's head, the curators at the NASM were compelled to fold and Harwit to resign.[17] *Enola Gay*'s restored fuselage ended up being displayed at the museum—in time for the fiftieth anniversary of the end of World War Two—essentially as a stand-alone celebratory ex-hibit of American might and technological ingenuity, completely be-reft of any historical context.[18] In other words, the exhibit had turned out to be precisely what the mayors of Hiroshima and Nagasaki had originally feared it would be.[19]

I had already been living in Japan for some eight years when all of this was happening, and I have a slew of memories of the excoriat-ing coverage the story received in the Japanese media that still make me cringe three decades later. As *The Asahi Shimbun* remarked at the time, "This is an exhibit without any record of the damage the bomb caused. . . . Two aspects of the bomb that cannot be ignored— the birth of the atomic age and the idea of 'never again'—have been yanked out completely."[20] Much Japanese commentary harped—not unreasonably—on the hypocrisy of a country always quick to criticize others' inability to satisfactorily deal with painful aspects of their past conveniently succumbing to historical amnesia when it was time to face and sort out its own.[21]

Most bitterly, the complete absence of any mention of the victims of Hiroshima and Nagasaki in the NASM exhibit led many Japa-nese to the shocking realization that their country and culture were apparently still despised by a significant segment of the American people—a revelation that threatened several generations' worth of painstaking transpacific postwar fence-mending and PR work between the two countries.[22] The denial of Japanese humanity implied in this blatant gesture of symbolic erasure was widely—and understandably— regarded by Japanese as a slap in their country's face. On reconsideration, it is remarkable that this did not metastasize into a more significant diplomatic incident—with recalled ambassadors, effigies burned in the street, and the like—and presumably it was only the peculiar neurotic anomalies of the two countries' postwar geostrategic accommodation that prevented this from happening.

In the meantime, on a personal level, I had numerous Japanese colleagues and other acquaintances express their disappointment to me—as a conveniently conspicuous (if not, often, the only) representative American / Westerner / white person in their respective social orbits—about my country's (civilization's/race's) handling of the issue. One such interaction that has stayed with me ever since was when a very urbane elderly gentleman—a language school student of mine— said to me: "You know, with all this carrying-on about a museum exhibit, you'd think it was the Americans who'd lost the war. . . ."

It was not until I had gotten a bit more intercultural savvy under my belt that I was able to flesh out the full meaning of that remark. From my superannuated student's to-the-marrow Japanese perspective—which saw every human interaction as playing out on a vertical social axis between upper and lower, stronger and weaker, senior and junior, parent and child, protector and protected—it was the place of the weak, not the strong, to throw resentful tantrums and the place of the strong to indulge these with either a pat on the head, a "this is going to hurt me more than it hurts you" spanking, or both. In this case, as my student obviously saw it, America—as the party holding the upper hand in its postwar power relationship with Japan—had displayed galling immaturity and dishonorable pettiness in having been presented with an opportunity to acknowledge shared humanity with a vanquished former enemy (and now important ally) and taken a hard pass.[23]

Nevertheless, I would like to think (in defiance of recent over-

EPILOGUE 377

whelming evidence to the contrary) that Americans can be bigger and better than that. It is my hope that the present volume and its *Embers* series companion, *Hiroshima: The Last Witnesses*, can help nudge us in that direction. In that sense—and toward that end—readers are encouraged to regard the books as an incarnation in literary form of the *Enola Gay* exhibit that never was.

North Field, Tinian

September 2, 1945

While Douglas MacArthur was accepting the Instrument of Surrender from the Japanese delegation on board the USS *Missouri* and my future Nagasaki hibakusha informants were taking their first steps toward rebuilding their Fat Man–shattered lives, several Manhattan Project scientists on Tinian were petitioning Colonel Tibbets for a ride. They were eager to get to Hiroshima and Nagasaki as soon as possible to survey bomb damage and radiation in the atom-bombed cities.

Tibbets communicated this request to General MacArthur's staff, and the expedition was cleared for disembarkation at Atsugi Airfield the next day.[24] In preparation for the trip, Tibbets ordered Major Sweeney to prepare two of the 509th's four-engine Douglas C-54 Skymasters. Onto each transport plane were loaded a jeep and a trailer filled with boxes of combat rations.[25] In addition to Tibbets, the Manhattan Project civilians, and a security detachment consisting of six "Nisei" Japanese American interpreters,[26] the Tokyo-bound aircraft would also be carrying some other 509th personnel members who were basically just coming along for the ride. These included Sweeney, Charles Albury, Kermit Beahan, and Jim Van Pelt from the *Bockscar* crew and Donald Lewis, Tom Ferebee, and Theodore "Dutch" Van Kirk from *Enola Gay*.[27]

After the arrival of the transport planes at the chaotically overcrowded Atsugi, Tibbets was informed that because the airstrip in Yoshijima was incapable of handling the big C-54s, Hiroshima would have to be scratched from the itinerary; Nagasaki, on the other hand, was accessible via the substantial IJN air base at Ōmura, some twenty-five kilometers north of the city.

While at Atsugi, the expedition ran into an additional problem: A young colonel was livid about Sweeney having parked his C-54 for unloading directly in front of the base's air operations building and he was threatening to have it bulldozed out of the way. After a conference with Tibbets, Sweeney offered that, rather than risking a security lapse by pulling rank with the 509th's carte blanche, Pentagon-backed credentials, he could defuse the situation by simply getting the offending C-54 out of there. He proposed that he and his crew chief fly it to Chōfu Airfield in northwest Tokyo—which was now occupied by an Army fighter wing—and then drive their jeep into the city to meet up with the rest of the expedition. Tibbets signed off on the plan, and Sweeney shortly thereafter flew to Chōfu without refueling first, only to be told when he landed that all of Chōfu's spare aviation gas had just been sent off to Atsugi.[28] With no other choice but to abandon the C-54 in place, Sweeney and his crew chief headed off to the city in their trailer-towing jeep. In their respective memoirs, neither Sweeney nor Tibbets recorded the latter's reaction to the news that his executive officer had just effectively lost one of the expedition's two transports.

While the Chōfu drama was unfolding, the expedition—minus Sweeney, his crew chief, and one jeep with a trailer rig—set off for the fifteen-kilometer trip to their billets at the Dai Ichi Insurance building, an imposing Art Deco edifice located directly across the eastern moat from the Imperial Palace.[29] During the drive into Tokyo—along roads now patrolled by gun-toting American MPs—the expedition members marveled at the destruction across the vast city, chafed at the intuitively incongruous traffic congestion, and playfully returned the military salutes given them by children as the convoy passed.[30]

As per the civilian scientists' request, the expedition's first official order of business in the city was to find Professor Tsuzuki Masao, a renowned Tokyo University radiation specialist (and reservist rear admiral in the IJN Medical Corps), and convince him to accompany them to

EPILOGUE

Nagasaki. Tsuzuki—who had just returned to Tokyo from a Japanese government survey of Hiroshima—was located in short order.[31] Although he acceded to the Americans' request, the rather fastidious professor—who even brought along a pair of boxed travel chopsticks for the trip—maintained a frostily formal and perceptibly begrudging attitude toward his erstwhile foes / new colleagues, Colonel Tibbets in particular.[32] The professor's demeanor was understandable, particularly in light of what had just happened to his country—and what he had just seen in Hiroshima—but Tibbets did not trust him, and he told his people to keep a close eye on the Japanese professor at all times. Outside of a short exchange with Tsuzuki on the plane to Nagasaki the next day, Tibbets would not speak to him for the rest of the trip.[33]

The next day, the expedition was confronted by a confusing and potentially dangerous situation as soon as they landed at Ōmura. Not only was there no American forward party there to greet them, but as they quickly ascertained, there were no American boots on the ground anywhere in the entire region.[34] The Allied occupation forces were still concentrated in the Tokyo-Yokohama area and weeks away from setting up any semblance of functioning military governance in the rest of the Home Islands. This meant that if the expedition members were going to venture into Nagasaki, they would be doing so at the mercy of the local Japanese authorities. And none of the 509th men needed an explanation as to what might happen to them if anyone in the atom-bombed city found out who they were and why they were there. Just in case, they kept their .45 automatic sidearms at the ready while hoping that they would not have occasion to draw them from their pistol belts.

In addition to these concerns, the expedition had lost their proprietary ground transportation. One of the vehicles was lost when Sweeney, in a likely rice-wine-fueled command decision, had traded his jeep (and its rations-stocked trailer) to some Marines in Tokyo for a consignment of "silk" kimonos (which turned out to be made of rayon). He thought that these garments would later come in handy for bartering purposes with the local populace.[35] Presumably, the other jeep and trailer rig—as well as the expedition's interpreter and security detail—were left back in Tokyo to compensate for cabin space and weight restrictions when the expedition had to load extra passengers and gear onto its sole remaining aircraft.[36]

After a round of haltingly communicated and likely pantomime-augmented negotiations with their nonplussed IJN counterparts—who were at first under the impression that the Americans had arrived to accept their formal surrender—the expedition's members were eventually able to explain their transportation situation.[37] For their troubles, they were provided with three archaic trucks[38] converted to run on charcoal-burning engines. Unfortunately, these rickety conveyances proved so prone to breakdown that they could not even reach Nagasaki on the first day; the expedition had to put up in a Japanese-style *ryōkan* inn for the night when they were still only halfway to the city.

The next morning, the expedition members were given a panoramic view of *Bockscar*'s handiwork when the trucks crested the last high ground north of the city before heading down into Urakami.[39] Sweeney recalled the scene in his 1997 memoirs:

> *The valley floor was a stretch of rubble dotted by grotesquely twisted lumps of steel beams and columns. A brick chimney rose here and there amid the wreckage where the munitions plants had once stood. From a distance, the destroyed armaments plants looked like erector sets a child had twisted and bent and carelessly tossed away. We had driven through the verdant hills to a wasteland. As we descended into the valley, we were the first Americans to set foot in Nagasaki and survey the damage.*[40]

About halfway through the valley, the three-truck convoy stopped on the Togitsu Road near a spot Sweeney guessed was very close to Ground Zero. Taking the opportunity to stretch his legs, he walked around the area for a bit before stopping at a spot that caught his eye:

> *On one corner I peered down into the cellar of what had been a fire station. It was then that I was struck by the significance of our*

weapon. In the cellar was a fire truck that had been crushed flat, as if a giant had stepped on it. In fact, the entire infrastructure of the city was flat—no water, no emergency facilities, no firefighters. Everything was gone.[41]

Once the expedition settled into its new lodgings, Tsuzuki and his Manhattan Project minders went off on their own to attend to their scientific fieldwork while the 509th men enjoyed two days of sightseeing and souvenir shopping around the CBD.[42] After their brief standoff with armed IJN personnel at Ōmura—which was really more a product of confusion than of rancor—no one with the expedition experienced another moment in Nagasaki in which they did not feel perfectly safe, and their pistol belts proved unnecessary after all. If the people they passed in the streets harbored any hostility toward these uniformed Americans in their midst, they were doing a very good job of hiding it.

In his 1998 memoirs, Tibbets recalled feeling "considerable respect for the people who had been our enemies such a short time before" as he walked through the city. "They were carrying on and trying to live as normally as possible. They were not unlike those I had seen in England during the German bombing attacks.[43]

"But while I felt no animosity" toward the Japanese, Tibbets was careful to add, "neither did I have a personal feeling of guilt about the terror that we had visited upon their land."[44]

Colonel Paul Tibbets and his second-in-command, Major Charles Sweeney, both went on to attain general officer ranks in the postwar U.S. Air Force. After their respective retirements from their military and post-military business careers, both men—and several other members of the Hiroshima and Nagasaki strike plane crews—would publish memoirs and become fixtures at American air shows, World War Two commemorative events, and the like.[45] Nearly without exception—and perhaps because the alternative was too terrible for them to contemplate—these men would defend for the rest of their lives what they saw as the moral justification for and the strategic necessity of dropping two atomic bombs on Japan.[46]

ACKNOWLEDGMENTS

THE RESEARCH AND writing of this book and its Embers series companion volume, *Hiroshima: The Last Witnesses*, has been the most challenging and grueling undertaking I have ever attempted. That said, the nine years I have devoted to this project also comprise the most rewarding and fruitful period of my life, bar none, and I would not trade an hour of it for anything.

But I have not done all of this alone. The people and institutions who have helped along the way are legion—far too numerous for all of them to be named here. Any list I might come up with will be incomplete, but I will attempt to do so, nevertheless, apologizing in advance to anyone I may have forgotten.

In the way of acknowledgments, I would first like to recognize the people who are most directly responsible for seeing my work eventually come to life in book form: my original acquiring editor for the project, Brent Howard; my editor at Penguin Random House/Dutton, Cassidy Sachs; and my agent (and dear friend of nearly half a century), Doug Grad of Doug Grad Literary Agency.

I would also like to acknowledge the contributions of my colleagues and students at Shizuoka University, the institution where I have spent nearly the entirety of my academic career, for their patience and understanding, and for providing me with a research environment that allowed me to immerse myself in this project at this level of detail—something I could never have done if I were a journalist writing against a deadline or a working author writing to put food on the table.

Additionally, the following institutions have also been indispensable in supporting my research and, ultimately, bringing the Embers series to fruition: the Japan Society for the Promotion of Science (JSPS); the Radiation Effects Research Foundation (RERF) at Nagasaki University School of Medicine; Nagasaki City Hall; Nagasaki Prefectural Office; Nagasaki Atomic Bomb Museum; the Catholic Archdiocese of Nagasaki; Hiroshima City Hall; Hiroshima Peace Memorial Museum; alumni of the former Hiroshima Prefectural Girls' School; the Tokyo and Yokohama/Kanagawa Prefectural branches and national headquarters of Hidankyō (Japan Confederation of A- and H-Bomb Sufferers Organizations—winners of the 2024 Nobel Peace Prize); the National Diet Library; Chugoku Shimbun: the Korean Red Cross; the Tri-Service General Hospital (Defense Ministry of the Republic of China); the Red Cross Society of the Republic of China; Junshin Joshi Gakuen (Girls School); Pearl Harbor Aviation Museum; Battleship *Missouri* Museum; and the library at Shizuoka University.

My project would have long ago been stopped dead in the water without the kind help of the following native Japanese speakers who volunteered their time and effort to help me transcribe the hundreds of hours of recorded survivor testimony I collected during the most intense period of my fieldwork research stage: Araki Paul Daisuke, Naomi Ellis, Itō Ryōko, Kawada Kō'ichi, Kusano Haruna, Kuwabara Moe, Murakoshi Masahiko, Nukaya Keiko, Onodera Shuko, Satō Shingo, Sawamura Midori, Sonoyama Akari, Sugaya Naomi, Suzuki Mayo, Suzuki Setsuko, Takechi Yuka, Tateno Kaori, Tōyama Sayaka, Toyohara Chie, Tsuda Kotomi, Yamahana Alice, Yokoi Yuko, Yamao Minamo, Kiyofuji Suzune, and particularly Sayaka Jess Kankolongo Watanabe, who used her extensive personal contact network to recruit at least half of the volunteers listed here.

ACKNOWLEDGMENTS

I would also like to thank the following friends and colleagues in academia, the fourth estate, and the professional English-Japanese translation community who have helped me with their guidance, expertise, and encouragement throughout this project: Tomonaga Masao, MD, Mine Mariko, Seki Chieko, Mordecai-Mark Mac Low, Takeuchi Yoshio, Morimoto Makoto, Shijō Chie, Tagawa Mari, Tado Yoshihiko, Tom Pyszcznski, James Orr, Mark R. Mullins, Jim Bowman, Debito Arudou, Arakawa Shōji, Maruyama Tomoni, Nishihara Jun, Sasahara Megumi, Kim Myungmi, Miyazaki Yoshinori, Sven Saaler, Roger Brown, Scott North, Nakano Ko'ichi, Watanave Hidenori, John Krinsky, Lee Dugatkin, Robert Hand, Eric Johnston, Jeff Kingston, Ran Zwigenberg, Robert "Bo" Jacobs, Lee Arnold, Mark Hudson, Steve McClure, Carl Freire, Jamie Findlay, M. Thomas Apple, Eugene Robinson, Perry Constantine, John Frederick Ashburne, Robert and Christina Hoover Moorehead, Todd Jay Leonard, the late Marc Helgesen, Jake Adelstein, Nevin Thompson, Eric M. Skier, Joel Sassone, Jeff Bryant, the late Burl Burlingame, North Compton, Hugh Graham-Marr, Mark Schilling, Katalin Ferber, Stafford Gregoire, Jacob Margolies, Noam Freedman, Garrett DeOrio, Walter Hatch, John Treat, Alex Wellerstein, Barrett Tillman, Andy Bienstock, Fred Uleman, Aaron Gerow, Jud Eri Magy, Michael Penn, David McNeill, Bill Snyder, Dwight Swift, Mark David Sheftall, Abram Hall, Gerry Mullany, Tom Gill, Mike Boyce, John Munroe, Michael Pinto, Justin McCurry, Alex Kerr, Ginny Tapley Takemori, C. A. Edington, Theodore F. Cook, James House, Mark Schreiber, Earl Hartman, Andre Hertrich, Marc Ward, Jon Bauer, Hank Shelton, Brian Prager, Simon Alexander Collier, Hugh Ashton, Richard Lloyd Parry, Philip Seaton, Daryl Bockett, Jerry Piven, Laura Kawaguchi, Rod Lange, Brant Vogel, Ria Coyne, Tom Yulsman, Kiridōshi Risaku, Wada Masako, and particular thanks for logistical assistance and encouragement throughout this project from William "Max" Maxwell.

I would also like to thank loved ones who have provided generous support throughout my long years of (too often obsessively self-centered) immersion in this project, when I could have—and probably should have—been paying more attention to matters closer to home.

In this latter category, I would include my wife, Nukaya Keiko, and sons, Levi Riku and Benjamin Dan Sheftall; my parents, George and Louise Sheftall; and my sister, Amelia Sheftall.

Finally, I would like to express my most heartfelt gratitude to the following hibakusha—many of whom are now no longer with us—who generously shared their precious time to sit for interviews and respond to follow-up information requests over the years: Chai Tsong Chin, Gunge Norio, Mayor Hiraoka Takashi, the late Ikeda Masaho, the late Sister Itonaga Yoshi, the late Ishida Jō'ichi, Kano (Kiridōshi) Michiko, Katayama Noboru, Kawada Kazuko, Lee Mi Cha*, Sister Kunihiro Setsuya, Edwin D. Lawson, the late Lee Jongkeun, the late Sister Matsushita Miya, Minematsu Ieko, the late Misaki Susumu, Mori Shige'aki, Murata Michiko (Tokyo Hidankyō), Nakamura Yūko, Ogura Keiko, Okuda Hagiko, the late Ōishi Matashichi, the late Ōiwa Kōhei, Ōiwa (Nakamura) Kazuko, Pak Nam Ju, Sakamoto Toyoko, the late Sano Hirotoshi, the late Seki (Tomonaga) Chieko, Shimohira (Kawasaki) Sakue, Tado (Yamaguchi) Sayoko, Archbishop Joseph Mitsuaki Takami, Tanaka Terumi, Tateno Sueko, Tomonaga Masao, Toyonaga Keisaburō, Tsuchiya Keiji, the late Yamamoto Hidenori, Yamamoto Mutsuko, the late Yanagawa (Ishida) Masako, and Zhen Su Bing. They have been a steady, reassuring, and inspiring wind at my back throughout this nine-year-long project. Without their help and cooperation, none of this would have been possible.

---

* Pseudonym

Grants and Research Funding

This research was made possible in part through regular research funding from Shizuoka University and by the following JSPS grants: (C)24520726 "Postwar Memorialization Discourses in Defeated Communities: An International Comparative Study" (2012–2017); and (C)18K00908 "Hibakusha Lives and Collective Memory Communities in the 21st Century" (2018–present).

M. G. Sheftall
Shizuoka University
Spring 2025

APPENDIX A

Proclamation Defining Terms for Japanese Surrender
Issued at Potsdam, July 26, 1945

1. We, the President of the United States, the President of the National Government of the Republic of China, and the Prime Minister of Great Britain, representing the hundreds of millions of our countrymen, have conferred and agree that Japan shall be given an opportunity to end this war.
2. The prodigious land, sea and air forces of the United States, the British Empire and of China, many times reinforced by their armies and air fleets from the west, are poised to strike the final blows upon Japan. This military power is sustained and inspired by the determination of all the Allied Nations to prosecute the war against Japan until she ceases to resist.
3. The result of the futile and senseless German resistance to the might of the aroused free peoples of the world stands forth in awful clarity as an example to the people of Japan. The might that now converges on Japan is immeasurably greater than that which, when applied to the resisting Nazis, necessarily laid waste to the lands, the industry and the method of life of the whole German people. The full application of our military power, backed by our resolve, will mean the inevitable and complete destruction of the

Japanese armed forces and just as inevitably the utter devastation of the Japanese homeland.

4. The time has come for Japan to decide whether she will continue to be controlled by those self-willed militaristic advisers whose unintelligent calculations have brought the Empire of Japan to the threshold of annihilation, or whether she will follow the path of reason.

5. Following are our terms. We will not deviate from them. There are no alternatives. We shall brook no delay.

6. There must be eliminated for all time the authority and influence of those who have deceived and misled the people of Japan into embarking on world conquest, for we insist that a new order of peace, security and justice will be impossible until irresponsible militarism is driven from the world.

7. Until such a new order is established and until there is convincing proof that Japan's war-making power is destroyed, points in Japanese territory to be designated by the Allies shall be occupied to secure the achievement of the basic objectives we are here setting forth.

8. The terms of the Cairo Declaration shall be carried out and Japanese sovereignty shall be limited to the islands of Honshu, Hokkaido, Kyushu, Shikoku and such minor islands as we determine.

9. The Japanese military forces, after being completely disarmed, shall be permitted to return to their homes with the opportunity to lead peaceful and productive lives.

10. We do not intend that the Japanese shall be enslaved as a race or destroyed as a nation, but stern justice shall be meted out to all war criminals, including those who have visited cruelties upon our prisoners. The Japanese Government shall remove all obstacles to the revival and strengthening of democratic tendencies among the Japanese people. Freedom of speech, of religion, and of thought, as well as respect for the fundamental human rights shall be established.

APPENDIX A 391

11. Japan shall be permitted to maintain such industries as will sustain her economy and permit the exaction of just reparations in kind, but not those which would enable her to re-arm for war. To this end, access to, as distinguished from control of, raw materials shall be permitted. Eventual Japanese participation in world trade relations shall be permitted.

12. The occupying forces of the Allies shall be withdrawn from Japan as soon as these objectives have been accomplished and there has been established in accordance with the freely expressed will of the Japanese people a peacefully inclined and responsible government.

13. We call upon the government of Japan to proclaim now the unconditional surrender of all Japanese armed forces, and to provide proper and adequate assurances of their good faith in such action. The alternative for Japan is prompt and utter destruction.[1]

APPENDIX B

Emperor Hirohito's "Jewel Voice Broadcast" (surrender speech) to the nation
Broadcast over NHK network, medium-wave and shortwave bands,
1200 Japan Time, August 15, 1945

TO OUR GOOD and loyal subjects:

After pondering deeply the general trends of the world and the actual conditions obtaining to our empire today, we have decided to effect a settlement of the present situation by resorting to an extraordinary measure.

We have ordered our government to communicate to the governments of the United States, Great Britain, China, and the Soviet Union that our empire accepts the provisions of their Joint Declaration.

To strive for the common prosperity and happiness of all nations as well as the security and well-being of our subjects is the solemn obligation which has been handed down by our imperial ancestors, and which we lay close to heart. Indeed, we declared war on America and Britain out of our sincere desire to ensure Japan's self-preservation and the stabilization of East Asia, it being far from our thought either to infringe upon the sovereignty of other nations or to embark upon territorial aggrandizement.

But now the war has lasted for nearly four years. Despite the best that has been done by everyone—the gallant fighting of the military and naval forces, the diligence and assiduity of our servants of the state, and the devoted service of our 100 million people—the war situation has developed not necessarily to Japan's advantage, while the general trends of the world have all turned against her interest.

Moreover, the enemy has begun to employ a new and most cruel bomb, the power of which to damage is indeed incalculable, taking the toll of many innocent lives.

Should we continue to fight, it would not only result in an ultimate collapse and obliteration of the Japanese nation, but also it would lead to the total extinction of human civilization.

Such being the case, how are we to save the millions of our subjects or to atone ourselves before the hallowed spirits of our imperial ancestors? This is the reason why we have ordered the acceptance of the provisions of the Joint Declaration of the Powers.

We cannot but express the deepest sense of regret to our allied nations of East Asia, who have consistently cooperated with the empire towards the emancipation of East Asia. The thought of those officers and men as well as others who have fallen in the fields of battle, those who died at their posts of duty, or those who met with untimely death and all their bereaved families, pains our heart day and night.

The welfare of the wounded and the war sufferers, and of those who have lost their homes and livelihood, are the objects of our profound solicitude.

The hardships and sufferings to which our nation is to be subjected hereafter will certainly be great. We are keenly aware of the inmost feelings of all [of] you, our subjects.

However, it is according to the dictate of time and fate that we have resolved to pave the way for a grand peace for all the generations to come by enduring the unendurable and suffering what is insufferable.

Having been able to safeguard and maintain the structure of the imperial state, we are always with you, our good and loyal subjects, relying upon your sincerity and integrity. Beware most strictly of any outbursts of emotion which may engender needless complications, or any fraternal contention and strife which may create confusion, lead you astray, and cause you to lose the confidence of the world.

Let the entire nation continue as one family from generation to generation, ever firm in its faith of the imperishableness of its divine land, and mindful of its heavy responsibilities, and the long road before it.

Unite your total strength to be devoted to the construction for the future. Cultivate the ways of rectitude; foster nobility of spirit; and work with resolution so that you may enhance the innate glory of the imperial state and keep pace with the progress of the world.

14th day of the 8th month of the 20th year of Showa.[1]

APPENDIX C

Imperial Surrender Rescript to Japanese Armed Forces
August 17, 1945

TO THE OFFICERS AND MEN OF THE IMPERIAL FORCES:

Three years and eight months have elapsed since we declared war on the United States and Britain. During this time our beloved men of the army and navy, sacrificing their lives, have fought valiantly on disease-stricken and barren lands and on tempestuous waters in the blazing sun, and of this we are deeply grateful.

Now that the Soviet Union has entered the war against us, to continue the war under the present internal and external conditions would be only to increase needlessly the ravages of war finally to the point of endangering the very foundation of the Empire's existence.

With that in mind and although the fighting spirit of the Imperial Army and Navy is as high as ever, with a view to maintaining and protecting our noble national policy we are about to make peace with the United States, Britain, the Soviet Union and Chungking.

To a large number of loyal and brave officers and men of the Imperial forces who have died in battle and from sicknesses goes our deepest grief. At the same time we believe the loyalty and achievements of you officers and men of the Imperial forces will for all time be the quintessence of our nation.

We trust that you officers and men of the Imperial forces will comply with our intention and will maintain a solid unity and strict discipline in your movements and that you will bear the hardest of all difficulties, bear the unbearable and leave an everlasting foundation of the nation.[1]

APPENDIX D

Announcement

THE NORWEGIAN NOBEL COMMITTEE has decided to award the Nobel Peace Prize for 2024 to the Japanese organisation Nihon Hidankyo. This grassroots movement of atomic bomb survivors from Hiroshima and Nagasaki, also known as Hibakusha, is receiving the Peace Prize for its efforts to achieve a world free of nuclear weapons and for demonstrating through witness testimony that nuclear weapons must never be used again.

In response to the atomic bomb attacks of August 1945, a global movement arose whose members have worked tirelessly to raise awareness about the catastrophic humanitarian consequences of using nuclear weapons. Gradually, a powerful international norm developed, stigmatising the use of nuclear weapons as morally unacceptable. This norm has become known as "the nuclear taboo."

The testimony of the Hibakusha—the survivors of Hiroshima and Nagasaki—is unique in this larger context.

These historical witnesses have helped to generate and consolidate widespread opposition to nuclear weapons around the world by drawing on personal stories, creating educational campaigns based on their own experience, and issuing urgent warnings against the spread and use of nuclear weapons. The Hibakusha help us to describe the indescribable, to think the unthinkable, and to somehow grasp the incomprehensible pain and suffering caused by nuclear weapons.

The Norwegian Nobel Committee wishes nevertheless to acknowledge one encouraging fact: No nuclear weapon has been used in war in nearly 80 years. The extraordinary efforts of Nihon Hidankyo and other representatives of the Hibakusha have contributed greatly to the establishment of the nuclear taboo. It is therefore alarming that today this taboo against the use of nuclear weapons is under pressure.

The nuclear powers are modernising and upgrading their arsenals; new countries appear to be preparing to acquire nuclear weapons; and threats are being made to use nuclear weapons in ongoing warfare. At this moment in human history, it is worth reminding ourselves what nuclear weapons are: the most destructive weapons the world has ever seen.

Next year will mark 80 years since two American atomic bombs killed an estimated 120 000 inhabitants of Hiroshima and Nagasaki. A comparable number died of burn and radiation injuries in the months and years that followed. Today's nuclear weapons have far greater destructive power. They can kill millions and would impact the climate catastrophically. A nuclear war could destroy our civilisation.

The fates of those who survived the infernos of Hiroshima and Nagasaki were long concealed and neglected. In 1956, local Hibakusha associations along with victims of nuclear weapons tests in the Pacific formed the Japan Confederation of A- and H-Bomb Sufferers Organisations. This name was shortened in Japanese to Nihon Hidankyo. It would become the largest and most influential Hibakusha organisation in Japan.

The core of Alfred Nobel's vision was the belief that committed individuals can make a difference. In awarding this year's Nobel Peace Prize to Nihon Hidankyo, the Norwegian Nobel Committee wishes to honour all survivors who, despite physical suffering and painful memories, have chosen to use their costly experience to cultivate hope and engagement for peace.

APPENDIX D 401

Nihon Hidankyo has provided thousands of witness accounts, issued resolutions and public appeals, and sent annual delegations to the United Nations and a variety of peace conferences to remind the world of the pressing need for nuclear disarmament.

One day, the Hibakusha will no longer be among us as witnesses to history. But with a strong culture of remembrance and continued commitment, new generations in Japan are carrying forward the experience and the message of the witnesses. They are inspiring and educating people around the world. In this way they are helping to maintain the nuclear taboo—a precondition of a peaceful future for humanity.

The decision to award the Nobel Peace Prize for 2024 to Nihon Hidankyo is securely anchored in Alfred Nobel's will. This year's prize joins a distinguished list of Peace Prizes that the Committee has previously awarded to champions of nuclear disarmament and arms control.

The Nobel Peace Prize for 2024 fulfils Alfred Nobel's desire to recognise efforts of the greatest benefit to humankind.

Oslo, 11 October 2024[1]

REFERENCES

Abe, S. (2006). *Utsukushii Kuni E (For a Beautiful Country)*. Tokyo: Bunshun Shinsho.

Adams, P. D. (2000). "An Army Air Corps Test of Strategic Power" [Strategy Research Project]. Carlisle Barracks, PA: U.S. Army War College.

Allam, C. M. (1990). "The Nichiren and Catholic Confrontation with Japanese Nationalism." *Buddhist-Christian Studies* 10, 35–84.

Allied Operational and Occupational Headquarters, World War II. (No date). "Tokyo Kempei Tai Cases, 1945–47, Fujihara to Kenichi." Box 1851, Supreme Commander for the Allied Powers, Legal Section, Investigation Division.

Alperovitz, G. (1995). *The Decision to Use the Atomic Bomb* (Kindle version). New York: Alfred A. Knopf.

Alvarez, L. M. (1987). *Alvarez: Adventures of a Physicist*. New York: Basic Books.

American Institute of Physics. (No date). "Topic Guide: The Manhattan Project and Predecessor Organizations." https://history.aip.org/phn/manhattan -project.html.

American POWs in WWII Hiroshima. (No date). "Lt. Thomas C. Cartwright." https://hiroshima-pows.org/tc-cartwright.

American Presidency Project. (No date). "The President's News Conference." https://www.presidency.ucsb.edu/documents/the-presidents-news -conference-494.

Anderson, D. (1942, October 20). "Japan Is Punishing Seized U.S. Fliers; Death Penalty Is Threatened to All Allied Aviators for 'Inhuman' Acts." *New York Times*. https://www.nytimes.com/1942/10/20/archives/japan-is-punishing -seized-us-fliers-death-penalty-is-threatened-to.html.

Archdiocese of Nagasaki. (2007, June 1). *Yokiotozure*.

REFERENCES

Army Map Service. (1945). "Nagasaki (Japan City Plans 1:12,500)." Washington, DC: U.S. Army.

Asada, S. (1998). "The Shock of the Atomic Bomb and Japan's Decision to Surrender: A Reconsideration." *Pacific Historical Review* 67(4), 477–512.

Ashworth, F. L. (2005). "Frederick L. Ashworth." In R. Krauss & A. Krauss (eds.), *The 509th Remembered: A History of the 509th Composite Group as Told by the Veterans That Dropped the Atomic Bombs on Japan* (pp. 15–20). Buchanan, MI: private publication.

Atomic Heritage Foundation. (No date–a). Abe Spitzer Diary. https://ahf .nuclearmuseum.org/wp-content/uploads/2016/11/Abe%20Spitzer%20Diary.pdf.

Atomic Heritage Foundation. (No date–b). "Bernard Waldman." https://ahf .nuclearmuseum.org/ahf/profile/bernard-waldman/.

Atomic Heritage Foundation. (No date–c). "The Jewel Voice Broadcast." https:// ahf.nuclearmuseum.org/ahf/key-documents/jewel-voice-broadcast/.

Atomic Heritage Foundation. (No date–d). "Voices of the Manhattan Project: Ray Gallagher's Accounts of the Hiroshima and Nagasaki Missions." https://ahf .nuclearmuseum.org/voices/oral-histories/ray-gallaghers-accounts-hiroshima -and-nagasaki-missions/.

Atomic Heritage Foundation. (2014, June 5). "The Interim Committee." https:// ahf.nuclearmuseum.org/ahf/history/interim-committee/.

Atomic Heritage Foundation. (2016, April 27). "Hiroshima and Nagasaki Missions—Planes & Crews." https://ahf.nuclearmuseum.org/ahf/history /hiroshima-and-nagasaki-missions-planes-crews/.

Atomi no Juku. (2000). *Atomi no Juku Kiroku no Kai.* Tokyo: private publication.

Ballhatchet, H. J. (2003). "The Modern Missionary Movement in Japan." In M. R. Mullins (Ed.), *Handbook of Christianity in Japan* (pp. 35–68). Leiden, The Netherlands: Brill.

"Bamboo Houses Easy Prey." (1923, September 3). *New York Times.*

Barrett, D. D. (2023). "Cities Reduced to Ashes." *American Heritage* 68(5). https:// www.americanheritage.com/cities-reduced-ashes.

Barshay, A. (1988). *State and Intellectual in Imperial Japan: The Public Man in Crisis.* Berkeley: University of California Press.

Beahan, K. (2005). "Kermit B. Beahan." In R. Krauss & A. Krauss (eds.), *The 509th Remembered: A History of the 509th Composite Group as Told by the Veterans That Dropped the Atomic Bombs on Japan* (p. 31). Buchanan, MI: private publication.

Beasley, W. G. (ed.). (1977). *Modern Japan: Aspects of History, Literature and Society.* Berkeley: University of California Press.

Beillevaire, P. (2018). "Father Louis Furet, Missionary of the Paris Foreign Missions Society: His Life and Scientific Observations on Okinawa (1855–1862)." *Journal of Geography (Chigaku Zasshi)* 127(4), 483–501.

Bernstein, A. (2006, September 28). "Iva Toguri D'Aquino, 90." *Washington Post.* https://www.washingtonpost.com/archive/local/2006/09/28/iva-toguri -daquino-90/49fae285-9b55-46c4-96b0-a49f025b9393/.

REFERENCES

Bernstein, B. J. (1977). "The Perils and Politics of Surrender: Ending the War with Japan and Avoiding the Third Atomic Bomb." *Pacific Historical Review* 46(1), 1–27.

Bernstein, B. J. (1991). "Eclipsed by Hiroshima and Nagasaki: Early Thinking About Tactical Nuclear Weapons." *International Security* 15(4), 149–173.

Beser, J. (1988). *Hiroshima & Nagasaki Revisited.* Memphis: Global Press.

Beser, J., & Spangler, J. (Eds.). (2007). *The Rising Sun Sets: The Complete Story of the Bombing of Nagasaki.* Bloomington, IN: AuthorHouse.

Bevacqua, M. L. (No date). "Taotaomo'na." Guampedia. https://www.guampedia .com/taotaomona-taotaomona/.

Bix, H. P. (1995). "Japan's Delayed Surrender: A Reinterpretation." *Diplomatic History* 19(2), 197–225.

Blackwell, W. (2003). "398th Bomb Group Combat Formations." 398th Bomb Group Memorial Association. https://www.398th.org/Research/8th_AF _Formations_Description.html.

Boku, K. (1965). *Chōsenjin kyōseirenkō no kiroku* (*A Record of the Forcible Conscription of Korean* [*Workers*]). Tokyo: Miraisha.

Bowen, L., R. D. Little et al. (1959). *A History of the Air Force Atomic Energy Program, 1943–1953*, vol. 3, *Building an Atomic Air Force.* Washington, DC: U.S. Air Force Historical Division.

Boxer, C. R. (1967). *The Christian Century in Japan, 1549–1650.* Berkeley: University of California Press.

Braw, M. (1991). *The Atomic Bomb Suppressed: American Censorship in Occupied Japan.* Armonk, NY: M. E. Sharpe.

Broderick, M., and D. Palmer. (2015). "Australian, British, Dutch and U.S. POWs: Living Under the Shadow of the Nagasaki Bomb." *Asia-Pacific Journal: Japan Focus* 13(3). https://af.org/2015/13/32/Mick-Broderick/4358.

Burke-Gaffney, B. (2015). *The Glover House of Nagasaki: An Illustrated History.* Nagasaki: Flying Crane Press.

Burke-Gaffney, B. (2019). *The Nagasaki British Consulate, 1859–1955.* Nagasaki: Flying Crane Press.

Burrett, J., and J. Kingston (eds.). (2023). *Routledge Handbook of Trauma in East Asia.* London: Routledge.

Butow, R. J. C. (1954). *Japan's Decision to Surrender.* Stanford, CA: Stanford University Press.

Byas, H. (1942). *Government by Assassination.* New York: Alfred A. Knopf.

CAF Media. (2020, November 10). *CAF Oral Histories—Charles Chauncey* [Video]. YouTube. https://www.youtube.com/watch?v=tfVkydGFCBs.

Cahill, W. M. (2012). "Imaging the Empire: The 3d Photographic Reconnaissance Squadron in World War II." *Air Power History* 50(1), 12–19.

Caidin, M. (1960). *A Torch to the Enemy.* New York: Bantam Books.

Caiger, J. G. (1966). *Education, Values and Japan's National Identity: A Study in the Aims and Content of Courses in Japanese History, 1872–1963* [Unpublished doctoral thesis]. Australian National University, Open Research Repository. https://openresearch-repository.anu.edu.au/items/54413089-47a5-47a1-874d -9004e26d575a.

Catholic News Agency. (No date). "St. Paul Miki and Companions." https://www .catholicnewsagency.com/saint/st-paul-miki-and-companions-139.

Cheney, D. M. (No date). "Bishop Januarius Kyunosuke Hayasaka." Catholic Hierarchy. https://www.catholic-hierarchy.org/bishop/bhayasaka.html.

Chilstrom, J. S. (1992). "Mines Away! The Significance of U.S. Army Air Forces Minelaying in World War II." Maxwell Air Force Base, AL: School of Advanced Airpower Studies, Air University, U.S. Air Force.

Chinnock, F. W. (1969). *Nagasaki: The Forgotten Bomb*. New York: New American Library.

Ciardi, J. (1988). *Saipan: The War Diary of John Ciardi*. Fayetteville: The University of Arkansas Press.

Clarke, H. V. (1984). *Last Stop Nagasaki!* London: Allen & Unwin.

Clulow, A. (2013). "Commemorating Failure: The Four Hundredth Anniversary of England's Trading Outpost in Japan." *Monumenta Nipponica*, 68(2), 207–231.

Cohen, J. B. (2000). *Japan's Economy in War and Reconstruction*. London: Routledge. (Original work published 1949)

Correll, J. T. (2004, September 14). "Revisiting *Enola Gay*" [Conference presentation]. AFA Air & Space 2004 Conference, Washington, DC. https:// secure.afa.org/media/scripts/Correll_Conf.asp.

Correll, J. T. (2011, July). "Near Failure at Nagasaki." *Air Force Magazine*, 94(7), 60–64.

Craig, W. (1967). *The Fall of Japan*. New York: Dial Press.

Craven, W. F., and J. L. Cate (eds.). (1953). *The Army Air Forces in World War II*, vol. 5, *The Pacific: Matterhorn to Nagasaki June 1944 to August 1945*. Chicago: University of Chicago Press.

CriticalPast. "Re-enacted Radio Tokyo broadcast featuring Iva Ikuko Toguri as 'Orphan Ann.'" (1945). https://www.criticalpast.com/video/65675043006 _Japanese-Station-announcer_Zero-Hour_Tokyo-Rose_sacrifices-of-Americans.

Cummings, W. K. (1980). *Education and Equality in Japan*. Princeton, NJ: Princeton University Press.

Dallek, R. (2013, August). "JFK vs. The Military." *The Atlantic*. https://www .theatlantic.com/magazine/archive/2013/08/jfk-vs-the-military/309496/.

Daniels, G. (1977). "The Great Tokyo Air Raid, 9–10 March 1945." In W. G. Beasley (ed.), *Modern Japan: Aspects of History, Literature and Society* (pp. 113–131). Berkeley: University of California Press.

Davis, W. (1976). "The Civil Theology of Inoue Tetsujirō." *Japanese Journal of Religious Studies* 3(1), 5–40.

Dawsey, J. (2022, January 31). "Exposing Atrocity: The Davao Dozen and the Bataan Death March." National WWII Museum. https://www.nationalww2 museum.org/war/articles/davao-dozen-bataan-death-march.

REFERENCES 407

Diehl, C. R. (2011). *Resurrecting Nagasaki: Reconstruction, the Urakami Catholics, and Atomic Memory, 1945–1970* [Unpublished doctoral dissertation]. Columbia University.

Diehl, C. R. (2018). *Resurrecting Nagasaki: Reconstruction and the Formation of Atomic Narratives.* Ithaca, NY: Cornell University Press.

Dietz, S. S. (2016). *My True Course: Dutch Van Kirk, Northumberland to Hiroshima.* Lawrenceville, GA: Red Gremlin Press.

Doak, K. M. (Ed.). (2011). *Xavier's Legacies: Catholicism in Modern Japanese Culture.* Vancouver: UBC Press.

Dore, R. P. (1952). "The Ethics of the New Japan." *Pacific Affairs* 25(2), 147–159.

Dorr, R. F. (2012). *Mission to Tokyo: The American Airmen Who Took the War to the Heart of Japan.* Minneapolis, MN: Zenith.

Dorr, R. F. "Pathfinder Fire Storm: The B-29s over Tokyo That Helped End the War." Warfare History Network. https://warfarehistorynetwork.com /pathfinder-fire-storm-the-b29s-over-tokyo-that-helped-end-the-war/.

Dower, J. W. (1986). *War Without Mercy: Race and Power in the Pacific War.* New York: Pantheon Books.

Dower, J. W. (1995). "Triumphal and Tragic Narratives of the War in Asia." *Journal of American History* 82(3), 1124–1135.

Dower, J. W. (2000). *Embracing Defeat: Japan in the Wake of World War II.* New York: W. W. Norton & Co.

Dower, J. W. (2010). *Cultures of War: Pearl Harbor / Hiroshima / 9-11 / Iraq.* New York: W. W. Norton & Co.

Ealey, M., and A. Yoshimura. (2005). "One Man's Justice." *Asia-Pacific Journal: Japan Focus, 3*(2). https://apjjf.org/mark-ealey/1884/article.

Earhart, D. C. (2008). *Certain Victory: Images of World War II in the Japanese Media.* Armonk, NY: M. E. Sharpe.

Earns, L. (1994). "The Foreign Settlement in Nagasaki, 1859–1869," *The Historian* 56(3), 483–500.

Earns, L. (2015). *Nagasaki Kyoryūchi no Seiyōjin (Westerners of the Nagasaki Foreign Settlement)* (F. Fukuta & K. Yanatori, Trans.). Nagasaki: Nagasaki Bunkensha.

Eatherly, C., & Anders, G. (1962). *Burning Conscience.* New York: Monthly Review Press.

Ezumi, M. (1961). *"Ano hi no mae no koto"* ("Before That Day"). In Junshin Joshi Gakuen (eds.), *Junjo gakutai jun'nan no kiroku (The Martyrdom of the Junshin Mobilized Students Group)* (pp. 1–6). Nagasaki: private publication.

Ezumi, M. (2018). "Toward the End of the War." In Nagasaki Junshin Educational Corporation (eds.), *A Resurrection: Nagasaki August 9, 1945* (pp. 27–29). Nagasaki: private publication.

Farrell, D. A. (2021). *Atomic Bomb Island: Tinian, the Last Stage of the Manhattan Project, and the Dropping of the Atomic Bombs on Japan in World War II.* Guilford, CT: Stackpole Books.

Fedman, D., and C. Karacas. (2012). "A Cartographic Fade to Black: Mapping the Destruction of Urban Japan During World War II." *Journal of Historical Geography* 38(3), 306–328.

Feis, H. (1966). *The Atomic Bomb and the End of World War II*. Princeton, NJ: Princeton University Press.

41st Bomb Group. (1945, August 3). "Kyushu Mission: Nagasaki Marshalling Yards" (After Action Report for Group Mission 41–37).

Francis, T. L. (1997). "'To Dispose of the Prisoners': The Japanese Executions of American Aircrew at Fukuoka, Japan, During 1945." *Pacific Historical Review* 66(4), 469–501.

Frank, B. M., & Shaw, H. I. (1968). *History of U.S. Marine Corps Operations in World War II*, vol. 5, *Victory and Occupation*. Quantico, VA: Historical Branch, G-3 Division, Headquarters, U.S. Marine Corps.

Frank, R. B. (1999). *Downfall: The End of the Imperial Japanese Empire*. New York: Random House.

Frank, R. B. (2016). "Ending the Asia-Pacific War: New Dimensions." In International Forum on War History (eds.), *The Termination of Wars in Historical Perspective: Proceedings* (pp. 41–55). Tokyo: National Institute for Defense Studies. https://www.nids.mod.go.jp/english/event/forum/pdf/2015/04.pdf.

Friedrich, J. (2006). *The Fire: The Bombing of Germany, 1940–1945* (A. Brown, trans.). New York: Columbia University Press.

Fujitani, T. (1996). *Splendid Monarchy: Power and Pageantry in Modern Japan*. Berkeley: University of California Press.

Fukuoka 14B. (No date). "Ronald Scholte." https://fukuoka14b.org/ronald-scholte-2/.

Futrell, F., and J. Taylor. (1953). "Reorganization for Victory." In W. F. Craven and J. L. Cate (eds.), *The Army Air Forces in World War II*, vol. 5, *The Pacific: Matterhorn to Nagasaki June 1944 to August 1945* (pp. 676–702). Chicago: University of Chicago Press.

Genbaku Fukkō 70-shūnen Kinen Jigyo Jikkō I'inkai (eds.). (2016). *Genbaku fukkō 70-shūnen kinenshi: Shōgen; Nagasaki Ikadaigaku* (*Volume Commemorating the Seventieth Anniversary of Recovery from the Atomic Bomb: Testimony from Nagasaki Medical College*). Nagasaki: Nagasaki University School of Medicine.

"Genbaku wo aruku: Himeguri an'nai: 3" ("Walking the Atomic Bomb [Trail]: A Memorial Pilgrim's Guide, Number 3"). (2005, July 7). *Nagasaki Shimbun*. https://www.nagasaki-np.co.jp/peace_article/2332/.

Giancreco, D. M. (1997). "Casualty Projections for the U.S. Invasions of Japan, 1945–1946: Planning and Policy Implications." *Journal of Military History* 61(3), 521–582.

Giangreco, D. M. (2009). *Hell to Pay: Operation Downfall and the Invasion of Japan, 1945–1947*. Annapolis, MD: Naval Institute Press.

REFERENCES

Gladwell, M. (2021). *The Bomber Mafia: A Dream, a Temptation, and the Longest Night of the Second World War.* New York: Little, Brown and Company.

Glantz, D. M. (2014). *August Storm: Soviet Tactical and Operational Combat in Manchuria, 1945* (Kindle version).

Gluck, C. (1985). *Japan's Modern Myths: Ideology in the Late Meiji Period.* Princeton, NJ: Princeton University Press.

Grayling, A. C. (2006). *Among the Dead Cities: Was the Allied Bombing of Civilians in WWII a Necessity or a Crime?* London: Bloomsbury.

Great Tokyo Air Raid / War Damage Records Editorial Committee (eds.). (1973). *Great Tokyo Air Raid / War Damage Records*, vols. 1–5. Tokyo: Association to Record for Posterity the Great Tokyo Air Raid.

Groves, L. M. (1962). *Now It Can Be Told: The Story of the Manhattan Project.* New York: Harper & Row.

Guillain, R. (1981). *I Saw Tokyo Burning: An Eyewitness Narrative from Pearl Harbor to Hiroshima* (trans. W. Byron). New York: Doubleday.

Gunge, N. (2016). *"Heisei 24-nendo 8-gatsu 9-ka kōwa"* ("August 9, 2012, Memorial Lecture"). In Genbaku Fukkō 70-shūnen Kinen Jigyo Jikkō I'inkai (eds.), *Genbaku fukkō 70-shūnen kinenshi: Shōgen; Nagasaki Ikadaigaku* (*Volume Commemorating the Seventieth Anniversary of Recovery from the Atomic Bomb: Testimony from Nagasaki Medical College*) (pp. 24–26). Nagasaki: Nagasaki University School of Medicine.

Hachida, K. (1961). *"Wareria Fukahori Hatsuno-ane"* ("Sister Valeria Fukahori Hatsune"). In Junshin Joshi Gakuen (eds.), *Junjo gakutai jun'nan no kiroku* (*The Martyrdom of the Junshin Mobilized Students Group*) (pp. 145–150). Nagasaki: private publication.

Hachiya, M. (1955). *Hiroshima Diary.* Chapel Hill: University of North Carolina Press.

Hall, R. K. (1949). *Shūshin: The Ethics of a Defeated Nation.* New York: Bureau of Publications, Teachers College, Columbia University.

Halloran, R., and C. Marshall. (2011). *Hap's War: The Incredible Story of a P.O.W. Slated for Execution* (Kindle version). Collierville, TN: Global Press.

Hamada, Y. (2017). *"[Ohara/Reddhi shikyō no Nihon shisatsu hōkoku sho—1946-nen 7-gatsu] honbun shiyaku"* ("A Partial Translation of the 'Report of the Visit of Bishop O'Hara of Buffalo and Bishop Reddy of Columbus to Japan—July, 1946'"). *Junshin Jinbun Kenkyū* 23, 301–328.

Hammer, J. (2006). *Yokohama Burning: The Deadly 1923 Earthquake and Fire That Helped Forge the Path to World War II.* New York: Free Press.

Harrington, A. M. (2011). "Catholic Women Religious Orders and Catholicism in Japan: 1872–1940." In K. M. Doak (ed.), *Xavier's Legacies: Catholicism in Modern Japanese Culture* (pp. 31–46). Vancouver: UBC Press.

Harris, A. (1947). *Bomber Offensive.* London: Collins.

Hartman, A. "Hell for Honshu." *Brief Magazine*, April 24, 1945, 3–6.

Harwit, M. (1996). *An Exhibit Denied: Lobbying the History of* Enola Gay. New York: Springer-Verlag.

Hasegawa, T. (2007). "The Atomic Bombs and the Soviet Invasion: What Drove Japan's Decision to Surrender?" *Asia-Pacific Journal: Japan Focus* 5(8). https://apjjf.org/tsuyoshi-hasegawa/2501/article.

Hatanaka, Y. (1961). *"Gakuen hibaku no kiroku"* ("A Record of the School's Atomic Bombing Experience"). In Junshin Joshi Gakuen (eds.), *Junjo gakutai jun'nan no kiroku (The Martyrdom of the Junshin Mobilized Students Group)* (pp. 7–20). Nagasaki: private publication.

Havens, T. R. H. (1975). "Women and War in Japan, 1937–45." *American Historical Review* 80(4), 913–934.

Hersey, J. (1946). *Hiroshima.* New York: Alfred A. Knopf.

Hesselink, R. H. (2016). *The Dream of Christian Nagasaki: World Trade and the Clash of Cultures, 1560–1640.* Jefferson, NC: McFarland & Company.

"Hibakusha: Nagasaki Doctor Feels Growing Urgency for Elimination of Nuclear Weapons." (2017, November 16). *Mainichi.* https://mainichi.jp/english/articles/20171116/p2a/00m/0na/024000c.

Hiraoka, T. (1996). *"Kibō no Hiroshima: Shichō wa uttaeru"* ("*Hiroshima, City of Hope: A Mayor's Plea*"). Tokyo: Iwanami Shoten.

Hiraoka, T. (2016). *"Urami ya ikari wa heiwa wo tsukuru gendōryoku"* ("Channeling Resentment and Anger to Create Peace"). In Asahi Shimbun Shuzai Han (eds.), *Hiroshima ni kita daitōryō: [Kaku no genjitsu] to Obama no risō (The President Who Came to Hiroshima: "Nuclear Realities" and Obama's Ideals)* (pp. 158–161). Tokyo: Chikuma Shobō.

Hirohiro's Homepage. (No date). "About Kokokyu." https://sites.google.com/site/kokokyohomepage/liao-shao-jie?authuser=0.

Hiroshima City (eds.). (1971). *Hiroshima genbaku sensaishi (Record of the Atomic Bombing of Hiroshima)*, vols. 1–5. Hiroshima: Hiroshima City. ("*Hiroshima Sensai*" in all notes and other in-text citations).

Hiroshima Jogakuin University. (No date). "History." https://www.hju.ac.jp/eng/history/.

Hiroshima/Nagasaki Editorial Committee for the Record of Atomic Bomb Damage (eds.). (1979). *Hiroshima/Nagasaki no genbaku saigai (Hiroshima/Nagasaki Atomic Bomb Damage)*. Tokyo: Iwanami Shoten.

Historical Studies Branch, United States Air Force Historical Division. (1968). "Combat Crew Rotation: World War II and Korean War." Maxwell Air Force Base, AL: Aerospace Studies Institute, Air University, U.S. Air Force.

"*Hiroshima wo shōbaku*" ("Hiroshima Hit with Incendiaries"). *Asahi Shimbun,* August 7, 1945.

Home Ministry. (1944). *Tonarigumi bōkū kaikai (An Illustrated Guide for Neighborhood Association Air Defense Measures)*. Tokyo: Dai Nippon Bōkū Kyōkai Teito Shibu.

REFERENCES

411

Hoshina, Z. (1975). *Daitō'a sensō hishi: Ushinawareta wahei kōsaku (Secret History of the Greater East Asia War: Squandered Peace Operations)*. Tokyo: Hara Shobo.

Hotei, A. (2020). *Fukugen! Hibaku chokuzen no Nagasaki (Restoration! Nagasaki Immediately Before Its Atomic Bombing)*. Nagasaki: Nagasaki Bunkensha.

Huie, W. B. (1964). *The Hiroshima Pilot*. New York: G. P. Putnam's Sons.

Hulen, B. D. (1943, April 22). "President Aghast; He Says Civilized People Will Share Horror at Act of Japanese." *New York Times*.

Ide, I. (2016). *"Heisei 21-nendo 8-gatsu 9-ka kōwa"* ("August 9, 2009, Memorial Lecture"). In Genbaku Fukkō 70-shūnen Kinen Jigyo Jikkō I'inkai (eds). (2016). *Genbaku fukkō 70-shūnen kinenshi: Shōgen; Nagasaki Ikadaigaku (Volume Commemorating the Seventieth Anniversary of Recovery from the Atomic Bomb: Testimony from Nagasaki Medical College)* (pp. 17–18). Nagasaki: Nagasaki University School of Medicine.

Inoguchi, R., and T. Nakajima. (1951). *Shinpū Tokubetsu Kogeki Tai (The Shinpū Special Attack Unit[s])*. Tokyo: Nihon Shuppan Kyōdō.

International Campaign to Abolish Nuclear Weapons (ICAN). (No date). "Hiroshima and Nagasaki Bombings." https://www.icanw.org/hiroshima _and_nagasaki_bombings.

International Military Tribunal for the Far East. (1946). "Summary Brief re HIROTA (Koki)." Roy L. Morgan Papers (Box 3, Folder "1946 [IMTFE] [IPS] Translations of Interrogations"), University of Virginia Law Library, Charlottesville, VA. http://imtfe.law.virginia.edu/collections/page-1-5422.

Ishida, H. (1937). *Ōbei no Meguri (Travels in the West)*. Tokyo: private publication.

Ishida, H. (1949). *"Omoide wo kataru"* ("Recounting My Recollections"). In M. Ishida, *Masako Taorezu (Masako Is Still Standing)* (pp. 63–116). Nagasaki: Fujin Taimuzu Sha.

Ishida, J. (1962, February 1). *"Chichi, Ishida Hisashi wo kotaru (1)"* ("Talking About My Father, Ishida Hisashi (Part 1)"). *Hanretsu Jihou* 359, 13040–13041).

Ishida, J. (2010). *Hirota Kōki no egao to tomo ni: Watashi ga ikita Shōwa (The Shōwa Era I Lived Next to Hirota Kōki's Smiling Face)*. Tokyo: Gen Shobō.

Ishida, M. (1949). *Masako Taorezu ("Masako Is Still Standing")*. Nagasaki: Fujin Taimuzu Sha.

Itoh, E. (2007). "The Danish Monopoly on Telegraph in Japan: A Case Study of an Unequal Communication System in the Far East." *Keio Communication Review* 29, 85–105.

Itonaga, Y. (1961). *"Ato shimatsu"* ("Cleaning Up"). In Junshin Joshi Gakuen (eds.), *Junjo gakutai jun'nan no kiroku (The Martyrdom of the Junshin Mobilized Students Group)* (pp. 27–54). Nagasaki: private publication.

Japan Customs. (No date). "History of Japan Customs." https://www.customs.go .jp/english/zeikan/history_e.htm.

Japan Dam Federation. (2015a). Hongōchi Kobu Dam. http://damnet.or.jp/cgi-bin /binranA/enAll.cgi?db4=3620.

Japan Dam Federation. (2015b). Nishiyama Dam. http://damnet.or.jp/cgi-bin
/binranA/All.cgi?db4=2572

Japan Heritage Portal Site. (No date). *"Satō bunk wo hirometa Nagasaki kaidō"*
("The Nagasaki Kaido, the Road That Spread Sugar Culture [in Japan]").
https://japan-heritage.bunka.go.jp/ja/stories/story103/speciality/.

Japan Kyushu Tourist. (No date). "Santo Domingo Church, Built in 1609." https://
www.japan-kyushu-tourist.com/santo-domingo-church-built-in-1609/.

Jōbōji, A. (1981). *Nihon Bōkūshi (A History of Japanese Air Defenses)*. Tokyo: Hara
Shobo.

Joint Chiefs of Staff. (1943). "Casablanca Conference, January 1943: Papers
and Minutes of Meetings." Washington, DC: Office of the Joint Chiefs of
Staff. https://www.jcs.mil/Portals/36/Documents/History/WWII
/Casablanca3.pdf.

Jones, V. C. (1985). *Manhattan: The Army and the Atomic Bomb (United States Army
in World War II: Special Studies)*. Washington, DC: Center of Military History,
United States Army.

Jungk, R. (1961). *Children of the Ashes: The Story of a Rebirth*. New York: Harcourt,
Brace & World.

Junshin Joshi Gakuen. (No date). *"Nagasaki Junshin Kōtō Gakkō no kaisetsu"* ("The
Founding of Nagasaki Junshin Girls' School"). https://www.n-junshin.ac.jp
/official/summary/history/.

Junshin Joshi Gakuen (eds.). (1961). *Junjo gakutai jun'nan no kiroku (The Martyrdom
of the Junshin Mobilized Students Group)*. Nagasaki: private publication.

Junshin Seibokai. (No date–a). *"Shisutā e no michi"* ("The Road to Becoming a
[Junshin] Sister"). https://n-junshinseibokai.or.jp/pages/20/.

Junshin Seibokai. (No date–b). *"Shisutā Ezumi no shōkai"* ("An Introduction to
Sister Ezumi"). https://n-junshinseibokai.or.jp/pages/6/.

Kamogawa, A. (1961). *"Kiba no yama e; Kaikon to matsuyani saishū"* ("To the
Mountain in Kiba; Cultivation and Pine Sap Collection"). In Junshin Joshi
Gakuen (eds.), *Junjo gakutai jun'nan no kiroku. (The Martyrdom of the Junshin
Mobilized Students Group)* (pp. 103–106). Nagasaki: private publication.

Kano, M., and R. Kiridōshi. (2016). *Jūgosai no hibakusha: Rekishi wo kesanai
tame ni (A Hibakusha at Fifteen: So That History Will Not Be Erased)*. Tokyo:
Sairyūsha.

Kataoka, C. (ed.). (1996). *Hibakuchi Nagasaki no saiken (The Rebuilding of Atom-
Bombed Nagasaki)*. Nagasaki: Nagasaki Junshin Daigaku Hakubutsukan.

Kataoka, Y. (1976). "Foreword." In T. Nagai, *Nagasaki no Kane (The Bells of
Nagasaki)*. Tokyo: Hibiya Shuppansha. (Original work published in 1949.)

Katō, N. (1997). *Haisengoron. (On the Post-Defeat Era)*. Tokyo: Kōdansha.

Katsuta, K. (1991). "Swift's Japan in His *Gulliver's Travels*." *Toyo Review* 23,
99–110.

Kawamura, N. (2015). *Emperor Hirohito and the Pacific War*. Seattle: University of
Washington Press.

REFERENCES 413

Kemp, K. (2017, July 11). "Imprisoned at Ground Zero: American POWs in Hiroshima." HistoryNet. https://www.historynet.com/imprisoned-ground-zero-american-pows-hiroshima/.

Kennedy, J. F. (1962, October 22). "Address During the Cuban Missile Crisis." John F. Kennedy Presidential Library & Museum. https://www.jfklibrary.org/learn/about-jfk/historic-speeches/address-during-the-cuban-missile-crisis.

Kerr, A. (1993). *Critical Assembly: A Technical History of Los Alamos During the Oppenheimer Years, 1943–1945.* Cambridge, UK: Cambridge University Press.

Kerr, E. B. (1991). *Flames over Tokyo: The U.S. Army Air Forces' Incendiary Campaign Against Japan, 1944–1945.* New York: Donald I. Fine.

Kirshner, H. (2021, August 6). "The Secret History of Japanese Wine: One Writer Traces the Surprisingly Deep Roots of Winemaking in the Heart of Japan's Modern-Day Wine Country." *Food & Wine.* https://www.foodandwine.com/drinks/the-secret-history-of-japanese-wine.

Kitajima, N. (ed.). (1977). *Bessatsu Ichiokunin no Shōwashi: Gakuto sokai.* (*Supplementary Volume of the Shōwa Era History of a Hundred Million: Student Evacuations*). Tokyo: Mainichi Shimbunsha.

Knebel, F., and C. W. Bailey II. (1960). *No High Ground.* New York: Harper & Row.

Kobayashi, K. (No date). *"Mukaijima horyo shuyōjō no memoriaru purēto jomakushiki"* ("Unveiling of the Mukaijima POW Camp Memorial Plates"). http://powresearch.jp/news/wp-content/uploads/mukaijima_memorial.pdf.

Kobayashi, S. (2022, March). *"Kankoku hibakusha kyūen wo meguru Nikkan kōshō: 1960s–1970s"* ("Japan–South Korea Negotiations over Aid for Korean Hibakusha: 1960s–1970s") [Conference presentation]. Japan Institute of International Affairs History Center Conference on International Political and East Asian History. https://www.jiia.or.jp/JIC/pdf/2-4.pdf.

Kort, M. (2007). *The Columbia Guide to Hiroshima and the Bomb.* New York: Columbia University Press.

Kōyūkai, S. (ed.). (2016). *Hiroshima/Nagasaki hibakusha no taikendan to omoi* (*Hiroshima and Nagasaki Hibakusha Testimonies and Memories*). Tokyo: private publication.

Krauss, R., and A. Krauss (eds.). (2005). *The 509th Remembered: A History of the 509th Composite Group as Told by the Veterans That Dropped the Atomic Bombs on Japan.* Buchanan, MI: private publication.

Kristof, N. D. (2003, August 5). "Blood on Our Hands?" *New York Times.* https://www.nytimes.com/2003/08/05/opinion/blood-on-our-hands.html.

Kubo, R. (1990). "Yoshio Nishina: The Pioneer of Modern Physics in Japan." In Suzuki, M., and R. Kubo (eds.), *Evolutionary Trends in the Physical Sciences: Proceedings of the Yoshio Nishina Centennial Symposium, Tokyo, Japan, December 5–7, 1990* (pp. 3–12). Berlin: Springer-Verlag.

Kunaichō (Imperial Household Agency). (2016). *Shōwa ten'nō jitsuroku dai kyū* (*The Record of Emperor Shōwa*, vol. 9). Tokyo: Tōkyō Shoseki.

REFERENCES

Kushner, B. (2005). *The Thought War: Japanese Imperial Propaganda*. Honolulu: University of Hawai'i Press.

Kye, J. L. (2019). "The Supreme Court Decision on the Liability of Japanese Company for Forced Labor During the Japanese Colonial Era and Its Implications." *Journal of Korean Law* 18(2), 335–363.

LaFeber, W. (1998). *The Clash: U.S.–Japanese Relations Throughout History*. New York: W. W. Norton & Company.

Laurence, W. L. (1945, September 9). "Atomic Bombing of Nagasaki Told by Flight Member." *New York Times*. https://www.nytimes.com/1945/09/09/archives /atomic-bombing-of-nagasaki-told-by-flight-member-aftermath-of.html.

Laurence, W. L. (1946). *Dawn over Zero*. New York: Alfred A. Knopf.

Laures, J. (1954). *The Catholic Church in Japan: A Short History*. Rutland, VT: Charles E. Tuttle Company.

LeMay, C. E., and M. Kantor. (1965). *Mission with LeMay*. New York: Doubleday & Company.

LeMay, C.E., and B. Yenne. (1988). *Superfortress: The B-29 and American Air Power*. New York: McGraw-Hill.

Lifton, R. J. (1963). "Psychological Effects of the Atomic Bomb in Hiroshima: The Theme of Death." *Daedalus* 92(3), 462–497.

Lifton, R. J. (1968). *Death in Life: Survivors of Hiroshima*. New York: Random House.

Lifton, R. J., and G. Mitchell. (1995). *Hiroshima in America: A Half Century of Denial*. New York: Avon Books.

Linenthal, E. T. (1995). "Struggling with History and Memory." *Journal of American History* 82(3), 1094–1101.

"Lord Cheshire, World War II Hero Who Founded Homes for Sick, 74." (1992, August 2). *New York Times*. https://www.nytimes.com/1992/08/02/world/lord -cheshire-world-war-ii-hero-who-founded-homes-for-sick-74.html.

Malloy, S. (2009). "Four Days in May: Henry L. Stimson and the Decision to Use the Atomic Bomb." *Asia-Pacific Journal: Japan Focus* 7(2). https://apjjf.org/sean -malloy/3114/article.

The Manhattan Project. (No date–a). "The Atomic Bombing of Nagasaki." U.S. Department of Energy. https://www.osti.gov/opennet/manhattan-project -history/Events/1945/nagasaki.htm.

The Manhattan Project. (No date–b). "Implosion Becomes a Necessity." U.S. Department of Energy. https://www.osti.gov/opennet/manhattan-project -history/Events/1942-1945/implosion_necessity.htm.

The Manhattan Project. (No date–c). "Order to Drop the Bomb: Handy to Spaatz, National Archives (July 25, 1945)." U.S. Department of Energy. https://www .osti.gov/opennet/manhattan-project-history/Resources/order_drop.htm.

The Manhattan Project. (No date–d). "Robert Serber." U.S. Department of Energy. https://www.osti.gov/opennet/manhattan-project-history/People/Scientists /robert-serber.html.

REFERENCES

Mann, R. A. (2009). *The B-29 Superfortress Chronology, 1934–1960* (Kindle version). Jefferson, NC: McFarland & Company.

Martin, M. (1987). *The Jesuits.* New York: Simon & Schuster.

Marx, J. L. (1971). *Nagasaki: The Necessary Bomb?* New York: Macmillan Co.

Mason, G. A. (2002). "Operation Starvation." Maxwell Air Force Base, AL: Air University, U.S. Air Force.

Matsui, T. (1966). *Zeno shinu hima nai (Zeno, the Man Too Busy to Die).* Tokyo: Shungeisha.

Mayr, O. (1998). "The 'Enola Gay' Fiasco: History, Politics, and the Museum." *Technology and Culture* 39(3), 462–473.

McKelway, S. C. (1945a, June 8). "A Reporter with the B-29s, Part II: The Doldrums, Guam, and Something Coming Up." *New Yorker.*

McKelway, S. C. (1945b, June 15). "A Reporter with the B-29s, Part III: The Cigar, the Three Wings, and the Low-Level Attacks." *New Yorker.*

McRaney, W., and J. McGahan. (1980). "Radiation Dose Reconstruction, U.S. Occupation Forces in Hiroshima and Nagasaki, Japan, 1945–1946." Washington, DC: Defense Nuclear Agency.

Milam, D. C. (2001). *The Last Bomb: A Marine Remembers Nagasaki.* Austin, TX: Eakin Press.

Miller, E. S. (1991). *War Plan Orange: The U.S. Strategy to Defeat Japan, 1897–1945.* Annapolis, MD: Naval Institute Press.

Miller, M., and A. Spitzer. (1946). *We Dropped the A-Bomb.* New York: Thomas Y. Crowell Company. (Republished in an Uncommon Valor Series public domain edition as *We Dropped the Atom Bomb*)

Ministry of Education, Culture, Sports, Science and Technology–Japan. (2008). *"Senji kyōiku taisei no shinkō"* ("The Progress of the Wartime Education System"). https://www.mext.go.jp/b_menu/hakusho/html/others/detail /1317693.htm.

Ministry of Land, Infrastructure, Transport and Tourism. (No date). "Santo Domingo Church Museum." https://www.mlit.go.jp/tagengo-db/common /001564007.pdf.

Miskow, C. M. (2011). "The Chrysanthemum and the Butterfly: What, if Anything, Remains of Pierre Loti in the *Madame Butterfly* Narrative." *Utah Foreign Language Review, 19*, 15–31.

Miyazaki, K. (2003a). "The Kakure Kirishitan Tradition." In M. R. Mullins (Ed.), *Handbook of Christianity in Japan* (pp. 19–34). Leiden, The Netherlands: Brill.

Miyazaki, K. (2003b). "Roman Catholic Mission in Pre-Modern Japan." In M. R. Mullins (Ed.), *Handbook of Christianity in Japan* (pp. 1–18). Leiden, The Netherlands: Brill.

Mizukawa, K. (2024, August 30). "Documenting Hiroshima of 1945: August 30, 'This Is Not Going to Be Easy.'" *Chūgoku Shimbun.* https:// www .hiroshimapeacemedia.jp/? p= 146345.

Montane, C. (2012). *Sacred Space and Ritual in Early Modern Japan: The Christian Community of Nagasaki (1569–1643)* [Unpublished doctoral dissertation]. University of London.

Morris, E. (Director). (2003). *The Fog of War: Eleven Lessons from the Life of Robert S. McNamara* [Film]. RadicalMedia; SenArt Films.

Morrison, W. H. (1979). *Point of No Return: The Story of the Twentieth Air Force*. New York: Times Books.

Mullins, M. R. (1994). "Ideology and Utopianism in Wartime Japan: An Essay on the Subversiveness of Christian Eschatology." *Japanese Journal of Religious Studies* 21(2–3), 261–280.

Mullins, M. R. (Ed.). (2003). *Handbook of Christianity in Japan*. Leiden, The Netherlands: Brill.

Murdoch, J., and I. Yamagata. (1903). *A History of Japan During the Century of Early Foreign Intercourse (1542–1651)*. Kobe: The Kobe Chronicle.

Nagae, M. (2018). "A Letter of 35 Years." In Nagasaki Junshin Educational Corporation (eds.), *A Resurrection: Nagasaki August 9, 1945* (pp. 5–6). Nagasaki: private publication. (Original work published in 1980.)

Nagai, T. (1949). *Nagasaki no Kane* (*The Bells of Nagasaki*). Tokyo: Hibiya Shuppansha.

Nagasaki City. (No date–a). *"Dai 3-kai (Heisei 26-nendo dai 1-kai) Nagasaki shi genshibakudan hōshasen eikyō kenkyūkai"* ("Third Session [First Session of 2015]: Nagasaki City Atomic Bomb Radiation Effect Research Symposium). https://www.city.nagasaki.lg.jp/syokai/760000/763000/p026241.html.

Nagasaki City. (No date–b). *"Gaikai kara Gotō e; Senpuku, ijū ni yoru denpa"* ("To Gotō from the Sea; Proselytization Through Stealth and Migration"). *Nagajin* 7. https://www.city.nagasaki.lg.jp/nagazine/church/7/index.html.

Nagasaki City. (No date–c). *"Ōura tenshudō no sōken to shintohakken"* ("The Construction of Ōura Cathedral and the Discovery of Believers"). *Nagajin* 9. https://www.city.nagasaki.lg.jp/nagazine/church/9/index.html.

Nagasaki City. (No date–d). *"Toki wo kizanda Nagasaki no tokei"* ("The Nagasaki Clock That Carved Time"). https://www.city.nagasaki.lg.jp/nagazine/hakken0908/index.html.

Nagasaki City (eds.). (1977). *Nagasaki genbaku sensaishi* (*Record of the Atomic Bombing of Nagasaki*), vols. 1–5. Nagasaki: Nagasaki City. (*"Nagasaki Sensai"* in all notes and other in-text citations.)

Nagasaki City (eds.). (1990). *Shisei Hyakunen: Nagasaki Nenpyō* (*One Hundred Years of Municipality: A Nagasaki Chronology*). Nagasaki: Nagasaki City.

Nagasaki Denki Kidō (Nagasaki Streetcar Company). (2024). *"Kaisha Gaiyō"* ("Corporate Overview"). https://www.naga-den.com/relays/download/24/143/86//?file=/files/libs/4429/202406280921049352.pdf.

"Nagasaki/Hiroshima shi no hibakushiryō, Bei no kinenten ni kashidashi" ("Nagasaki and Hiroshima Will Lend Atomic Bomb–Related Materials for American Exhibit"). (1993, November 30). *Asahi Shimbun*.

REFERENCES 417

Nagasaki Junshin Educational Corporation (eds.). (2018). *A Resurrection: Nagasaki August 9, 1945*. Nagasaki: private publication.

Nagasaki National Peace Memorial Hall for the Atomic Bomb Victims. (No date). "The Nagasaki Atomic Bomb Damage Records: Part 2 The Atomic Bomb." https://www.peace-nagasaki.go.jp/abombrecords/b020101.html.

Nagasaki no Heiwa. (No date–a). *"Shiroyama Kokumin Gakkō."* https://nagasakipeace.jp/search/about_abm/gallery/shiroyama.html.

Nagasaki no Heiwa. (No date–b). *"Yamazato Kokumin Gakkō (Yamazato Elementary School)."* https://nagasakipeace.jp/search/about_abm/gallery/yamazato.html.

Nagasaki Prefectural Government Culture, Tourism, and International Affairs Department, World Heritage Registration Division. (No date). "A Dedication Ceremony Without Japanese People." https://oratio.jp/p_column/kendoshiki?type=c_en.

Nagasaki Prefecture. (2021, December 7). "The Former Site of the Nagasaki Prefectural Office in Historical Photos." https://www.pref.nagasaki.jp/shared/uploads/2021/12/1638848700.pdf.

Nagasaki Zainichi Chōsenjin no Jinken wo Mamoru Kai (eds.). (1989). *Chōsenjin Hibakusha: Nagasaki kara no Shōgen (Korean Hibakusha: Testimony from Nagasaki).* Tokyo: Shakai Hyōron Sha.

Nakajima, N. (2019). *"Ajia taiheiyō sensō no kaisen to kōkoku gyōkai: Nihon senden bunka kyōkai wo jirei ni"* ("The Advertising Industry and the Outbreak of the Pacific War: The Case of Activities of the Japan Association of Propaganda Culture." *Studies in Urban Cultures* 21, 55–65.

National Archives of Japan. (2007). *Kokumin Chōyō Rei* ("National Service Draft Ordnance"). https://www.archives.go.jp/ayumi/kobetsu/s14_1939_01.html.

National Defense Research Committee (1946). *Fire Warfare: Incendiaries and Flamethrowers.* New York: Columbia University Press.

National Diet Library. (No date). "Text of the Constitution and Other Important Documents." https://www.ndl.go.jp/constitution/e/etc/c06.html.

National Opinion Research Center. (1946). "Japan and the Post-War World." Denver: University of Denver. https://www.norc.org/content/dam/norc-org/pdfs/NORCRpt_32.pdf.

National WWII Museum. (No date). "WWII Veteran Statistics: The Legacy of the WWII Generation." https://www.nationalww2museum.org/war/wwii-veteran-statistics.

Naval Medical Research Institute. (1945, September 1). "Series of Japanese Reports on the Atomic Bomb, No. 29, Daily Weather Data, Nagasaki City, 11 July–31 August 1945." Bethesda, MD: National Naval Medical Center.

NHK. (2005). *NHK Supesharu: Tōkyō Daikūshū 60-nen me no hisai chizu ("NHK Special: A Disaster Map of the Great Tokyo Air Raid Sixty Years Later")* [Film].

NHK Museum of Broadcasting. (2022, July 19). *"Ano hi hōsō ha nani wo tsutaeta ka dai 7 kai: 1942-nen 7-gatsu 8-ka 'Taishōhōtaibi' no tokubetsu hensei"* ("What Was Broadcast on That Day? Part 7: July 8, 1942, Imperial Proclamation Veneration

Day Special Programming Schedule"). https://www.nhk.or.jp/museum/topics /2022/20220719.html.

Nihon Chishi Kenkyūjō. (1978). *Nihon chishi: Dai 17-kan Okayama-ken; Hiroshima-ken; Yamaguchi-ken (Japanese Geological History: Vol. 17, Okayama, Hiroshima, Yamaguchi Prefectures)*. Tokyo: Nihon Chishi Kenkyūjō.

Nihon Hōrei Sakuin (Japan Legal Database). (No date). *"Shisōhan Hogo Kanshisatsu Hō"* ("Security Surveillance of Thought Crime Law"). https:// hourei.ndl.go.jp/simple/detail?lawId=0000025502&current=-1.

Nishimori, I. (1995). "Pathological Effects." Atomic Bomb Disease Institute, Nagasaki University. https://www.genken.nagasaki-u.ac.jp/abcenter /nishimori/index_e.html.

Nobel Prize. (2024, October 11). "Press Release." https://www.nobelprize.org /prizes/peace/2024/press-release/.

Nolte, S. H., and Ō. Hajime. (1983). "National Morality and Universal Ethics. Ōnishi Hajime and the Imperial Rescript on Education." *Monumenta Nipponica* 38(3), 283–294.

Nosaka, A. (1997). *Kono Kuni no Nakushimono: Nani ga Warera wo Kyosei Shita no ka (What Our Nation Has Lost: What Emasculated Us?)*. Tokyo: PHP Kenkyūjo.

Office of the Assistant Chief of Air Staff, Intelligence. (1943). "Air Objective Folder No. 90.17 Tokyo Area." Washington, DC: United States Army Air Forces.

Office of the Assistant Chief of Air Staff, Intelligence. (1944). "Air Objective Folder No. 90.36 Sasebo Area; No. 90.39 Tsushima Area." Washington, DC: United States Army Air Forces.

Oguma, E. (2002). *A Genealogy of 'Japanese' Self-Images* (David Askew, trans.). Melbourne: Trans Pacific Press.

Okada, S. (2014, July 14–26). *"'Masako Taorezu': Ken'etsu wo koete: Yanagawa Masako-san (1931nen umare)"* ("'Masako Is Still Standing': Overcoming Censorship: Yanagawa Masako-san [born 1931]"). *Asahi Shimbun*. http://www .asahi.com/hibakusha/shimen/nagasakinote/note90-08.html.

Okahata, T. (2012, August 1). "History of Hiroshima: 1945–1995 (Part 1, Article 1)." *Chūgoku Shimbun*. https://www.hiroshimapeacemedia.jp/?p=27413.

Olivi, F. J. (1998). *Decision at Nagasaki: The Mission That Almost Failed*. Private publication.

Ōmori, J. (2023). *Rajio sensō: Hōsōjin tachi no "hōkoku" (Radio War: How Broadcasters "Performed Their Patriotic Duty")*. Tokyo: NHK Shuppan.

Osada, S. (ed.). (1951). *Genbaku no ko: Hiroshima no shōnen shōjo no uttae (Children of the Atom Bomb: The Plea of the Boys and Girls of Hiroshima)*. Tokyo: Iwanami Shoten.

Ōta, A. (2022). *"Sensō to watashitachi no kurashi 19"* ("War and Our Lifestyle 19"). Fukuoka City Museum. https://museum.city.fukuoka.jp/archives/leaflet/364 /index02.html.

Ōta, Y., M. Mine, and E. Yoshimine. (2014). *Genshiya no Torauma* ("Trauma Amidst Fields of Atom-Bombed Rubble"). Nagasaki: Nagasaki Shimbunsha.

REFERENCES

Otake, T. (2015, August 7). "Nagasaki's 'Providential' Nightmare Shaped by Religious, Ethnic Undercurrents." *Japan Times*. https://www.japantimes .co.jp/news/2015/08/07/national/history/nagasakis-providential-nightmare -shaped-religious-ethnic-undercurrents/.

Otsuki, T. (2016). "Reinventing Nagasaki: The Christianization of Nagasaki and the Revival of an Imperial Legacy in Postwar Japan." *Inter-Asia Cultural Studies* 17(3), 395–415.

Pappas, C. (1998). *Law and Politics: Australia's War Crimes Trials in the Pacific, 1943–1961* [Unpublished doctoral thesis]. University of New South Wales.

Patch, N. S. (2014). "Mission: Lifeguard." *Prologue* 46(3). https://www.archives .gov/files/publications/prologue/2014/fall/lifeguard.pdf

Perera, G. R. (1944). "History of the Organization and Operations of the Committee of Operations Analysts, 16 November 1942–10 October 1944." Doc. 118.01, Vol. II, Tab 22. Maxwell Air Force Base, AL: USAF Historical Research Agency.

Plutschow, H. E. (1983). *Historical Nagasaki*. Tokyo: Nippon Shuppan Hanbai.

Ralph, W. W. (2006). "Improvised Destruction: Arnold, LeMay, and the Firebombing of Japan." *War in History* 13(4), 495–522.

Reid, T. R. (1995, June 28). "Japanese Media Decry *Enola Gay* Exhibition." *Washington Post*. https://www.washingtonpost.com/archive/politics/1995/06 /29/japanese-media-decry-enola-gay-exhibition/0dbcb4fd-0604-4d49-b0a4 -62cf779bf7b4/.

Rhodes, R. (1986). *The Making of the Atomic Bomb*. New York: Simon & Schuster.

Rhodes, R. (1995, June 19). "The General and World War III." *New Yorker*. https://www.newyorker.com/magazine/1995/06/19/the-general-and-world -war-iii.

Robbins, J. M. J. (1997). *Tokyo Calling: Japanese Overseas Radio Broadcasting 1937–1945* [Doctoral dissertation, University of Sheffield].

Robertson, G. B. (2018). *Bringing the Thunder: The Missions of a World War II B-29 Pilot in the Pacific*. Oklahoma City: Wide Awake Books.

Russell, E. F. L. (2002). *The Knights of Bushido: A Short History of Japanese War Crimes*. London: Greenhill Books / Lionel Leventhal.

Sams, R. (2016). "Perdition: A Forgotten Tokyo Firebombing Raid." *Asia-Pacific Journal: Japan Focus* 14(3). https://apjjf.org/2016/12/Sams.

Sanger, D. E. (1994, August 4). "Hiroshima Journal; Museum's A-Bomb Message: There's More to It." *New York Times*. https://www.nytimes.com/1994/08 /04/world/hiroshima-journal-museum-s-a-bomb-message-there-s-more-to-it .html.

Saotome, K. (1971). *Tōkyō daikūshū: Shōwa 20-nen 3-gatsu 10-nichi no kiroku*. (*The Great Tokyo Air Raid: A Record of March 10, 1945*). Tokyo: Iwanami Shoten.

Saotome, K. (1987). *Shashinban Tōkyō daikūshū no kiroku* (*Photographic Version: A Record of the Great Tokyo Air Raid*). Tokyo: Shinchō Bunko.

Schwabe, D. T. (2015). *Burning Japan*. Lincoln, NE: Potomac Books.

Scott, J. M. (2015). *Target Tokyo: Jimmy Doolittle and the Raid That Avenged Pearl Harbor.* New York: W. W. Norton & Co.

Seidensticker, E. (1983). *Low City, High City—Tokyo from Edo to the Earthquake: How the Shogun's Ancient Capital Became a Great Modern City, 1867–1923.* New York: Alfred A. Knopf.

Sellagar, F. M. (1974). "Lessons from an Aerial Mining Campaign ('Operation STARVATION')." Santa Monica, CA: Rand Corporation.

Serber, R. (1992). *The Los Alamos Primer: The First Lectures on How to Build an Atomic Bomb.* Berkeley: University of California Press.

Sheftall, M. G. (2005). *Blossoms in the Wind: Human Legacies of the Kamikaze.* New York: NAL Caliber.

Sheftall, M. G. (2023). "Surviving a World Destroyed: Existential Trauma in *Hibakusha* Experience," 11–22 in Burrett, J., and J. Kingston (eds.) *Routledge Handbook of Trauma in East Asia.* London: Routledge.

Sheftall, M. G. (2024). *Hiroshima: The Last Witnesses.* New York: Dutton.

Sherry, M. S. (1989). *The Rise of American Air Power: The Creation of Armageddon.* New Haven: Yale University Press.

Shibusawa, N. (2006). *America's Geisha Ally: Reimagining the Japanese Enemy.* Cambridge, MA: Harvard University Press.

Shirabe, R. (1972). *Nagasaki bakushinchi fukugen no kiroku* (*A Record of Rebuilding Nagasaki's Zone of Total Atomic Bomb Destruction*). Tokyo: Nippon Hōsō Shuppan Kyōkai.

Smethurst, R. J. (1974). *A Social Basis for Prewar Japanese Militarism: The Army and the Rural Community.* Berkeley: University of California Press.

Smith, C. R. (1997). "Securing the Surrender: Marines in the Occupation of Japan." Washington, DC: Marine Corps Historical Center.

Smith, G. S. (1998). "Beware, the Historian! Hiroshima, the 'Enola Gay,' and the Dangers of History." *Diplomatic History* 22(1), 121–130.

Smithsonian Institution Archives. (2020, June 25). "Exhibiting the *Enola Gay*." https://siarchives.si.edu/blog/exhibiting-enola-gay.

Statista. (No date). "Estimated Annual Gross Domestic Product (GDP) of the Second World War's Largest Powers from 1938 to 1945 (in Billions of 1990 International Dollars)." https://www.statista.com/statistics/1334676/wwii -annual-war-gdp-largest-economies/.

Stewart, H. A., and J. E. Power. (1947). "The Long Haul: The Story of the 497th Bomber Group (VH)." *World War Regimental Histories,* 106, Bangor Public Library, Bangor, ME. https://digicom.bpl.lib.me.us/ww_reg _his/106.

Stimson, H. L., and M. Bundy. (1947). *On Active Services in Peace and War* (Kindle version). New York: Harper & Brothers.

Storry, R. (1957). *The Double Patriots: A Study of Japanese Nationalism.* Westport, CT: Greenwood Press.

REFERENCES 421

"Survivors' Statements on Japanese Abuse of Prisoners on Bataan." (1944, January 27). *New York Times.* https://www.nytimes.com/1944/01/28/archives/survivors-statements-on-japanese-abuse-of-prisoners-on-bataan.html.

Suzuki, M., and R. Kubo (eds.). (1990). *Evolutionary Trends in the Physical Sciences: Proceedings of the Yoshio Nishina Centennial Symposium, Tokyo, Japan, December 5–7, 1990.* Berlin: Springer-Verlag.

Sweeney, C. W. (1997). *War's End: An Eyewitness Account of America's Last Atomic Mission.* New York: Avon Books.

Szasz, R. J. (2015, April 16). "Part II—Ramou: Calm Before the Storm." https://shatteredjewels.wordpress.com/2015/04/06/264/.

Taiwan Documents Project. (No date). "Emperor Hirohito's Surrender Rescript to Japanese Troops." http://www.taiwandocuments.org/surrender07.htm.

Takagi, T. (1980). *Shōshin: Nagasaki no genbaku; Junjo gakutai no jun'nan (Burnt Offering: The Atomic Bombing of Nagasaki and the Sacrifice of the Junjo Mobilized Student Corps).* Tokyo: Kadokawa Bunko.

Takase, T. (2009). *Nagasaki: Kieta mō hitotsu no "Genbaku Dōmu" (Nagasaki: The Lost "Second Atomic Dome").* Tokyo: Heibonsha.

Takazane, Y. (2016). *"Nagasaki to Chōsenjin Kyōseirenkō: Chōsa kenkyū no seika to kadai"* ("Nagasaki and Forcible Korean Conscription: Survey Research Results and Topics"). *Ōhara Shakai Mondai Kenkyūjo Zasshi* 687(1), 1–14.

Takemae, E. (2002). *Inside GHQ: The Allied Occupation of Japan and Its Legacy* (R. Ricketts and S. Swann, trans.). London: Continuum.

Takeuchi, Y. (2020). *Kankoku chōyōkō saiban to wa nanika (What Is the Korean Forced Labor Trial All About?).* Tokyo: Iwanami Shoten.

Target Committee. (1945, May 10–11). "Minutes of Second Meeting of the Target Committee, Los Alamos." Washington, DC: National Archives.

Tateno, S. (2016). *"Hibaku taiken wo kataritsugu 17; Mirai wo ikiru mina sama"* ("Telling the Hibakusha Experience, No. 17: To You Who Will Live in the Future"). In S. Kōyūkai (ed.), *Hiroshima/Nagasaki hibakusha no taikendan to omoi (Hiroshima and Nagasaki Hibakusha Testimonies and Memories)* (pp. 52–61). Tokyo: private publication.

Thomas, E. (2023). *Road to Surrender: Three Men and the Countdown to the End of World War II.* New York: Random House.

Thornton, F. B. (1963). *Our American Princes.* New York: G. P. Putnam's Sons.

Tibbets, P. W. (1998). *The Return of the* Enola Gay. Columbus, OH: Private printing.

Tillman, B. (2007). *Lemay.* New York: Palgrave Macmillan.

Tillman, B. (2010). *Whirlwind: The Air War Against Japan, 1942–1945.* New York: Simon & Schuster.

Tobacco & Salt Museum. (No date). *"Tabako to shio arekore"* ("Various Topics of Tobacco and Salt"). https://www.tabashio.jp/collection/tobacco/t9/index.html.

Tōgō, S. (1956). *The Cause of Japan* (T. Fumihiko and B. B. Blakeney, trans.). New York: Simon & Schuster.

Tōkai, U. (2010, March 1). *"'Kuroi ame' kai'u'iki no jikan henka wo suikei; gen'i kenkyūra"* ("Atomic Medicine Researcher Chronologically Maps the Change of 'Black Rain' Fall Areas"). *Chūgoku Shimbun.* https://www.hiroshimapeacemedia.jp/?p=2300.

Toland, J. (1970). *The Rising Sun: The Decline and Fall of the Japanese Empire, 1936–1945.* New York: Random House.

Touken World. (No date). *"Sengoku shōgun ni eikyō wo ataeta Nanban no ishō"* ("The Nanban Clothing That Influenced Warring States Period Warlords"). https://www.touken-world.jp/tips/94856/.

Tsuchiyama, I. (2016). *"Heisei 23-nendo 8-gatsu 9-ka kōwa"* ("August 9, 2011, Memorial Lecture"). In Genbaku Fukkō 70-shūnen Kinen Jigyo Jikkō I'inkai (eds.), *Genbaku fukkō 70-shūnen kinenshi: Shōgen; Nagasaki Ikadaigaku* (*Volume Commemorating the Seventieth Anniversary of Recovery from the Atomic Bomb: Testimony from Nagasaki Medical College*) (pp. 21–23). Nagasaki: Nagasaki University School of Medicine.

Tsurumi, K. (1970). *Social Change and the Individual: Japan Before and After Defeat in World War II.* Princeton, NJ: Princeton University Press.

Tsutsui, H. (director). (2021). *Kienai kurokemuri: Genbaku wa naze Nagasaki e* (*The Black Smoke That Will Not Fade Away: Why Was Nagasaki Atom-bombed?*) [Film]. RKB Mainichi Broadcasting. https://rkb.jp/article/26719/.

Twentieth Air Force. (1945a). "Field Order Number 16, August 7." Guam: Twentieth Air Force.

Twentieth Air Force. (1945b). "Field Order Number 17, August 8." Guam: Twentieth Air Force.

Twentieth Air Force. (1945c). "Mission Resume, Mission Number 319, August 16." Guam: Twentieth Air Force.

Twentieth Air Force, A-2 Section. (1945). "Tactical Report: Mission No. Special."

Twentieth Air Force, XX Bomber Command, Target Unit, Intelligence Section. (1945, April). "Nagasaki Area (Urban), Target No. 90.36-542; Target Chart No. 22A."

Twentieth Air Force, XXI Bomber Command. (1945). "Phase Analysis: Incendiary Operations." Curtis LeMay Papers, Library of Congress, Washington, DC.

Twentieth Air Force, XXI Bomber Command, A-2 Section. (1945). "Tactical Mission Report Field Orders No. 39, Mission No. 38; Target: Urban Area TOKYO, JAPAN, 25 February 1945."

Uchino, C. (1961). *"Byōin meguri"* ("Visiting Hospitals"). In Junshin Joshi Gakuen (eds.), *Junjo gakutai jun'nan no kiroku* (*The Martyrdom of the Junshin Mobilized Students Group*) (pp. 55–61). Nagasaki: private publication.

United States Army Air Forces, Joint Target Group. (1945, April 24). "Urban Information Sheet: Tokyo No. 7 (Provisional Edition)." Washington, DC: Office of AC/AS Intelligence.

"Urusura Itonaga Yoshi shūdōin" ("Sister Ursula Itonaga Yoshi"). (2022, November 1). *Katorikku Kyōhō,* (1109).

U.S. Strategic Bombing Survey, Office of the Chairman. (1946) *Report 3: The Effects of the Atomic Bomb on Hiroshima and Nagasaki.* Washington, DC: United States Government Printing Office.

U.S. Strategic Bombing Survey, Civilian Defense Division. (1947). *Report 4: Field Report Covering Air Raid Protection and Allied Subjects, Tokyo, Japan.* Washington, DC: Government Printing Office.

U.S. Strategic Bombing Survey, Civilian Defense Division. (1947). *Report 5: Field Report Covering Air Raid Protection and Allied Subjects in Nagasaki, Japan.* Washington, DC: Government Printing Office.

U.S. Strategic Bombing Survey, Manpower, Food and Civilian Supplies Division. (1947). *Report 42: The Japanese Wartime Standard of Living and Utilization of Manpower.* Washington, DC: Government Printing Office.

U.S. Strategic Bombing Survey, Medical Division. (1947). *Report 13: The Effects of Atomic Bombs on Health and Medical Services in Hiroshima and Nagasaki.* Washington, DC: Government Printing Office.

U.S. Strategic Bombing Survey, Military Analysis Division. (1946). *Report 66: The Strategic Air Operation of Very Heavy Bombardment in the War Against Japan (Twentieth Air Force).* Washington, DC: U.S. Government Printing Office.

U.S. Strategic Bombing Survey, Military Analysis Division. (1947). *Report 70: The Seventh and Eleventh Air Forces in the War Against Japan.* Washington, DC: U.S. Government Printing Office.

U.S. Strategic Bombing Survey, Morale Division. (1947). *Report 14: The Effects of Strategic Bombing on Japanese Morale.* Washington, DC: U.S. Government Printing Office.

U.S. Strategic Bombing Survey, Naval Analysis Division. (1946a). *Report 73: Campaigns of the Pacific War (Final Report).* Washington, DC: U.S. Government Printing Office.

U.S. Strategic Bombing Survey, Naval Analysis Division. (1946b). *Report 78: The Offensive Mine Laying Campaign Against Japan.* Washington, DC: U.S. Government Printing Office.

U.S. Strategic Bombing Survey, Office of the Chairman. (1946). *Report 2: Japan's Struggle to End the War.* Washington, DC: Government Printing Office.

U.S. Strategic Bombing Survey, Over-all Economic Effects Division. (1946). *Report 53: The Effects of Strategic Bombing on Japan's War Economy.* Washington, DC: U.S. Government Printing Office.

U.S. Strategic Bombing Survey, Physical Damage Division. (1947). *Report 90: Effects of the Incendiary Attacks on Eight Cities.* Washington, DC: U.S. Government Printing Office.

U.S. Strategic Bombing Survey, Physical Damage Division. (1947). *Report 93: Effects of the Atomic Bomb on Nagasaki, Japan.* Washington, DC: Government Printing Office.

U.S. Strategic Bombing Survey, Transportation Division. (1946). *Report 54: The War Against Japanese Transportation 1941–1945*. Washington, DC: U.S. Government Printing Office.

U.S. Strategic Bombing Survey, Urban Areas Division. (1947). *Report 59: The Effects of Air Attack on the City of Nagasaki*. Washington, DC: U.S. Government Printing Office.

Van Pelt, J. F., and C. D. Albury. (2005). "James F. Van Pelt and Charles D. Albury." In Krauss, R., and A. Krauss (eds.), *The 509th Remembered: A History of the 509th Composite Group as Told by the Veterans That Dropped the Atomic Bombs on Japan* (pp. 187–199). Buchanan, MI: private publication.

Van Wolferen, K. (1989). *The Enigma of Japanese Power*. London: Macmillan.

"Vast Repair Bases Keep B-29's Tuned: Depot Handles 425,000,000 Spare Parts—Ground Crews, Gear Mesh in Vital Work." (1945, March 14). *New York Times*.

Vespa, J. E. (2000). "Those Who Served: America's Veterans from World War II to the War on Terror (American Community Survey Report)." United States Census Bureau. https://www.census.gov/content/dam/Census/library/publications/2020/demo/acs-43.pdf.

"VOX POPULI: Warship *Yamato* Remembered on 77th Anniversary of Its Sinking." (2022, April 7). *Asahi Shimbun*. https://www.asahi.com/ajw/articles/14592451.

Walker, J. S. (1997). *Prompt and Utter Destruction: Truman and the Use of Atomic Bombs Against Japan*. Chapel Hill: University of North Carolina Press.

Washburn, W. E. (1995). "The Smithsonian and the *Enola Gay*." *National Interest* 40, 40–49.

Wellerstein, A. (2014). "The Kyoto Misconception." Restricted Data: A Nuclear History Blog. https://blog.nuclearsecrecy.com/2014/08/08/kyoto-misconception/.

White Sands Missile Range Museum. (No date). "Special Mission 16: Fat Man and the Atomic Bombing of Nagasaki." https://wsmrmuseum.com/2024/01/31/special-mission-16-fat-man-and-the-atomic-bombing-of-nagasaki/5/.

Williams, H. S. (1958). *Tales of the Foreign Settlements in Japan* (Kindle version). Rutland, VT: Charles E. Tuttle Company.

Wilson, M. R. (2011). "Making 'Goop' out of Lemons: The Permanente Metals Corporation, Magnesium Incendiary Bombs, and the Struggle for Profits During World War II." *Enterprise & Society* 12(1), 10–45.

Yamaguchi, T. (1996). *"Meiji Matsunen no Shūkyō to Kyōiku: Sankyō Kaidō wo Megutte"* ("Religion and Education in the Late Meiji Era: Considering the 1912 Conference of Three Religions"). *Tōkyō Daigaku Shi Kiyō* 14, 1–17.

Yamazaki, M. (2016). *Nippon Kaigi: Senzen Kaiki e no Jōnen* (*Nippon Kaigi: Yearning to Return to the Prewar Past*). Tokyo: Shū'eisha.

Yellen, J. A. (2013). "The Specter of Revolution: Reconsidering Japan's Decision to Surrender." *International History Review* 35(1), 205–226.

REFERENCES

Yokote, K. (2010). *Nagasaki: Sono toki no hibaku shōjo: Rokujūgo me no "Masako Taorezu"* (*Nagasaki: A Young Girl Hibakusha at the Time: "Masako Is Still Standing" at Sixty-five*). Tokyo: Jijitsūshin Shuppankyoku.

Yoshino, K. (1992). *Cultural Nationalism in Contemporary Japan*. London: Routledge.

Yūkan Fukunichi Shinbunsha Furusato Jinbutsuki Kankōkai (eds.). (1956). *Furusato Jinbutsuki* (*Hometown Who's Who*). Fukuoka: Yūkan Fukunichi Shinbunsha.

Zellen, B. S. (2020). "Hansai or the Cleansing Fire: How the Interplay of Fog, Friction, and Faith Resulted in the Unintended Annihilation of Nagasaki's Christian Community." Wild Blue Yonder. https://www.airuniversity.af.edu /Wild-Blue-Yonder/Articles/Article-Display/Article/2362769/hansai-or-the -cleansing-fire-how-the-interplay-of-fog-friction-and-faith-result/.

Zwigenberg, R. (2014). *Hiroshima: The Origins of Global Memory Culture*. Cambridge, UK: Cambridge University Press.

NOTES

"THERE ARE NO CIVILIANS IN JAPAN"

1. Glantz, 2014, Loc 607 of 3742.
2. The Americans feared the presence of the Kwantung (Kantō) Army in Manchuria—specifically because with its independent command status and proprietary on-site industrial base, it would be able to continue fighting long after the Home Islands were subdued by invasion (or prior political surrender). This is the primary reason Roosevelt wanted the Russians to come into the war—to neutralize the Manchuria threat by destruction of the Kwantung Army's military capability and by nailing it to the spot and preventing it from shipping forces to help shore up defenses in the Home Islands should ground combat in that theater still be underway. See Bowen, Little, et al., 1959, p. xvi.
3. Rhodes, 1986, p. 737. As discussed in Sheftall, 2024, Project Alberta was a division within the Manhattan Project responsible for the nuts-and-bolts technology and operational deployment of the atomic bombs.
4. See Groves, 1962, p. 344; Olivi, 1998, p. 91; and Beser, 1988, p. 128.
5. Farrell, 2021, p. 273.
6. Twentieth Air Force, 1945b; et al. Presumably this was for the sake of poststrike reconnaissance photography.
7. U.S. Secretary of War Henry L. Stimson, in his postwar memoirs, described the strategic aim of this urgent schedule thusly: "So far as the Japanese could know, our ability to execute atomic attacks, if necessary by many planes at a time, was unlimited. As Dr. Karl Compton has said, 'It was not one atomic bomb, or two, which brought surrender; it was the experience of what an

428 NOTES

atomic bomb will actually do to a community, plus the dread of many more, that was effective.'" Stimson and Bundy, 1947, Loc 10317 of 12038. See also Correll, 2011, p. 60; Walker, 1997, p. 147. Attempts were made to see that the bluff reached the Japanese populace via propaganda leaflets dropped over the main cities of the archipelago in early August; the leaflets were full of threats to use atomic bombs "again and again." For this and other details of atom bomb propaganda leaflets, see Twentieth Air Force, A-2 Section, 1945, pp. 60–61. See also Bix, 1995. The full text of the Potsdam Declaration is in appendix A of this volume.

8. Twentieth Air Force, A-2 Section, p. 60.

9. See B. J. Bernstein, 1977; B. J. Bernstein, 1991.

10. For accessible treatments of the highly complex story of the internecine skulduggery between the hard-line militarists and the "peace faction" at the Imperial Palace in the final days of the war (and the role of the atomic bombs in the same), see Feis, 1966; R. B. Frank, 1999; and Asada, 1998. See also Butow, 1954.

11. Joint Chiefs of Staff, 1943, p. 152.

12. See U.S. Strategic Bombing Survey, Office of the Chairrman, 1946, p. 23; Feis; Bix, especially p. 207; et al.

13. General Carl Spaatz wanted to drop a third atomic bomb on Tokyo. See B. J. Bernstein, 1977, p. 13.

14. Truman's decision: "At an afternoon Cabinet meeting on August 10 [according to the diary of Commerce Secretary Henry Wallace], 'Truman said he had given orders to stop atomic bombing. He said the thought of wiping out another 100,000 people was too horrible. He didn't like the idea of killing, as he said, 'all those kids.'"Alperovitz, 1995, pp. 416–417. See also Walker, p. 86. Bombs for invasion: This was according to a production estimate made by Manhattan Project boss General Leslie Groves in a July 30 response to a query by Army chief of staff General George C. Marshall, two weeks after the first successful testing of an atomic bomb at Alamogordo. See B. J. Bernstein, 1991, p. 161.

15. The Fifth was one of the Far East Air Forces (FEAF) flying out of recently captured Okinawa. In addition to the Fifth, this primarily tactical air command consisted of the Seventh, the Eighth (recently transferred from the European Theater), and the Thirteenth Air Forces of the U.S. Army Air Forces.

16. This passage from the "Fifth Air Force Weekly Intelligence Review, No. 86, 15-21 July 1945" was written by Colonel Henry F. Cunningham. Craven and Cate, 1953, pp. 696n–697n.

17. Operation STARVATION was the U.S. Army Air Forces' primary (and highly effective) contribution to the U.S. Navy's overall strategic campaign to block Japan's access to maritime supply lines—particularly food and other raw materials from the Asian continent. The operation employed B-29s of the

NOTES

313th Bombardment Wing, XXI BC, Twentieth Air Force that flew out of North Field, Tinian, and dropped aerial mines in Japanese waterways, concentrating on the Shimonoseki Straits, the Bungo Channel, and the Seto Inland Sea. See: U.S. Strategic Bombing Survey, Transportation Division, 1947; Sellagar, 1974; Chilstrom, 1992; Mason, 2002.

18. "Interdiction of the railroad system, had it been undertaken, would have deprived Japan of all significant transportation and left the nation industrially and militarily almost completely immobile." U.S. Strategic Bombing Survey, Transportation Division, p. 6. "[These f]oodstuffs [would have included]: agricultural products of the interior transported to coastal cities—rice, other grains, potatoes and soybeans, and fish from seaports to interior consuming centers." U.S. Strategic Bombing Survey, Transportation Division, p. 28. See also U.S. Strategic Bombing Survey, Over-all Economic Effects Division, 1946, p. 53. "[F]rom Okinawa airfields, the 'Greater East Asia Co-Prosperity Sphere' would feel the knife of complete dismemberment. The remaining tentacles of the Japanese Imperial octopus, the shipping lanes to Formosa, China, and Korea, could now be severed." U.S. Strategic Bombing Survey, Military Analysis Division, 1947, p. 13. See also R. B. Frank, 2016.

19. For an analysis of the effects of Japanese attempts to counter this threat through dispersal of their industries into caves, etc., see U.S. Strategic Bombing Survey, Over-all Economic Effects Division, 1946; Twentieth Air Force, A-2 Section.

20. Twentieth Air Force, A-2 Section, p. 3. The "thirteen consequences" reference is to the Potsdam Declaration issued by the Allies (including the theretofore Japan-neutral Soviet Union) on July 26, 1945. Punctuation and formatting of the leaflet text is per original.

21. U.S. Strategic Bombing Survey, Morale Division, 1947, p. 34.

22. For an overview of this campaign from the perspective of its commander, see Harris, 1947. For a German perspective, see Friedrich, 2006, and Grayling, 2006.

23. Ralph, 2006, p. 517.

24. Schwabe, 2015, p. 115.

25. See Wilson, 2011.

26. "Vast Repair Bases Keep B-29's Tuned," 1945.

27. For a summary of studies on psychological stress experienced by B-29 crews, see XXI Bomber Command, 1945, pp. 38–41. For personal testimony on Saipan B-29 base life, see Ciardi, 1988.

28. Thinking along these lines was widespread among Twentieth Air Force aircrews. See Robertson, 2018, p. 112, and Francis, 1997, p. 474.

29. In a June 1945 White House planning conference for the scheduled invasion of Japan, the deputy commander of Army Air Forces, Lieutenant General Ira Eaker, reported a 2 percent casualty rate for combat missions then being flown in the Pacific Theater. This was a total figure, including not only losses

430 NOTES

for B-29s but also those for smaller tactical aircraft flying in typically more hazardous combat environments (low altitudes as per ground support missions; being exposed to more antiaircraft fire; etc.). See Giancreco, 1997, p. 559.

30. "On 5 August 1945, the day before the first atomic bomb was dropped on Japan, Twentieth Air Force published a regulation which made B-29 and F-13 [the photo reconnaissance version of the B-29] crewmen eligible for consideration for rotation when they completed 35 combat sorties." Historical Studies Branch, United States Air Force Historical Division, 1968, p. 18.

31. For personal testimony about the alcohol habits of B-29 crews on Tinian, see Robertson, pp. 100–101.

HIGH CITY, LOW CITY

1. I owe this topographical visualization device to Edwin Seidensticker, who uses it in his excellent *Low City, High City.*

2. U.S. Strategic Bombing Survey, Physical Effects Division, 1947a, p. 67.

3. "Bamboo Houses Easy Prey," 1923. See also Miller, 1991, p. 349; Hammer, 2006.

4. Sherry, 1989, p. 58.

5. Mitchell's 1924 article (possibly lecture notes) "Strategical Aspect of the Pacific Problem."

6. Mitchell, 1928, "America, Air Power and the Pacific." Both of these typewritten and hand-annotated documents are to be found in the William Mitchell Papers, Library of Congress, Washington, DC, and are also available for download in pdf form at www.scribd.com.

7. Sherry, p. 54. The original article is in the July 24, 1934, edition of *The New York Times* on page 6.

8. George Marshall's November 1941 quotes, paraphrased by journalists at the meeting as "burning the wood and paper cities of Japan," are in Dower, 2010, p. 168.

9. Anderson, 1942.

10. Hulen, 1943.

11. Hulen.

12. Dawsey, 2022.

13. "Survivors' Statements," 1944.

14. See Dower, 1986.

15. Sherry, p. 169.

16. Marshall and staffer quotes: Sherry, p. 169.

17. See National Defense Research Committee, 1946.

18. See Sweeney, 1997; Tibbets; Robertson, et al. Cigar- and rum-fueled runs to Cuba were one of the favorite destinations for Stateside B-29 crewmen undergoing this training.

NOTES

19. The report on a study begun in May 1943 was published by the Army Air Forces on October 15, 1943, as *Japan—Incendiary Attack Data* by S. de Palma and Raymond H. Ewell. See Fedman and Karacas, 2012, p. 312.

SHITAMACHI GIRL

1. E. B. Kerr, 1991, p. 153.
2. Atomi no Juku, 2000. Koishikawa Ward now lies within the new Tokyo administrative unit of Bunkyō Ward.
3. This was apparently a rather common reaction among Tokyo residents to the sound of sirens on this particular day. See Scott, 2015, p. 210.
4. Although no Doolittle bombs fell on Ginza during the raid, there were numerous civilian casualties on the ground around Tokyo that day due to short-falling or malfunctioning antiaircraft fire (similar to many Honolulu casualties during the Pearl Harbor attack), and the Atomi girl might have been one of these (amateur historian and Doolittle Raid expert Morimoto Makoto—personal correspondence).
5. The next American bombs on the Japanese Home Islands would fall somewhat ironically on Nagasaki in June 1944—news that at the time was largely drowned out by D-Day in Europe.
6. Robbins, 1997, p. 101.
7. See Scott.
8. "Akebono"—like "Akatsuki"—is one of the myriad idiomatic Japanese expressions for "rising sun."
9. See U.S. Strategic Bombing Survey, Manpower, Food and Civilian Supplies Division, 1947, especially p. 75.
10. United States Air Forces, Joint Target Group, 1945, p. 6.

A YOUNG MAN OF PROMISE

1. Laures, 1954, p. 207, et al.
2. Montane, 2012, p. 9.
3. See LaFeber, 1998.
4. E.g., British merchant Thomas Blake Glover. See Burke-Gaffney, 2015.
5. Cummings, 1980, p. 16.
6. Although I have been using the term independently for decades in my teaching, I will give William Cummings credit for reminding me of the relevance of "samuraization" in this context. Cummings, p. 83.
7. Cummings, p. 43.
8. See Cummings.
9. See J. Ishida, 2010. For Okayama origins, see J. Ishida, 1962.
10. J. Ishida, 2010, p. 27.
11. This system is also explained in Sheftall, 2024.
12. Yūkan Fukunichi, 1956, p. 75.
13. Oguma, 2002, p. 18. See also Yoshino, 1992, pp. 90–94.

432 NOTES

14. See Nolte and Hajime, 1983.
15. See Davis, 1976. For an examination of postwar Japanese cultural fallout from the rescinding of the rescript, see Dore, 1952.
16. See also Van Wolferen, 1989, pp. 369–370.
17. See Davis; Oguma, p. 25.
18. Yokote, 2010, p. 191.
19. Yokote, p. 83.

YAMANOTE GIRL

1. U.S. Strategic Bombing Survey, Office of the Chairman, 1946, p. 25.
2. Yūkan Fukunichi, p. 5; see also J. Ishida, 2010.
3. See J. Ishida, 1962.
4. J. Ishida, 2010, p. 72.
5. For a detailed autobiographical account of the judge's overseas travels as Hirota's emissary, see H. Ishida, 1937.
6. This is now Ochanomizu University in Otsuka, Bunkyō Ward.
7. See Ōmori, 2023, pp. 152–153.
8. See U.S. Strategic Bombing Survey, Medical Division, 1947, particularly p. 85.
9. See U.S. Strategic Bombing Survey, Civilian Defense Division, 1947, p. 32, et al.
10. Yokote, p. 191.
11. The Hiroshima Court of Appeals was some five hundred thirty meters southeast of what would become Little Boy's Ground Zero a year and a half later.
12. In the prewar Japanese education system, *jogakkō* were the equivalents of the nation's male-only junior high schools.
13. See Kitajima, 1977, p. 168. Elementary school student evacuation began in Japan's main cities on the Tokyo-to-Osaka Pacific Coast corridor on July 8, 1944, the day after the fall of Saipan put them within range of B-29s. Similar evacuations from smaller regional cities like Hiroshima did not occur until nearly a year later.
14. Cahill, 2012, p. 14.
15. Adams, 2000, p. 14.
16. Nocturnal "weather strike missions"—small formations of B-29s—began flying out of the Marianas against Tokyo and other Home Island targets in December 1944. The intention of these was to collect data on weather conditions over Japan, to give crews experience in night navigation during long flights to Japan, and, ostensibly, to adversely affect the morale of the increasingly sleep-deprived Japanese population. See Stewart and Power, 1947, p. 85.

NOTES

433

NORTH FIELD, GUAM

1. This is near the present-day Tokyo Dome stadium.
2. This raid—a high-altitude, daylight incendiary mission flown by 172 XXI BC bombers—occurred on February 25, 1945. It destroyed more than two kilometers of Kanda and Shitaya Wards and can be regarded, in a sense, as a trial run for mass use of incendiary tactics perfected by the March 9 and 10 raid two weeks later. See Sams, 2016.
3. J. Ishida, 2010, p. 65. Adachi Denki was in Tengenji in Minami-Azabu—not Yotsuya. Masako had started working there in January 1945.
4. Great Tokyo Air Raid / War Damage Records Editorial Committee, 1973, vol. 1, p. 19. See also Guillain, 1981, p. 181; and Saotome, 1971, p. 20.
5. The 314th BW still did not have its full complement of B-29s by the time of the March 9 to 10, 1945, raid. The remainder of its aircraft would arrive on Guam the following month.
6. See McKelway, 1945b.
7. Richard Rhodes suggests this malady might have been a legacy of LeMay's earlier career as a full-time high-altitude pilot.
8. See Blackwell, 2003.
9. See Tillman, 2007.
10. For the Robert McNamara interview, see Morris, 2003.
11. President John F. Kennedy and LeMay—by then chief of staff of the U.S. Air Force—shared a mutual antipathy that famously came to a head during the Cuban Missile Crisis of October 1962. Theodore Sorensen, Kennedy's speechwriter and alter ego, called LeMay "my least favorite human being." See Dallek, 2013.
12. See McKelway, 1945b.
13. Tillman, 2010, p. 137.
14. "MEETINGHOUSE" was Twentieth Air Force code for "Tokyo."
15. See Rhodes, 1995.
16. See Caidin, 1960, p. 69.
17. See LeMay and Yenne, 1988.
18. Some of the B-29s took off with a weight of up to 138,000 pounds for this mission—some 13,000 pounds over design safety restrictions. See Robertson, p. 2.
19. Each B-29 for this particular mission was tanked up with more than 6,800 gallons of fuel. "Tactical Mission Report," Mission No. 40, Twentieth Air Force, XXI Bombing Command, p. 3.
20. Twentieth Air Force, XXI Bombing Command, "Tactical Mission Report, Mission No. 40," p. 6. The B-29s of 314th Bombing Wing flying out of Guam were loaded out with closer to five tons of bombs to compensate for the longer distance they had to fly to Tokyo.

21. "It was the mission on which many B-29 Superfortress crew members were certain LeMay was going to get them killed" (crew anger at LeMay). Dorr, 2018, p. 4.
22. Caidin, p. 120.
23. E. B. Kerr, p. 158.
24. The armorers in some squadrons interpreted the gun-stripping directive somewhat creatively, leaving tail armament on their bombers.
25. "I chose General Tommy Power of the 314th Bomb Wing, who I felt was my best wing commander, to lead the mission and to remain over Tokyo and observe the attack as it developed. He drew a series of sketches—every 10 minutes—as the fires spread, and this furnished invaluable information for planning future missions." LeMay and Yenne, pp. 123–124.
26. Twentieth Air Force, XXI BC, Mission 40.
27. These capabilities were believed to be surprisingly limited, especially given the city's experience with the Great Kantō Earthquake barely twenty years before.
28. Twentieth Air Force, XXI BC, Mission 40; see also Twentieth Air Force, XXI Bomber Command, p. 33.
29. Great Tokyo Air Raid / War Damage Records Editorial Committee, vol. I., p. 34.
30. Twentieth Air Force, XXI BC, Mission 40.
31. Twentieth Air Force, XXI Bomber Command, p. 47.
32. This is based on COA and XXI BC Shitamachi population density estimates of 103,000 people per square mile.

MEETINGHOUSE

1. Twentieth Air Force, XXI BC, Mission 40.
2. "Tinian-based chaplains were always on the scene to bless each plane and crew just at the start of the takeoff roll. Chaplains appeared similarly at Guam and Saipan." Dorr, 2018, p. 70. See also Halloran and Marshall, 2011, Loc 507.
3. McKelway, 1945a. LeMay started back to XXI BC HQ at Tumon Bay at sundown.
4. Since 1964, the site has been occupied by a young-learner-oriented science museum administered by the Japan Science Foundation.
5. Jōhōji, 1981, pp. 68–69.
6. Jōhōji, pp. 68–69.
7. Saotome, 1987, p. 73. This was the Imperial Army's counterpart war-trophy engagement to the Navy's glorious Battle of Tsushima Strait (which was commemorated on Navy Day—May 28—also a national holiday until the end of the Imperial Era).
8. Robbins, p. 140,
9. See A. Bernstein.

NOTES   435

10. CriticalPast, 1945. Similar to the (successful) postwar treason court-martial defense of her Australian POW collaborator at NHK, Major Charles Cousens, Orphan Annie / Tokyo Rose—Los Angeles–born Iva Ikuko Toguri—claimed in her own postwar treason trial that she had performed her disc jockey / announcer services for NHK under duress. As evidence for this claim, her lawyers made use of the hidden innuendos and inside jokes at the expense of the Japanese with which she and Cousens peppered her nightly scripts. While an Australian court-martial failed to find Cousens guilty of treason, an American court found Toguri guilty of one count of the same and gave her a $10,000 fine and a ten-year prison sentence (of which she served six in a federal penitentiary in West Virginia). She was pardoned by President Gerald R. Ford in 1977 after a CBS broadcast of *60 Minutes* featured a segment on her story that won widespread public sympathy for the legendary wartime radio announcer.
11. Caidin, p. 130.
12. Hartman, 1945, p. 4. See also Barrett, 2023.
13. Great Tokyo Air Raid / War Damage Records Editorial Committee, vol. I, p. 19.
14. See Guillain, p. 181.
15. Saotome, 1987, p. 73.
16. Caidin, p. 132. Cabin depressurization and oxygen masks were not necessary, as the planes never flew at high altitude for the entirety of the mission.
17. XXI Bomber Command, pp. 16–17.
18. Saotome, 1971, pp. 21, 26, et al.
19. See Great Tokyo Air Raid / War Damage Records Editorial Committee, vol. I, p. 20; XXI BC, Mission 40, p. 14.
20. NHK, 2005.
21. See Dorr, 2012, pp. 150–151; Hartman; and LeMay and Yenne, pp. 123–124.
22. Hartman, p. 4.
23. Several Japanese incendiary raid survivors I have interviewed over the years described this sound as a rapid, distant popping, not unlike a giant sheet of sailcloth being ripped.
24. Guillain, p. 184.
25. U.S. Strategic Bombing Survey, Physical Damage Division, 1947a, p. 94.
26. Great Tokyo Air Raid / War Damage Records Editorial Committee, vol. I, p. 20.
27. U.S. Strategic Bombing Survey, Physical Damage Division, 1947a, p. 97.
28. NHK.
29. See Dorr, 2018; Caidin, p. 146.
30. Caidin, p. 147, et al.
31. Saotome, 1971, p. 22.
32. NHK.
33. NHK.

NOTES

34. NHK.
35. U.S. Strategic Bombing Survey, Physical Damage Division, 1947a, p. 102.
36. Twentieth Air Force, XXI BC, Mission 40, pp. 7–8.
37. Tillman, 2010, pp. 137–142.

TRAVEL ORDERS

1. This is based on an eyewitness account of such a scene in the Yamanote by a French journalist. See Guillain, p. 182.
2. J. Ishida, 2010, p. 123.
3. J. Ishida, 2010, p. 124.
4. To accompany the rest of their family on the move, Shizuko and Yasuyo would have been called back from the rural evacuation sites where they had been living with elementary school classmates since the previous summer.
5. The Kurofuchis' youngest daughter, Sumiko, was the only family member who survived March 9 and 10. Kano and Kiridōshi, 2016, p. 167.
6. Kano and Kiridōshi, p. 166. These girls were Japanese—not Mongolian or Korean—and their families were likely in these continental postings either as colonial administrators (Korea), corporate executives (Korea or Mongolia), or entrepreneurs (Korea or Mongolia).
7. Kano and Kiridōshi, p. 168.
8. See Guillain, p. 194.
9. See Daniels, 1977, p. 122.
10. Kano and Kiridōshi, p. 169.

GEOGRAPHICAL DESTINY

1. See U.S. Strategic Bombing Survey, Office of the Chairman, p. 9.
2. Otsuki, 2016, p. 399.
3. Hotei, 2020, p. 17.
4. Today, this track is used by the JR Nagasaki Nagayo Branch Line.
5. "Nagaden" is the popular local moniker for Nagasaki's streetcar lines. The term is an abbreviation of the name of the company that built and has run the system since 1914, Nagasaki Denki Kidō. See Nagasaki Denki Kidō, 2024. Today, the northern terminus is Akasako, 1.65 kilometers north of Ōhashi Station.
6. See *Nagasaki Sensai*, 1977, vol. 2, p. 14. In its official Ministry of Transportation designation, this stretch of the modern-day National Highway 206 connects Nagasaki (via Togitsu) and the naval harbor of Sasebo some fifty kilometers to the north. On modern maps, this section of 206 is sometimes referred to as New Urakami Road (*Shin Urakami Kaidō*), but this was not in usage in 1945, so for the sake of historical accuracy and clarity, this thoroughfare—limited to its stretch between Nagasaki and Togitsu—will be referred to in this volume as the Togitsu Road.

NOTES

7. Prewar, Sasebo was the third-largest naval base in Japan, behind Yokosuka and Kure. See C. R. Smith, 1997. Today, it is still a vitally important facility for the Japan Maritime Self-Defense Force.

8. Japan Dam Federation, 2015a.

9. Japan Dam Federation, 2015b.

10. Laures, p. 209.

11. Itoh, 2007, p. 89.

12. This inbound Chinese traffic has yet to fully return to pre-COVID-19 pandemic levels.

13. Japan's 1940 GDP was $192 billion (in 1990 U.S. dollars). Statista, no date. The construction of the *Yamato*, the more famous identical sister ship of the *Musashi*, cost $3.23 billion (in 2022 U.S. dollars). "Vox Populi," 2022.

14. *"Nanban"* was an early pejorative applied to the Portuguese as they were foreigners (i.e., "barbarians") whose ships always approached Japan from the south. The chronological definition of the *Nanban Bōeki* Era I use here is based on Murdoch and Yamagata, 1903.

15. Hesselink, 2016, et al.

16. Hesselink et al.

17. See Japan Heritage Portal Site, no date; Touken World, no date; Nagasaki City, no date–d; Kirshner, 2021; Tobacco & Salt Museum, no date; Boxer, 1967, p. 26.

18. Boxer provides a comprehensive history of Portuguese Christian activity in Japan during this period.

19. Catholic News Agency, no date. This would have constituted about 1 percent of the population of the Japanese archipelago at the time. Interestingly—and perhaps tellingly in terms of the resilience of the native culture—the percentage of Japanese who are Christians has never surpassed this tiny fraction over the subsequent four centuries.

20. Mullins, 1994, p. 262.

21. A similar ban against Christianity had been promulgated in the 1590s by Toyotomi Hideyoshi, the political precursor to the Tokugawa Shogunate.

22. Miyazaki, 2003a, p. 13. See also Hesselink, p. 221.

23. Hesselink, p. 116.

24. One of these ceremonies is dramatically depicted in the 2016 Martin Scorsese film *Silence*, which is set in seventeenth-century Nagasaki after the Shogunate's official ban of Christianity. The annual *efumi* ceremonies were finally ceased in 1857 because of the Shogunate's concern that continuation of the practice would bring Western condemnation. See Plutschow, 1983, p. 124.

25. Cited in Katsuta, 1991, pp. 99–100.

26. Katsuta, pp. 99–100.

27. Dejima was manned by a full-time facility staff of Dutchmen who had to make annual pilgrimages to Edo to supplicate the Shogun.

28. Earns, 2015, p. 98.
29. Williams, 1958, Loc 314 of 4251. See also Burke-Gaffney, 2015, et al.
30. Burke-Gaffney, 2015, et al.
31. The first of these treaties was concluded between Japan and the United States in July 1858, largely through the efforts of Townsend Harris, who had been dispatched by President Millard Fillmore as the first American consul to Japan. The second raft of unequal treaties between Japan and Britain, Russia, France, and the Netherlands came into effect a year later. See Burke-Gaffney, 2015, p. 6.
32. See Williams.
33. U.S. Strategic Bombing Survey, Physical Damage Division, 1947b, p. 28. See also Burke-Gaffney, 2019, pp. 80–81.
34. U.S. Strategic Bombing Survey, Urban Areas Division, 1947, p. 1.
35. U.S. Strategic Bombing Survey, Physical Damage Division, 1947, vol. I, p. 18.
36. See U.S. Strategic Bombing Survey, Office of the Chairman, p. 9; U.S. Strategic Bombing Survey, Urban Areas Division, pp. 3–4.
37. See U.S. Strategic Bombing Survey, Office of the Chairman, p. 9; U.S. Strategic Bombing Survey, Urban Areas Division, pp. 3–4.
38. U.S. Strategic Bombing Survey, 93, vol. I, p. 99.

ACCULTURATION

1. Kano and Kiridōshi, p. 53.
2. Junshin Joshi Gakuen, 1961, sec. I, p. 5.
3. U.S. Strategic Bombing Survey, Medical Division, pp. 74, 76.
4. This was of course a problem for Japan as a whole, because the country was particularly dependent on overseas food sources. Once the IJN ceded command of the Western Pacific and Indies to the Allies, these sources were steadily cut off, with serious consequences for public health in Japan. See Perera, 1994.
5. Craven and Cate, p. 666.
6. U.S. Strategic Bombing Survey, Medical Division, pp. 74 ("Doctor Akizuki, physician to the Urakami hospital in Nagasaki, stated that during the war, most of his patients [private practice] had beriberi."), 76 ("The most important of the deficiencies in the diet appear to have been deficiencies of calories, high-quality proteins and members of the vitamin B complex, particularly thiamine and niacin.").
7. Kano and Kiridōshi, p. 149.
8. Kano and Kiridōshi, p. 149.
9. Kano and Kiridōshi, p. 150.
10. U.S. Strategic Bombing Survey, Urban Areas Division, p. 7.
11. The bomber in question—probably a Great Tokyo Air Raid veteran—was from the 39th BG of the 314th BW, which had taken part in XXI BC Mission Number 106 targeting Kokubu Airfield, Kyushu (XXI BC Target 2527). Having

NOTES

failed to drop its payload on the primary target, it attacked Nagasaki as a target of opportunity, probably for more than any other reason just to lighten its load for the long flight back to its home base in Guam. Mann, 2009, Loc 2550 of 5874.

12. U.S. Strategic Bombing Survey, Urban Areas Division, pp. 5–6. Sightings of American planes anywhere in Kyushu could set off sirens in Nagasaki City, but Nagasaki authorities sounded sirens only on orders from Fukuoka. Poor coordination of the air raid alert/alarm system at the prefectural level caused the triggering of an excessive number of alerts/alarms that, in turn, resulted in considerable sleep deprivation and daytime disruption for city residents throughout the spring and summer of 1945, up to the atomic bombing. This eventually led to many of those citizens generally regarding air raid alerts and warnings with boy-who-cried-wolf apathy.

13. On Nagasaki apathy and laxness in regard to air defense, see U.S. Strategic Bombing Survey, Urban Areas Division, pp. 5–6, et al.

14. "Kenjo" was a contraction of Nagasaki Kenritsu Jogakkō (Nagasaki Prefectural Girls' School).

15. Michiko's younger sister Yasuko—who had already been living in the city for a year—had won admission to Kenjo as a first-grader through the conventional written exam route a month or two before Michiko's arrival.

16. XX Bomber Command, Target Unit, Intelligence Section, 1945.

17. Particulars of Michiko's daily work uniform are based on Kano and Kiridōshi, p. 40.

18. U.S. Strategic Bombing Survey, Urban Areas Division et al.

19. Office of the Assistant Chief of Air Staff, Intelligence, 1944, p. 13. See also U.S. Strategic Bombing Survey, Urban Areas Division, p. 4.

20. The official USAAF name designation for this facility was Mitsubishi Urakami-Ohashi War Plant. For brevity's sake, we will refer to it as its wartime employees and other associates referred to it, i.e., simply as "Ōhashi" (with a macron on the capital "O" for pronunciation accuracy). For details on the construction and wartime expansion of the Ōhashi facility, see *Nagasaki Sensai*, vol. 1, pp. 35–36.

21. U.S. Strategic Bombing Survey, Urban Areas Division, p. 1.

22. *Nagasaki Sensai*, vol. 1, p. 283.

23. *Nagasaki Sensai*, vol. 1, pp. 65–66.

FACTORY GIRL

1. See Nagasaki Zainichi Chōsenjin no Jinken wo Mamoru Kai, 1989.

2. Boku, 1965, p. 49.

3. Takazane, 2016, p. 2.

4. Takeuchi, 2020, p. 5.

5. Takazane, p. 2.

440 NOTES

6. See Nagasaki Zainichi Chōsenjin no Jinken wo Mamoru Kai.

7. See Clarke, 1984.

8. The camp had this particular nomenclature because it was the fourteenth camp under jurisdiction of Western Army HQ in Fukuoka (the same HQ that covered the air defense of the district, inclusive of Nagasaki). Dutch East Indies POWs at Fukuoka Camp No. 14: Fukuoka 14B, no date.

9. See Clarke.

10. Hotei, p. 82. The map on that page shows the finishing building as having approximate dimensions of two hundred meters by twenty-five meters, so, in terms of square meters, almost exactly the area of an American football field. Also, in an interview, Kano (Kiridōshi) Michiko likened the space to "six or so high school gymnasiums" (ostensibly lined up end to end).

11. U.S. Strategic Bombing Survey, Office of the Chairman, p. 13; U.S. Strategic Bombing Survey, Physical Damage Division, 1947b, vol. I, p. 14.

12. Kano and Kiridōshi, p. 33.

13. Kano and Kiridōshi, p. 66.

14. Kano and Kiridōshi, p. 88.

15. Kano and Kiridōshi, p. 25.

16. U.S. Strategic Bombing Survey, Urban Areas Division, pp. 13–14.

17. U.S. Strategic Bombing Survey, Over-all Economic Effects Division, p. 44.

18. U.S. Strategic Bombing Survey, Office of the Chairman, p. 15.

ŌHASHI

1. *Nagasaki Sensai*, vol. I, p. 84.

2. *Nagasaki Sensai*, vol. I, p. 84.

3. U.S. Strategic Bombing Survey, Military Analysis Division, 1947, p. 15.

4. Target Committee, 1945. In May 1945, the Target Committee consisted of three Pentagon men from General Arnold's office and three Manhattan Project scientists, including William Penney, a British member of Oppenheimer's research team at Los Alamos. See Groves, p. 268.

5. According to historian Alex Wellerstein, no official paper trail has ever been found leading to the removal of Yokohama from the Reserved Area list. Niigata, for its part, seems to have initially been withdrawn from consideration—like Nagasaki earlier being determined not to be worth a bomb—before being restored to the list. By the eve of the actual atomic bombings in early August, however, it seems to have been removed yet again from serious consideration, as it did not even receive weather reconnaissance for either of the eventual atomic attacks. See Wellerstein, 2014.

6. Wellerstein.

7. See Stimson and Bundy, Loc 10260 of 12038. See also Malloy, 2009.

8. See Target Committee.

9. See Stimson and Bundy, Loc 10230 of 12038. See also Groves, pp. 273–274, 275.

NOTES

10. See Atomic Heritage Foundation, 2014.
11. The Manhattan Project, no date–c.
12. U.S. Strategic Bombing, Military Analysis Division, 1947, p. 15
13. See Friedrich; also Gladwell, 2021.
14. This is modern-day Wuhan, incubator community for the COVID-19 virus.
15. See E. B. Kerr, p. 115; Craven and Cate, p. 144.
16. *Nagasaki Sensai*, vol. 1, p. 283.
17. Government guidelines limited female *teishintai* personnel at munitions plants to day shift work. See U.S. Strategic Bombing Survey, Manpower, Food and Civilian Supplies Division, p. 59
18. See National Archives of Japan, 2007. See also Kye, 2019, and Havens, 1975, especially pp. 924–925.
19. Army Map Service, 1945.
20. For detailed descriptions of Japan's late-war industrial-dispersal program, see U.S. Strategic Bombing Survey, Over-all Economic Effects Division.
21. *Nagasaki Sensai*, vol. 2, p. 501; see also Itonaga, 1961. For elementary school facilities usage, see *Nagasaki no Heiwa*, no date–a, and *Nagasaki no Heiwa*, no date–b.
22. See Nagasaki Zainichi Chōsenjin no Jinken wo Mamoru Kai, pp. 102–105.
23. U.S. Strategic Bombing Survey, Civilian Defense Division, p. 52. See also Shirabe, 1972, p. 57.
24. Shirabe, p. 58.
25. See Nagasaki Zainichi Chōsenjin no Jinken wo Mamoru Kai, pp. 102–105.
26. The August 1 bombing of Mori-machi was actually accidental. The attacking planes in question, B-25s of the 41st Bomb Group flying out of Kadena Air Base in Okinawa, had, in fact, been tasked on August 1 with hitting the marshaling yards to the north of Nagasaki Station. During the confusion of the raid, several of the 41st BG bombardiers, unable to distinguish the industrial sprawl of the marshaling yard from the immediately adjacent Mori-machi works, landed their payloads—or part of their payloads—on the latter instead of the former. See 41st Bomb Group, 1945. See also U.S. Strategic Bombing Survey, Urban Areas Division, p. 8.
27. J. Ishida, 2010, p. 128. This raid also destroyed Atomi Jogakkō.
28. This dormitory, the Kōkōkyo, was established by Hirota Kōki in 1899 during his own time at the university, and it still stands today at its original Suginami Ward location. See Hirohiro's Homepage, no date.
29. J. Ishida, 2010, p. 128.
30. *Nagasaki Sensai*, vol. 1, p. 283.
31. Kenjo was amalgamated into the new coed Nagasaki High School after the 1948 education reforms, and perhaps for this reason, little in the way of detailed numerical data records about its student body seems to have still existed when Nagasaki City (following Hiroshima's lead) began compiling its official record of the atomic bomb attack in the early 1970s. I offer this

NOTES

estimate of two hundred based on two known facts and an educated guess: An entire class year group was involved; Masako was in third-year homeroom #6 (implying at least five other and possibly more homerooms); and I assumed a homeroom size of about twenty-five to thirty girls.

32. *Nagasaki Sensai*, vol. I, p. 340.

33. The name "Keiho" derives from the *onyomi* reading of the kanji ideograms used to write "Tamano'ura," the ancient name of Nagasaki.

34. *Nagasaki Sensai*, vol. I, p. 348.

35. This is present-day Nagasaki Prefectural Road No. 113, a.k.a., Nagayo Ōhashi-machi Road (a.k.a. Bunkyō Street for the stretch of the thoroughfare that runs through Urakami).

36. Some secular "civilians" were brought onto the faculty to teach specialty subjects—such as higher math, science, or PE—that the nuns deemed themselves less qualified to handle.

37. See Takagi, 1980, pp. 119–121, and Takase, 2009.

HIDDEN CHRISTIANS

1. See Miyazaki, 2003a, p. 16. These three ports were joined, in short order, by Hyogo, Osaka, and Niigata. See also Japan Customs, no date.

2. Nagasaki City, no date-c.

3. Plutschow, p. 124.

4. See Miyazaki, 2003a, pp. 15–17.

5. Laures, p. 221.

6. Beillevaire, 2018, pp. 483–501, especially p. 497.

7. Takagi, p. 71.

8. After massive landfill work during the early twentieth century to expand the CBD and provide space for the second iteration of Nagasaki Station, Nishizaka is now some six hundred fifty meters northeast of the Nagasaki harbor waterfront. Today, the erstwhile bluff is the site of the Nagasaki branch office and transmitter tower of NHK, and there is a bronze frieze monument and museum dedicated to the Twenty-Six Martyrs.

9. For a thorough examination of Hideyoshi's anti-Christian campaign, see Boxer.

10. One of the Westerners—Felipe de Jesús, a Mexican priest of the Franciscan order—was actually beatified by Pope Urban VIII more than two hundred years earlier, and he became the patron saint of his birthplace, Mexico City. Catholic News Agency.

11. Earns, 2015, p. 76.

12. Earns, 1994, pp. 491–492.

13. Earns, 1994, p. 493.

14. For Furet as architect of Ōura *Tenshudō* (Church), see Beillevaire, p. 498. See also Plutschow, p. 121.

15. Earns, 1994, p. 493.

NOTES

16. Nagasaki Prefectural Government Culture, Tourism, and International Affairs Department World Heritage Registration Division, no date.

17. Snitches were ubiquitous in Japanese society during the early modern era after the establishment of the Tokugawa Shogunate, and they were not limited to professional police informants. Their function was also performed by ordinary local neighborhood residents fearful of running afoul of the *goningumi seido*. The coercive power of the system lay in the archaic Japanese legal concept of collective criminal liability, whereby communities were held responsible for reporting suspicious activities to the authorities. The members of those communities could have been prosecuted for any offense committed by one of them or even for one that had merely been committed by a criminal or other troublemaker who just happened to pass through their villages. This policy—the trans-generational psychological legacy of which continues to influence Japanese sociocultural space even today—was originally instituted in the seventeenth century to augment the scope and granularity of the Shogunate's surveillance network during the early years of the state's nationwide anti-Christian pogrom and to dissuade among the common people any tolerance of Christianity in any symbolic or practiced form, no matter how trivial or personal. See Nagasaki City, no date.

18. Laures, pp. 209–210.

19. Laures, pp. 210–211.

20. Diehl, 2011, p. 15.

21. See Miyazaki, 2003a, pp. 16–17; Plutschow, p. 124; et al.

22. Laures, p. 223.

23. Ballhatchet, p. 40.

24. Miyazaki, 2003b, p. 19. See also Laures, p. 236.

25. From the late 1870s, a quarter century of proselytization efforts to spread the faith more thoroughly throughout the Home Islands met with mixed results. At the end of the nineteenth century, Nagasaki Prefecture remained overwhelmingly demographically dominant in Japanese Catholicism; it was home to some 60 percent of the nation's faithful. See Ballhatchet, p. 40.

26. Cheney, no date.

27. Allam, 1990, p. 42.

28. Junshin Seibokai, no date–b.

29. Junshin Seibokai, no date–b.

THE NOVICE

1. See Harrington, 2011.

2. See Byas, 1942, et al.

3. The national daily *Asahi Shimbun* was something of an outlier in this respect; well into the late 1930s, it was critical of this ultraright movement, which it saw (correctly) as threatening the rule of parliamentary law in the country.

During this period, the paper was, however, unbending in its populist-flavored celebration of the Japanese military's feats of arms on the Asian continent—acts that, of course, eventually steered Japan onto its catastrophic collision course with the West.

4. See Hall, 1949, especially pp. 22–39.

5. This nomenclature can cause some confusion among laypeople, as both nuns and members of apostolic orders use the term "Sister" in their formal titles as well as in referring to one another in interactions "on the job"—usually in combination with either a name in religion (a female saint's name, e.g., "Sister Segunda," "Sister Clothilda," etc.) for nuns or, in the case of apostolics, given birth names (e.g., "Sister Stacy," "Sister Kathy," etc.). The usage by generations of American Catholic parochial school students in referring to their female faculty tormentors as "nuns" (cf. *The Blues Brothers*) is, in fact, mistaken, as these teachers are almost certainly always members of apostolic orders and therefore "Sisters" in terms not only of appellation but also of office.

6. In spite of the fact that both nuns and Sisters devote their lives to religious work and take vows of poverty and chastity, they are still considered "laypersons" according to strict Church definition because women cannot be ordained as priests and are thus not allowed to perform the Holy Sacraments in mass or other liturgical services.

7. Junshin Seibokai, no date–a.

8. Junshin Joshi Gakuen, no date.

9. Ezumi, 1961, p. 2.

10. Ezumi, 1961, p. 3. See also Havens, especially pp. 930–931.

11. Ezumi, 1961, p. 3.

12. This mission was codified by the 1936 passage of the *Shisōhan Hogo Kanshisatsu Hō* (Security Surveillance of Thought Crime Law).

13. Takagi, p. 119; Ezumi, 1961, p. 1.

14. Ezumi, 1961, p. 2; Takagi, p. 120.

15. Takagi, pp. 120–121. Ise Shrine, a Shintō facility near the major city of Nagoya, holds central importance in the ancient Japanese national foundation myth; as such, it was and continues to be the holiest of holy venues for veneration in the Shintō religion, and it is the location of the most important of a complicated series of ceremonies performed during the enthronement of new emperors.

16. Takagi, p. 121.

17. As Itonaga had yet to finish her novitiate at this point, she did not have a canonical name in religion.

18. See Takagi, p. 174; also Boxer, p. 144. See also Clulow, 2013.

19. Ezumi, 1961, p. 3.

20. Ezumi, 1961, p. 2.

21. Ezumi, 1961, pp. 3–4.

NOTES 445

22. These cabinets were standard-issue to primary and secondary schools from the end of the Meiji Period until 1945. Usually located near the front gates so that students could bow to them coming and going, they were typically a little larger than old-fashioned closable-door telephone booths. Any readers who have visited Père Lachaise Cemetery in Paris and seen the phone-booth-style standing crypts there may find the *hōanden* very similar to those in size, shape, and gray masonry appearance.

23. The somewhat (and perhaps purposely) nebulous term *Kokutai* (literally, "national body") is typically translated into English as "national polity" (see Bix). In ideological terms, it raises the concept of Japan above the mere political-ethnic formulation of "nation" to the level of a living religious and supernatural entity due veneration and ultimate loyalty by all imperial subjects. The term "ultranationalism," as employed to describe early- to mid-twentieth-century Japanese ideology, should be understood as being based upon this concept.

24. Itonaga, p. 28. Sister Uchino (1920–2007) took the name in religion of Sabina after her final vows in 1955. She spent the rest of her life with the Junshin Sisters, serving in important training and pedagogical posts. Her younger sister, Teiko, was a Junshin student killed at Ōhashi. See Archdiocese of Nagasaki, 2007.

FIRST BRIEFING

1. Twentieth Air Force, 1945b.
2. Farrell, p. 291.
3. Atomic Heritage Foundation, 2016.
4. Beser and Spangler, 2007, pp. 132–133.
5. Twentieth Air Force, 1945b.
6. Twentieth Air Force, 1945b. These cities were conglomerated after the war into the metropolis of Kitakyūshū.
7. Twentieth Air Force, 1945b.
8. Sweeney, p. 194.
9. U.S. Strategic Bombing Survey, Transportation Division, especially p. 69.
10. Farrell, p. 292.
11. U.S. Strategic Bombing Survey, Urban Areas Division, p. 7.
12. Nagasaki Aiming Point: Twentieth Air Force, 1945b, p. 1; Office of the Assistant Chief of Air Staff, Intelligence, 1944, p. M-4.
13. As noted in this book's companion volume, *Hiroshima: The Last Witnesses*, the 393rd Bomb Squadron was the official designation of the 509th Composite Group's B-29 element.
14. This was the result of a deliberate psychological tactic employed by the XXI BC during the weeks leading up to the Hiroshima mission. See LeMay and Yenne, p. 150.
15. Beser and Spangler, p. 132.

446 NOTES

16. U.S. Strategic Bombing Survey, Physical Damage Division, 1947b, vol. I, p. 30.
17. See Tibbets, pp. 148–149, and Sweeney, 100–101.
18. See Sheftall, 2024.
19. Olivi, p. 179.
20. Power was provided by the aircraft's onboard generators during the ingress flight and by the bomb's own self-contained batteries during its final drop. See Ashworth, 2005, p. 19.
21. Sweeney, p. 191.
22. Olivi, p. 97. Commander Ashworth inserted the red firing plugs around 0400 on August 9, fifteen minutes after wheels up from Tinian.
23. Sweeney, pp. 195–196.

REPORTS FROM HIROSHIMA

1. See Nakajima, 2019; also Gluck, 1985; Fujitani, 1996; et al.
2. Daniels, p. 120.
3. See Ōta, 2022.
4. See Kushner, 2005.
5. Coincidentally, this was the day Nazi Germany invaded Poland, igniting World War Two.
6. See Ōta.
7. Ide, 2016, p. 17.
8. See *Hiroshima Sensai*, 1971, vol. 3, p. 260.
9. Tsuchiyama, 2016, pp. 22–23.
10. *"Hiroshima wo shōbaku"("Hiroshima hit with incendiaries"*), August 7, 1945.
11. Braw, 1991, p. 16.
12. U.S. Strategic Bombing Survey, Physical Damage Division, 1947b, vol. I, p. 14 (medical college buildings hit by earlier raids [Aug 1]); U.S. Strategic Bombing Survey, Medical Division, p. 3 (three students at the medical college killed in the August 1 raid).
13. Ide, p. 17.
14. Ministry of Education, Culture, Sports, Science and Technology–Japan, 2008.
15. This is the same plant that was responsible for the mercury poisoning of Minamata Bay in the 1950s and 1960s.
16. See Nishimori, 1995.
17. Nagasaki Junior High School was consolidated with Kenjo to become the coed Nagasaki Higashi High School in 1948.
18. The Gunges' home was only a few blocks east of Judge Ishida's first official residence in Katsuyama-machi.
19. See Japan Kyushu Tourist, no date; Ministry of Land, Infrastructure, Transport and Tourism, no date.
20. This was (and is) the Japanese equivalent of the U.S. Federal Reserve System.

NOTES

21. U.S. Strategic Bombing Survey, Office of the Chairman, p. 6. See also U.S. Strategic Bombing Survey, Civilian Defense Division, p. 85.

DIGGING

1. U.S. Strategic Bombing Survey, Civilian Defense Division, p. 68.
2. These were civilians not already engaged in full-time munitions plant work, et al.
3. Some more sophisticated variants of L- or U-shaped shelters (with two entranceways—one on either end of the main gallery) had what were known as "baffle walls," freestanding surfaces usually constructed of concrete or thick wood beams and set in front of the entranceways for an added layer of protection. These were similar in appearance and sheltering function to the wooden walls provided in rodeo rings or bullfight arenas for people to run to and hide behind when being pursued by enraged bulls.
4. U.S. Strategic Bombing Survey, Office of the Chairman, p. 3.
5. U.S. Strategic Bombing Survey, Civilian Defense Division, p. 12.
6. U.S. Strategic Bombing Survey, Urban Areas Division, p. 5. See also U.S. Strategic Bombing Survey, Civilian Defense Division, 1947, pp. 12–13: Nagasaki City received siren-sounding orders from three sources: (1) the prefectural office (when cleared by Western Army HQ); (2) the local army garrison HQ (ditto); and (3) Western Army HQ; p. 13: "Radio announcements [regarding air raid threats] were made by the Western Army headquarters, from which a transmitter broke into the normal public [NHK] broadcasts."
7. This may be merely anecdotal, but I have heard that there are only a handful of *yuiwata*-qualified hairdressers still alive today.
8. Szasz, 2015.
9. See Kushner et al.
10. *Akagami* literally means "red paper"—and was so named after the pink color of the stationery on which draft notices were printed.

NERVES AND GUILT

1. Tibbets, p. 246.
2. Sweeney, p. 200.
3. Sweeney, p. 200.
4. Sweeney, pp. 185–186.
5. Sweeney, p. 195.
6. Alvarez, pp. 144–145.
7. Alvarez, p. 144.
8. Knebel and Bailey, 1960, p. 223. (N.B.: "Atomic Bomb Command" was a spurious military organization.)
9. *Hiroshima Sensai*, vol. 1, p. 82; Kubo, 1990, p. 7.
10. Hiroshima/Nagasaki Editorial Committee for the Record of Atomic Bomb Damage, 1979, p. 488.

448 NOTES

11. This is only conjecture on the author's part, but a likely reason for Nishina's sense of urgency in this matter might have been because he wanted civilian authorities to know about the bomb in case the Japanese military tried to bury the investigation team's findings in the interest of maintaining national fighting morale.

12. *Hiroshima Sensai*, vol. 1, p. 82.

13. See Hasegawa, 2007.

14. *Nagasaki Sensai*, vol. 1, p. 142.

15. This directive was codified in the following line of the Home Ministry's "Air Defense Creed for Final Victory": "We are all warriors defending our nation. We shall remain at our posts even at the cost of our lives." See Home Ministry, 1944.

16. *Nagasaki Sensai*, vol. 1, p. 142.

17. *Nagasaki Sensai*, vol. 1, p. 143.

18. *Nagasaki Sensai*, vol. 1, p. 143.

TAKEOFF

1. Olivi, p. 114.

2. Olivi, p. 97.

3. Beser, p. 129.

4. Atomic Heritage Foundation, 2016.

5. Beser, p. 101.

6. Krauss and Krauss, 2005, pp. 66–67.

7. "Lord Cheshire, World War II Hero Who Founded Homes for Sick, 74," 1992.

8. Laurence, 1945. Beser and Spangler, p. 125.

9. Atomic Heritage Foundation, 2016.

10. After its declassification, this volume was eventually published by the University of California Press as *The Los Alamos Primer*.

11. Krauss and Krauss, pp. 175–176.

12. Waldman participated in the Hiroshima mission as the photography plane's designated Fastax operator, but the six feet of film he purportedly shot were never successfully developed. Atomic Heritage Foundation, no date-b.

13. Farrell, p. 300.

14. Atomic Heritage Foundation, no date-a, p. 20.

15. Tibbets, p. 247.

16. Tibbets, p. 247.

17. Sweeney, p. 198.

18. Olivi, p. 95. As Olivi states in his memoir, this is a "to the best of my memory" quotation.

19. The Pumpkin bombs were the exact weight and shape of the Fat Man design, although filled with conventional Torpex explosive compound in lieu of a plutonium core. Each crew in the 393rd Bomb Squadron qualified for strike

NOTES

plane duty by flying multiple Pumpkin missions. Another objective of these missions was to saturate the Japanese air defense grid with single-plane and small-formation daytime penetrations in the weeks leading up to the actual atomic missions in the hope of inducing laxity and exhaustion on the part of Japanese observation post personnel and radar watchers.

20. Until Sweeney received his mission command orders on August 7, he had actually expected—from the beginning and as a matter of course—that Tibbets would repeat his role of mission commander and strike plane pilot for the second mission.

21. See Zellen, 2020.

22. Doll was Project Alberta's "fusing team leader." See American Institute of Physics, no date.

23. Beser, p. 131.

24. Tibbets, p. 247.

25. Beser, p. 131.

26. Weather planes and a spare takeoff at 0230: Craven and Cate, p. 719. Weather conditions over North Field: Beser, p. 135.

27. Isolated from the rest of the aircraft's pressurization system, the tail gunner's position maintained its own pressurization behind an airtight hatch. The unpressurized forward bomb bay was separated from the flight deck by a similar hatch, a good view of the operation of which is provided in the film *The Right Stuff* when Chuck Yeager uses the hatch to access the cockpit of his Bell X-1 rocket plane.

28. Tibbets, p. 247.

29. Tibbets, p. 247.

30. Laurence, 1945.

31. White Sands Missile Range Museum, no date.

INGRESS

1. Olivi, p. 96.

2. Laurence, 1945.

3. Laurence, 1945.

4. Sweeney, p. 209; Olivi, p. 98.

5. Beser, p. 132.

6. Laurence, 1945.

7. The aircraft was still flying at a relatively low altitude at this point, so its crew cabins were not yet pressurized.

8. Tibbets, p. 248.

9. Olivi, p. 97.

10. Olivi, p. 97.

11. Fat Man fusing details after Ashworth et al.

12. Ashworth, p. 20.

13. Sweeney, p. 210.

14. Ashworth, p. 20, and Sweeney, p. 210.
15. Ashworth, p. 20.
16. Tōgō, 1956, p. 316.
17. U.S. Strategic Bombing Survey, Office of the Chairman, pp. 31–32.
18. See R. B. Frank, 1999, et al.
19. R. B. Frank, 1999, p. 297.
20. See Sheftall, 2005.
21. Toland, 1970, p. 957.
22. See Butow; R. B. Frank (1999, 2016); et al. The War Department order authorizing the 509th CG to begin deploying the bombs against Japanese targets "after about August 3" was actually issued one day before the Potsdam Declaration. From this wording, it can be interpreted that America was giving Japan a one-week grace period to accept the Potsdam Declaration's "unconditional" surrender terms before—as per President Truman's Potsdam warning—the atomic "rain of ruin" was set to commence. The Manhattan Project, no date–C.
23. U.S. Strategic Bombing Survey, Office of the Chairman, p. 13.
24. Tōgō, pp. 289, 296, 298–299, 301–302.
25. Kort, 2007, p. 371.
26. Butow, p. 145; Toland, p. 986.
27. Farrell, p. 308. See also Glantz.
28. Frontline Kwantung Army units had been stripped to 30-percent-strength levels by this point. Toland, p. 986.
29. U.S. Strategic Bombing Survey, Office of the Chairman, p. 8.
30. U.S. Strategic Bombing Survey, Office of the Chairman, p. 8.
31. Sweeney, p. 211; Beser & Spangler, p. 136.
32. Olivi, p. 118.
33. Sweeney, p. 212. "According to [Group Captain Leonard] Cheshire, [Major] Hopkins climbed to 39,000 feet approaching Yakoshima [sic] and stayed at that altitude, which was 9,000 feet higher than where he should have been. He commenced making fifty-mile doglegs in the area of Yakoshima [sic], instead of circling the southwest corner of the island [as Sweeney had directed him to do in the briefing hut at the end of the final briefing]."
34. Sweeney, p. 211; Tibbets, p. 248. In most historical accounts of the mission, Sweeney has tended to take blame for ignoring Tibbets' fifteen-minutes directive. However, Ashworth later confessed in a 2005 memoir that he was also responsible for pressuring Sweeney to loiter so long over the rallying point, as he had wanted "to get all three planes together and make the mission perfect" (Ashworth, p. 20). Amazingly, neither this—nor the other snafus that were to follow in the mission—ended up adversely affecting the careers of the two officers. Both went on to achieve flag rank postwar.

NOTES   451

A PEACEFUL THURSDAY MORNING

1. This is the same facility where Professor Mimura Yoshitaka of Hiroshima University of Literature and Science delivered his prophetic lecture on the feasibility of atomic weapons to a gathering of Akatsuki officers on the evening of August 5. See Sheftall, 2024.
2. *Hiroshima Sensai*, vol. 1, p. 84.
3. *Hiroshima Sensai*, vol. 1, p. 85.
4. *Nagasaki Sensai*, vol. 1, p. 138.
5. *Nagasaki Sensai*, vol. 1, p. 144.
6. *Nagasaki Sensai*, vol. 1, p. 144.
7. H. Ishida, 1949, p. 67.
8. H. Ishida, 1949, p. 64.
9. M. Ishida, 1949, p. 3.
10. M. Ishida, p. 3.
11. Kano and Kiridōshi, p. 102.
12. Hatanaka, 1961, p. 7.
13. Kamogawa, 1961, p. 104.
14. See Sheftall, 2005.
15. Hatanaka, p. 7.
16. In Junshin practice, Sisters would receive their Christian names after taking their final lifetime vows—the last step to completing their process of becoming full-fledged members of the order. After the final lifetime vow ceremony, they would be referred to as "Sister (Christian name)" in daily order life as well as by their students, while the order members who had yet to take their final vows would be referred to as "Sister (Japanese family name)." For example, in the summer of 1945, Tagawa was already "Sister Christina" ("Kuristina-ane"), while Sister Yoshi was "Sister Itonaga" ("Itonaga-ane").
17. Hatanaka, p. 7.

"CAN ANY OTHER GODDAMNED THING GO WRONG?"

1. See Tsutsui, 2021.
2. Beahan, p. 31.
3. See Olivi, p. 121.
4. Olivi, p. 121; Atomic Heritage Foundation, no date–a, p. 23.
5. Sweeney, p. 213.
6. Sweeney, p. 213.
7. Sweeney, p. 213.
8. Beser, p. 132.
9. Sweeney, p. 214.
10. Olivi, p. 121.
11. Beser, p. 133.
12. Atomic Heritage Foundation, no date–a, p. 23.

NOTES

13. Beser, p. 133.
14. Sweeney, p. 215.
15. Sweeney, p. 215.
16. Sweeney, p. 215.
17. See Olivi.
18. Van Pelt and Albury, 2005, p. 197.
19. In his testimony, Albury mentions several Japanese towns the strike formation passed over during its southerly ingress toward Nagasaki after leaving Ashiya airspace. However, the geographical names that he recalled incorrectly and accordingly transcribed incorrectly correspond to no locations either in northern Kyushu or in Japan itself.
20. *Nagasaki Sensai*, vol. 1, p. 162.
21. *Nagasaki Sensai*, vol. 1, p. 159.
22. Twentieth Air Force, 1945b.
23. Beahan, p. 31.
24. In one of the many mysteries surrounding the Nagasaki bombing, all local meteorological records (see *Nagasaki Sensai*, vol. 1, p. 137) and survivor testimony references to the weather on August 9 report clear skies over the city at the time of the attack. It is possible—if not likely—that the poor visibility reported by Beahan and others on *Bockscar* might have been caused by normal summertime high humidity and airborne particulates—an effect that would have been greatly magnified by distance and the relatively shallow downward angle of the line of sight from the approaching aircraft during most of its bomb run.
25. Atomic Heritage Foundation, no date–a, p. 24.
26. Beahan, p. 31.
27. Tibbets, pp. 249–250; Atomic Heritage Foundation, no date–a, p. 24.
28. Groves describes the original AP as being "in the city, east of the harbor" (Groves, p. 343). According to Tibbets (pp. 249–250), "The approach over the target—and there was fuel enough for but one—was made on radar. The aiming point in the center of the city of Nagasaki was missed by almost a mile and a half, the weapon detonating over the Urakami river valley instead of the heart of town."
29. Sweeney, p. 217.
30. Beser, pp. 133–134.
31. Sweeney, p. 217; Atomic Heritage Foundation, no date–a, p. 25.
32. Atomic Heritage Foundation, no date–a, p. 25; Beahan, p. 31; Ashworth, p. 20.
33. Atomic Heritage Foundation, no date–a, p. 25.
34. Sweeney, p. 218.

DETONATION

1. *Nagasaki Sensai*, vol. 1, p. 137.
2. Tateno, 2016, p. 52.

NOTES 453

3. Hatanaka, p. 8.
4. Hatanaka, p. 8.
5. Takagi, p. 170.
6. Takagi, p. 170.
7. *Nagasaki Sensai*, vol. 2, p. 401.
8. M. Ishida, p. 4.
9. M. Ishida, p. 4.
10. Kano and Kiridōshi, p. 29.
11. Kano and Kiridōshi, p. 30.
12. *Nagasaki Sensai*, vol. 1, p. 144.
13. U.S. Strategic Bombing Survey, Civilian Defense Division, 1947, p. 83.
14. See Sheftall, 2024.
15. U.S. Strategic Bombing Survey, Civilian Defense Division, 1947, p. 84.
16. *Nagasaki Sensai*, vol. 1, p. 145.
17. *Nagasaki Sensai*, vol. 1, p. 145.
18. *Nagasaki Sensai*, vol. 1, p. 182.
19. *Nagasaki Sensai*, vol. 1, pp. 145–146.
20. Hiroshima/Nagasaki Editorial Committee for the Record of Atomic Bomb Damage, p. 6.
21. "four thousand degrees Celsius": International Campaign to Abolish Nuclear Weapons (ICAN), no date. "Roof tiles": U.S. Strategic Bombing Survey, Office of the Chairman, 1946, p. 25.
22. See Nagasaki National Peace Memorial Hall for the Atomic Bomb Victims, no date.
23. ICAN.
24. ICAN.
25. U.S. Strategic Bombing Survey, Office of the Chairman, 1946, p. 33.
26. See Nagasaki National Peace Memorial Hall for the Atomic Bomb Victims.
27. Olivi, p. 125.
28. Laurence, 1945.
29. Atomic Heritage Foundation, no date–a, p. 25.
30. Olivi, p. 125; Beser, p. 134; Laurence, 1945; et al.
31. Sweeney, p. 219.
32. Laurence, 1945.
33. Sweeney, p. 219.

A SEA OF FIRE

1. There were other shelters for Mori-machi's seventeen-hundred-fifty-odd employees (and POWs) in Yanagawa Park on the opposite bank of the Urakami. This spot was accessed by a bridge whose eastern foot was on the southwestern corner of the plant compound.

2. U.S. Strategic Bombing Survey, Civilian Defense Division, 1947, p. 47.
3. Kano and Kiridōshi, p. 35.
4. Kano and Kiridōshi, p. 43.
5. J. Ishida, 2010, p. 134.
6. J. Ishida, 2010, p. 135.
7. M. Ishida, pp. 6–7.
8. M. Ishida, p. 12.
9. Kamogawa, p. 104.
10. Kamogawa, p. 105.

THE NAGASAKI CABLE

1. *Nagasaki Sensai*, vol. 1, p. 183.
2. U.S. Strategic Bombing Survey, Civilian Defense Division, 1947, p. 41.
3. The witness—cited in Asada, p. 490—was the emperor's grand chamberlain, Fujita Hisanori.
4. Asada, p. 490.
5. Hoshina, 1975, p. 239; Tōgō, p. 315.
6. Tōgō, p. 315.
7. Kawamura, 2015, pp. 185–186.
8. Kawamura, p. 186.
9. "The one hundred million" (*ichioku*) was metaphorical shorthand for "the Japanese people" in contemporary propaganda sloganeering. The population of the Home Islands at the time was, in fact, more on the order of seventy million, with another twenty million nominal Korean "subjects" on the Korean Peninsula.
10. For a discussion of Japanese leadership's fears of Communist revolution as a result of such chaos, see R. B. Frank, 2016, and Yellen, 2013.
11. U.S. Strategic Bombing Survey, Office of the Chairman, p. 9.
12. U.S. Strategic Bombing Survey, Office of the Chairman, p. 9; R. B. Frank, 1999, p. 291.
13. Craig, 1967, pp. 73–74.
14. R. B. Frank, 1999, p. 290. See also Marx, pp. 59–60; and Kristof, 2003. Of McDilda's testimony, Kristof writes: "One of the great tales of World War II concerns an American fighter pilot named Marcus McDilda who was shot down on Aug. 8 and brutally interrogated about the atomic bombs. He knew nothing, but under torture he 'confessed' that the U.S. had 100 more nuclear weapons and planned to destroy Tokyo 'in the next few days.' The war minister informed the Cabinet of this grim news—but still adamantly opposed surrender."
15. Craig, p. 134; *Nagasaki Sensai*, vol. 1, p. 188.
16. R. B. Frank, 1999, p. 290.
17. *Nagasaki Sensai*, vol. 1, pp. 181–182.
18. *Nagasaki Sensai*, vol. 1, p. 188.

NOTES

IN KONPIRA'S SHADOW

1. Laurence, 1945.
2. Sweeney, p. 220.
3. Sweeney, p. 220.
4. Sweeney, p. 220.
5. See Tibbets, Sweeney.
6. Sweeney, p. 222; Olivi p. 132.
7. During normal 509th operations (e.g., training missions, Pumpkin bomb missions, etc.), First Lieutenant Albury and Second Lieutenant Olivi were the aircraft commander/pilot and copilot, respectively, of *The Great Artiste* (which had been so named in recognition of bombardier Beahan's skills behind the Norden bombsight). For Special Mission #16, the entire crew of *Bockscar*, outside of Sweeney and the Project Alberta people, was, in fact, Albury's team from *The Great Artiste*, which on this day was being flown by the normal *Bockscar* crew and commanded by Captain Fred Bock. During the Hiroshima mission, when *The Great Artiste* first performed its instrumentation-plane role and was commanded/piloted by Sweeney and copiloted by Albury, Olivi had been unceremoniously bumped from the flight to make way for extra Project Alberta passengers.
8. Olivi, p. 132.
9. Sweeney, p. 223.
10. Olivi, p. 133.
11. Sweeney, p. 224.
12. Sweeney, p. 225.
13. Olivi, p. 133; Beser, p. 135.
14. Beser, p. 135.
15. Sweeney, p. 225.
16. Laurence, 1946, p. 242.
17. See Gunge, 1962.
18. U.S. Strategic Bombing Survey, Civilian Defense Division, 1947, p. 41. "Since the city was in the 'release-from-alarm' or 'alert' stage at the time the atomic bomb was dropped, the entire guard rescue unit (*keibitai*) was concentrated at its headquarters (which was not damaged) directly across from the control center. . . . This unit was one of the first civilian defense services to arrive at the incident, but due to lack of training and proper equipment, plus the extremely small number of available personnel, approximately 60 men, very little actual rescue work could be accomplished, so the men were used principally to control traffic (personnel and vehicular); to maintain a semblance of order; to provide information; and to help in road clearance.
19. U.S. Strategic Bombing Survey, Physical Damage Division, 1947b, vol. I, p. 12. "The city's new and yet untested professional fire department was unable to

NOTES

penetrate north of the railroad station, 8,000 feet from GZ, due to debris and intense fire." See U.S. Strategic Bombing Survey, Physical Damage Division, 1947b, vol. III, p. 120.

20. See Matsui, 1966.

21. Tateno-san recalls only Mitsuko's workplace as having been heavily industrial in nature; the only sites on the eastern side of Nagasaki harbor that fit that criterion and were close enough to commute to on foot from Fukuro-machi for a lunch break would have been Mori-machi or the main Kawanami shipyard facility near Ōura (which also employed large numbers of POWs from Fukuoka Camp No. 14). See Clarke; Broderick & Palmer, 2015; et al.

22. If Mr. Tateno had, in fact, been at his workplace at the Mitsubishi shipyards, it is highly doubtful that he would have walked from there to Fukuro-machi. It is possible that to reach the eastern shore, he rode across Nagasaki harbor in a company boat—a conveyance that the author has heard mentioned in other testimony (interview with Nagasaki survivor and former Mitsubishi shipyard employee Okuda Hagiko in Katsumata, Tokyo, in September 2017).

23. Tateno, p. 53.

24. Tateno, p. 53.

FALSE TWILIGHT INTO NIGHT

1. Itonaga, p. 29.

2. Itonaga, p. 29.

3. Itonaga, p. 29.

4. Itonaga, p. 31.

5. *Nagasaki Sensai*, vol. 1, pp. 360–361. Assumption of Mary preparations: Takase, p. 78.

6. A full discussion of the theological, cultural, and psychological ramifications of Urakami Cathedral's destruction—and of its eventual contested reconstruction—is, unfortunately, beyond the scope of this already lengthy volume. Readers who are interested in this subject are encouraged to consult: Diehl, 2011; Diehl, 2018; C. Kataoka, 1996; Nagai, 1949; Takase; et al.

7. Itonaga, p. 30.

8. Itonaga, p. 30.

9. Itonaga, p. 30.

10. Takagi, p. 200.

11. Hatanaka, pp. 9–10.

12. The crude slit trenches dug at various points on the school grounds were to be used by people caught in the open by surprise air raids. When campus personnel had the forewarning of sirens, they were supposed to use the riverbank dugout shelter.

13. Takagi, p. 204.

14. M. Ishida, p. 13.

NOTES

15. M. Ishida, p. 14.
16. M. Ishida, p. 15.
17. M. Ishida, p. 19.

THE LONGEST NIGHT

1. Beser, p. 136.
2. Beser, pp. 135–136; Olivi, pp. 135–136.
3. From 1942 to 1945, the "Mighty Eighth"—operating from bases in England—single-handedly carried the U.S. strategic bombing effort in Northern Europe, with Doolittle in command for the latter half of that period. After the Nazi surrender, the Eighth Air Force was redeployed to Okinawa to begin bombing operations against the Japanese Home Islands. Visiting Doolittle: Sweeney, pp. 226–227.
4. It can be reasonably assumed that the discussion used as reference material the 1944 air objective folder maps for the Sasebo-Tsushima area (inclusive of Nagasaki), which would have been found in any in-theater USAAF headquarters at the time. As noted in earlier chapters, the Mitsubishi facilities in both Mori-machi and Ōhashi were prominently indicated on these maps as high-priority Nagasaki-area targets.
5. Olivi, p. 136.
6. Olivi, p. 136.
7. Sweeney, p. 229.
8. Olivi, p. 137; Beser, p. 137.
9. Olivi, p. 137.
10. Beser, p. 137; Sweeney, p. 230.
11. Tibbets was famously resentful of—and seemingly incensed by—what he saw as Sweeney's attempts to whitewash embarrassing details out of his accounts of the Nagasaki mission. In his third autobiography, *Return of the* Enola Gay (1998), for example, Tibbets makes numerous objections to—and refutations of—claims made in Sweeney's autobiographical apologia, *War's End*, published one year earlier.
12. Beahan, p. 31.
13. Tibbets, p. 250. See also Dietz, 2016, p. 491.
14. Tibbets, p. 250.
15. Tōgō, p. 317.
16. Kunaichō, 2016, p. 753.
17. Asada, p. 494.
18. Asada, p. 494.
19. Asada, p. 494.
20. Asada, pp. 494–495.
21. U.S. Strategic Bombing Survey, Office of the Chairman, p. 8.
22. Barshay, 1998, p. 55.
23. International Military Tribunal for the Far East, 1946.

24. This was a fate that befell Suzuki's Navy minister, Yonai Mitsumasa, during his own brief tenure as premier in 1940. See Storry, 1957, pp. 264–265.
25. The privy council was a traditionally archconservative advisory body that consulted directly with the emperor on critical matters of state. Many of its members were former prime ministers. What remained of this body's influence over matters of the state, particularly regarding the war, was largely usurped by the formation of the Supreme War Council in August 1944.
26. Paraphrased from memory by Sakomizu in postwar interrogation. U.S. Strategic Bombing Survey, Office of the Chairman, p. 9.
27. U.S. Strategic Bombing Survey, Office of the Chairman, p. 9.
28. Thomas, 2023, p. 163.
29. U.S. Strategic Bombing Survey, Office of the Chairman, p. 9.
30. Tōgō, p. 321.
31. Kunaichō, p. 755.
32. Nagasaki Prefecture, 2021.
33. The same phenomenon occurred on the high roof of Nagasaki Station some nine hundred meters to the northwest. *Nagasaki Sensai*, vol. 1, p. 192.
34. *Nagasaki Sensai*, vol. 1, p. 191.
35. *Nagasaki Sensai*, vol. 1, p. 193.
36. *Nagasaki Sensai*, vol. 1, p. 195.
37. H. Ishida, 1949, pp. 75–76.
38. H. Ishida, 1949, p. 81.
39. H. Ishida, 1949, p. 83.

THE DAY AFTER

1. The Nagasaki temperature at midnight on August 9 to 10, 1945, was 24.5 degrees Celsius (Naval Medical Research Institute, 1945). This temperature would not have been experienced as cold or even chilly by an uninjured, healthy individual. But it is likely that Masako experienced it as such in her injured and exhausted state at the time, with the sensation of cold probably also exacerbated by the damp, clammy air in the tunnel.
2. M. Ishida, p. 22.
3. This soldier might have been from the nearby Konpira-summit-based 4th Company of the 130th Antiaircraft Artillery Regiment. See *Nagasaki Sensai*, vol. 1, p. 162.
4. Kano and Kiridōshi, p. 49.
5. This "numbing" is an initial psychological response to the horror of the bombing that is very common in hibakusha testimony, as well as in that of combat veterans and disaster survivors in general. See Lifton, 1963; Lifton, 1968; Ōta, Mine, and Yoshimine, 2014; Sheftall, 2023; Sheftall, 2024; et al.
6. M. Ishida, p. 26.

NOTES

7. M. Ishida, pp. 26–27. The Inasa Bridge was an Urakami River crossing near the southern edge of the Mitsubishi Mori-machi compound.
8. U.S. Strategic Bombing Survey, Civilian Defense Division, 1947, p. 47.
9. M. Ishida, p. 31.
10. M. Ishida, p. 33.
11. M. Ishida, p. 34.
12. M. Ishida, p. 35.

RUINS

1. There are substantial passages and explanations of this in Sheftall, 2024.
2. Another forty thousand bomb victims in Hiroshima would die by the end of the 1945, bringing the total number of deaths caused by Little Boy to 140,000.
3. In terms of actual distance over roads extant at the time, Ōmura was thirty-three kilometers from Nagasaki, Isahaya was thirty kilometers, and Sasebo was sixty-four kilometers.
4. U.S. Strategic Bombing Survey, Civilian Defense Division, 1947, p. 48.
5. U.S. Strategic Bombing Survey, Civilian Defense Division, 1947, p. 36.
6. Milam, 2001, p. 28, et al. Milam, a U.S. Marine Corps corporal with the occupation forces, claims that this smell lingered over the Urakami Valley until the following winter—testimony that is corroborated by that of U.S. Strategic Bombing Survey teams that visited the city.
7. Nagasaki Prefecture reported a total of 19,743 dead as of September 1, 1945. This number was calculated by the number of cremation permits issued by police as required by law. *Nagasaki Sensai*, vol. 1, p. 389.
8. The Manhattan Project, no date–a.
9. Shirabe, pp. 145–146. See also Kanō and Kiridōshi, p. 69. Kiridōshi (Kanō) Michiko recalls that families in Nagasaki after the bombing burned their own dead. No one had "funerals" worthy of the name.
10. Milam, p. 28.
11. Itonaga, p. 32.
12. Takagi, p. 221.
13. Itonaga, p. 41.
14. Uchino, 1961, p. 55.
15. Hachida, p. 150.
16. Very few mothers came to the site in the early period, because the Urakami area was still perceived by the public as being dangerous. It was almost all fathers who came. Almost all, to a man, expressed their thanks to Ezumi and to the school. Many of them urged Ezumi to rebuild the school, stating that this was not only their own hope but that of their daughters as well.
17. U.S. Strategic Bombing Survey, Office of the Chairman, p. 9.
18. Stimson and Bundy, p. 741.
19. LeMay and Yenne, p. 202.

NOTES

20. U.S. Strategic Bombing Survey, Office of the Chairman, p. 9.
21. U.S. Strategic Bombing Survey, Office of the Chairman, p. 9.
22. Asada, p. 496.
23. U.S. Strategic Bombing Survey, Office of the Chairman, p. 9. This semi-verbatim quotation is based on the postwar interrogation of Chief Cabinet Secretary Sakomizu.
24. U.S. Strategic Bombing Survey, Office of the Chairman, p. 9.
25. The full text of the surrender broadcast is included in this volume in appendix B. Appendix C contains the text of the emperor's parallel surrender order to his Army and Navy personnel. Unlike the NHK broadcast, this message makes no mention of the atomic bomb as a reason for the cessation of hostilities, instead emphasizing the Soviet threat as the primary justification for this decision.
26. The American Presidency Project, no date.
27. The American Presidency Project.

AUGUST 15

1. Tateno, p. 55.
2. See Smethurst, 1974.
3. C. R. Smith, p. 27. See also Sheftall, 2005; Sheftall, 2024.
4. The attribution of humanlike sentiment to inanimate objects has roots in ancient native animist beliefs and is still quite common among Japanese today.
5. Tateno, p. 57.
6. U.S. Strategic Bombing Survey, Office of the Chairman, 1946, p. 8.
7. H. Ishida, 1949, p. 91.
8. H. Ishida, 1949, p. 92.
9. H. Ishida, 1949, p. 96.
10. H. Ishida, 1949, p. 93.
11. M. Ishida, p. 44.
12. M. Ishida, p. 45.
13. M. Ishida, p. 45.

LEARNING TO LOVE COCA-COLA

1. M. Ishida, p. 46.
2. M. Ishida, p. 46.
3. See Hachiya, 1955.
4. M. Ishida, p. 48. The hospital and its parent institution would shortly lose the "Imperial" designation from their respective names.
5. Yokote, p. 191; Okada, 2014.
6. Recognition—and simmering resentment—of the realities of this arrangement has been a driving psychological force behind Japanese conservative politics and sociocultural commentary ever since.

NOTES

461

7. C. R. Smith, p. 24.
8. C. R. Smith, p. 24.
9. For comprehensive studies of the policies and effects of the Allied occupation of Japan, see Takemae, 2002; Shibusawa, 2006; Dower, 2000; and Tsurumi, 1970.
10. C. R. Smith, p. 25.
11. C. R. Smith, p. 29.
12. C. R. Smith, p. 28.
13. C. R. Smith, p. 29.
14. Itonaga, pp. 48–49.
15. While the brunt of this typhoon bypassed Nagasaki—aside from producing torrential rains in the area—it landed a direct hit on Hiroshima, causing several thousand deaths among atom-bomb survivors there, as well as among Japanese first responders and International Red Cross personnel; see Sheftall, 2024. Somewhat ironically, the impact of the Makurazaki Typhoon on Hiroshima had the add-on effect of scouring away much of the city's fallout-contaminated topsoil—a windfall benefit, so to speak, that was denied Nagasaki, with effects that continue to linger to this day.
16. Kano and Kiridōshi, p. 109.
17. U.S. Strategic Bombing Survey, Office of the Chairman, p. 19.
18. Kano and Kiridōshi, p. 68.
19. Kano and Kiridōshi, p. 256.
20. This film with English subtitles is viewable as *Nagasaki: Memories of My Son* on Amazon Prime Video.
21. Kano and Kiridōshi, pp. 303–305.

DR. NAGAI'S FOOTPRINTS

1. *Nagasaki Sensai*, vol. 1, p. 635.
2. C. Kataoka, p. 73.
3. Translation from Diehl, 2018, p. 73.
4. Nagai converted to Christianity during his courtship of his future wife, Midori, the daughter of an old Urakami *kakure Kirishitan* family.
5. Diehl, 2018, pp. 74–75, et al.
6. Another critical—and likely related—step in raising awareness among American Catholics of Urakami's plight was made when two American prelates—Bishop (later Cardinal) John F. O'Hara of Buffalo, New York, and Bishop Michael J. Reddy of Columbus, Ohio—visited Nagasaki and the ruins of Urakami Cathedral and donated funds for the construction of a temporary chapel on the site in July 1946. See Thornton, 1963, p. 259, and Hamada, 2017.
7. Y. Kataoka, 1976, pp. iii–iv. This same photographic appendix was also forced on the Occupation Era Japanese publishers of a bestselling 1951 volume of kamikaze memoirs. (See Inoguchi & Nakajima, 1951.)

8. See Braw; Diehl, 2011, 2018.
9. See Otake, 2015.
10. *"Genbaku wo aruku: Himeguri an'nai: 3,"* 2005.
11. This is a reference to Fr. Francis Xavier's first landfall in Kagoshima in 1549.
12. As Sister Itonaga Yoshi later explained to me, when the Junshin pyre site was being cleared away after the final cremation, it was noticed that there were still small bits of bone mixed in with the ashes on the ground. The Junshin Sisters saved this material, which is now interred under the Holy Mother of Mercy statue.
13. Note the school's new post-1948 national-education-reforms naming.
14. *"Urusura Itonaga Yoshi shūdōin,"* 2022.

NEGOTIATED MEMORY

1. *"Urusura Itonaga Yoshi shūdōin."*
2. J. Ishida, 2010, p. 139.
3. Braw, p. 92.
4. Quoted in Braw, pp. 92–93.
5. Quoted in Braw, p. 93.
6. Yokote, pp. 205–206.

THE OTHER SIDE OF KONPIRA

1. Author interviews with former Komaba resident Shimohira Sakue at RECNA Nagasaki in August 2018 and August 2019.
2. Shirabe, p. 154.
3. Shirabe, p. 155.
4. See Sheftall, 2024.
5. Shirabe, p. 155.
6. Shirabe, pp. 155–156. For details on the 1949 Atom-bombed Cities Reconstruction Law, see Sheftall, 2024; Zwigenberg, 2014; et al.
7. This ossuary, and its symbolic importance, is discussed at length in Sheftall, 2024.

EPILOGUE

1. Nobel Prize, 2024.The full text of this announcement is in appendix D of this volume.
2. See Katō, 1997; Nosaka, 1997; et al.
3. See Yamazaki, 2016; Abe, 2006; Sheftall, 2005; et al.
4. Correll, 2004.
5. See Washburn, 1995, et al.
6. See Linenthal, 1995.

NOTES

7. See Harwit, 1996. For an account of the NASM Hiroshima negotiations from the Japanese side, see T. Hiraoka, 1996. Historian John Dower also identifies the Peace Museum artifacts as the most symbolically and emotionally problematic aspect of the NASM's proposal from the perspective of its critics. See Dower, 1995.
8. Harwit, pp. 238–245.
9. Some letters to the museum from angry veterans cited hyperinflated figures of one to two million American casualties purportedly saved by the bombs. See Harwit, pp. 239–240. On a personal note, and for what it is worth, I would be remiss if I did not mention here that, on a handful of occasions during my thirty-eight-year-long sojourn in Japan, elderly Japanese of war-service age—including several trained kamikaze pilots and an actual Hiroshima survivor whose mother was gravely wounded by Little Boy—have told me, sotto voce, that they have no doubt that their own lives were saved by the bombs.
10. Harwit, p. 239.
11. See Lifton and Mitchell, 1995, pp. xiv–xv.
12. See G. S. Smith.
13. My characterization of Harwit and his colleagues as "tweedy" is based on Hiraoka's remembered observations of his Smithsonian counterparts from their early-1990s meetings as related to me in an interview I had with His Honor in Hiroshima in February 2017. Although he believed in their moral sincerity and good intentions, he feared they were out of their depth in terms of the political skills and sheer chutzpah that would be necessary to pull off such an ambitious and controversial exhibit as the one they were proposing. See also Hiraoka, p. 6. Republican backlash: Harwit, pp. 245–250, et al.
14. For a useful analysis of the marshaling of these forces against the NASM, see Washburn.
15. In the midst of the controversy, Clinton went on record saying that he approved of Truman's decision to use atomic weapons to end the war. (Whether Truman actually "decided" anything about Hiroshima is a discussion for another time.) That statement caused great consternation in Japan at the time. In 1995, there were probably on the order of seven or eight million World War Two veterans still alive in the United States. Alienating this voting bloc would have been political suicide for a mid-1990s presidential candidate. "Between 2000 and 2018, the number of living World War II veterans in the United States declined from 5.7 million to fewer than 500,000" (Vespa, 2000). By 2022, the number of living American World War Two veterans had dipped to under 168,000. The National WWII Museum, no date.
16. See Mayr, 1998. The U.S. Senate condemned the NASM's proposed exhibit by a rare unanimous vote. Dower, 1995, p. 1125.
17. See Washburn.

464   NOTES

18. Smithsonian Institution Archives, 2020. For a monograph-length treatise on the proposed exhibit and resulting scandal written by the NASM director at the time, see Harwit.

19. Mayor Hiraoka intimated this to me during a February 2017 interview in Hiroshima.

20. Reid, 1995.

21. Reid.

22. John Dower's *Embracing Defeat* is the seminal monograph treatment of the nascent stage of this postwar strategic arrangement between Japan and the U.S., which was motivated more by Cold War enemy-of-my-(Soviet)-enemy realpolitik pragmatism than it was by some desire for genuine rapprochement between the two countries and their respective peoples.

23. As a Smithsonian official read the lay of the land at the time, "[Americans] wanted the exhibit to stop when the doors to the bomb bay opened. . . . And that's where the Japanese wanted it to begin." Sanger, 1994.

24. Tibbets, p. 252.

25. Dietz, p. 499; Sweeney, p. 247.

26. Dietz, p. 498.

27. Dietz, p. 498; Sweeney, p. 247.

28. Sweeney, pp. 249–250.

29. Tibbets, p. 253. This facility would shortly be converted into MacArthur's headquarters–cum–personal residence.

30. Tibbets, p. 253; Sweeney, p. 250.

31. Mizukawa, 2024; Tibbets, p. 253.

32. Tibbets, p. 253.

33. Tibbets, p. 253.

34. Sweeney, p. 255. There were, at the time, several U.S. Navy vessels in the Nagasaki offing—possibly engaged in mine clearing in preparation for the arrival of American forces—but none of their crews would go ashore for nearly another two weeks, as they were waiting for the city to be tested and OK'd for residual radiation levels.

35. Sweeney, p. 253.

36. In his 1997 memoirs, Sweeney claims that both of the 509th's jeeps were lost in the kimono transaction, but after nine years spent attempting to peer into Paul Tibbets' mind, I find it next to impossible to accept that the typically hidebound colonel would have signed off on such a stunt. My aircraft-weight-compensation theory to explain the absent second jeep makes much more sense, and it would also explain the disappearance of the interpreter-security detail from Sweeney's, Tibbets', and Van Kirk's accounts of their Nagasaki sojourn, which feature numerous scenes in which they are shown being unable to communicate with the local Japanese—including during the initial tense standoff scene at Ōmura, when their trained interpreters, had

NOTES   465

they been present, would have certainly stepped up to do their job and
defuse the situation (as well as arrange for transportation later). It is possible
that, after getting some idea of Japanese man-on-the-street attitudes toward
their new American occupiers during the expedition's overnight in Tokyo,
Tibbets might have felt it safe to dispense with the security detail, and
perhaps he felt they would just be able to "muddle through" with the
language issues once there were boots on the ground in Nagasaki (which
turned out to be the case).

37. Sweeney, p. 253.
38. Sweeney, p. 253; Dietz, p. 500.
39. Sweeney, p. 255.
40. Sweeney, p. 255.
41. Sweeney, p. 255.
42. Dietz, p. 500.
43. Tibbets, pp. 254–255.
44. Tibbets, pp. 254–255.
45. See Tibbets, Sweeney, Dietz, Olivi, et al.
46. One notable exception here was Claude Eatherly, the pilot of the 509th
    CG weather reconnaissance plane that cleared Hiroshima for the atomic
    bombing on the morning of August 6, 1945. In 1962, a volume of his
    correspondence with journalist Gunther Anders—in which Eatherly
    repeatedly expressed remorse for the Hiroshima and Nagasaki bombings—
    was published to great controversy in the United States. The conservative
    outcry over Eatherly's statements was so great that it prompted William
    Bradford Huie—author of the renowned *The Execution of Private Slovik* and
    The Americanization of Emily (both of which were made into films)—to
    publish a book-length refutation of Eatherly's claims, the basis of which
    included searing criticisms of the former pilot's character and suggestions
    of mental instability that Huie claimed should have negated Eatherly's
    testimony. Additionally, 509th CG radio operator Abe Switzer's memoir—
    coauthored by Merle Miller and published in 1946 as *We Dropped the
    A-Bomb*—contains numerous passages and comments hinting at
    a degree of remorse over the bombings, although these come nowhere near
    the candor of Eatherly's remarks. It is important to note the Spitzer memoirs'
    1946 publication date, which, in chronological terms of the evolution of
    American bomb-interpretive discourse, makes it a contemporary of John
    Hersey's seminal *Hiroshima*. Both Spitzer's and Hersey's works appeared
    before the effective locking down of this discourse by the conservative
    interpretation of the atomic bombs as having been fully justified—an
    interpretation that subsequently went on to become the canonically
    approved narrative in mainstream American public discourse over ensuing
    decades and still holds considerable sway in American historical
    consciousness to this day.

NOTES

APPENDIX A

1. National Diet Library, no date.

APPENDIX B

1. Atomic Heritage Foundation, no date–c.

APPENDIX C

1. Taiwan Documents Project, no date.

APPENDIX D

1. Nobel Prize.

INDEX

Note: Italicized page numbers indicate material in photographs or illustrations.

Abe Shinzō, 363–64
acute radiation syndrome (ARS), 224, 264, 268, 284, 300, 303, 316–18, 325–26, 329, 336–38
Air Defense Law, 150
Akabane Kazuo, 65–66
Akabane Tokiko, 65
akagami draft notices, 165
Akatsuki Command, 173, 197–98, 298, 451n1
Akebono Squad, 30, 47, 431n8
Akuno'ura shipyard, 85, 100, 104, 303
Akutagawa Prize, 357
Albury, Charles, 185–86, 211, 377, 452n19
Allied occupation of Japan, 322–25, 344–45, 366, 377–81, 464n34
Alvarez, Luis, 171–72, 174
The Americanization of Emily (Huie), 465n46
Anami Korechika, 193, 195, 242, 243–44, 246, 274–78, 305
Anders, Gunther, 465n46
Anritsu Electrical Company, 48
Ansei Five-Power Treaties (Unequal Treaties), 33–34, 39, 89–91, 119, 438n21
antiaircraft artillery, 11, 143, 209, 431n4
Anti-Comintern Pact, 43
Ariake Sea, 211
Arima Setsuko, 258
Armed Forces Radio, 271
Arnold, Henry "Hap," 49
Asahi Shimbun, 153–54, 375, 443n3
Asakusa, 66, 74
Asakusa quarter, Tokyo, 25
Ashworth, Frederick L., 178, 180, 182, 184, 188, 189–90, 213
Atom-bombed Cities Reconstruction Law, 361
Atomi Jogakkō, 26–31, 47, 60–61, 73–75, 94–95
Atsugi Airfield, 377–78
Attlee, Clement, 179

B-17 bombers, 20–21, 23, 49
B-24 bombers, 23
B-25 bombers, 21
B-29 ("Superfortress") bombers
accounts of Nagasaki bombing, 245
attacks on Japanese supply lines, 428n17, 430n18

casualty rates, 429n29, 430n29, 434n21
combat status of crew members, 430n30
crew requirements, 10–11
execution of Nagasaki bombing, 187, 207, 210, 212, 215–16
F-13 photoreconnaissance craft, 45–46
"flying on the step," 248–49
Hiroshima bombing, 137, 154
incendiary campaign against Japan, 23, 50, 53–56, 59–60, 62–63, 65, 71, 96–97
loadout for bombing missions, 433nn18–20
and National Air and Space Museum controversy, 372–73
and Operation STARVATION, 95, 428n17
"over the hump" flights, 166
preparations for "Fat Man" mission, 142, 144–46, 149, 169–70, 182, 184
return from Nagasaki mission, 247–50
and significance of Saipan bases, 432n13
and surrender deliberations in Japan, 305
target selection for bombing missions, 4, 111
and weather conditions for missions, 5, 432n16
See also specific aircraft names
"Ballad of the Mobilized Students," 136
Barnes, Philip, 178, 186, 188, 190
barometric sensors, 189
Battle of Mount Song, 166
Battle of Mukden, 58
Beahan, Kermit, 143, 208–10, 213–14, 223, 377, 452n24, 455n7
Beser, Jacob, 178–79, 182–84, 187, 189, 195, 210, 250
Big Stink, 142, 179, 183, 185, 196, 270, 271
USS *Biloxi*, 323
birth defects, 339
black rain, 255, 284. *See also* radiation exposure
blast effects, 224
blockade of Japan, 106, 152, 204, 243, 275, 428n17
Bock, Fred, 142, 187, 195, 270, 271, 455n7
Bockscar
assessment of "Fat Man" mission, 273
crew for Special Mission #16, 455n7
execution of Nagasaki bombing, 186–90, 195–96, 207–11, 212–14, 452n24

468 INDEX

Bockscar (*cont.*)
  and National Air and Space Museum controversy, 374
  and post-bombing survey mission, 377
  preparations for "Fat Man" mission, 141–42, 146, 149, 169–71, 178–79, 181, 184
  return from Nagasaki mission, 224–25, 247–50, 271
Bōsō Peninsula, 62
Buckley, Ed, 178, 210, 213
Buddhism, 367
Bungo Channel, 429n17
Burma Road, 166
buyō dance, 338

Casablanca Conference, 7
Catholic Church, 80, 81, 83, 84, 87, 98, 117–18, 119–26, 127–37. *See also* Christianity in Japan; Nagasaki Sisters of the Sacred Heart of Mary (Junshin Sisters)
censorship, 22, 344
Central Business District (Hiroshima), 359
Central Business District (Nagasaki)
  and aftermath of Nagasaki bombing, 281, 286, 315, 359
  aiming point for "Fat Man" mission, 171, 212
  air raid alerts, 108, 199
  and Allied occupation of Japan, 324
  Christian churches in, 130
  day of Nagasaki bombing, 224, 231, 233, 253–54, 256
  and disparity in Hiroshima vs. Nagasaki bomb discourse, 363
  and food shortages, 96
  and geography of Nagasaki, 79–83, 84
  and Keiho Girls' School, 117
  and memorialization of bomb victims, 361
  modern configuration of, 442n8
  and Nagasaki Kunchi festival, 338
  and Nagasaki's streetcar system, 99, 116
  and post-bombing survey mission, 381
  and recovery efforts after Nagasaki bombing, 297, 300, 313, 317, 328
  Rokasu-machi neighborhood, 157
  shopkeepers' district, 160–61
  and surrender announcement, 318
  and target selection for bombing missions, 110
Cheshire, Leonard, 179
Chiang Kai-shek, 112, 166
China, 89, 96–97, 130
Chisso Minamata chemical plant, 156
Chōfu Airfield, 378
chōrei assemblies, 114, 200, 204, 235
Chōshū, 34
chōyōkō adult laborers, 112
Christianity in Japan, 39, 87–89, 437n19, 437n21. *See also* Catholic Church
Chūō Line, 334
Churchill, Winston, 4, 179
Civil Information and Education Section (CIE), 354–55

Clinton, Bill, 375, 463n15
cluster munitions, 55
Coca-Cola, 328
Committee of Operations Analysts (COA), 23–24, 144
Communications Corps, 165
Compton, Karl, 427n7
Convent of the Sacred Heart (Marmoutier, France), 126
coup fears, 192, 242, 243
Cousens, Charles, 435n10
C rations, 367
cremations, 198, 264, 266, 297–300, 303–4, 325–26, 336, 337, 459n7, 462n12
Cuban Missile Crisis, 433n11

Daigō Kōtō Gakkō (National High School Number Five), 37
Dai Ichi Insurance, 378
Daiwa Textile, 198
Dehart, Albert "Pappy," 185, 209, 210
Dejima, *x–xi*, 89, 437n27
Denmark, 85
Diocese of Nagasaki, 126
Dogpatch Inn, 182
dō'in gakuto student laborers, 30, 112, 117–18
Doll, Ed, 183
Dōmei News Agency, 28
Doolittle, James, 21, 270–71, 272, 457n3
Doolittle Raid, 21, 28–29, 431n4
Douglas C-54 Skymasters, 377–78
Dower, John, 464n22
Downey, William, 182
Dugway Proving Ground, 23
Dury, Léon, 122

Eaker, Ira, 429n29
earthquakes, 19–20, 234
East China Sea, 78, 85, 95, 212
Eastern Military District Headquarters, *viii*, 57, 58, 61–62
Eatherly, Claude, 465n46
Edo Castle, 18
efumi apostasy rituals, 88, 120, 124
Eighth Air Force, 11, 49, 270, 457n3
Embracing Defeat (Dower), 464n22
Enola Gay, 3, 4, 141, 183, 184, 195, 271, 273, 372–75, 377
Etajima (imperial service academy), 37
European Age of Exploration, 80
The Execution of Private Slovik (Huie), 465n46
Ezumi (Mary Maddalena) Yasu, 126, 128–32, 132–36, 203–5, 260, 262, 302, 324, 345, 347, 350–51

F-13 photoreconnaissance aircraft, 45–46
fallout, 256. *See also* radiation exposure
Far East Air Forces (FEAF), 9, 428n15
Farrell, Thomas, 185, 272
Fastax high-speed camera, 142, 180, 183, 185, 224
"Fat Man" bomb

INDEX

"Black Box" monitoring device, 178, 187–88, 190
bomb-drop procedure, 208–9, 214
detonation, 223–24, 260
fusing system, 179, 183, 187–90
and long-term effects of bomb, 341
plans for tactical deployments, 8
power compared with Hiroshima bomb, 299
preparations for bombing mission, 147–49, 169–70
and Project Alberta, 4
triggering mechanism, 148–49
Ferebee, Tom, 377
Fiedler, Arthur, 58
Field Order Number 17, 212
Fifth Air Force, 8–9, 428n15
56th Infantry Division (IJA), 155, 164, 166, 336
Fillmore, Millard, 438n31
firebreaks, 54, 65, 157, 222, 359
First Opium War, 32
509th Composite Group
and American remorse over atomic bombings, 465n46
and assessment of "Fat Man" mission, 271–73
and authorization for atomic bomb missions, 450n22
and execution of Nagasaki bombing, 208, 211
and incendiary campaign against Japan, 9
normal crew assignments, 455n7
and operational security around bombing missions, 270
and post-bombing survey mission, 377–79, 381, 464n36
preparations for "Fat Man" mission, 141–44, 146, 169–70, 180–82, 185
and rules for atomic bomb missions, 5
Ford, Gerald R., 435n10
Foreign Ministry, 38, 306
Foreign Settlement Districts, 90, 120, 122, 123
41st Bomb Group, 441n26
43rd Squadron, 53, 63
Frankl, Viktor, xiii
Fu-Gō paper balloon bombs, 30
Fujin Taimuzu Sha (Women's Times), 354
Fukagawa, 54, 63
Fukahori Fujiko, 262
Fukahori-kun, 268–69, 282–83, 288–89
Fukui, 174
Fukuoka, 25, 91–92, 111, 115, 315, 321, 324
Fukuoka District Court, 317
Fukuoka POW Camp No. 14, 103, 156, 323
Fukushima nuclear plant disaster, 331, 356
Full House, 141, 142, 183
Furet, Louis-Theodore, 120–21, 122
Futaba Elementary School, 65–66

gamma radiation, 198, 202, 224
genbaku byō, 330
geography of Nagasaki, 78–83, 83–85, 85–92
Gingrich, Newt, 374
Ginza district (Tokyo), 28
Glover, Thomas Blake, 84

Glover Garden, 90
goningumi seido ("five-household system"), 120, 443n17
Goodman, Walter, 179
Gotō Islands, 124
gozen kaigi, 277
The Great Artiste, 142, 171, 179, 187, 195–96, 210, 214, 225, 247, 250, 455n7
Great Kantō Earthquake, 19–20, 234
Great Northern Telegraph Company, 85
Ground Zero, x–xi, 380
Groves, Leslie R., 8, 109–10, 272, 428n14, 452n28
Gunge Norio
and aftermath of Nagasaki bombing, 286–87, 314–16
and Allied occupation of Japan, 324
author's interview with, 365–69
day of Nagasaki bombing, 206, 215–16, 251–54
and housing evictions, 157–58
life before Nagasaki bombing, 3
and memorialization of bomb victims, 364–65
postwar career, 348
relationship with brother, 156–58
Gunge Yoshio
and aftermath of Nagasaki bombing, 286–87
day of Nagasaki bombing, 206, 215, 253–54
education, 154–56
and Gunge family's postwar life, 366–69
and housing evictions, 157–58
and memorialization of bomb victims, 365
missing after bombing, 314–15
relationship with brother, 156–58
Gunkanjima coal mines, 102

Haha to kuraseba (film), 332
Hakodate, 119
Hankow, China, 112
"Hansai no Uta" (Nagai), 346–48
hansai setsu ("burnt offering theory"), 343–44, 346–48, 359–60
Hansell, Haywood S., 46
Harris, Townsend, 438n31
Harwit, M., 374–75, 463n13
Hatanaka Yoshino, 205, 217–18
Hayasaka (Januarius) Kyūnosuke, 125–26, 205, 345
Hayashi Akiko, 73, 116, 281
Hayashi Kyōko, 356–57
Hersey, John, 465n46
hibakusha (atomic bomb survivors)
and Nihon Hidankyō, 339–40, 356, 363, 370, 399–401
and Nobel Peace Prize, 370–71, 399–401
and peace activism, 339–40
and trajectory of postwar atomic bomb discourse, 344–45
See also specific individuals
Himosashi Elementary School, 134
Hirado, 124, 133–34
Hiranuma Ki'ichirō, 277
Hiraoka Takashi, 373, 463n13

INDEX

Hirohito, Emperor, 7–8, 72, 191, 241–43, 277, 308, 393–95, 460n25
Hiroshima
  atomic bombing of, 192, 202, 203
  death toll compared with Nagasaki, 224
  and decision to drop second bomb, 4–5
  Hiroshima Castle, 153
  Hiroshima Peace Museum, 373
  Hiroshima Peace Park, 371–72
  and post-bombing survey mission, 377–79
  and target selection for bombing missions, 109
  topography contrasted with Nagasaki, 297–98
  and trajectory of atom-bomb-memory discourse, 358–63
Hiroshima: The Last Witnesses (Sheftall), 359, 377
Hirota Kōki, 38, 42–43, 91, 193–94, 276
Hitler, Adolf, 43–44, 147, 192, 194
hōanden, 136, 445n22
Hōkayama, 94
Holy Mother of Mercy statue, 348, 352
Home Ministry, 131, 174–75, 448n11
Honda Sawa, 104–5, 202, 229–30, 232–33, 280, 284–86
hondo kessen, 7
Honshu, 17, 21, 57, 87, 92
Hopkins, James, 141, 142, 180, 183, 185, 195–96, 211, 272, 448n33
Huie, William Bradford, 465n46

Ichigaya (imperial service academy), 37
Immaculate Conception (Urakami) Cathedral, *x–xi*, 81–82, 88, 118–19, 135–36, 152, 259, 342, 461n6
Imperial General Headquarters (IGHQ), 173, 197
Imperial Japanese Army (IJA)
  and aftermath of Nagasaki bombing, 283, 297–98
  and Akatsuki Maritime Command, 197–98
  and Allied occupation of Japan, 322–23
  Imperial Rescript to Soldiers and Sailors, 397–98
  imperial service academy, 37
  and Ishida family background, 43
  and Japan's surrender, 309
  and kamikaze tactics, 192
  and labor mobilization, 101–2
  Nagasaki garrison, 296
  and Operation MATTERHORN, 111–12
  and recovery efforts after Nagasaki bombing, 329
  and Supreme War Council, 193, 195
  and target selection for "Fat Man" mission, 143
  Tateno Chūtarō's enlistment, 164
Imperial Japanese Navy (IJN)
  and aftermath of Nagasaki bombing, 268–69
  and Allied occupation of Japan, 322–23
  disbanding of, 351–52
  and economic history of Nagasaki, 92
  Imperial Rescript to Soldiers and Sailors, 397–98
  imperial service academy, 37

  and incendiary campaign against Japan, 97
  and kamikaze tactics, 192
  and labor mobilization, 101–2
  Medical Corps, 378
  and post-bombing survey mission, 378, 380–81
  and Supreme War Council, 195
  Suzuki's service, 191
  and target selection for "Fat Man" mission, 143
  and wartime manufacturing in Nagasaki, 99–100
Imperial Palace, 17, 274
Imperial Rescript on Education, 39
Imperial Rescript to Soldiers and Sailors, 230, 397–98
imperial service academies, 37
Imperial Way (*Kōdō*) movement, 127–28, 191
Inasa Bridge, *x–xi*, 288, 290
Incendiary Zone #1, 24, 30, 47, 53, 55, 62–63, 65, 67, 73, 144, 161
Inoue Sueko, 76–77
Inoue Takako, 39, 42
Inoue Tetsujirō, 38–39, 45, 72, 91, 115
Instrument of Surrender, 377
International Red Cross, 461n15
Isahaya, 80, 219, 263, 268–69, 288, 298, 301–3, 459n3
Ise Shrine, 444n15
Ishida Hisashi ("judge Ishida")
  and aftermath of Nagasaki bombing, 269, 280–81, 316–17
  and Allied occupation of Japan, 323
  and daughter's radiation sickness, 320–21
  day of Nagasaki bombing, 199
  and economic history of Nagasaki, 91
  and evacuations from Tokyo, 75
  family background and education, 37–39
  and family's move to Nagasaki, 115–16
  and incendiary campaign against Japan, 61, 72
  and Ishida family background, 43, 45
  official residence in Nagasaki, 83
  and postwar military governance of Japan, 353–54
  and Tokyo air raids, 46
Ishida Jō'ichi
  and author's research, 41
  birth of, 39
  education, 72–73
  and family's move to Nagasaki, 115–16
  and Ishida family background, 44–46
  and sister's memoirs, 321–22, 353, 355
  and Tokyo air raids, 47
Ishida Masako
  and aftermath of Nagasaki bombing, 264–65, 265–69, 282–83, 288–89, 289–92
  and Allied occupation of Japan, 324
  author's interview with, 42–46, 352–57
  birth of, 39
  day of Nagasaki bombing, 199–201, 219–20, 234–38, 281
  family background, 40–42
  and family's move to Nagasaki, 114–17

INDEX

and incendiary campaign against Japan, 52,
61, 71–72
life before Nagasaki bombing, 3
memoirs, 321–22, 353, 355
and radiation sickness, 316–19, 320–22, 329–30
and Tokyo air raids, 47
and trajectory of postwar atomic bomb
discourse, 344
wartime labor, 112
Ishida Shizuko, 39, 44, 116
Ishida Takako, 39, 42, 45
Ishida Times, 322
Ishida Yasuyo, 39, 44, 116
Itonaga (Ursula) Yoshi
and Allied occupation of Japan, 324–25
author's interview with, 350–52
background with Junshin Sisters, 133–36
day of Nagasaki bombing, 203–5, 218,
257–61, 264
final vows, 136–37, 451n16
life before Nagasaki bombing, 3
and memorialization of bomb victims, 342
and postwar atomic bomb discourse, 347
and recovery efforts after Nagasaki bombing,
301–4, 462n12
Iwaya Bridge, 302
Iwo Jima, 141, 181, 184–85, 212

Japan Coast Guard, 84
Japan Confederation of A- and H-Bomb
Sufferers Organizations, 339–40, 356, 363,
370, 399–401
Japanese Communist Party, 364
Japan Women's Patriotic Association, 165
Jesuits, 33, 86–87, 121, 124, 133
jogakkō (girls' school), 45
Johnston, Lawrence, 179
jokō (adult *teishintai* women), 101, 105, 112
Jūgosai no hibakusha: Rekishi wo kesanai tame ni
(Kiridōshi and Kiridōshi), 332
Junshin Girls' School, x–xi, 3, 98, 119, 129–32,
203–5, 236–37, 301–4, 344, 350. *See also*
Nagasaki Sisters of the Sacred Heart of
Mary (Junshin Sisters)

Kadena Air Base, 441n26
Kaigun-san, 282, 283, 288
Kaiten manned torpedoes, 100, 105, 106, 112
kakure Kirishitan community, 121–22, 124, 133,
203, 342
kamikaze attacks, 7, 146, 192
Kanda Ward, 47
Kanmon railway tunnel, 143
Kano Michiko. *See* Kiridōshi Michiko
Kantō Plain, 17, 18, 62, 334, 368
Kazagashira Hill, 79, 83, 90, 161, 255
keibitai guard units, 240, 290, 455n19
Keiho Girls' School, x–xi, 117, 161, 167–68, 326, 338
Keiho Prefectural Junior High School, 117
keikai keihō air raid alerts, 60
Keio University, 331

Kempeitai, 131–32, 175, 202, 205, 244–45, 296,
309, 313, 329
Kenjo (Nagasaki Prefectural Girls' School)
and 1948 education reforms, 441n31, 446n17
admission procedures, 439n15
calligraphy teacher, 157
day of Nagasaki bombing, 200–201, 220, 229,
235
full name of, 439n14
and Ishida Masako's postwar life, 353–54, 356
Kiridōshi Michiko's admission to, 97–98
location, x–xi
and radiation sickness cases, 316, 329–30
and wartime labor, 101, 105–6, 116, 117
Kennedy, John F., 433n11
kinkyōrei ban, 88, 133
Kiridōshi Kunitake, 27
Kiridōshi Michiko
and aftermath of bombing, 284–86, 459n9
and Allied occupation, 324
author's interview with, 14–17
and culture of Nagasaki, 93–97
day of Nagasaki bombing, 220–21, 229–33,
264, 280
evacuation to Nagasaki, 73–77
family background, 25–31
and geography of Nagasaki, 78
and incendiary campaign against Japan, 52, 61
and radiation sickness, 316, 329–32
and surrender announcement, 312–14
and wartime labor, 47, 97–99, 101, 103–7, 113,
116, 201–2, 440n10
Kiridōshi Risaku, 331–33
Kiridōshi Teruko, 285, 329
Kiridōshi Tetsurō, 4, 329
Kiridōshi Yasuko, 285, 314
Kirishitan Japanese, 87–88, 121–22, 124, 133, 203,
342, 363, 461n4
Kōenji, 334
Koishikawa Ward, Tokyo, 60, 61, 71–77
Koiso Kuniaki, 191–92
kokuminfuku ("national people's clothing"), 151
Kokura, 4, 110, 141–45, 171, 178, 181, 185, 190,
194–96, 207–10, 211
Kokura Arsenal, 109, 209
Kokutai, 242–43, 445n23
Kokutetsu (National Railways), 75–77, 80, 238,
265, 289
Kōmei, Emperor, 34
Korean Peninsula, 194
Korean workers, 101–3, 114
Kōryū (two-man midget submarines), 100
Kōtaiji, x–xi, 255–56, 295–96
Ko'ura Sōhei, 222
Kōyūkai, 339–40
Kuchinotsu, 86
Kuharek, John, 184, 196, 209, 249
Kumamoto, 331
Kupferberg, Jesse, 179
Kurashi no Techō, 356
kūshū keihō air raid alerts, 60

INDEX

Kwantung (Kantō) Army, 194, 427n2
Kyōdomari village, 312
Kyoto, 109–11, 121
Kyushu, 7–8, 27–28, 78–79, 87, 119, 121, 143, 194, 323, 353–54
Kyushu University, 315, 321, 353, 368

Laggin' Dragon, 141, 183, 195
Laucaigne, Joseph, 122
Laurence, William, 179, 187, 211, 225, 247
Lawrence, Ernest, 171
leaflet drops, 5–6
LeMay, Curtis E.
  antipathy for JFK, 433n11
  and assessment of "Fat Man" mission, 273–74
  Bell's palsy, 48, 433n7
  and casualty rates among bomber crews, 11
  and execution of Nagasaki bombing, 208
  and incendiary campaign against Japan, 9, 56, 62, 65, 67, 192, 434n21
  military background, 48–49
  and operational security around bombing missions, 270
  preparations for "Fat Man" mission, 141
  and target selection for bombing missions, 111
leukemia, 344
leukopenia, 320, 330
Lewis, Donald, 377
Library of Congress, 356
Limbaugh, Rush, 374
Lion Toothpaste Company, viii, 30, 47–48, 54, 74, 94
Little Boy bomb, 5, 146, 147–48, 170, 188
Los Alamos, New Mexico, 109–10, 270. See also Manhattan Project
Lucke, Edward, 180

M47A2 incendiary bombs, 53, 67
M69 incendiary bombs, 23, 53, 55, 63, 66–67, 71
MacArthur, Douglas, 270, 323, 360, 377
Main Torpedo Assembly Shop, 112, 117, 219–20
Makurazaki Typhoon, 325, 461n15
Malik, Jacob, 194
Manchuria, 4, 7, 191, 194, 309, 427n2
Manhattan Project, 4, 8, 109, 144, 147, 178–80, 187, 377, 381, 428n14
Mariana Islands, 45
Marshall, George C., 20–21, 23, 143, 428n14
Marure special-attack motorboat, 100
Masaji Yoshio, 155
Masako Taorezu, 353–54, 356
Matsuba-chō, Asakusa, 25–26
Matsuba Elementary School, 26
Matsugae International Terminal, 85
Matsuoka Yōsuke, 21
Matsuri no Ba (Hayashi), 357
McDilda, Marcus, 244–45, 454n14
McKelway, St. Clair, 50
McNamara, Robert S., 10, 49
Megami Bridge, 85
Megumi no Oka Nagasaki Genbaku Home, 348

Meiji Era
  architectural style, 73, 279
  Constitution of 1889, 132, 276, 372
  and geography of Tokyo, 18–19
  and history of Christianity in Japan, 124–25
  and hōanden, 445n22
  and Japanese Christianity, 39
  and Kiridōshi's family background, 25–26
  and Kokura's growth, 142
  and modernization of Japan, 34–36
  and Tateno family background, 162
memoirs of Nagasaki bombing, 322, 344, 353–57
memorial ceremonies, 340, 342, 345–46, 360–61, 363–65
Mercurochrome, 267
Michino'o, 137, 204, 238, 257–59, 262, 264–69, 311
Midway, 28
Miller, Merle, 465n46
Mindanao, 22
Mine Mariko, 364
Ministry of Education, 37, 125, 134–35
Ministry of Health and Welfare, 102
Ministry of Justice, 38, 43, 45, 72–73, 201, 355
minisubs, 104–6, 112
USS Missouri, 377
Mitchell, William "Billy," 20
Mitsubishi
  aircraft designs, 146, 210
  and Allied occupation of Japan, 324
  and assessment of "Fat Man" mission, 271
  and demographics of atomic bomb victims, 359
  and economic history of Nagasaki, 92
  and geography of Nagasaki, 85
  and incendiary campaign against Japan, 97
  and industrialization of Japan, 80
  and Ishida Hisashi's background, 38
  and Kiridōshis' home in Nagasaki, 94
  location of Nagasaki facilities, x–xi
  and Meiji Era modernization, 35
  and recovery efforts after Nagasaki bombing, 301–3
  and targets of bombing missions, 111, 143–44, 214
  and Tateno Sueko's postwar life, 337
  and wartime patriotism, 341
  See also specific facility names
Mitsubishi Electric Corporation, 337
Mitsubishi Raiden, 210
Mitsubishi shipyards, x–xi, 94, 99–100, 111–12, 167, 219–20, 234. See also Ōhashi plant (Mitsubishi Urakami-Ohashi War Plant)
Mitsubishi Steel and Arms Works, 98, 103, 220–21
Mitsuyama Hill, 238, 351
Miyashiro Satoru, 207
Moji neighborhood, 143
Mori-machi works (Mitsubishi facility)
  and aftermath of Nagasaki bombing, 326
  day of Nagasaki bombing, 215, 220–21, 229–39, 253

INDEX

and incendiary campaign against Japan,
441n26
location, *x–xi*
and memoirs of Nagasaki bombing, 332
and Nagasaki's streetcar system, 98–100
and POW labor, 456n21
and target selection for bombing missions,
111, 457n4
and wartime manufacturing in Nagasaki,
101–7, 112–13, 115, 156–58, 167, 201–2
Morrison, Philip, 171
Motoshima Hitoshi, 373
Mount Hōka, 79, 83, 84
Mount Konpira
and aftermath of Nagasaki bombing, 264,
284–86, 289–90, 315, 326
day of Nagasaki bombing, 215, 218, 223–24,
230–33, 234, 240–41, 251–54, 256, 261, 280
and disparity in Hiroshima vs. Nagasaki
bomb discourse, 363
and geography of Nagasaki, 79, 81, 82, 83, 84
and Gunge Norio's return to Nagasaki, 369
Musashi (ship), 85
Mussolini, Benito, 43–44, 192

Nabekanmuri Hill, 83–85, 90, 122
Nagaden Military District, 137
Nagai Midori, 342
Nagai Takashi, 342–43, 346, 351, 354, 359–60
Nagano Wakamatsu, 174–76, 199, 222–23,
240–41, 245, 280, 298, 316
Nagasaki Appellate Court, *x–xi*, 73, 200
Nagasaki Atomic Bomb Museum, 373
Nagasaki Commercial School, 268, 304
Nagasaki Ground Zero memorial ceremony,
360–61
Nagasaki Harbor, 84, 108, 110
Nagasaki Junshin Kōtō Jogakkō, 117–18
Nagasaki Medical College, *x–xi*, 82, 152,
154–55, 161, 175, 286, 287, 330, 342, 348,
359, 364–65, 367
Nagasaki Middle School, *x–xi*
Nagasaki Military Government Team (NMGT)
HQ, *x–xi*, 328, 353, 360, 367
Nagasaki Nippō, 175
Nagasaki no Kane (Nagai), 344, 346–47
Nagasaki Peace Park, *x–xi*, 340, 345–48, 361, 363,
371–72
Nagasaki Prison, *x–xi*
Nagasaki School for the Blind and Deaf, *x–xi*, 113
Nagasaki Sisters of the Sacred Heart of Mary
(Junshin Sisters)
and aftermath of bombing, 301–4
and Allied occupation of Japan, 324
assisted-living facility, 348–49
Christian given names, 451n16
day of Nagasaki bombing, 217, 263–64
founding of, 126
and Ieno-machi campus, 118
lay status of, 444n6
and memorialization of bomb victims, 342–48

Mother Ezumi's leadership of, 127–32
"Sister" appellation, 444n5
See also Junshin Girls' School; *specific
individuals*
Nagasaki Station, *x–xi*, 97, 99, 164–65, 223, 286,
290, 320, 442n8
Nagasaki Teachers College, 235–36
Nagasaki University, 82, 364–65, 368
Nagasaki Youth Association, 317
Nagatani Martina, 351
Nakajima Aircraft Engine Factory, 46
Naka-machi Catholic Church, *x–xi*, 130, 290
Nakashima Mitsuno, 261
Nakashima River, 82, 89, 171, 255
napalm, 23, 50, 53, 63, 71, 149, 175
National Air and Space Museum (NASM),
372–77
National Air Defense Law, 61, 65, 150
National Highway 206, 81, 436n6
National Service Draft Ordinance, 112
Netherlands, 33, 82, 89
New Yorker, 50
New York Times, 20, 22, 179, 187, 211, 225
NHK radio, 57, 58, 61, 151, 153, 307, 435n10, 442n8
Nigiwai Bridge, *x–xi*, 82, 212–13, 299, 336
Nihonbashi, 54, 63
Nihon Hidankyō, 339–40, 356, 363, 370, 399–401
Nihon Joshi Daigaku (Japan Women's
University), 134
Niigata, 109, 440n5
Nimitz, Chester, 270
Nippon Kaigi, 371
"Nisei" Japanese American, 377
Nishida Saburō, 260
Nishina Yoshio, 173–74, 197, 245, 448n11
Nishioka Takejirō, 175
Nishizaka, *x–xi*, 121, 122
No. 617 "Dambusters" Squadron, 179
Nobel Peace Prize, 356, 370, 399–401
Norden bombsights, 54, 111, 208, 213–14
Norstad, Lauris, 67, 111
North Field, Tinian, 9, 47–55, 56, 142, 149, 170,
270–71, 377–81, 429n17

Obama, Barack, 340, 356, 372
Obunko fuzoku ko (Imperial Library annex), 241,
274–79, 304–7
O'Hara, John F., 461n6
Ōhashi Bridge, *x–xi*, 238
Ōhashi plant (Mitsubishi Urakami-Ohashi War
Plant)
and aftermath of Nagasaki bombing, 264–65,
266–68, 326
and Allied occupation of Japan, 324–25
day of Nagasaki bombing, 199–201, 203–4, 219,
234–38, 260–63
location, *x–xi*
and memorialization of bomb victims, 348
and recovery efforts after Nagasaki bombing,
301–3
student laborers lost at, 351, 445n24

Ōhashi plant (Mitsubishi Urakami-Ohashi War Plant) (*cont.*)
and target selection for bombing missions, 439n20, 457n4
and wartime manufacturing in Nagasaki, 99–100, 103, 112–18, 136, 137
Ōhato Wharf, 97, 164, 324
Okada Jukichi, 298
Okinawa, 7, 212, 225, 247–50
Old Edo, 18–19, 54–55
Olivi, Fred, 185–86, 188, 248–50
Ōmura Bay, 78, 80–81, 145
Ōmura City, 80, 97, 298, 316, 323–24, 351, 366, 378–79, 381, 464n36
Ōmura Naval Air Station, 145
Operation Ichi-gō, 112
Operation MATTERHORN, 111
Operation MEETINGHOUSE, 50, 56–67
Operation STARVATION, 9, 95, 428n17
opium trade, 90
Oppenheimer, J. Robert, 109, 146–47, 180
Orphan Annie / Tokyo Rose, 59–60, 177, 435n10
orphans, 253
Osaka, 24, 121
Osaka Imperial University (Handai), 164
Ōura Church (later Cathedral), *x–xi*, 125–26, 136

Padroado patronage, 86–87
Pathfinder squadrons, 53–54, 55, 62–63
Pati Point, 56
Payette, Hazen, 143, 145, 180
Peace God statue, 363–64
Pearl Harbor, 20–21, 44, 114, 152, 164, 309, 373
Penney, William, 180
Père Lachaise Cemetery, 445n22
Permanente Metals, 10
Perry, Matthew C., 32
Petitjean, Bernard, 122, 123–25
Philippines, 20–22
photoreconnaissance missions, 45–46, 284, 448n12
Pius IX, pope, 121, 124
Pius XI, pope, 126
plutonium, 8, 147–48, 299
Potsdam Declaration, 5, 110, 193, 195, 241–44, 274, 275, 277, 279, 305–6, 389–91, 429n20, 450n22
Power, Thomas, 53, 56, 64, 434n25
precision bombing tactics, 46, 50, 54, 67, 111, 113
prisoners of war, 22–23, 28, 103, 156, 234, 290, 323–24, 373
Project Alberta, 4, 149, 171, 178, 180, 182–83, 190, 427n3, 449n22, 455n7
propaganda, 5–6, 57–60, 95, 107, 150–53, 177, 428n7, 435n10, 454n9
"Pumpkin" bombs, 182, 448n19
Purnell, William, 272

radar, 160, 179, 195, 213
radiation exposure
acute radiation syndrome (ARS), 224, 264, 268, 284, 300, 303, 316–18, 325–26, 329, 336–38

and Allied occupation forces, 464n34
fallout, 256
gamma radiation, 198, 202, 224
and investigation of Hiroshima bombing, 197–98
and Nobel Peace Prize announcement, 400–401
post-bombing survey mission, 377–81
and rumors about "new-type bomb," 202
symptoms of radiation illnesses, 320–21
Radio Moscow, 190
radiosondes, 171, 179, 208
Radio Tokyo, 58, 61
railroad system of Japan, 75–77, 79, 80, 91–92, 106, 153, 202, 301–2, 329, 334, 429n18. *See also Kokutetsu* (National Railways)
Reddy, Michael J., 461n6
Religious Legislation Investigation Commission, 125
Research Center for Nuclear Weapons Abolition (RECNA), 364
Reserved Area list, 109–10, 440n5
Return of the Enola Gay (Tibbets), 457n4
Rising Asia Service Day, 151–52
"Ro'ei no Uta" ("Song of the Field Encampment"), 341
Rogers, Irvin W., 353
Roosevelt, Franklin, 4, 427n2
Royal Air Force (RAF), 9, 11, 23, 67, 179
royal roads (*ōdō*), 37
Russo-Japanese War, 35, 58

Sagane Ryōkichi, 171–73
Saint Elmo's fire, 189
Saipan, 7, 29, 51, 56, 275, 309, 432n13
Sakomizu Hisatsune, 174, 195, 277, 306
samurai, 17–19, 25–26, 33–37, 39, 86–87, 142
San'yō Line, 153
Sasebo Naval Anchorage, 104, 298
School Sisters of Notre Dame, 126, 129
Sea of Japan, 106, 194
2nd Marine Division, 323, 324
2nd Marine Regiment, 324
Second Sino-Japanese War, 151, 164
Seikei High School, 45
Seki Chieko, 13–16, 332
Serber, Robert, 171, 180, 183, 185, 224
Seto Inland Sea, 143, 429n17
Seventh Air Force, 108, 110
73rd Bombardment Wing, XXI BC, 53, 54
Sherry, Michael, 22
Shimonoseki Straits, 143, 429n17
Shinagawa-sensei (calligraphy teacher), 157, 215, 251, 253–54
Shinkōzen Elementary School, *x–xi*, 164, 165, 330, 338
Shintoism, 26, 127–28, 132, 136, 152, 157, 205, 338, 444n15
Shin'yō special-attack motorboat, 100
Shiroyama Elementary School, *x–xi*, 113
Shitamachi ("Low City")

INDEX

and geography of Tokyo, 18–20
and incendiary campaign against Japan, 24, 54–55, 63–67, 71–74
and Ishida Masako's family background, 44
and Kiridōshi family background, 25–27, 30
population density, 434n32
and wartime student labor, 47
Shizuoka University, 370–77
Shogunate, 17, 18, 33–34, 36, 39, 82, 87–90, 119–24, 157, 163, 338
shortwave radio, 58–60
Shotokuji Temple, 231
Shōwa Period, 334
Shūyūkan Junior High, 37
Signal Corps, 272
Silence (film), 437n24
Simeral, George, 56
Sino-Japanese War, 21, 35, 130–31
6th Marine Regiment, 324
60 Minutes, 435n10
Smithsonian Institution, 372–73, 463n13, 464n23
Snatch Blatch (B-29), 53, 55–56, 63–64
Société des Missions Étrangères de Paris (MEP), 120
"Song of the *Hansai*" (Nagai), 346–48
Sonoda Foundries, 218, 257–58
Sorensen, Theodore, 433n11
Soviet-Japanese Neutrality Pact, 21, 194
Soviet Union, 4, 7, 190, 194–95, 242, 271, 275, 329, 397
Spaatz, Carl, 110
Special Higher Police *(tokkō keisatsu),* 131
Special Mission #16, 141, 211
Spitzer, Abe, xiii, 178, 188, 195, 208, 225, 247, 272
Stalin, Joseph, 4, 7, 194
Stimson, Henry, 109, 111, 427n7
submarines, 95, 99–100
Sugimoto Kamekichi, 360–61
Sugiyama Shigeo, 318
Sumida River, 18, 19, 54–55, 66
Supreme War Council, 193, 195, 241–44, 246, 272, 274, 276–77, 458n25
surrender of Japan, 241–43, 274–75, 308, 318, 393–95, 460n25. *See also* Potsdam Declaration
Suwa Shrine, x–xi, 157, 234, 338
Suzuki Kantarō, 191–95, 243, 246, 274–79, 305–6
Sweden, 279
Sweeney, Charles
    and assessment of "Fat Man" mission, 271–74
    and casualties of Nagasaki bombing, 299
    and command of bombing mission, 449n20
    crew for Special Mission #16, 455n7
    and execution of Nagasaki bombing, 186, 188, 190, 196, 208–11, 212–14, 450n33, 450n34
    and operational security around bombing missions, 270
    and post-bombing survey mission, 377–81, 464n36
    preparations for "Fat Man" mission, 142, 145, 149, 169–71, 174, 180, 182, 184

return from Nagasaki mission, 224–25, 247–51
tensions with Tibbets, 457n11
Swift, Jonathan, 88
Switzer, Abe, 465n46
Switzerland, 279, 306

Tachibana Bay, 78, 313–14
Tagami Village, 317–19
Tagawa (Christina) Tadako, 204, 263, 268, 303
Taishō Era, 19
Takao Clinic, 300, 308, 337
Takarazuka Revue Theater, 30
Takigawa Masaru, 360–61
Tamaki Vocational College, 338
Tamano'ura, 78
Tamaya Fusakichi, 260
Tanizaki Jun'ichirō, 28
Target Committee, 109–10
Tategami shipyard, 85, 100, 102–4
Tateno Asao, 162, 164–65
Tateno Chūtarō, 162, 164, 166, 309, 336–37
Tateno Mitsuko, 162, 254–55
Tateno Seijirō, 162, 167, 295, 328
Tateno Shimi, 162, 165, 167, 327–28
Tateno Sueko
    acceptance at Keiho Girls' School, 167–68
    and aftermath of Nagasaki bombing, 310–12
    and Allied occupation of Japan, 324
    author's interview with, 334–37
    day of Nagasaki bombing, 205–6, 216–17, 252, 254–56
    family background, 162–65
    and Japan's surrender, 308–9
    life before Nagasaki bombing, 3
    postwar life, 337–41
    radiation sickness, 296, 325–28
    and recovery efforts after Nagasaki bombing, 300
    and wartime labor in Nagasaki, 161–62, 456nn21–22
Tateno Yoshiko, 162, 167
Tatsuno Kingo, 279–80
313th Bombardment Wing, XXI BC, 9, 53–54, 149
314th Bombardment Wing, 48, 51, 53, 56, 144, 177, 182, 445n13, 448n19
Tibbets, Paul
    on aiming point at Nagasaki, 452n28
    and assessment of "Fat Man" mission, 272–73
    and execution of Nagasaki bombing, 194, 196, 449n20, 450n34
    mission briefing, 181–82
    and post-bombing survey mission, 377–79, 381, 464n36
    preparations for "Fat Man" mission, 141–42, 144–45, 149, 169–70, 178–79, 184–85
    return from Nagasaki mission, 248–49
    tensions with Sweeney, 457n11
Tinian, 51, 56, 185, 208, 271, 434n2
Tōdai Faculty of Law, 355
Tōgō Shigenori, 190–91, 193, 242–43, 274–77, 279, 304–5

476   INDEX

Tokiwa Bridge, 255
Tokugawa Shogunate, 437n21, 443n17
Tokusanji, 317–19
Tokuseidō, 162–63, 167
Tokyo
  Air Defense Headquarters, *viii*, 57, 58
  air raids, 46
  District Court, 72
  and Doolittle Raid, 21, 431n4
  and economic history of Japan, 92
  and Great Kantō Earthquake, 19–20, 234
  and incendiary campaign against Japan, 24,
    30, 54–55, 63–67, 71–74
  layout of, 17–18
  and Operation MEETINGHOUSE, 57–67
  and target selection for bombing missions,
    23–24
Tokyo Bay, 17–18, 19, 32, 54, 62
Tokyo Rose (aircraft), 45–46
Tokyo Rose (broadcaster), 59–60, 177, 435n10
Tokyo University, 378
Tokyo Women's Teachers College, 44, 45
Tomihisa Taue, 363–64
Tomonaga Masao, 348
Torpedo Finishing Room, 103–4, 156, 221, 229
tōsuiken, 276–77
Toyoda Soemu, 193, 195, 243, 245, 277–78, 305
Toyotomi Hideyoshi, 121
Treaty of Versailles, 191–92
Trinity test, 179
Truman, Harry, 5, 110, 242, 270–71, 279, 306–7,
  428n14
Tsuno'o Susumu, 153–54, 161, 175
Tsuzuki Masao, 378–79, 381
Twentieth Air Force, 5, 9, 67, 95, 111, 144, 149,
  166, 212, 428n7, 429n17, 430n30
XX Bomber Command, 49, 51, 111–12, 166
XXI Bomber Command
  and assessment of "Fat Man" mission, 273
  and casualty rates among bomber crews, 11
  and execution of Nagasaki bombing, 208
  and incendiary campaign against Japan,
    48–52, 60, 62, 64, 67, 433n2, 438n11
  merged with XXI BC, 112
  and Operation STARVATION, 428n17
  preparations for "Fat Man" mission, 146, 180,
    445n14
  and target selection for bombing missions,
    109–10
  Tokyo air raids, 46
Twenty-Six Martyrs of Nishizaka, 121, 126,
  442n8
typhoons, 181, 325, 461n15

Uchino Chito, 137
Umaya Bridge, 47
Umezu Yoshijirō, 193, 195, 243, 277–78, 305
University of Tokyo (Tōdai)
  and Ishida Jō'ichi's education, 72–73, 115–16,
    353, 355

and Ishida Masako's family background,
  42–45
location, *viii*
main campus, 74
Nagano Wakamatsu's background, 174
and "royal roads" to social advancement,
  37–38
Uragawa Kazusaburō, 342
Urakami Cathedral. *See* Immaculate Concep-
  tion (Urakami) Cathedral
Urakami River, 79, 95, 99, 117, 130, 214, 237, 325,
  452n28, 459n7
uranium, 147
Urban VIII, pope, 442n10
U.S. Army, 49, 352
U.S. Army Air Force (USAAF), 73
U.S. Marine Corps, 323, 324, 327, 352, 367, 379
U.S. Navy, 32
U.S. Strategic Bombing Survey (USSBS), xiii, 330,
  335, 429n18, 438n6, 439n12, 447n6, 455n19

Van Kirk, Theodore "Dutch," 377, 464n36
Van Pelt, James, 184, 210, 211, 213, 250, 377
Vatican, 86, 120–21
Veneration of the Imperial Rescript Day, 152, 161

Waldman, Bernard, 180, 448n12
war crimes trials, 243, 323
Warring States period, 87, 121
weather conditions, 4–5, 58, 180–81, 183, 185, 212,
  432n16, 452n24, 458n1, 465n46
We Dropped the A-Bomb (Switzer and Miller),
  465n46
Wellerstein, Alex, 440n5
Western Army HQ, 97, 157, 160, 245
USS *Wichita*, 323
Will, George, 374
Workman, E. J., 145–46
World War One, 99, 191–92

Yahata Steel Works, 92
Yakushima Island, 181, 184, 195–96
Yalta Conference, 4, 193
Yamada Shichigorō, 279–80
Yamaguchi Shige, 200, 234, 281
Yamanote ("High City"), 18–19, 71, 74
Yamato-class battleships, 85
Yamazato Elementary School, *x–xi*, 113
Yanagawa Masako. *See* Ishida Masako
Yanagawa Toshikazu, 355–56
Yasuda, 35
Yokohama, 19–20, 23, 109, 119, 121, 234, 440n5
Yonai Mitsumasa, 243, 246, 275
Yontan, Okinawa, 247–50, 270–74

Zebrowski, Zeno, 253
Zero fighters, 146, 210
Zero Hour program, 58–60
Zone of Total Destruction (ZTD), 144, 223, 241,
  256, 289, 297, 300, 310, 324

ABOUT THE AUTHOR

M. G. SHEFTALL has lived in Japan since 1987. He has a PhD in international relations / modern Japanese history awarded by Tokyo's Waseda University. Since 2001, he has been a professor of modern Japanese cultural history and communication at the Faculty of Informatics of Shizuoka University, which is an institution in the Japanese national university system. Sheftall is married, with two adult sons, and makes his home in Hamamatsu, Japan.